Jonas' Introduction to the U.S. Health Care System
Seventh Edition

Raymond L. Goldsteen, DrPH, is the Founding Director of the Master of Public Health program (MPH North Dakota) and Professor in the Department of Family and Community Medicine at the University of North Dakota School of Medicine and Health Sciences. He was also the Founding Director of the Graduate Program in Public Health at the State University of New York, Stony Brook. He received his doctoral degree from the Columbia University Mailman School of Public Health. Dr. Goldsteen has an extensive background in health care research and policy and was formerly director of the health policy research centers at the University of Illinois in Urbana-Champaign, University of Oklahoma College of Public Health, and the West Virginia University School of Medicine. He is co-author of the highly acclaimed *An Introduction to the U.S. Health Care System*, 6th Edition, and *Introduction to Public Health*.

Karen Goldsteen, PhD, MPH, is a Research Associate Professor in the Center for Rural Health at the University of North Dakota School of Medicine and Health Sciences. She was previously a Research Associate Professor in the Graduate Program in Public Health at the State University of New York, Stony Brook. She received an MPH from the Mailman School of Public Health at Columbia University and a PhD in Community Health from the University of Illinois at Urbana-Champaign. She was a Pew Health Policy Fellow at the University of California, San Francisco. Dr. Goldsteen is a co-author of the bestselling *An Introduction to the U.S. Health Care System*, 6th Edition, and co-author of *Introduction to Public Health*.

Jonas' Introduction to the U.S. Health Care System

Seventh Edition

Raymond L. Goldsteen, DrPH,
Karen Goldsteen, PhD, MPH

Founding Author, Steven Jonas, MD, MPH

SPRINGER PUBLISHING COMPANY

NEW YORK

Springer Publishing Company, LLC
11 West 42nd Street
New York, NY 10036
www.springerpub.com

Acquisitions Editor: Sheri W. Sussman
Composition: Newgen Imaging

ISBN: 978–0-8261–0930-9
E-book ISBN: 978–0-8261–0931-6

12 13 14 15 / 5 4 3 2 1

The author and the publisher of this Work have made every effort to use sources believed to be reliable to provide information that is accurate and compatible with the standards generally accepted at the time of publication. The author and publisher shall not be liable for any special, consequential, or exemplary damages resulting, in whole or in part, from the readers' use of, or reliance on, the information contained in this book. The publisher has no responsibility for the persistence or accuracy of URLs for external or third-party Internet Web sites referred to in this publication and does not guarantee that any content on such websites is, or will remain, accurate or appropriate.

Library of Congress Cataloging-in-Publication Data
CIP data is available at the Library of Congress.

Special discounts on bulk quantities of our books are available to corporations, professional associations, pharmaceutical companies, health care organizations, and other qualifying groups.

If you are interested in a custom book, including chapters from more than one of our titles, we can provide that service as well.

For details, please contact:
Special Sales Department, Springer Publishing Company, LLC
11 West 42nd Street, 15th Floor, New York, NY 10036–8002s
Phone: 877–687-7476 or 212-431-4370; Fax: 212–941-7842
Email: sales@springerpub.com

Printed in the United States of America by Bang Printing.

This book is dedicated to our children—Jon, Ben, and Sune Goldsteen—and to our grandaughter—Eliza Grace Goldsteen

Contents

Abbreviations

AALL	American Association for Labor Legislation
AAMC	Association of American Medical Colleges
ACA	Accountable Care Organizations (see PPACA)
AHA	American Hospital Association
ALOS	Average Length of Stay
AMA	American Medical Association
ANA	American Nurses Association
ASTHO	Association of State and Territorial Health Officials
CAT	Computerized Axial Tomography
CCMC	Committee on the Costs of Medical Care
CDC	Centers for Disease Control and Prevention
CHC	Community Health Center
CHSS	Cooperative Health Statistics System
CME	Continuing Medical Education
CMS	Centers for Medicare and Medicaid Services
CPO	Combined Provider Organization
DHHS	Department of Health and Human Services
DO	Doctor of Osteopathy
DOD	Department of Defense
DRG	Diagnosis-Related Group
EAP	Employee Assistance Program
ED	Emergency Department
EMS	Emergency Medical Service (or System)
EMT	Emergency Medical Technician
EPA	Environmental Protection Agency
EPO	Exclusive Provider Organization
FDA	Food and Drug Administration
GAO	General Accounting Office
GPO	Government Printing Office

GDP	Gross Domestic Product
GMENAC	Graduate Medical Education National Advisory Committee
GNP	Gross National Product
GPEP	General Professional Education of the Physician Panel
HCFA	Health Care Financing Administration
HIV	Human Immunodeficiency Virus
HMO	Health Maintenance Organization
HRSA	Health Resources and Services Administration
IDS	Integrated Delivery System
IOM	Institute of Medicine
IPA	Individual/Independent Practice Association
IPO	Independent Practice Organization
JCAHO	Joint Commission on Accreditation of Healthcare Organizations
LCME	Liaison Committee on Medical Education
LPN	Licensed Practical Nurse
MC	Managed Care
MCH	Maternal and Child Health
MCO	Managed Care Organization
MEPS	Medical Expenditure Panel Survey
MHS	Marine Hospital Service
MMWR	Morbidity and Mortality Weekly Report
MRI	Magnetic Resonance Imaging
MVSR	Monthly Vital Statistics Report
NCHS	National Center for Health Statistics
NHANES	National Health and Nutrition Examination Survey
NHIS	National Health Interview Survey
NIH	National Institutes of Health
NIMH	National Institute of Mental Health
NIOSH	National Institute of Occupational Safety and Health
NLN	National League for Nursing
NP	Nurse Practitioner
OMB	Office of Management and Budget
OPD	Outpatient Department
OSHA	Occupational Safety and Health Administration
PA	Physician Assistant
PHO	Physician–Hospital Organization
PHS	Public Health Service
POS	Point of Service

PPACA	Patient Protection and Affordable Care Act of 2010
PPGP	Prepaid Group Practice
PPO	Preferred Provider Organization
RBRVS	Resource-Based Relative Value System
RN	Registered Nurse
SAMSHA	Substance Abuse and Mental Health Services Administration
UR	Utilization Review
USDA	United States Department of Agriculture
USPHS	United States Public Health Service
VA	United States Department of Veterans Affairs
WHO	World Health Organization
WIC	Women, Infants, and Children Supplemental Nutrition Program

Foreword

This is the seventh edition of *An Introduction to the U.S. Health Care System*. It was my privilege, and indeed it was an honor, with the third edition to have succeeded the late Dr. Milton Roemer as the principal author of this book. In 1966, then a student at the Yale School of Public Health, I went to my first American Public Health Association Annual Meeting, held that year in Los Angeles. My mentor, the late Dr. E. Richard Weinerman, had me in tow and introduced me to all the greats, the luminaries of the field that was then called "medical care." None shone more brightly than Dr. Roemer. As I said in a letter to him after we came to a final agreement on doing the third edition of this book together, I felt like a kid who idolized the superstar baseball player and then grew up to play on the same team with him.

The third edition of *An Introduction* was a substantial revision of Dr. Roemer's previous work, but it drew significantly on that work. The bulk of the writing in the fourth edition and even more so in the fifth edition was mine. With the publication of the sixth edition, the book took yet another turn in its authorship. My dear friends and colleagues, Drs. Raymond and Karen Goldsteen, agreed to take over responsibility for the book for the foreseeable future. Just as the third edition marked a transition from Dr. Roemer's work to mine, so did the sixth edition mark a transition from my work to that of the Goldsteens. With the publication of this edition, the transition is now complete, and I could not be happier with the result.

This book describes the U.S. health care delivery system in broad outline. It focuses on principles, basic structures, and important unsolved problems. It takes care to discuss these matters in the historical context that is essential for understanding them. It takes primarily a qualitative rather than a quantitative approach. Thus, although it uses some numbers, it uses them lightly. It is referenced, but it does not have a profusion of citations. As were the first six editions of this book, this one is intended primarily for use in undergraduate courses on the U.S. health care delivery system, in graduate survey courses, for teaching the subject to medical students (who usually do not cover it in any depth, if they cover it at all), and for the practicing health professional who simply wants a relatively brief overview of the system.

Although *An Introduction* is not primarily a policy book, it does deal with policy to the extent that an understanding of it is essential to understanding how the U.S. health care system works, and doesn't. Roemer, I, and the Goldsteens have published elsewhere a great deal on policy. Thus, this book has a political and philosophical point of view. Although it always attempts to be objective, it is not neutral. Its primary social value is that the principal purpose of the U.S. health care delivery system, taking precedence over any other purpose, should be to meet and serve the health care needs of the American people. If other purposes, such as the production of private profit, power, prestige, and political advantage for individuals and organizations, are achieved at all, they should very much take a back seat to the stated primary purpose.

At various points in the book, especially in Chapters 1, 7, and 8, proposals and legislation for U.S. health care delivery system policy and program changes, old and new, are described. Very occasionally, some are recommended. I hope that, after assimilating the factual material presented, you will be able to come to your own conclusions about what is being done and what further is to be done, if anything. I am certain that, if nothing else, you will agree with the majority of the American people, when they are asked in detail, not in generalities and slogans, that something must be done to reform both the structure and the functions of the system, well beyond what we have now, even with the changes that are taking place and are scheduled to take place under the Affordable Care Act of 2009.

Steven Jonas, MD, MPH
Professor of Preventive Medicine
Graduate Program in Public Health
State University of New York, Stony Brook

Preface

This is the seventh edition of *An Introduction to the U.S. Health Care System*, now titled *Jonas' Introduction to the U.S. Health Care System*. It was our privilege, and indeed it was an honor, to be asked by Dr. Steven Jonas to coauthor the sixth edition with him in preparation for assumption of full authorship of subsequent editions. Now the intended transition from Dr. Jonas to us has come about, and we hope that the seventh and future editions of this classic text about the health care system in the United States carries on the tradition of excellence begun more than 30 years ago by Dr. Milton Roemer and continued by Dr. Jonas.

In the seventh edition, we continue the practice of Drs. Roemer and Jonas, providing both description and commentary on the health care system. As Dr. Jonas wrote in the Preface to the sixth edition, "... this book has a political and philosophical point of view. Although it always attempts to be objective, it is not neutral. Its primary social value is that the principal purpose of the U.S. health care delivery system, taking precedence over any other purpose, should be to meet and serve the health care needs of the American people. If other purposes, such as the production of private profit, power, prestige, and political advantage, are achieved at all, they should very much take a back seat to the stated primary purpose."

The seventh edition updates the description of the health care system, as well as efforts to make it responsive to the health care needs of all Americans. Two significant developments in the period since the sixth edition—the rise of the Tea Party and the passage of the Affordable Care Act (ACA)—encapsulate the dysfunction and conflict within the larger society, which continue to prevent the health care system from fully achieving equity, quality, and efficiency; the criteria used to evaluate all health systems (Aday et al., 1993). The Tea Party's success at rousing public opinion against government assured that in health care, as in all other areas of society, private-sector interests would be defended even if doing so maintained inequity, inefficiency, and poor quality care. The ACA represents the best efforts of those who believe that governments have a responsibility to assure an equitable, efficient, and quality health care system, but who were constrained by rabid anti-government sentiment.

Their options for public action were limited during development of the legislation and, even now, the most important facets of the legislation for bringing about needed reforms—the individual mandate and funding for prevention—may be overturned. The tension between public and private action continues to define the kind of health care system we have in the United States.

As were the first six editions of *An Introduction to the U.S. Health Care System*, this edition is intended primarily for use in undergraduate courses on the U.S. health care delivery system, in graduate survey courses, for teaching the subject to medical, nursing, and other clinical students (who usually do not cover it in any depth, if they cover it at all), and for the practicing health professional who simply wants a relatively brief overview of the system. The subject matter has been reorganized. In this edition, Chapter 1 provides an overview of the system. Chapter 2 covers the settings for health care delivery—hospitals, long-term care, and ambulatory care. Chapter 3 discusses the professions and training of people who deliver health care. Chapter 4 describes the role of government in the health care system. In Chapter 5, the financing and cost of health care are reviewed. In Chapter 6, the principles and practices of performance improvement and quality assurance are presented. Chapter 7 is devoted to the subject of managed care, beginning with an examination of its historical forebear, pre-paid group medical practice. The history of and prospects for national health insurance and health care system reform in the United States are covered in Chapter 8, including the Affordable Care Act passed by the Obama administration. Chapter 9 summarizes important themes in the development of the U.S. health care system and prospects for the future. Finally, we have interjected a bit of humor into the seventh edition in the form of cartoons that capture a theme, highlight an issue, or point out an absurdity or contradiction in policy or practice. We hope these add to the readers' understanding of the material.

Raymond L. Goldsteen, DrPH
Professor of Family & Community Medicine
Founding Director, North Dakota MPH
University of North Dakota
Professor Emeritus of Preventive Medicine
State University of New York, Stony Brook
Karen Goldsteen, PhD, MPH
Research Associate Professor
Center for Rural Health
University of North Dakota

Acknowledgments

For their assistance in research and preparation of the manuscript, we wish to thank Skye Ostreicher, Haseeb Shahid, and Sune Goldsteen, MA. Benjamin Goldsteen, MBA, provided Chapter 5 (Financing).

At Springer Publishing Company, we thank Jennifer Perillo, Former Acquisitions Editor, and Executive Editor Sheri W. Sussman for their enthusiastic support of this project and technical expertise in seeing it through, swiftly to its end. And following Dr. Jonas' lead taken in preceding editions, we thank the woman without whom none of this work would ever have seen the light of day, Dr. Ursula Springer, Honorary Chair to Springer Publishing Company, and as well to Theodore Nardin, CEO and Publisher, who is shepherding the company so well into the 21st century.

ONE

Introduction

"Come back in three months because you're perfectly healthy which means a WHOLE LOT can go wrong with you."

©Artizans Entertainment Inc. By Chris Wildt.

Each nation has a health care system, but as a knowledgeable colleague said, "When you've seen one health care system, you've seen one health care system. No two are exactly the same." Every country's health care system is organized to provide the diagnosis and treatment of individuals' health problems and consists of a health care workforce, practice setting, suppliers of therapeutics, and organizations responsible for workforce training, research, and system oversight. However, there is enormous variation in how this important societal function is actually realized. The variation arises from differences in fundamental beliefs about what constitutes a health problem, who are legitimate health care providers, what are fitting and effective methods of diagnosis and treatment, what are suitable settings for the provision of health care, how health care should be financed, and what constitutes appropriate oversight and evaluation of health care providers and the health care system. Differences also result from variation in national resources, which differentiate nations' health care systems, even if their fundamental beliefs about health and health care are similar.

In general, all societies designate some persons or positions as legitimate providers of health care. These designated providers are empowered in their society to determine the causes of ill health and provide alleviation or cure. Some providers are designated as dominant, or vie with others for dominance. There is also a defined role for the recipients of health care services: for example, the "sick role," as defined by Parsons (1951), which posits the rights and obligations of sick persons in Western societies. The sum of all the institutions and processes that support the work of diagnosis and healing can be called the health care system of that society. The system is organized to facilitate the diagnosis and treatment of legitimized patients by appropriate providers.

We also recognize that conditions defined as health problems may differ from society to society. In the United States today, people who are obese are considered in poor health, and they are treated with everything from diet to bariatric surgery. In other societies, obesity is a desirable trait, emulated if possible by those who are thin. Diagnosis and treatment models may differ between societies. The social position, training, and authority of healers may differ. The organization of the system and the expected outcomes may differ among countries and among cultures.

Let us consider an example of fundamental differences in beliefs about what constitutes a health problem, a legitimate provider, and appropriate methods of treatment of health problems. Traditional Chinese medicine (Liu, 1988) offers an entirely different perspective on health and health care than the model developed in the Western European countries. Written records about the origins of traditional Chinese medicine can be traced back further than 200 BCE According to Chinese medicine, the human body must maintain homeostasis in order to maintain a state of health, that is, an internal, bodily balance between two inseparable and opposing forces of nature: yin and yang. Yin represents the cold, or passive, principle whereas yang represents the hot, or active, principle. Any imbalance of these two forces can lead to a blockage of flow in the qi (vital energy) or in the blood, both of which run along interconnected channels in the body called meridians. When there is a disturbance in the energy flow, the appropriate type of treatment is selected to unblock the flow through the meridians: materia medica (herbology), acupuncture, bodywork (massage and manipulation), or health-benefiting exercises (exercising the body–mind connection). This is quite different from the Western approach to understanding health problems and their treatment. Western medicine perceives the human body as a collection of interconnected health systems—heart, circulatory, endocrine, reproductive, and so forth—each with a set of functions and normal operating processes. Health problems result from dysfunction in a system or systems, due to injury, infection, toxic exposure, or other cause. They are treated with surgery and/or medication to restore normal functioning (cure), if possible, or to interrupt a downward spiral and provide rehabilitation, stabilization, or comfort care.

The focus of this book is the U.S. health care system, with some comparisons to certain peer industrialized countries including Western European nations, Canada, Australia, and Japan. The United States shares with these nations (as well as many others around the globe) the same basic understanding of health and health care, including what constitutes a health problem; what are legitimate and effective diagnostic and treatment theories, methods, and tools; and what persons should be designated as health care providers, with physicians dominant among them. This set of beliefs about health and health care, which originated and developed over a period of centuries in Western Europe, is generally referred to as "Western medicine." Western medicine is also called allopathic medicine after the medical faction (allopaths) that gained dominance in the 19th century over groups of healers including homeopaths, chiropractors, and osteopaths (Starr, 1982). Among the countries in which Western medicine is the primary means of dealing with the problems of health and disease, there are also certain similarities in the basic structures and organization used to deliver health care. Moreover, the United States and its peer nations have similar economies and abilities to finance their health care systems. However, as we will discuss, there are very real differences between the United States and its peer nations relating to the methods of paying for health care, the equity and efficiency of health care as provided, and population health outcomes. These differences make the U.S. health care system unique, even among its peer nations.

HEALTH AND HEALTH CARE

What Is Health?

The most famous and influential definition of health is the one developed by the World Health Organization (WHO): "Health is a state of complete physical, mental, and social well-being and not merely the absence of disease or infirmity." It was adopted in 1946 and has not been amended since 1948 (WHO, 1946). Many subsequent definitions have taken an equally broad view of health, including that of the International Epidemiological Association:

> A state characterized by anatomical, physiological and psychological integrity; ability to perform personally valued family, work, and community roles; ability to deal with physical,

biological, psychological and social stress; a feeling of well-being; and freedom from the risk of disease and untimely death.

Both definitions exemplify the tendency over the second half of the 20th century to enlarge the definition of health beyond morbidity, mortality, and disability to include sense of well-being, ability to adapt to change, and social functioning. However, in practice, the more limited view of health usually guides the provision of health services and efforts to improve health status. As Young (1998) writes: "Indeed, the WHO definition is 'honored in repetition, rarely in application.' Health may become so inclusive that virtually all human endeavors, including the pursuit of happiness, are considered within its domain" (p. 2).

Determinants of Health

Individual and population health are determined by many factors, only one of which is health care. It is generally accepted that the determinants of health include genetic inheritance, the physical environment—natural and built—and the social environment. The impact of these factors on health is mediated by an individual's response to them, both behavioral and biologic. This concept is argued well by Evans and Stoddart (1994) and more recently in Marmot and Wilkinson's (2006) *Social Determinants of Health*. Note that although we talk about the "determinants of health," they are usually discussed in terms of how they are related to poor health. A brief overview of the determinants of health follows.

Genetic Inheritance

Our knowledge about the effects of genetic inheritance on health is growing rapidly. It is understood that, with few exceptions, disease processes are:

determined both by environmental and by genetic factors. These often interact, and individuals with a particular set of genes may be either more or less likely, if exposed, to be at risk of developing a particular disease. These effects can be measured by showing that the relative risk of exposure to the environmental factor is significantly greater (or lesser) for the subgroup with the abnormal gene, than the risk in those without. (Pencheon, Guest, Melzer, & Gray, 2001, p. 544)

Physical Environment

Physical environment factors include health threats from exposure to toxins and unsafe conditions, particularly in occupational and residential settings. Many occupations can expose workers to disease-causing substances, high risk of injury, and other physical risks. For example, the greatest health threats to U.S. farm workers are injuries from farm machinery and falls that result in sprains, strains, fractures, and abrasions (Myers, 2001). There are well-documented health threats to office workers from indoor air pollution, found by research beginning in the 1970s, including passive exposure to tobacco smoke, nitrogen dioxide from gas-fueled cooking stoves, formaldehyde exposure, "radon daughter" exposure, and other health problems encountered in sealed office buildings (Samet, Marbury, & Spengler, 1987; U.S. Environmental Protection Agency, 2006). In residential settings, exposure to pollutants from nearby industrial facilities, power plants, toxic waste sites, or a high volume of traffic presents hazards for many. In the United States, these threats are increasingly known to have a disproportionately heavy impact on low-income and minority communities (Centers for Disease Control and Prevention [CDC], 2003; Institute of Medicine [IOM], 1999).

Social Environment

Sociodemographic characteristics, particularly race, ethnicity, and socioeconomic status, are associated with significant variations in health status and risk for health problems. There is a large literature demonstrating the relationship between low socioeconomic status and poor health, including a gradient in which the higher the socioeconomic status, the better the health (e.g., Lynch & Kaplan, 2000; Williams, 1990).

Similarly, much research indicates that disparities in health status exist between racial and ethnic groups. Minority Americans, including African Americans, Hispanics/Latinos, Native Americans, and Pacific Islanders, generally have poorer health outcomes than do Whites. The preventable and treatable conditions for which disparities have been shown include cardiovascular disease, diabetes, asthma, cancer, and HIV/AIDS (U.S. Department of Health and Human Services [DHHS], 1998). Although race and ethnicity do not "explain" these disparities, they point to the need for explanations. Discrimination and its consequences are a recent focus for investigations attempting to explain racial and ethnic disparities (Krieger, 2000; Mays, 2007).

Nonphysical occupational factors also affect health. For example, a great deal of research demonstrates the relationship between poor health outcomes and the psychosocial work environment. The demand-control model is one well-known theory, hypothesizing that employees with the highest psychological demands and the lowest decision-making latitude are at the highest risk for poor health outcomes (Theorell, 2000). In addition, job loss and threat of job loss have a negative impact on health (Kasl & Jones, 2000).

Another large body of research on the social environment and health focuses on social integration, social networks, and social support

(Berkman & Glass, 2000). For example, numerous studies over the past 20 years have found that people who are isolated or disengaged from others have a higher risk of premature death. Also, research has found that survival of cardiovascular disease events and stroke is higher among people with close ties to others, particularly emotional ties. Social relations have been found to predict compliance with medical care recommendations, adaptation to adverse life events such as death of a loved one or natural disaster, and coping with long-term difficulties such as caring for a dependent parent or a disabled child.

In 2008, the WHO released a major report on the social determinants of health, *Closing the Gap in a Generation: Health Equity Through Action on the Social Determinants of Health* (WHO, 2008). The premise and evidence of the report are that "Social justice is a matter of life and death. It affects the way people live, their consequent chance of illness, and their risk of premature death. We watch in wonder as life expectancy and good health continue to increase in parts of the world and in alarm as they fail to improve in others." Areas studied include early child development, globalization, urbanization, employment conditions, social exclusion, priority public health conditions, and women and gender equity.

Health Behavior

The term *health behavior* can refer to behaviors that are beneficial to health. However, the term is generally used in the negative to refer to behaviors that harm health, including smoking, abusing alcohol or other substances, failing to use seat belts or other poor safety behaviors, making unhealthy food choices, and not engaging in adequate physical activity.

The effect of health behaviors on health status has been widely studied and found to be an important determinant of health. For example, most of the leading causes of death in the United States can be explained largely in terms of health behaviors that relate to them. Consider the 10 leading causes of death, as of 2007, as characterized by diagnosed disease or condition: diseases of the heart, malignant neoplasms, cerebrovascular diseases, chronic lower respiratory diseases, unintentional injuries (accidents), Alzheimer's disease, diabetes mellitus, influenza and pneumonia, nephritis, nephrotic syndrome and nephrosis, and septicemia. The next five leading causes of death were intentional self-harm (suicide), chronic liver disease and cirrhosis, essential hypertension and hypertensive renal disease, Parkinson's disease, and assault (homicide) (National Center for Health Statistics [NCHS], 2010).

In one way or another, personal health behavior has an impact on the occurrence in any given individual of most of the diseases and conditions on this list. Looking at the cause of death in a different way, that is, by major contributing cause of the disease to which the death was attributed rather than by the disease itself, in the first study of its kind, McGinnis and Foege (1993) showed that, as of 1990, the leading factors were tobacco use, dietary patterns, sedentary lifestyle, alcohol consumption, microbial agents, toxic agents, firearms, sexual behavior, motor vehicles, and use of illicit drugs. As of 2002, the situation remained the same (McGinnis, Williams-Russo, & Knickman, 2002).

Even though there is widespread agreement that health is a response to the physical and social environments in which the individual lives and is influenced by the individual's genetic inheritance, health behaviors are often seen as the best target for health improvement efforts. For example, the emphasis of *Healthy People 2010* (DHHS, 2000), which is the U.S. nationwide health promotion and disease prevention agenda, is on health behaviors and medical care. The leading health indicators cited in *Healthy People 2010* are level of physical activity, overweight and obesity, tobacco use, substance abuse, responsible sexual behavior, mental health, exposure to injury and violence, environmental quality, immunization status, and access to health care. Only the environmental quality indicator deals substantially with factors other than personal behavioral change or the availability of medical care.

Health Care as a Determinant of Health

The central focus of health care is to restore health or prevent exacerbation of health problems. If we argue that health is the product of multiple factors including genetic inheritance, the physical environment, and the social environment, as well as an individual's behavioral and biologic response to these factors, we see that health care has an impact late in the causal chain leading to disease, illness, and infirmity. Often by the time the individual interacts with the health care system, the determinants of health have had their impact on his or her health status, for better or worse. Thus, the need for health care may be seen as a failure to prevent the determinants of health from adversely affecting the individual patient.

Health care can be categorized in terms of its relationship to prevention—primary, secondary, and tertiary. Fos and Fine (2000) define these terms as follows: "Primary prevention is concerned with eliminating risk factors for a disease. Secondary prevention focuses on early detection and treatment of disease (subclinical and clinical). Tertiary prevention attempts to eliminate or moderate disability associated with advanced disease" (Fos & Fine, 2000, pp. 108,109).

Primary prevention intends to prevent the development of disease or injury before it occurs in individuals, and thus to reduce the incidence of disease in the population. Examples of primary prevention include the use of automobile seat belts, condom use, skin protection from ultraviolet light, and tobacco-use cessation programs. Secondary prevention is concerned with reducing the burden of existing disease after it has developed; early detection is emphasized. Secondary prevention activities are intended to identify the existence of disease early so treatments that might not be as effective when applied later can be of benefit. Tertiary prevention focuses on the optimum treatment of clinically apparent, clearly identified disease so as to reduce the incidence of later complications to the greatest possible degree. In cases where disease has been associated with adverse effects, tertiary prevention involves rehabilitation and limitation of disability.

Health care is primarily concerned with (a) secondary and tertiary prevention: early detection, diagnosis, and treatment of conditions that can be cured or limited in their consequences (secondary prevention); and (b) treatment of chronic diseases and other conditions to prevent exacerbation, stabilize conditions, and minimize future complications (tertiary prevention).

The health care system undoubtedly has its smallest impact on primary prevention; that group of interventions that focus on stopping the development of disease and illness and the occurrence of injury. And as Evans and Stoddart (1994) argue, other than for immunization, the major focus of the health care system's primary prevention activities is on the behavioral determinants of health, rather than the physical and social environments:

> The focus on individual risk factors and specific diseases has tended to lead not away from but back to the health care system itself. Interventions, particularly those addressing personal life-styles, are offered in the form of "provider counseling" for smoking cessation, seatbelt use, or dietary modification. These in turn are subsumed under a more general and rapidly growing set of interventions attempting to modify risk factors through transactions between clinicians and individual patients.

> The "product line" of the health care system is thus extended to deal with a more broadly defined set of "diseases": unhealthy behaviors. The boundary becomes blurred between, e.g., heart disease as manifest in symptoms, or in elevated serum cholesterol measurements, or in excessive consumption of fats. All are "diseases" and represent a "need" for health care intervention.... The behavior of large and powerful organizations, or the effects of economic and social policies, public and private, [are] not brought under scrutiny. (pp. 43,44)

The success of any health care system is also affected by the other determinants of health. Genetic predisposition to breast cancer may limit the long-term success rates of cancer treatment. Continued exposure to toxins in the environment or at work may decrease the likelihood that the physician can stabilize an individual with allergies. Health behaviors, such as smoking or substance abuse, may stymie the best health care system when treating an individual with lung disease. The lack of support at home for changes in behaviors or adherence to medical regimens may undermine the ability of the health care system to treat an individual with diabetes successfully. Poverty, race, and ethnicity often limit access to health care, and therefore the ability of physicians to diagnose and treat health problems effectively (IOM, 2003). We recognize that health, as well as health care, exist within a biological, physical, and social context, and all of these factors influence the health care system's probability of success.

HEALTH CARE SYSTEMS

Components of Health Care Systems

All health care systems have five major components: the facilities where health care is provided; the workforce that provides health care services; the providers of health care therapeutics, such as, in Westernized countries, pharmaceuticals and medical equipment; and the educational and research institutions that train the health care workforce and produce knowledge to improve health care services, and the financing mechanisms. In addition, some kind of organizational structure stands at the system's center, like the trunk of a tree. Besides this organizational structure, in any country's health care system there may be other loci of power and control. But wherever they exist, they are central to the system. They enable the system's components to interact and function to produce health services for the people.

Organization of Health Care Systems

The five components of the system—facilities, workforce, suppliers of therapeutics, education and research organizations, and financing mechanisms—are organized to produce health services. The forms and proportionate role of each differ among national systems. In the United States, as in most industrialized countries, there are three sectors that combine to organize the health care system: the governmental health agencies with health care functions, the private, nonprofit health care sector, and the private, profit-making, or commercial sector with health care functions.

Health Care System Management

If institutions, workforce, and financing are to be brought together in order to provide health care, they must be managed. System management includes four major activities: administration, planning, regulation, and evaluation. Each is closely related to the others. It should be noted that these terms are not used consistently in the description and analysis of the operations and functions of all the health care system sectors. A given action may be termed deliberate planning in one, normal administration in a second, and official regulation in a third. Additionally, the generic term management is often used interchangeably with the technically more narrow term administration.

Health Care System Performance

Health care systems can be judged on the following criteria: (a) the quality of the health care provided; (b) the equity achieved in the provision of health care; and (c) the efficiency with which health care is provided.

U.S. HEALTH CARE SYSTEM

We now turn to a brief overview of the U.S. health care system. In many ways, the U.S. health care system is similar to that in other countries where the allopathic medical model predominates. Yet it is also unique among those countries in several major ways. It is a truism that "when you've seen the U.S. health care system, you've seen the U.S. health care system." There are many different perspectives from which we could begin an examination of this extremely complex health care system. One is to look at its major features in the context of those of the health care systems of the other major industrialized countries.

In the United States, there is no one central "trunk" of the "tree," mentioned earlier, but multiple ones. For the United States, think of a banyan tree, not an oak. For example, there is no national Ministry of Health, or its equivalent, playing a central role in either the operation or the financing of health services. In the other industrialized countries, even if a ministry does not operate the health care system directly, at the least it creates and supervises the structure within which the system functions, and it customarily runs the national organization that pays for health care at the personal, institutional, and community-wide levels.

In the United States, the health care system is highly decentralized and fragmented. Its role and function focus significantly on producing outcomes, such as power and profits for providers and payers, in addition to the provision of patient and community health services. Care is provided, and it is paid for. Top-quality health sciences research is carried out, and education is provided. There are certainly loci of power and control. But it is amazing how much money and time these other areas of power and control, such as the pharmaceutical and insurance industries, spend to make sure that the United States does not have a single national structure for paying for, much less operating, its health care system. This was evident most recently during efforts to achieve health care reform, which resulted in the Affordable Care Act (ACA) on March 24, 2010.

The United States has had a private fee-for-service system of medical practice that, certainly since the end of World War II, has produced, among other things, high incomes for many physicians. Although private medical practice is also common in most of the other industrialized countries, physician income in the United States has been significantly higher in relative terms than the income of most physicians in other industrialized countries. Since the mid-1980s, however, the U.S. health care system has become a major venue for the generation of corporate profits from the direct provision of health care services (Himmelstein & Woolhandler, 2001). This, too, is a unique feature of the U.S. health care system.

Next we will consider briefly each of the five major operating components of the health care system: workforce, facilities, suppliers of therapeutics, training and research, and financing, each of which is treated in more detail in later chapters.

Health Care System Components

Health Care Workforce

In 2009, about 15.5 million people worked in the health care system, up from 12.2 million in 2000 (NCHS, 2011, Table 105). As of 2010, the largest groups, aside from technicians such as radiologic and emergency medical technicians, were nurses, physicians, pharmacists, physical therapists, and dentists, in that order (United States Department of Labor, 2010). The physicians, of whom there were 784,199 active in 2008, up from 692,368 in 2000 (NCHS, 2011, Table 107), by tradition and by license have been the most powerful, dominant group. In the mid-1990s, however, a major change in the locus of control over medical practice did take place, as a significant portion of it moved to the managed care companies.

Health Care Facilities

Health care facilities are generally one of two types: inpatient and outpatient. Of the institutions housing and caring for patients in bed (inpatients), acute-care community hospitals are the most numerous. The American Hospital Association defines the *community hospital* as a nonfederal, short-term general or other special hospital. In 2008, there were about 5,010 acute-care community hospitals, with 808,069 beds—up from 4,915 hospitals in 2000, but down in number of beds from 823,560 (NCHS, 2011, Table 113). This is the predominant type of hospital in the United States. Other types of hospitals include psychiatric, tuberculosis and other respiratory disease hospitals, and long-term and short-term general and other specialty hospitals.

Hospitals are categorized in a variety of ways—for example, by control, size, function, and average length of patient stay. There are four functional categories: general, special, rehabilitation and chronic disease, and psychiatric. There are four principal types of control or ownership: government, nonfederal (state, local, county, city-county, or hospital district); government, federal; private, not-for-profit (sometimes called voluntary); and private, for-profit (also called investor-owned or proprietary) (American Hospital Association, 2010). Nursing homes are a separate category of health care facilities, which numbered 15,700 in 2009 with 1,705,808 beds (NCHS, 2011, Table 117). Nursing homes and other long-term care institutions are also described briefly in a later chapter.

Ambulatory or *outpatient* care is health care not delivered to inpatients. There were 1,189,619 ambulatory visits in physician offices, hospital outpatient departments, and hospital emergency departments in 2008, up from 1,014,848 in 2000 (NCHS, 2011, Table 91). This represented 393 visits per 100 persons (age adjusted), up from 374 visits per 100 persons in 2000. About 80% of ambulatory care was delivered in private doctors' offices rather than hospital outpatient and emergency departments. This percentage was slightly less than in 2000.

Suppliers of Therapeutics

A variety of therapeutics, including equipment and pharmaceuticals, are required in the health care system. Many kinds of equipment and supplies for the diagnosis and treatment of disease are produced by hospital and medical supply manufacturers. These items range from gauze pads, hospital furniture, sterile needles, laboratory chemicals, and anesthetic gases to diagnostic imaging and laboratory equipment, surgical instruments, orthopedic appliances, eyeglasses, hearing aids, and dental prostheses. The other major category of health therapeutics is pharmaceuticals (see Strongin, 2002). An indicator of the importance of this sector is the amount expended on therapeutics. Retail outlet prescription drugs and other medical products alone cost $299.6 billion in 2008, up from $169.8 billion in 2000. This category accounted for 12.8% of the total national health expenditures in 2008, similar to the percentage in 2000 (12.6%) (NCHS, 2011, Table 126). This category of health care expenditures, although very important, is not covered in any detail in this book.

Health Care Training and Research

The scientific basis of every health care system is the fund of knowledge about health and disease, as well as the understanding of how to apply that knowledge to prevention and treatment through various interventions. A vast store of knowledge has been accumulated from the observations and experiences of past centuries. In our era, both the scientific knowledge base and our understanding of the best means for applying it to health maintenance and disease treatment are expanding at an ever-increasing rate through evidence-based medical research. The primary function of the biomedical research and medical technology systems is to continue this expansion of knowledge.

Health sciences knowledge and technology are put to use by the large number of people who work in the health care system in its myriad professions and occupations. The health sciences education system educates and trains these professionals and technicians. In health care, how someone carries out a particular set of tasks and the nature of his or her motivation and attitude are sometimes as critical to success as what it is that he or she actually does. "How" can be taught as well as "what" can be. Thus, the health sciences education system plays a role in determining the character of the health care system that goes well beyond the mere technical and scientific content of the educational programs.

Health Care Financing and Cost

In 2009, the United States spent over $2.486 trillion on health care, or 17.6% of the gross domestic product (GDP). This amount published annually by the U.S. Department of Health and Human Services and called the National Health Expenditures, includes health consumption expenditures, "as well as the dollar amount invested in medical sector structures and equipment and noncommercial research to procure health services in the future" (Centers for Medicare and Medicaid Services, 2010, p. 3). The average annual percent change in National Health Expenditures has been declining since 1990, when it was 11.9%. In 2000, the average percent change was 7.1%, in 2005 it was 6.7%, in 2008 it was 4.7%, and in 2009 the average annual percent change was 4%. However, despite a steady decline in average annual percent change in the last 20 years, health expenditures in 2000, for example, were substantially lower than today and accounted for a considerably smaller percent of the GDP. We spent $1.378 trillion on health care in 2000, which was 13.8% of the GDP (U.S. Census Bureau, 2012, Table 135).

About 84% of the National Health Expenditures are for personal health care, which includes hospital care, physician and clinic services, other professional services, home health care, nursing care facilities and continuing care retirement communities, prescription drugs, durable medical equipment, and other nondurable medical products. The distribution of personal health care expenditures has stayed fairly constant since 2000 with some increase in hospital care and prescription drugs and decreases in professional services, nursing home and home health care, and medical equipment. In 2009, 36.3% was spent on hospital care (35.7% in 2000), 32.3% on professional services including physicians and other professionals (33.4% in 2000), 9.8% on nursing home and home health care (10.1% in 2000), 12.0% on prescription drugs (10.4% in 2000), and 3.7% on durable and nondurable medical equipment (4.9% in 2000) (U.S. Census Bureau, 2012, Table 134).

The sources of funding for National Health Expenditures can be categorized as: (a) out-of-pocket; (b) private health insurance; (c) public health insurance; (d) other third-party payers and programs; (e) public health activity; and (f) investment in research, structures, and equipment. "Public health insurance" sources include Medicare, Medicaid, the Children's Health Insurance Program (CHIP), Department of Defense, and Department of Veterans Affairs. "Other third party payers and programs" include other federal sources, community and neighborhood clinics, state and local health departments, Indian health services, and Workers' Compensation. Public health activity includes services such as epidemiological surveillance, inoculations, immunizations, disease prevention programs, and public health laboratories. In 2009, for persons of all ages, 12% of the National Health Expenditures were paid out-of-pocket, 32.2% were paid by private insurance, 38.9% were paid by a public insurance program, 7.5% were paid by other third-party payers and programs, 3.1% were paid through public health activities; and 6.3% were investments in research, structures, and equipment. This compares to 2000 when 14.7% of the National Health Expenditures were paid out-of-pocket, 33.3% were paid by private insurance, 33.4% by public insurance, 9% by other programs and third-party payers, 3.1% by public health activities; and 6.5% as investments in research, structures and equipment (U.S. Census Bureau, 2012, Table 135). The greatest change in source of funds for health care expenditures between 2000 and 2009 was in the contributions of the public insurance programs—Medicare, Medicaid, CHIP, and the Departments of Defense and Veterans Affairs—which increased from 33.4% to 38.9% of the total.

Financing Mechanisms. The largest source of health care funds is health insurance—private and public—which currently pays about two-thirds of health care costs. The term *health insurance* is customarily applied to a system under which an insurance company is paid money (a premium) in advance for agreeing to pay for the costs or some proportion of them of a specified list of health services provided to a named beneficiary during a specified period of time. Under traditional health insurance, the care is not provided by the insurance company itself. Under managed care, either the "insurance" and the care are provided by the same company, or the insurer and provider are very closely connected, usually by contract. The reason the word *insurance* is put in quotation marks above is that the customary use of the term health insurance is not in accord with the usual meaning of the word *insurance*. Customarily, the term describes an arrangement under which members of a group pay a premium to a financial entity to protect themselves against the financial consequences of the occurrence of a relatively rare event, such as premature death or the loss of a dwelling to fire. The use of health services over a lifetime, by the members of any covered group of beneficiaries, is not a rare event, however. Thus the term *insurance* is inappropriately used in the health care sector. What is going on, rather, is prepayment for at least some services that one can expect to use at some time in the future. Nevertheless, because the term *health insurance* has a customary meaning, even though it is at variance with the true meaning of *insurance* we will use it in a similar way.

Although health insurance has traditionally been a major payer of health care costs, the enactment of the Health Maintenance Organization Act of 1973 brought about a major change in how health insurance pays for health care, called managed care.

> Managed care plans are health insurance plans that contract with health care providers and medical facilities to provide care for members at reduced costs. These providers make up the plan's network. How much of your care the plan will pay for depends on the network's rules. Restrictive plans generally cost you less. More flexible plans cost more. There are three types of managed care plans:
>
> * Health Maintenance Organizations (HMO) usually only pay for care within the network. You choose a primary care doctor who coordinates most of your care
> * Preferred Provider Organizations (PPO) usually pay more if you get care within the network, but they still pay a portion if you go outside
> * Point of Service (POS) plans let you choose between an HMO or a PPO each time you need care. (MedlinePlus, 2011)

Managed care organizations (MCOs) enter into contracts with hospitals, physicians, and other providers to deliver health care to their enrollees (or beneficiaries) at what the MCO believes will be a favorable rate per enrollee for their care (capitated). Key attributes of managed care plans are (a) selecting providers who will then deliver a comprehensive range of services to enrollees at the agreed upon rate; (b) giving economic incentives to providers to choose less costly care; and (c) reviewing providers' utilization and quality of care, formally and regularly, through data mining claims data and chart review. Typically, the primary care provider is the "gatekeeper" who must approve the use of specialists. There are controls on inpatient hospital care and length of stay; and disease management, case management, wellness incentives, and patient education are used to control costs and quality.

This matter-of-fact description of managed care disguises the transformational change that it brought about in the U.S. health care system. Managed care shifted the balance of power from providers to payers. Payers entered "the treatment room" with providers, influencing their treatment patterns through reimbursement rates that affect patient flow; through provider incentives that favor certain tests and procedures over others; and through utilization and quality reviews that further constrain provider autonomy in decision making.

Managed care has been a very controversial practice from the start. Critics say it restricts needed access to health care and adversely affects health care quality. The use of economic incentives to providers for limiting certain kinds of health care and the restraint on their fees concern detractors. Proponents argue that managed care reduces inefficiencies and, thereby, costs of the health care system without affecting quality or access. However, two factors make it difficult to evaluate the effects of managed care on cost, quality, and access. First, managed care is almost invisible now because it is so pervasive. All payers—for-profit, nonprofit, and government—have adopted managed care principles and practices to some extent. As an example, the health care reform legislation passed under President Obama in 2010—the Affordable Care Act—put managed care principles and practices into place by its focus on effectiveness and efficiency.

Second, managed care plans are so varied that it is difficult to generalize about their effects on cost, quality, and access. The criteria for selection of providers, the limitations on covered services, the reimbursement rates negotiated with providers, and the ways that utilization and quality reviews are used differ widely across plans. Thus, we should expect that the actual quality of care received and the costs of that care will differ, as well. These factors—reimbursement rates, favored services, and utilization review criteria—may be more predictive of quality and cost of health care than whether or not the care was "managed."

Nevertheless, we refer to managed care throughout this book because of its singular influence on the way health care is delivered today in the United States, although its influence on costs, quality, and access appears not to be uniform.

Organization of Health Care Services

The components of a health care system are organized to provide health care services. The forms and proportionate role of each component differ among national systems. In the United States, as in most industrialized countries, there are three major sectors involved in organizing health care services: the principal governmental health authorities and other agencies of government with health care functions (government sector), the private, nonprofit health care sector, which includes the voluntary health care agencies and professional associations, and the private, for-profit enterprises with health care functions.

Government Sector

In the United States, each of the three levels of government—federal, state, and local—directly operates certain health services programs. For example, there are the federal Department of Veterans Affairs hospital system, the state mental hospitals, and the local government public hospitals. Furthermore, by being the conduit for almost half of the money paid for health services, by collecting and disseminating health and health services information, by educating and training personnel directly, by providing financial support for many private health sciences educational institutions, and by being the largest player in the biomedical research arena, government is closely involved with virtually all health services delivery.

The principal health agency of the U.S. federal government is the Department of Health and Human Services, headed by a cabinet-level secretary. The agency is responsible for the federal Social Security program, the federal role in the state-run public assistance programs, and the main federal programs in biomedical research, regulation, financing, and public health. Many of the department's responsibilities are met by allocation of money and delegation of authority to the many other public and private entities throughout the nation that are concerned with health matters.

In each of the 50 states there is a major health agency that is part of state government. As at the federal level, in some states the agency is combined with agencies for social welfare or other functions. The administrative configuration and scope of functions of the state health care agencies are highly variable. The heads of these agencies are ordinarily appointed by the state's governor. Administratively, they are responsible entirely to the governor and not at all to the Department of Health and Human Services. Only insofar as certain standards must be met as a condition for receipt of certain federal monies or in times of declared national emergency must the states accept national direction.

Similarly, below the level of state government, there are units of local government—counties, cities, and occasionally special health services districts—that also have major health care agencies. Most of these have a great deal of operational autonomy, although on certain health matters the local health department may carry out functions delegated by the state agency.

Finally, a variety of health-related functions are carried out by non–health care government agencies. For example, at the federal level, the Department of Labor administers the Occupational Safety and Health Administration, and the Department of Agriculture sets national nutrition standards in cooperation with the Department of Health and Human Services. At all three levels of government, environmental protection services are often provided by an independent agency, for example, the Environmental Protection Agency at the federal level.

Private, Nonprofit Sector

The U.S. health care system traditionally has been dominated by private medical, and other health professional, practices, as noted earlier. At present, system trends have begun changing some of these relationships. Office and in-hospital medical, dental, chiropractic, and medical and nonmedical psychotherapeutic care, pharmacy, optical, speech and audiology services, and the fitting of prosthetic appliances, among other services, have been furnished primarily by private practitioners. However, this is changing. The following report on physicians is an example:

> Traditionally, American medicine has been largely a cottage industry. Most doctors cared for patients in small, privately

owned clinics—sometimes in rooms adjoining their homes. But an increasing share of young physicians, burdened by medical school debts and seeking regular hours, are deciding against opening private practices. Instead, they are accepting salaries at hospitals and health systems. And a growing number of older doctors—facing rising costs and fearing they will not be able to recruit junior partners—are selling their practices and moving into salaried jobs, too. As recently as 2005, more than two-thirds of medical practices were physician-owned—a share that had been relatively constant for many years, the Medical Group Management Association says. But within three years, that share dropped below 50 percent, and analysts say the slide has continued. (Harris, 2010)

It is especially noteworthy that even when the financial support for health services in the United States has been collectivized, as in the various public and private health insurance programs, the direct provision of health services to patients has remained substantially in the markets created by individual practitioners. In private medical practice, for example, whether it is carried out in the physician's office or at a hospital, the service is rendered by an individual physician to a private patient. The responsible third-party payer, if any, pays a private fee to the provider. The "participation" of the insurance companies in the provision of services is limited to making sure that the payments for care, in whole or in part, for the individual patient are covered by the company's policy, and that the care given is "appropriate" as a covered item of care, in terms of the insurance company's prewritten guidelines.

Voluntary Agencies. In all countries, there are nongovernmental agencies that play a role in the health care system. They are commonly known as *voluntary agencies.* In the United States, the group includes the American Heart Association, the Red Cross, and the Visiting Nurse Association. Voluntary health agencies have a wide variety of functions: to perform services not rendered by other health care agencies, to pursue certain research or service objectives with special vigor and dedication, to advance or protect the interests of a certain population subgroup, to engage in public and political education and advocacy, and to carry out certain tasks at the behest of governmental agencies.

Like corporations, in order to stay in business voluntary agencies must take in more money than they spend. In a voluntary agency, however, the excess of income over expenses does not accrue to any individual(s) but rather is used to support the expansion of that agency's work. A voluntary agency is thus labeled "not-for-profit" or "nonprofit." The voluntary agency may be devoted exclusively to health care delivery, or health services may be incidental to certain larger purposes, such as those of religious missions (domestic or foreign).

A subset of voluntary health care agencies is comprised of health professional organizations, for example, the American Medical Association (AMA), the American Nurses Association (ANA), the American Public Health Association (APHA), the American Hospital Association (AHA), the Association of American Medical Colleges (AAMC), and the American Medical Athletic Association (AMAA). In this nation of organizations, they are in fact legion. They are financed by individual and institutional membership dues, journal subscriptions and advertising fees and, on occasion, research grants and contracts. They are primarily concerned with advancing the perceived professional and economic interests of their members, both individual and institutional. They do this through, for example, public education, continuing professional education, litigation, legislative and political action and, on occasion, trade union–like activity. They also may focus on advancing scientific knowledge and understanding, setting and maintaining professional standards, and educating the public about health and disease.

Private, For-Profit Sector

There are two distinct ways in which for-profit enterprises provide health services. There are for-profit health services providers and suppliers, and there are corporations that deliver health services to their employees as a benefit of employment, a diminishing area of the private, for-profit health care sector.

For-Profit, or "Proprietary," Health Services Enterprises. These enterprises are playing an increasingly significant role in the U.S. health care system. There are five subgroups of for-profit health services enterprises. First are those engaged in therapeutics production, as mentioned earlier. Most significant in terms of its impact on national health policy is the pharmaceutical industry (Strongin, 2002). Second are the commercial health insurance companies, as well as those insurance companies providing professional liability (malpractice) coverage. Third are nursing homes for the aged and chronically ill, which have long been predominantly proprietary. There were about 1.7 million nursing home beds in 16,000 certified nursing homes in 2009 (NCHS, 2011, p. 7), with about 67% operated for-profit (Harrington, Carrillo, Blank, & O'Brian, 2010). Fourth are the for-profit, proprietary, general hospitals; those that are part of a managed care company and those that are independent. They accounted for about 17% of the nonfederal, short-term hospitals and 13.4% beds in 2008. This is an increase over 2000 in the number of hospitals and number of beds—13.5% and 11.8%, respectively (NCHS, 2011, Table 113). Fifth is the for-profit managed care sector (the MCOs), which has grown rapidly and is now the dominant nongovernmental actor on the health care system stage. It has developed mainly from the proprietary hospital sector and commercial health insurance.

Employee Health Services. In the United States, in-plant employee health services are generally of circumscribed scope, except in large establishments (more than 500 workers). In smaller factories, they are usually limited to the provision of first-aid by an industrial nurse or perhaps only a medicine chest for self-use. Large plants or mines may maintain a staff of physicians and nurses who perform preplacement and periodic health examinations, treat any work-related illnesses, disabilities, or injuries, and may engage in work site wellness activities (O'Donnell & Harris, 1994). Enterprises in isolated locations, such as rural railroad junctions or lumber mills, may operate comprehensive medical care programs. Industrial firms are obligated by law to protect workers from accidents and occupational diseases, although enforcement, carried out by the federal Occupational Safety and Health Administration (OSHA) and, in certain designated state agencies, is often weak.

Types of Health Services

The several components of the health care system work together to produce health services for individuals (personal health services) and population groups (community health services).[1] To distinguish the personal from other parts of the system, what happens in the former is customarily called the "delivery of health services." These services are usually further categorized as primary, secondary, or tertiary.

Primary Care

In functional terms, primary care is the care that most people need most of the time for most of their health and illness concerns, for patients who are not in institutional beds. Primary care includes a range of personal treatment and preventive measures. Common forms of personal preventive measures are the promotion of personal lifestyle/behavior change (e.g., becoming a regular exerciser), immunization, prenatal care, and periodic health examination for early disease detection. In industrialized countries, both treatment and preventive interventions are usually provided by a physician, although in some parts of the United States nurse practitioners and physician assistants also provide primary care.

Most of the major causes of acute and chronic morbidity (sickness) are treated in the primary care setting. As of 1996 (the most recent year for which the following data were available at the time of writing), the major causes of acute and chronic morbidity were respiratory conditions, influenza, the "common cold," injuries, other infective and parasitic diseases, hearing impairment, chronic sinusitis, arthritis, hypertension, heart conditions, orthopedic impairments (including low back pain), and asthma and hay fever (Adams, Hendershot, & Marano, 1999, Tables 1, 57).

Secondary and Tertiary Care

Secondary care (the most difficult level to define) includes services that are available in both community hospitals and physicians' offices. Ideally, they are arranged through referral or consultation after a preliminary evaluation by a primary care practitioner. Secondary services include most surgical procedures and the common diagnostic and treatment interventions of such specialists as radiologists, cardiologists, and ophthalmologists.

Tertiary care consists of highly specialized diagnostic, therapeutic, and rehabilitative services, requiring staff and equipment "that transcend the capabilities of the average community hospital" (Rogatz, 1970, p. 47). Such care, available largely at major medical centers, includes organ transplantation, open-heart surgery, and other technically complex procedures, complex chemo- and radio-therapy for cancer, and the preservation of very low birth-weight premature infants.

In the United States, both secondary and tertiary health services are highly developed. That development has not always occurred either in response to a well-documented need or in a planned way so as to make for the most efficient use of scarce resources.

Care of Special Populations and Diseases

In all health care systems there are special programs providing primary, secondary, and tertiary care for certain population subgroups that are defined by age, gender, or occupation, as well as the management of certain specific health disorders in the population as a whole. In the United States, many of the special programs for defined population groups are provided by government, such as those for military personnel and dependents, military service veterans, and Native Americans. Other U.S. population subgroups for which special programs of health care have been created include railroad workers, migrant farm workers, certain industrial workers, schoolchildren, and college and university students.

Special programs can also be organized by type of illness. Mental illness is the most important health disorder for which special subsystems of health care are organized in the United States. Historically, hospitalization for mental illness took place primarily in special mental hospitals, primarily financed and operated by state governments. However, throughout the country the state hospital systems have shrunk drastically since the mid-1960s in both the number and the size of the hospitals, with little replacement by alternative services such as community mental health centers. This long-term development has had increasingly negative effects for both patients and the communities in which they live, as well as for the nonspecialized hospitals to which they are forced to turn when no other alternative is available (DHHS, 1999; Haugh, 2002; Sharfstein, Stoline, & Koran, 2002).

Ambulatory care for mental illness and emotional problems can be provided in private practice by psychiatrists, clinical psychologists, psychiatric social workers, and other psychotherapists. There are also several thousand public or voluntary mental health clinics serving primarily low-income patients. As noted, a national community mental health center system, for which federal legislation was enacted back in the 1960s to replace the state mental hospital system, has never been developed. Nevertheless, as also noted, the state mental hospital system was sharply and steadily contracted over the last third of the 20th century.

Tuberculosis (TB), before the steep decline in its incidence and prevalence that occurred after the discovery at mid-20th century of antibiotics effective in treating it, also warranted a special network of clinics and hospitals for its detection and care. The current increase in the incidence of tuberculosis related to acquired immunodeficiency syndrome (AIDS), although a serious problem, is not of a magnitude that will lead to the reestablishment of anything like the old TB sanitarium system.

Health Care System Management

Administration

The administration of health services is a complex matter; the subject of many lengthy books (e.g., Shortell & Kaluzny, 2006). Although the principles of good administration and management apply equally, the many different types of health services organizations face different types of administrative problems.

For example, consider an administrative/management problem with which hospitals around the country are wrestling. Its resolution will require major changes in the way hospitals are structured. Those structural changes will in turn require major changes in the way people think and feel. The problem is that, with a few exceptions, hospitals are not used to mounting coordinated programs, but rather to delivering individual services, each component putting in its piece more or less as it judges to be best, and hoping that it fits. Medical staffs in hospitals in particular are often used to functioning independently, not as part of a team (Carpenter, 2002; Sanderson, 1996/1997).

Many of the contradictions that are evident in the role of service, teaching, and research in hospitals will have to be resolved before these administrative problems can be resolved. Managed care puts special strains on the administration and management of hospitals, although the problems raised by the for-profit and not-for-profit varieties are rather different.

Dominant Manager: Changes in the Physician–Patient Relationship. Traditionally, as noted, American physicians control the bulk of the decision-making process concerning the allocation and use of health care system resources, whether through scheduling visits to their offices, or the ordering of diagnostic tests, hospital admissions, surgical interventions, or the use of pharmaceuticals, for example. One of the major factors leading to the ever-rising costs of U.S. health care (U.S. Census Bureau, 2005, Table 118) has been this characteristic of independent physician decision making in resource allocation.

With the advent of managed care, that pattern began to change (Dudley & Luft, 2001; Kassirer, 1995). Traditionally, whether or not the service was paid for by the patient or a third party other than the patient or physician, medical care in the United States has been provided primarily on the basis of a private, direct (usually unwritten) contract between physician and patient. Under managed care, an MCO, usually for-profit (Dudley & Luft, 2001; Smits, 2002), contracts with patients, either directly or through their employers, to provide medical care. In the United States there is a clear distinction between managers and providers.

As MCOs increasingly became the primary contractor with patients for the provision of medical care, they took away from the physicians an increasing amount of the decision-making authority over how health care system resources are used and spent. This led to a degree of cost containment as utilization of certain resources declined (KPMG Peat Marwick, 1996). (By coincidence, the upward march of health care costs significantly in excess of the rise in the Consumer Price Index resumed in the early 2000s; Heffler et al., 2002, Table 2.) But it also led to a rising level of unhappiness and dissatisfaction, for somewhat different reasons, among both doctors and patients ("Can HMOs Help," 1996; "Hillary, you won the war," 2001). We will return to these themes at various points in this book.

Planning

Planning may be defined as any deliberate action to determine unmet needs, set goals and objectives, design a program to meet them, and allocate resources for implementing the program in a systematic way. In this sense, health and health care planning in the United States and elsewhere can be said to have occurred with the establishment of the first hospital or the organization of the first governmental office of public health.

Even though virtually all health care entities engage in some form of health services planning at some time or other, customarily the terms *health care planning* and *health services planning* refer to the actions of a governmental or quasigovernmental agency in carrying out the functions just described. The results of the activity can be applied at any health care system level, from the local to the national.

The findings and decisions of health care planning agencies have only in-frequently been backed by the force of law. Thus, health care planning in the United States has, for the most part, been very weak. Legally enforced planning has been largely confined to hospital construction. From the mid-1990s onward, in many parts of the United States, there was no official planning function in place at all. With the exception of antitrust considerations, major decisions, even on such matters as medical school mergers, the growth of the managed care approach to the delivery of health services, and the concomitant expansion of profit making in the health care field, for the most part have been left to the institutional/provider parties themselves.

Government Regulation

Somewhat paradoxically, in the U.S. health care system, government regulation of certain aspects of the system, other than prospective system planning, is highly developed. However, U.S. government regulation is primarily a reactive, not a proactive, process. In the health care system it usually occurs, for example, after serious financial problems have developed or serious defects in quality have been encountered. There is also regulation in the public health sector, for example, in response to the undertaking by a corporate entity of an activity that threatens the health, safety, or comfort of some significant group of people in society.

Because of the highly decentralized, primarily private administrative structure and the general absence of planning, many problems and abuses have developed in the system over time. In response, federal, state, and local governments from time to time have imposed health care system regulation in an attempt both to correct existing deficiencies, inefficiencies, and inequities and to prevent the development of new problems in the future. Presently, government regulation of the health care system operates at a modest level. Should the public find that the operations of the free market cannot meet all of their expressed needs, that level could rise again in the future, that is, if the expected opposition of those entities being regulated could be overcome (Blumenthal, 2001; Geyman, 2003).

Evaluation

Program evaluation technique is highly developed in the United States (Horn, 1997, 2002; IOM, 2000; Rossi & Freeman, 1993). A good deal of academic program evaluation is carried out. For a variety of public policy reasons, however, not the least of which is the absence of any national health care system or national health planning system, actual applied program evaluation is often not done in the United States. For example, from the mid-1990s onward, managed care development has moved swiftly ahead, with little applied evaluation of the effectiveness of the approach of its several different forms in meeting MCOs' stated goals and objectives, much less the objectively determined societal goals (Kodner, 1996). This may be changing with the development of "pay for performance," in which reimbursement rates are based on outcomes achieved. If the Medicare program adopts this strategy for improving health care outcomes, there will be a ripple effect on all providers, including MCOs (Rosenthal, Landon, Normand, Frank, & Epstein, 2006).

The Population Served

It can be argued that those people who use the health care system have as great an influence on the system as those who provide health care. What are some of the major characteristics of the U.S. population—the aggregate user of health care—that influence the health care system?

In 2010, the population of the United States was about 309 million (U.S. Census Bureau, 2005, Table 2). Many characteristics of the U.S. population differentiate us from other industrialized countries that have more homogenous populations, and these characteristics, in turn, contribute to shaping our health care system.

Unlike our peer countries, such as Germany, the United Kingdom, the Scandinavian countries, and Japan, the United States has a more racially and ethnically diverse population. In 2010, 72.4% of the U.S. population was White (includes persons of Hispanic or Latino origin), 12.6% was Black or African American, 4.8% was Asian, and 10.2% was some other race, or two or more races. About 16% of the population was of Hispanic or Latino origin. As a percent of total population, every racial and ethnic group increased between 2000 and 2010 except for non-Hispanic Whites (U.S. Census Bureau, Humes, Jones, & Ramirez, 2011). This is in contrast to the European nations, for example, that have an estimated 3% to 4% ethnic minorities of non-European origin. Lack of cultural competence among providers can lead to a decrease in the quality of care provided, thus contributing to the existing health disparities in minority populations in the United States (Betancourt, Green, Carrillo, & Park, 2005).

There is also a broad range of social classes with large income differentials, that are becoming wider over time (IOM, 2002; Reich, 1998; IOM, 2003; Thurow, 1995; "Who's Winning," 2001). Unfortunately, the United States has the greatest disparity between the rich and poor of all the Western European countries and Japan (*World Factbook*, 5 October 2006). These disparities add to the complexity and fragmentation of the U.S. health care system through effects such as differential care, payment issues, cost sharing, and access problems.

Age structure also affects the U.S. health care system. The population forecast for the year 2020 undoubtedly foreshadows major changes on the system, as the Baby Boomer generation ages. As a result, health care consumption patterns that have remained fairly constant over time will move more unevenly in the direction of elderly care. Physicians will need to spend more time providing services for the elderly, increasing from 32% of patient care hours in 2000 to 39% in 2020 (Bureau of Health Professions, 2003). Health care expenditures are also expected to increase because of the growing elderly population, putting greater pressures on Medicaid and Medicare to provide services for the increasingly large retired population.

As an example of how demographic and health characteristics of the population affect the health care system, consider the following findings about the variation in health care expenditures by chronic condition and age:

> Half of the population spends little or nothing on health care, while 5 percent of the population spends almost half of the total amount. In 2002, the 5 percent of the U.S. community (civilian non-institutionalized) population that spent the most on health care accounted for 49 percent of overall U.S. health care spending..... In contrast, the 50 percent of the population with the lowest expenses accounted for only 3 percent of overall U.S. medical spending, with annual medical spending below $664 per person. Thus, those in the top 5 percent spent, on average, more than 17 times as much per person as those in the bottom 50 percent of spenders....
>
> The elderly (age 65 and over) made up around 13 percent of the U.S. population in 2002, but they consumed 36 percent of total U.S. personal health care expenses. The average health care expense in 2002 was $11,089 per year for elderly people but only $3,352 per year for working-age people (ages 19–64)....However, within age groups, spending is less concentrated among those age 65 and over than for the under-65 population. The top 5 percent of elderly spenders accounted for 34 percent of all expenses by the elderly in 2002, while the top 5 percent of non-elderly spenders accounted for 49 percent of expenses by the non-elderly. A principal reason why health care spending is spread out more evenly among the elderly is that a much higher proportion of the elderly than the nonelderly have expensive chronic conditions. (Stanton & Rutherford, 2005, pp. 2,3)

Health Care System Performance

For all of its resources, workforce, facilities, skills, knowledge, money, and ability to do wondrous things to and with the human body, the U.S. health care system is plagued with problems. Some observers consider the situation a crisis. "Sudden worsening" is part of the definition of crisis, however, most of the observed problems have been around for a long time. Thus, it can be fairly stated that the health care system is not in crisis. Rather, it has serious problems, many of which are long-standing, but some of which, especially the increasing dominance of for-profit activities, are of recent origin—in particular, as Schiff and Young (2001, p. 401) put it, "the (modern) transformation of health care from a service into a business" (see also Himmelstein & Woolhandler, 2001; Lasser, Himmelstein & Woolhandler, 2006; Woolhandler & Himmelstein, 2006). Unfortunately, many of the problems, whether recent or long-standing, are, at present, seemingly intractable.

Health care systems performance is generally evaluated on three criteria: (a) quality of health care; (b) equity of health care; and (c) efficiency of health care (Aday, Begley, Lairson, & Balkrishnan, 2004; Aday, Begley, Lairson, & Slater, 1993). Health care performance may be assessed at the micro level—for physician practices, hospitals, or other health care settings—or at the macro level—for regions, states, and nations. We introduce these concepts here, and discuss them in more detail later in the book.

Quality of Health Care

Beginning with Donabedian and inspired by his work (1980–1985), there has been increasing effort to assess the quality of health care systematically in order to bring about continuous quality improvement. Health care outcomes and their relationship to structure and process are of major importance in health care today (e.g., IOM, 2001). In general terms, this kind of quality assessment is performed through the conduct of research that compares the clinical outcomes of providers, institutions, treatments, and procedures, and then translates these research findings into clinical guidelines. Later in the book, we discuss clinical outcomes research and evidence-based medicine, as well as the organizations that have been in the forefront of this movement to improve the quality of health care.

In addition, we briefly discuss the population health orientation and its indicators of health care quality. A health care system can be evaluated on the ultimate health outcome measure, that is, the health status of the population it serves. As David Kindig (1997) wrote:

> Despite the massive resources it consumes, the U.S. health care system remains under stress. While we are global leaders in technical accomplishments in medicine, the amount of health we achieve per dollar invested is far from optimal.... [W]e will not maximize the amount of health we achieve until a measure of health outcomes becomes the purchasing standard for both the private and public sectors. (p. 1)

Equity of Health Care

The distribution of and access to health services for the American people are significantly uneven (IOM, 2002; Wennberg et al., 1996, 1999). For many persons who live in the right geographic location, have the right health care cost coverage package, and have a disease or condition on which American medicine has chosen to focus, American medicine is, as it is said, "the best in the world." But for the person who lives in the wrong place (Wennberg et al., 1996, 1999), has no health care cost coverage (Schroeder, 2001), is, for example, someone other than a young White male (IOM, 2002, Marmot, 2001; Stolberg, 2002) and, even worse, has a disease or condition in which American medicine has limited interest, the saying may well not be true. Such a person may be in serious trouble in terms of his or her health care and his or her health.

Efficiency of Health Care

Efficiency is either allocative (attaining the most valued mix of health care services) or productive (producing a given level of health care services at minimum cost). An allocative efficiency issue is how much to invest in preventive versus curative medical services, whereas a productive efficiency issue might concern whether and where to substitute relatively low-cost nurses for physicians in the provision of medical care. At the micro level, efficiency is assessed using: (a) production functions; and (b) cost-effectiveness, cost-benefit, and cost-utility analysis. At the macro level, efficiency analysis is based on comparisons of the performance of health care systems (Aday et al., 2004). In many studies of macro-efficiency, the U.S. health care system is less efficient than those of other nations, spending more, providing fewer basic resources per capita, and having worse population health outcomes, such as life expectancy.

FUTURE OF THE U.S. HEALTH CARE SYSTEM

History of Change

As far back as 1932, the findings of the first comprehensive study of health care in the United States were summarized in these terms (Committee on the Costs of Medical Care [CCMC], 1970/1932, p. 2):

> The problem of providing satisfactory medical service to all the people of the United States at costs which they can meet is a pressing one. At the present time, many persons do not receive service which is adequate either in quantity or quality, and the costs of service are inequably distributed. The result is a tremendous amount of preventable physical pain and mental anguish, needless deaths, economic inefficiency, and social waste. Furthermore, these conditions are … largely unnecessary. The United States has the economic resources, the organizing ability, and the technical experience to solve this problem.

Reports have been issued ever since; changes have been called for, and some have been made—for example, the enactment of the Medicare and

Medicaid legislation to ensure health care for older Americans and those without means. These calls for change have set the stage for our present situation as well as the future.

The Present Situation

Today, the problem list for the financing, distribution, and delivery of services has changed little since the time of the publication of the Committee on the Costs of Medical Care (CCMC) final report (except that the costs are incredibly higher). Indeed, certain problems considered important by the CCMC that are still pressing today that originated in our country and those of our European forebears well before the CCMC's time, in the 17th, 18th, and 19th centuries (Freymann, 1974, pp. 3–97). This is the case even though the advances in the science and technology of medicine have gone well beyond the wildest dreams of anyone giving thought to the possibilities in 1932.

Future Directions

Although this book describes the dominant health care system in the United States today, changes are occurring rapidly. Other health care methods, including alternate methods originating in Western countries, such as chiropractic, and those originating in other parts of the world, such as Chinese medicine, are increasingly accepted by Americans. These are being developed as parallel systems, as well as incorporated into the allopathic health care system. New financing and organizational models and, along with these, new paradigms of dominance and legitimacy are coming about. As a result, it is not clear what the U.S. health care system will look like 10 years from now. Some of the major changes occurring now will be discussed in the final chapter.

NOTE

1. A personal health service is one given directly to an individual—for example, treatment for an upper respiratory infection or the setting and casting of a fractured ankle. The recipient is almost invariably aware that he or she is receiving the service. A community health service is one provided to a group of people. Each group member may be aware that he or she is receiving the service, for example, public health education on smoking cessation, but often the group member is unaware of the service received, for example, as in the provision of pure water supply and sanitary sewage disposal.

REFERENCES

Adams, P. F., Hendershot, G. E., & Marano, M. A. (1999). *Current estimates from the National Health Interview Survey, 1996* (Vital and Health Statistics, Series 10, No. 200). Washington, DC: National Center for Health Statistics.

Aday, L. A., Begley, C. E., Lairson, D. R., & Balkrishnan, R. (2004). *Evaluating the healthcare system: Effectiveness, efficiency, and equity.* Chicago, IL: Health Administration Press.

Aday, L. A., Begley, C. E., Lairson, D. R., & Slater, C. H. (1993). *Evaluating the medical care system: Effectiveness, efficiency, and equity.* Chicago, IL: Health Administration Press.

American Hospital Association (AHA). (2010). *AHA guide 2011.* Chicago, IL: Health Forum.

Berkman, L. F., & Glass, T. (2000). Social integration, social networks, social support, and health. In L. F. Berkman & I. Kawachi (Eds.), *Social epidemiology* (pp. 137–173). Oxford, UK: Oxford University Press.

Betancourt, J. R., Green, A. R., Carillo, J. E., & Park, E. R. (2005). Cultural competence and health care disparities: Key perspectives and trends. *Health Affairs, 24*(2), 499–505.

Blumenthal, D. (2001). Controlling health care expenditures. *New England Journal of Medicine, 344*(10), 766–769.

Bureau of Health Professions, Health Resources and Services Administration. (2003). *Changing demographics and the implications for physicians, nurses, and other health workers.* Retrieved February 2, 2012 from www.nachc.com/client/documents/clinical/Clinical_Workforce_Changing_Demographics.pdf

Can HMOs help solve the health-care crisis? (1996, October). *Consumer Reports,* pp. 28–35.

Carpenter, D. (2002, February 1). Hospital stocks prove health on Wall Street. *Hospitals and Health Networks,* p. 22.

Centers for Disease Control and Prevention (CDC). (2003). *Environmental public health indicators.* Atlanta, GA: National Center for Environmental Health, Division of Environmental Hazards and Health Effects.

Centers for Medicare and Medicaid Services (CMS). (2010). *National health expenditure accounts: Methodology paper, 2010.* Retrieved on June 4, 2012, from www.cms.gov/Research-Statistics-Data-and-Systems/Statistics-Trends-and-Reports/NationalHealthExpendData/downloads/dsm-10.pdf

Committee on the Costs of Medical Care. (1932). *Medical care for the American people.* Chicago, IL: University of Chicago Press. (Reprinted, Washington, DC: USDHEW, 1970.)

Donabedian, A. (1980–1985). *Explorations in quality assessment and monitoring. Vol. I: The definition of quality and approaches to its measurement; Vol. II: The criteria and standards of quality; Vol. III: The methods and findings of quality assessment and monitoring—An illustrated analysis.* Ann Arbor, MI: Health Administration Press.

Dudley, R. A., & Luft, H. S. (2001). Managed care in transition. *New England Journal of Medicine, 344*(14), 1087–1092.

Evans, R. G., & Stoddart, G. L. (1994). Producing health, consuming health care. In R. G. Evans, M. L. Barer, & T. R. Marmor (Eds.), *Why are some people healthy and others not?* (pp. 27–64). New York, NY: Aldine de Gruyter.

Fos, P. J., & Fine, D. J. (2000). *Designing health care for populations: Applied epidemiology in health care administration.* San Francisco, CA: Jossey-Bass.

Freymann, J. G. (1974). *The American health care system: Its genesis and trajectory.* New York, NY: Medcom.

Geyman, J. P. (2003). Myths as barriers to health care reform in the United States. *International Journal of Health Services, 33*(2), 315–329.

Harrington, C., Carrillo, H., Blank, B., & O'Brian, T. (2010). *Nursing, facilities, staffing, residents, and facility deficiencies, 2004 through 2009.* Retrieved December 29, 2011, from www.pascenter.org/documents/OSCAR_complete_2010.pdf

Harris, G. (March 25, 2010). More doctors giving up private practices. *The New York Times: Money & Policy Section.* Retrieved from www.nytimes.com/2010/03/26/health/policy/26docs.html?pagewanted=all

Haugh, R. (2002, April). Nowhere else to turn. *Hospitals and Health Networks,* p. 45.

Heffler, S., Smith, S., Won, G., Clemens, M. K., Keehan, S., & Zezza, M. (2002).Health spending projections for 2001–2011: The latest outlook. *Health Affairs, 21*(21), 207–218.

Hillary, you won the war. (2001, June 23). *The Economist,* p. 33.

Himmelstein, D. U., & Woolhandler, S. (2001). *Bleeding the patient: The consequences of corporate health care*. Monroe, ME: Common Courage Press.

Horn, S. D. (1997). *Clinical practice improvement methodology: Implementation and evaluation*. New York, NY: Faulkner.

Horn, S. D. (2002). Improving quality of care. In A. R. Kovner & S. Jonas (Eds.), *Jonas and Kovner's health care delivery in the United States* (7th ed.). New York, NY: Springer Publishing.

Institute of Medicine (IOM). (1999). *Toward environmental justice: Research, education, and health policy needs*. Washington, DC: National Academies Press.

Institute of Medicine (IOM). (2000). *To err is human: Building a safer health system*. Washington, DC: National Academies Press.

Institute of Medicine (IOM). (2001). *Crossing the quality chasm: A new health system for the 21st century*. Washington, DC: National Academies Press.

Institute of Medicine (IOM). (2003). *Unequal treatment: Confronting racial and ethnic disparities in health care*. Washington, DC: National Academies Press.

Kasl, S. V., & Jones, B. A. (2000). The impact of job loss and retirement on health. In L. F. Berkman & I. Kawachi (Eds.), *Social epidemiology* (pp. 118–136). Oxford, UK: Oxford University Press.

Kassirer, J. P. (1995). Managed care and the morality of the marketplace. *New England Journal of Medicine, 333*(1), 50–52.

Kindig, D. A. (1997). *Purchasing population health: Paying for results*. Ann Arbor, MI: University of Michigan Press.

Kodner, D. (1996, September–December). *Managed care* [Course]. New York University.

KPMG Peat Marwick. (1996). *The impact of managed care on U.S. markets* [Executive Summary]. Washington, DC: Author.

Krieger, N. (2000). Discrimination and health. In L. F. Berkman & I. Kawachi (Eds.), *Social epidemiology* (pp. 36–75). Oxford, UK: Oxford University Press.

Lasser, K. E., Himmelstein, D. U., & Woolhandler, S. (2006). Access to care, health status, and health disparities in the United States and Canada: Results of a cross-national population-based survey. *American Journal of Public Health, 96*(7), 1300–1307.

Liu, Y. (1988). *The essential book of traditional Chinese medicine*. New York, NY: Columbia University Press.

Lynch, J., & Kaplan, G. (2000). Socioeconomic position. In L. F. Berkman & I. Kawachi (Eds.), *Social epidemiology* (pp. 13–35). Oxford, UK: Oxford University Press.

Marmot, M. (2001). Inequalities in health. *New England Journal of Medicine, 345*(2), 134–136.

Marmot, M., & Wilkinson, R. G. (Eds.). (2006). *Social determinants of health*. Oxford, UK: Oxford University Press.

Mays, V. M. (2007). Race, race-based discrimination, and health outcomes among African Americans. *Annual Review of Psychology, 58*, 201–225.

McGinnis, J. M., & Foege, W. H. (1993). Actual causes of death in the United States. *Journal of the American Medical Association, 270*(18), 2207–2212.

McGinnis, J. M., Williams-Russo, P., & Knickman, J. R. (2002, March–April). The case for more active policy attention to health promotion. *Health Affairs, 21*(3), 78.

Myers, J. R. (2001). *Injuries among farm workers in the United States, 1995*. Washington, DC: U.S. Department of Health and Human Services, Centers for Disease Control and Prevention, National Institute for Occupational Safety and Health.

National Center for Health Statistics (NCHS). 2010. Deaths: Final data for 2007. *National Vital Statistics Reports, 58*(19), 1–117.

National Center for Health Statistics (NCHS). (2011). *Health, United States, 2010: With special feature on death and dying*. Hyattsville, MD: U.S. Department of Health and Human Services.

O'Donnell, M. P., & Harris, J. S. (1994). *Health promotion in the workplace*. Albany, NY: Delmar.

Parsons, T. (1951). *The social system*. London, UK: Routledge & Kegan Paul.

Pencheon, D., Guest, C., Melzer, D., & Gray, J. A. M. (Eds.). (2001). *Oxford handbook of public health practice*. Oxford, UK: Oxford University Press.

Reich, R. B. (1998, April 5). The care and feeding of the rich. *The New York Times*, p. A29.

Rogatz, P. (1970, April 16). The health care system: Planning. *Hospitals*, p. 47.

Rosenthal, M. B., Landon, B. E., Normand, S. L., Frank, R. G., & Epstein, A. M. (2006). Pay for performance in commercial HMOs. *New England Journal of Medicine, 355*(18), 1895–1902.

Rossi, P. H., & Freeman, H. E. (1993). *Evaluation: A systematic approach*. Newbury Park, CA: Sage.

Samet, J. M., Marbury, M. C., & Spengler, J. D. (1987). Health effects and sources of indoor air pollution. Part I. *American Review of Respiratory Diseases, 136*(6), 1486–1508.

Sanderson, S. C. (1996, December–1997, January). Collaboration and team-building are critical skills for up-and-coming faculty. *AAMC Reporter, 6*(4), 1.

Schiff, G. D., & Young, Q. D. (2001). You can't leap a chasm in two jumps: The Institute of Medicine Health Care Quality Report. *Public Health Reports, 116*(5), 396–403.

Schroeder, S. A. (2001). Prospects for expanding health insurance coverage. *New England Journal of Medicine, 344*(25), 847–852.

Sharfstein, S. S., Stoline, A. M., & Koran, L. M. (2002). Mental health services. In A. R. Kovner & S. Jonas (Eds.), *Jonas and Kovner's health care delivery in the United States*. New York, NY: Springer Publishing.

Shortell, S. M., & Kaluzny, A. D. (2006). *Health care management, organization design, and behavior* (5th ed.) Albany, NY: Delmar.

Smits, H. L. (2002). Managed care. In A. R. Kovner & S. Jonas (Eds.), *Jonas and Kovner's health care delivery in the United States*. New York. NY: Springer Publishing.

Stanton, M. W., & Rutherford, M. K. (2005). The high concentration of U.S. health care expenditures. *Research in Action*, Issue 19. AHRQ Pub. No.06–0060.

Starr, P. (1982). *The social transformation of American medicine*. New York, NY: Basic Books.

Strongin, R. J. (2002). Drugs. In A. R. Kovner & S. Jonas (Eds.), *Jonas and Kovner's health care delivery in the United States*. New York, NY: Springer Publishing.

Theorell, T. (2000). Working conditions and health. In L. F. Berkman & I. Kawachi (Eds.), *Social epidemiology* (pp. 95–117). Oxford, UK: Oxford University Press.

Thurow, L. C. (1995, September 3). Companies merge: Families break up. *The New York Times*. Final, Section 4, page 11, column 1.

U.S. Census Bureau. (2005). *Statistical abstract of the United States: 2006*. Washington, DC: U.S. Department of Commerce.

U.S. Census Bureau. (2012). *Statistical abstract of the United States: 2012*. Retrieved December 27, 2011, from www.census.gov/compendia/statab/2012/tables/12s0134.pdf

U.S. Census Bureau, Humes, K. R., Jones, N. A., & Ramirez, R. R. (2011). Overview of Race and Hispanic Origin: 2010. *2010 census briefs*. Retrieved December 29, 2011, from www.census.gov/prod/cen2010/briefs/c2010br-02.pdf

U.S. Department of Health and Human Services (DHHS). (1998). *Call to action: Eliminating racial and ethnic disparities in health*. Potomac, MD: U.S. Department of Health and Human Services.

U.S. Department of Health and Human Services (DHHS). (1999). *Mental health: A report of the surgeon general*. Rockville, MD: National Institute of Mental Health.

U.S. Department of Health and Human Services (DHHS). (2000). *Healthy people 2010* (2nd ed., Vols. 1 and 2). Washington, DC: U.S. Government Printing Office.

U.S. Department of Labor; Bureau of Labor Statistics. (May, 2010). *National occupational employment and wage estimates, United States*. Retrieved December 21, 2011, from www.bls.gov/oes/current/oes_nat.htm#29–0000

U.S. Environmental Protection Agency. (2006). *Indoor air quality in large buildings*. Retrieved October 23, 2006, from www.epa.gov/iaq/largebldgs

U.S. National Library of Medicine, MedlinePlus. (2011). *Managed care*. Retrieved December 31, 2011, from www.nlm.nih.gov/medlineplus/managedcare.html

Wennberg, J. E. & Members of the Dartmouth Atlas of Health Care Working Group. (1996). *The Dartmouth atlas of health care.* Chicago, IL: American Hospital Publishing.

Wennberg, J. E. & Members of the Dartmouth Atlas of Health Care Working Group. (1999). *The quality of medical care in the United States: The Dartmouth atlas of health care, 1999.* Chicago, IL: Health Forum.

Who's winning the class war? (2001, Summer). *Too much,* p. 1.

Williams, D. R. (1990). Socioeconomic differentials in health: A review and redirection. *Social Psychology, 53*(81), 81–89.

Woolhandler, S., & Himmelstein, D. U. (2006). The new Massachusetts health reform: Half a step forward and three steps back. *Hastings Center Report, 36*(5), 19–21.

World Factbook. 5 October 2006. Retrieved February 2, 2011, from www.cia.gov/library/publications/the-world-factbook

World Health Organization (WHO). (1946). *Preamble to the constitution of the world health organization* as adopted by the International Health Conference, New York, June 19-July 22, 1946; signed on July 22, 1946, by the representatives of 61 states (Official Records of the World Health Organization, no. 2, p. 100) and entered into force on April 7, 1948.

World Health Organization (WHO). (2008). *Closing the gap in a generation: Health equity through action on the social determinants of health.* Geneva, Switzerland: WHO Press.

Young, T. K. (1998). *Population health: Concepts and methods.* New York, NY: Oxford University Press.

TWO

The Settings for Health Care Delivery

"WE'VE UPGRADED YOUR CONDITION FROM 'CRITICAL' to 'COSTLY.'"

©Artizans Entertainment Inc. By Harley Schwadron.

HOSPITALS

Hospitals accounted for the largest portion of U.S. health care spending (31%) in 2008 (Agency for Healthcare Research and Quality [AHRQ], 2011). In this section, we will provide some historical background on this important health care sector and then describe its current form—its services, organization, structure, and trends.

Historical Background

Historically, for the provision of personal health care the hospital has been the institutional center of the health care delivery system (Knowles, 1965). In its teaching incarnation, the modern hospital is also the center of much undergraduate and graduate clinical training for many health professions, as well as continuing health sciences education, both formal and informal. In addition, some teaching hospitals are also major centers for medical research. For most U.S. physicians, in addition to their private offices, the hospital is an important workplace, and the only place where they are likely to be subject to peer review of their professional work.

The word *hospital* shares its Latin root with the words *hostel* and *hotel*. Most frequently under church sponsorship, the institution originated in the Middle Ages primarily as a place of refuge for the poor, the sick, and the weary, rather than as a place for treating illness. As recently as the turn of the 20th century, a person entering a hospital had less than a 50% chance of leaving it alive. By the beginning of the 21st century, most patients could expect to benefit from a hospital stay—about 97% of patients expect to leave the hospital alive. Even though the quality of care could still be significantly improved (Institute of Medicine, 2000, 2002), the hospital has evolved from a place where a person went to spare his family the anguish of watching him die to a multiservice institution providing interdisciplinary medical care, ambulatory as well as in-bed (Freymann, 1974, pp. 21–29; Rosenberg, 1979; Stern, 1946, chapters 2, 6).

In the European settlements in America the earliest hospitals were infirmaries attached to poorhouses. (A poorhouse was an institution operated by a local government authority to house persons who were unemployed, orphans or abandoned children, the mentally ill or retarded, the ill elderly, and those otherwise incapable of self-care.) The first of these was established at Henricopolis in Virginia (1612), and the second in 1732 in Philadelphia (Stern, 1946, chapter 6).

The first public institution established solely for the care of the sick was the "pest-house" built in 1794 on Manhattan Island. It was located north of midtown, at a place called Belle Vue ("beautiful vista"). In a reverse of the earlier pattern, the New York City public workhouse (a later version of the poorhouse) was moved to the grounds of the pest-house in 1816. New York City's famous Bellevue Hospital is still at that location. Nongovernment charity (private, voluntary) hospitals to care for the sick poor were first established in the American colonies during the 18th century (Freymann, 1974, pp. 22–24). The first was the Pennsylvania Hospital in Philadelphia, founded by Benjamin Franklin in 1751.

By 1873, there were an estimated 178 hospitals in the United States, many of them solely for the mentally ill (Stevens, 1971, p. 52). At about that time, however, the development of modern medical science was under way, and a general hospital building boom began. By the early 20th century, a patient admitted to a general hospital did, in fact, have a better-than-even chance of getting out alive. That milestone was achieved largely through the development of general hospital hygiene, surgical asepsis (keeping surgical sites scrupulously clean and free of microbial contamination), and surgical anesthesia.

After the turn of the 20th century, overall medical care quickly became far too complex for average physicians to be able to carry their entire armamentarium in a black bag. By 1910, general hospitals had been established in many communities. There were nearly 4,400 of them, with a total of 421,000 beds (Stevens, 1971, p. 52). It was the rapid advance of medical science that led to the expansion of the hospital system and of individual hospitals, as well as to the evolution of hospitals as the center of the medical care system (MacEachern, 1962, pp. 21–27; Rosenberg, 1979).

The mold from which today's health care system was cast took its shape around 1850. There were still relatively few general hospitals or health care facilities of any type in either Great Britain (our most important medical organizational forebear) or the fledgling United States, but the institutional organization of health care was already firmly established. The physical separation, for the most part, as well as separate provision for administration and staffing of the curative services for acute, chronic, and psychiatric illnesses became firmly established in the 19th century. That very strong precedent continues to control the physical and administrative design of the health care delivery system even when all three components have a common source of support, as they do now in Britain.

Data Sources

The American Hospital Association (AHA) is the primary agency that counts and classifies hospitals in the United States. The AHA regularly publishes the *AHA Guide* (AHA, 2011a) and the companion AHA *Hospital Statistics* (AHA, 2011b), referred to as *Hospital Statistics* in the text. The former lists each AHA-registered and osteopathic hospital in the United States, as well as U.S. government hospitals outside the United States. The *Guide* provides information on the basic characteristics of each hospital, as well as other valuable information on "Networks, Health Care Systems and Alliances," and "Health Organizations, Agencies, and Providers" at the international, national, state, and voluntary levels, including the various quality-assurance bodies. *Hospital Statistics* presents summary descriptive data about U.S. hospitals, nationally and by state and region. A few selected summaries of AHA and other hospital statistical data are also published in *Health, United States* (National Center for Health Statistics [NCHS], 2006, 2010, 2011) and the *Statistical Abstract of the United States* (U.S. Census Bureau, 2005). This chapter uses AHA definitions and data, except as otherwise noted.

Definitions

Community Hospital

In general, hospitals are classified as general, special, rehabilitation and chronic disease, and psychiatric. The AHA has an all-inclusive descriptor for the majority of hospitals: the *community hospital*, which is defined as follows:

> All nonfederal, short-term general, and special hospitals whose facilities and services are available to the public. (Special hospitals include obstetrics and gynecology; eye, ear, nose and throat; rehabilitation; orthopedic, and other individually described specialty services.) Short-term general and special children's hospitals are also considered to be community hospitals. (AHA, 2011b, p. 203)

In 2009, there were 5,008 community hospitals out of the 5,795 of all types (AHA, 2011b, Table 2).

Hospital Type by Medical Condition Treated

There are 13 types of hospitals, when classified by type of medical condition treated: psychiatric; tuberculosis and other respiratory diseases; obstetrics and gynecology; eye, ear, nose, and throat; rehabilitation; orthopedic; chronic disease; surgical; cancer; heart; acute long-term care; general; and all others. The most numerous type is the general hospital, of which there were 4,766 in 2009 out of the total of 5,795 U.S. registered hospitals (AHA, 2011b, Table 2). These can be either federal or nonfederal, short term or long term, public or private.

Hospital Type by Control or Ownership

There are two principal types of control or ownership: private and public. Control is defined by the AHA as "The type of organization responsible for establishing policy concerning the overall operation of hospitals" (AHA, 2011b, p. 204). In turn, there are two categories of private hospital differentiated by the mode of distribution of surplus income: investor-owned, for-profit (formerly called proprietary), which may be owned by an individual, a partnership, or a corporation, and not-for-profit (also called voluntary). There are also three categories of public hospital: federal, state, and local.

Hospital Beds

Hospitals are also classified by the "number of beds regularly maintained (set up and staffed for use) for inpatients as of the close of the reporting period. This excludes newborn bassinets" (AHA, 2011b, p. 202). The AHA groups hospitals into eight categories based on bed size: 6 to 24 beds; 25 to 49 beds; 50 to 99 beds; 100 to 199 beds; 200 to 299 beds; 300 to 399 beds; 400 to 499 beds; and 500 beds or more.

Length of Patient Stay

There are two categories of hospital, as defined by length of patient stay: long term and short term. Respectively, the terms refer to stays of 30 days or more and of less than 30 days. "The figure is derived by dividing the number of inpatient days by the number of admissions" (AHA, 2011b, p. 208). *Total facility length of stay* "includes admissions and inpatient days from nursing-home-type units under control of the hospital. In *hospital unit length of stay*, nursing home utilization is subtracted" (p. 208).

Average Daily Census

The average daily census is the "average number of people served on an inpatient basis on a single day during the reporting period; the figure is calculated by dividing the number of inpatient days by the number of days in the reporting period" (AHA, 2011b, p. 202).

Hospital Trends

Type and Size of Hospitals

As can be seen from the foregoing definitions, hospitals can be classified by type of medical conditions treated; number of beds; control or ownership; short term or long term (defined by length of patient stay); and average daily census (the average number of beds occupied on a given day). Table 2.1 presents these data for the major classes of hospital for 2009. Not-for-profit community hospitals are clearly dominant in the hospital market with the most hospitals, beds, and admissions, as well as the highest average daily census. In 2009, most hospitals were nonfederal (96% or 5,584 of the 5,795 hospital, which includes long-term general and other hospitals not included in Table 2.1). Of the nonfederal hospitals, most were community hospitals (86% or 5,008 hospitals). About 58% of these community hospitals were not-for-profit (2,918) and 22% were state or local government owned (1,092). Only about 20% were investor-owned (998) (AHA, 2011b, Table 2).

TABLE 2.1 Basic Characteristics of Major Hospital Groups, United States, 2009

CHARACTERISTIC	ALL FEDERAL	NON-FEDERAL PSYCHIATRIC	NOT-FOR-PROFIT COMMUNITY	FOR-PROFIT COMMUNITY	STATE AND LOCAL COMMUNITY
Number of hospitals	211	444	2,918	998	1,092
Beds	44,772	76,287	556,406	122,071	127,116
Annual admissions	1,047,238	763,208	25,783,321	4,886,943	4,857,113
Average daily census	30,945	67,205	690,103	70,457	82,635
Average length of stay (days)	NA	NA	5.3	5.3	6.2

Source: Adapted from AHA (2011b, Table 2).

The hospital profile has changed over time. In 1978, a peak year, when the U.S. population was close to 40,000,000 fewer than it was in 1994, there were almost 1.4 million beds in 7,015 hospitals of all kinds, with an average daily census of 1.04 million patients and an overall occupancy rate of 75.5%. As of 1990, there were about 1.2 million beds in a total of 6,649 hospitals, with an average daily census of about 844,000 patients and an overall occupancy rate of about 70%. As of 2009, there were about 944,277 beds in a total of 5,795 hospitals, with a total admission of 37,479,709 and a total expenses of $726,671,229 (AHA, 2011b, Table 1).

The peak number of nonfederal, short-term general and other special hospitals in the United States, 5,979, was reached in 1975 (AHA, 2011b, Table 1). Before that, the number of such hospitals had risen rather steadily since 1946, when there were 4,444. Between 1946 and 1983, the number of beds in these hospitals increased from 473,000 to 1,021,000 (the high point), or more than doubled. During the same period, reflecting the decline in the number of small hospitals, the average number of beds per hospital increased by 65%, from an average of 106 beds per hospital to 175 beds per hospital.

After 1975, the number of nonfederal, short-term general, and other special hospitals declined steadily through 2011 (AHA, 2011b, Table 1). In 1985, there were about 5,784 hospitals, with 1,003,000 beds, close to 34 million admissions, and an average daily census of 650,000. By 2009, the number of hospitals shrank to 5,023 (a 16% drop since 1975), with 807,000 beds, more than 35 million admissions, and an average daily census of 529,000. Thus, compared to 1975, a smaller number of hospitals were admitting more patients in 2009, a fact that is reflected in the drop in average length of stay from 7.7 days to 5.4.

There were (and are) multiple reasons accounting for this phenomenon. Among them are the higher fixed costs in staff, facilities, and equipment for hospitals of any size that adversely affect the smaller hospitals; the increasing difficulties of hiring and retaining appropriate staff in rural hospitals; the increasing economies of scale for larger and larger hospitals as the availability of technology, with its attendant costs, increases; and the fact that when hospitals perform various procedures more frequently, the quality of each one goes up.

Teaching Hospitals. In the past, the AHA used the term *teaching hospital* to refer to hospitals providing undergraduate or graduate teaching for medical students and medical house staff (interns, residents, and specialty fellows). The term was not applied to hospitals with teaching programs for other health care providers. Although the AHA formerly presented data for the teaching hospitals separately, those data are now subsumed under the general categories of hospital, of which the teaching hospitals are a part.

In one of the last years for which teaching hospital data were presented separately, 1989, there were 1,054 teaching community hospitals (about 19% of all community hospitals), with 393,000 beds (more than 42% of all beds in community hospitals) (AHA, 1990, Tables 6 and 8). Their average size was about 370 beds, whereas the average size for all community hospitals was about 170 beds. The teaching hospitals had more than 14 million admissions (almost 46% of the total of community hospitals) and, on an average day, cared for more than 47% of all community hospital patients. They represented almost half of all visits to community hospital outpatient departments. Their occupancy rate was 74.6%, and the average length of stay was 7.5 days. In terms of both professional education and service, teaching hospitals have an importance in the hospital system that is out of proportion to their number.

Public General Hospitals. The public general hospital was defined by the Commission on Public General Hospitals of the American Hospital Association (Commission on Public General Hospitals of the American Hospital Association, 1978, p. v) as "short-term general and certain special hospitals excluding federal (those operated by the Department of Defense and the Department of Veterans Affairs), psychiatric, and tuberculosis hospitals that are owned by state and local governments."

Public general hospitals provide care for many persons unable to be treated elsewhere: the poor, the uninsured, the homeless, alcoholics and other substance abusers, the disruptive psychiatric patients, and prisoners. In certain areas such as isolated rural areas, the public general hospital is also the only source of care for patients with special medical problems regardless of income: the badly burned, at-risk newborns, high-risk mothers, and victims of criminal or noncriminal life-threatening trauma. Although only a minority of hospitals are under public ownership, in a nation without universal health care coverage, they play an important role beyond their numbers (Felt-Lisk, McHugh, & Howell, 2002; Friedman, 1997; Huang, Silbert, & Regenstein, 2005; May, 2004; Verghese, 1996).

The public hospital sector is shrinking today. In 1975, there were 1,761 state and local general hospitals with 210,000 beds. As of 1990, there were 1,444 state and local general hospitals, with a total of about 169,000 beds (AHA, 2011b, Table 1). By 2009, the numbers had shrunk to 1,092 state and local hospitals, with about 127,116 beds. The average daily census for these hospitals had declined from 148,000 in 1975, to 111,000 in 1990, and to 82,635 in 2009.

Despite the low occupancy rate, public general hospitals are still the primary health services resource for the nation's poor and for those with no health insurance. As of 2002, these hospitals were in serious trouble. Noting the shrinking number of public general hospitals, Richard Haugh (2002), writing in the AHA's journal *Hospitals and Health Networks*, highlighted their financial straits:

> [In] an era of tax cuts and disappearing [budget] surpluses, the well is dry. Officials are recommending deep austerity measures...[that] might foreshadow a looming crisis throughout the nation. The U.S. health care safety net is frayed; without

changes, critics fear, it will unravel—and drag other hospitals down with it. (p. 44)

As the axe falls on mental health funding, hospitals EDs fill the gap-reluctantly. In many areas, officials are also recommending privatizing these hospitals.

Hospital Distribution and Bed Supply

In 1948, there were approximately 3.4 nonfederal general medical and surgical hospital beds per 1,000 civilian resident population (AHA, 1990, Table 1). By 1976, the community hospital bed-to-population ratio was 4.5 beds per 1,000. By 1989, the ratio had declined to 3.8, and by 1994 it had reached 3.5, about where it was in 1948. By 2009, that ratio had declined to 2.6 (AHA, 2011b). Primarily because of a post–World War II hospital construction program known as "Hill-Burton" (after its two original congressional sponsors), the geographical distribution of beds was quite different in 2005 from what it had been in 1948.

Under Hill-Burton, many rural hospitals were built in areas that previously had no direct access to modern health services. Improvements in bed distribution and increases in bed supply after World War II, which provided access for many persons for whom hospital services were formerly unavailable, has been regarded as an outstanding national achievement. However, this massive program of hospital construction was undertaken without any kind of a national, comprehensive health care planning system in place.

It turned out that the hospital industry created many hospitals, particularly in the West and South, that now have extraordinarily low occupancy rates and many permanently empty beds. Furthermore, under Hill-Burton, many relatively small hospitals were built, in rural and semirural areas. In the modern era of high-tech, labor-intensive, expensive medical care, small hospitals tend to become highly inefficient and noncompetitive. This is one reason why so many small hospitals have gone bankrupt in the past 20 years.

Hospital closure, secondary to community overbedding and hospital undersizing in terms of the types of procedures that could be carried out, is the reason why in recent years the national bed-to-population ratio has been declining. However, most of the shrinkage has occurred haphazardly. Just as there was no plan when the hospital industry was expanding, there is no plan now when it is contracting. Under the pressure of managed care and "free market" competition, the hospital bed supply will likely continue to shrink for some years to come, but not in anything approaching a rational way.

Health Conditions of Hospitalized Patients

Considerable data on the characteristics of hospitalized patients are available from the National Hospital Discharge Survey of community hospitals

(Hall & Owings, 2002, pp. 1–3), produced annually by the National Center for Health Statistics of the U.S. Department of Health and Human Services. (In certain cases, these data differ somewhat from those of the AHA in describing the same hospital and patient characteristics.) In 2009, excluding newborns, there were about 36 million discharges from nonfederal, short-stay hospitals, and the average length of stay was 4.9 days (NCHS, 2010). This is in contrast to 31 million discharges in 1990 and an average length of stay of 6.4 days, a continuing trend of increasing number of hospitalizations with shorter stays. Persons age 65 and over accounted for about 39% of all discharges in 2009 (13,935 in 2009), up from 34% in 1990. In 2009, a little more than one-fifth of the national hospital bill was for treatment of only six conditions: septicemia, osteoarthritis, coronary atherosclerosis, liveborn (newborn infant), acute myocardial infarction, and complication of device, implant or graft (AHRQ, 2009a).

The 10 diagnoses in Table 2.2 accounted for about 31% of all principal diagnoses for hospital stays in both 1997 and 2009. However, there were

TABLE 2.2 Number of Stays, Stays Per 10,000 Population, and Growth of the Most Frequent Principal Diagnoses for Hospital Stays, 1997 and 2009

PRINCIPAL CCS DIAGNOSIS	NUMBER OF STAYS IN THOUSANDS		STAYS PER 10,000 POPULATION		CUMULATIVE GROWTH IN RATE
	1997	2009	1997	2009	1997 to 2009
All stays	34,679	39,435	1,278	1,284	1%[a]
Liveborn (newborn infant)	3,777	4,159	139	135	-3%[a]
Pneumonia	1,232	1,165	45	38	-16%
Congestive heart failure	991	1,023	37	33	-9%
Osteoarthritis	418	921	15	30	95%
Mood disorders	641	873	24	28	20%
Coronary atherosclerosis	1,407	832	52	27	-48%
Septicemia	413	831	15	27	78%
Cardiac dysrhythmias	572	807	21	26	25%
Trauma to vulva and perineum due to childbirth	713	751	26	24	-7%[a]
Chronic obstructive pulmonary disease and bronchiectasis	551	733	20	24	18%

[a] 2009 stays per 10,000 population are *not* statistically different from 1997 stays per 10,000 population at $p < 0.05$.

Source: Adapted from AHRQ (2009b).

substantial changes in the impact of each diagnosis on the overall percentage of hospital stays over time. Osteoarthritis, septicemia, mood disorders, and chronic obstructive pulmonary disease (COPD) accounted for a greater percentage of stays in 2009 than in 1997, while congestive heart failure, pneumonia, and coronary atherosclerosis accounted for far less.

In 2003–2004, there was a change in the rates of various procedures performed in the hospital, compared to 1993–1994 (NCHS, 2006, Table 99). Many procedures increased in frequency, including cardiac catheterization (52.4 to 57.9 per 10,000 population), angiocardiography using contrast materials (44 to 48.4 per 10,000), operations on vessels of the heart (36.1 to 42.1 per 10,000), diagnostic procedures on the small intestines (43 to 48.7 per 10,000), and joint replacement of the lower extremities (23 to 41.1 per 10,000). Others decreased dramatically in frequency, including diagnostic radiology (67.3 to 35.5 per 10,000 population), diagnostic ultrasound (60.5 to 33.3 per 10,000), and cholecystectomy (24.7 to 19.5 per 10,000). These changes reflect innovations in technology, with newer and more effective treatments replacing older ones.

Hospital Structure

Hospitals have a complex structure and a variety of operating divisions. Traditionally, the principal divisions are administration, medical (physicians), nursing, and other diagnostic and therapeutic support. Most hospitals provide services both to inpatients and to outpatients who come to an emergency department, to an outpatient clinic, or to a diagnostic or therapeutic service (such as an ambulatory surgery unit) for a procedure not requiring hospitalization.

Hospital administration keeps the institution up and running in all areas other than direct patient care. Its major responsibilities include finance, both expense and capital; personnel; providing services—maintenance, housekeeping, laundry, and dietary (cooking and delivery of meals); community/public relations; and development (fund-raising).

The Medical Division

A hospital's medical division is usually organized along the lines of medical specialties. There is no universal logic to the standard categorization of the latter, which has developed haphazardly over time. Thus, there are certain crossovers and overlaps. Some specialties are defined by the types of interventions used, some by the age or gender of their primary patient population group, and some by the organ or organ system that is their purview.

The major medical departments are as follows:

- Internal medicine: diagnosis and therapeutic intervention for adults, involving one or more internal organs or the skin, not requiring physical alteration of the body by invasive technologies.
- Surgery: diagnosis and therapeutic intervention for persons of all ages, in which some physical alteration of the patient's body is the primary focus of the physician's activity.
- Pediatrics: diagnosis and therapeutic intervention for children, primarily using nonsurgical techniques.
- Obstetrics/gynecology: diagnosis and therapeutic intervention focusing on the female sexual/reproductive system using both surgical and nonsurgical modalities.
- Psychiatry: diagnosis and therapeutic intervention for persons of all ages with psychological and emotional problems, using primarily counseling and pharmaceuticals.

There are also medical specialties and departments organized around organs and organ systems in which physicians use both surgical and nonsurgical interventions. They include *ophthalmology* (eye), *otolaryngology* (ear, nose, and throat), *urology* (male sexual/reproductive system and the renal system for both males and females), *orthopedics* (bones and joints), and *neurology* and *neurosurgery* (respectively, nonsurgical and surgical attention to the nervous system).

Radiology, the use of x-ray and other radiation sources, is a medical department with a primarily diagnostic function, although radiotherapy has become an important function. In recent years, several non-x-ray internal diagnostic techniques such as computerized axial tomography (CAT) scanning and magnetic resonance imaging (MRI) have been developed. They are usually provided by the department of radiology (in some institutions, reflecting the new technologies, now called *diagnostic imaging* or a similar term). In some hospitals, radiotherapy (also called *therapeutic nuclear medicine* or similar) has been separated from diagnostic radiology and its newer diagnostic cousins.

In medical practice, the department of *pathology* provides only a diagnostic function, both before and after treatment. Traditionally, *anesthesiology* has been concerned with preparing patients to be operated on without pain or discomfort during the procedure. More recently, the scope of the work has been expanded to include participation in critical care medicine and the developing area of nonsurgical pain management.

Medical Staff Organization. The physician has traditionally been described both as a "guest in the hospital" and as its primary customer. The hospital has sometimes been described as the doctors' workshop. Except when a physician chooses to run a hospital for profit, however, he or she has no personal responsibility to see that the hospital is functioning and available to provide care for his or her patients. Nor does the individual physician carry any financial liability for the success or failure of the hospital, unless, again, he or she is an owner.

A physician traditionally has been largely free to order whatever tests or treatments he or she deems necessary for a particular patient. In recent years, certain limitations have been placed on this particular physician's freedom. An example is the use by hospitals of what are called *formularies*, which are limited lists of pharmaceuticals that will be provided by the hospital pharmacy for physician prescription. This is an attempt both to ensure that the medications used in the hospital are being used correctly and to keep the number of pharmaceuticals that need to be held in stock under control. Insurers may specify formularies as well, in the attempt to contain costs. Regardless of these kinds of limitations, however, because he or she orders all the hospital tests, services, and drugs provided to its patients, the individual physician is a major determinant of hospital costs, even though traditionally he or she has borne no personal responsibility for them. Physicians in a given specialty (e.g., cardiology/cardiac surgery, oncology/cancer surgery, or children's services) can also influence the direction of the growth and expansion of the institution, affecting costs in another way.

In the traditional hospital-medical staff arrangement, in exchange for the privilege of admitting patients, the physician participates in the self-governance of the medical staff. Physicians may have to share the load for providing care in areas of the hospital for which the medical staff accepts collective responsibility, such as the emergency room or outpatient clinics. A variety of medical staff patterns of organization exist. Roemer and Friedman's review of them (1971) is still largely valid, although some elements are beginning to change.

Under managed care, for example, in an arrangement called the physician–hospital organization (PHO), groups of medical staff are joining with hospital corporations to negotiate contracts with third-party payers, often a managed care organization (MCO), most often a health maintenance organization (HMO), to provide both medical and hospital services (Kongstvedt, Plocher, & Stanford, 2001). Assuming that the payments from the MCO to the PHO or HMO are made on an other than fee-for-service basis, and increasingly they are (Thrall, 1996), such an arrangement does put the medical staff at some financial risk should patient utilization exceed projections.

Responsible for overseeing the physicians' clinical work are a set of medical staff committees. These include the executive committee, which provides overall coordination and sets general policy; the joint conference committee, which serves as liaison between the medical staff and the hospital's governing board; the credentials committee, which reviews applications to join the medical staff and controls the periodic reappointment process; the infections control committee, which is responsible for preventing infections and monitoring and correcting any outbreaks that do occur; and the pharmacy and therapeutics committee, which reviews pharmaceutical agents for inclusion in the list of drugs approved for use in the hospital (that is, those included in the formulary).

There are also the tissue committee, which reviews all surgical procedures that produce "bodily tissues;" the medical records committee, which is responsible for certifying the completeness and clinical accuracy of the documentation of patient care; and the quality assurance committee, which has the overall responsibility for monitoring and correcting any deficiencies in the quality of care provided by the medical staff.

Other Hospital Divisions

Another principal health care organizational division besides the medical staff is nursing. The nonphysician diagnostic and therapeutic services, which may or may not be administratively attached to one of the medical departments, include laboratory (usually under the direction of the department of pathology); electrocardiography (usually a part of internal medicine); electroencephalography (part of neurology); radiotherapy technology (supporting diagnostic imaging); pharmacy; clinical psychology; social service; inhalation therapy (usually part of either anesthesiology or pulmonary medicine); nutrition as therapy; physical, occupational, and speech therapy (often attached to the department of rehabilitation medicine, if there is one); home health care; medical records; adult day care; screening; end-of-life/hospice services; pain management; sports medicine/fitness center; and women's health services (AHA, 2007b, Table 7).

Hospital Governance in the Private Sector[1]

The typical not-for-profit hospital has a board of trustees. Usually prominent in its membership are persons who give or raise substantial sums of money for the hospital or represent important community institutions, such as major employers and banks. The person carrying the title of president of the hospital can be either the leader of the board of trustees, or the paid chief executive officer (CEO) of the hospital. In the former case, the top operations person is usually called the executive director or executive vice-president. If the hospital CEO carries the title of president, then the head of the board usually carries the title of chairman. In theory, the board of directors sets policy, and the chief executive officer carries it out. In practice, the situation is often as complex as it is in any modern corporation.

For-profit hospitals may have a governance structure similar to that of the voluntaries, with board seats held by the owners or their representatives, or they may be run directly by the owners. All hospitals operate under the licensure and supervision of an agency of state government.

Trends in the Hospital Sector

Hospital Systems and Integration

Increasingly, individual hospitals must affiliate with other hospitals to form systems if they are to remain financially viable. For example, in New York City in 2010, there were 43 general hospitals. Of these, only 17 were independent, and the remaining 26 were members of just 5 hospital systems (AHA, 2011a). This is not unique to New York, and it is a trend that has been going on since the 1970s, as discussed by Prybil in 1982:

> The growth of multiunit hospital systems (organizations that include two or more acute-care hospitals owned, leased, or managed by a single corporate entity) and their impact on health care are described. In 1970, there were fewer than 50 nongovernmental multiunit hospital systems in the United States. By 1981, this figure increased to 256; 53% of the systems included only two or three hospital units, while 13% included 11 or more units. Approximately one third of all nongovernmental hospitals in 1981 were included in multiunit systems. About 12% of the systems, which included 39% of the hospitals, were owned or operated by investor-owned firms. Multiunit hospital systems can improve the hospital industry's overall effectiveness and efficiency by achieving economies of scale and by developing hospital performance criteria and standards. In the future, the number and size of U.S. multiunit hospital systems most likely will continue to increase. The nation's multiunit hospital systems vary enormously in size and composition, as well as in their mission, goals, values, and approaches to governance and management.

In addition, hospitals are increasingly seeking affiliations with nonhospital medical providers in order to coordinate care better across sectors—ambulatory care, home care, and long-term care—and achieve better outcomes. For example, the American Hospital Association's report, *AHA Environmental Scan 2011*, projects that in the future:

> There will be widespread use of ambulatory, home and community care in place of traditional inpatient services and expanded use of new communication and monitoring techniques.
>
> • Medical devices have become more portable and sophisticated (AHA, 2011c).

Complementary Medicine

A tremendous amount of out-of-pocket money is being spent by Americans each year on complementary or alternative medical care, that is, non-allopathic medicine. A growing trend in hospitals is to add complementary medical therapies to their offerings. These include acupuncture, massage therapy, guided imagery for stress reduction, pet therapy, and music/art therapy.

> As hospitals elbow one another to attract patients, increasingly they're hoping to tap into Americans' interest in—and willingness to spend money on—complementary and alternative therapies such as acupuncture and massage.
>
> According to a recent survey by the American Hospital Assn. and the Samueli Institute, a nonprofit research group focusing on complementary medicine, 42% of the 714 hospitals that responded offered at least one such therapy in 2010; five years earlier, only 27% of hospitals offered such treatments.
>
> Experts say hospitals are embracing these therapies for many reasons, including a growing recognition that some integrative therapies, as they're also called, are very effective in certain instances.
>
> In addition, hospitals aren't blind to the opportunity these therapies present to attract patients and perhaps make some money. According to the most recent report from the National Center for Health Statistics, Americans spent $33.9 billion on integrative therapies in 2007—with most of the money coming out of their own pockets, since the majority of these treatments aren't covered by insurance. That figure includes fees for about 354 million visits to complementary and alternative medical practitioners, and it represents about 11% of total out-of-pocket expenditures on healthcare. (Andrews, 2012)

Luxury Medicine

Another trend among hospitals is to compete for patients, worldwide, through extremely luxurious hospital accommodations and service. For example, as reported in the *New York Times*:

> The feverish patient had spent hours in a crowded emergency room. When she opened her eyes in her Manhattan hospital room last winter, she recalled later, she wondered if she could be hallucinating: "This is like the Four Seasons—where am I?"
>
> The bed linens were by Frette, Italian purveyors of high-thread-count sheets to popes and princes. The bathroom gleamed with polished marble. Huge windows displayed panoramic East River views. And in the hush of her $2,400 suite, a man in a black vest and tie proffered an elaborate menu and told her, "I'll be your butler."
>
> It was Greenberg 14 South, the elite wing on the new penthouse floor of NewYork-Presbyterian/Weill Cornell Hospital. Pampering and décor to rival a grand hotel, if not a Downton Abbey, have long been the hallmark of such "amenities units," often hidden behind closed doors at New York's premier hospitals. But the phenomenon is escalating here and around the country, health care design specialists say, part of an international competition for wealthy patients willing to pay extra, even as the federal government cuts back hospital reimbursement in pursuit of a more universal and affordable American medical system.
>
> "It's not just competing on medical grounds and specialties, but competing for customers who can go just about anywhere," said Helen K. Cohen, a specialist in health facilities at the international architectural firm HOK, which recently designed luxury hospital floors in Singapore and London and renovated NewYork-Presbyterian's elite offerings in the McKeen Pavilion in Washington Heights. "These kinds of patients, they're paying cash—they're the best kind[s] of patient to have," she added. "Theoretically, it trickles down." (Bernstein, 2012)

Luxury medicine represents the consumerist trend, when the consumer is well-to-do, also exemplified by the incorporation of complementary medicine into hospital offerings.

Current Issues in the Hospital Sector

First, hospitals have been relatively costly to build and maintain. They still are, even as their numbers shrink and the pace of new construction and renovation slows markedly. Also, there is an imbalance in the hospital sector in the provision of acute, long-term, and ambulatory care. The high costs of in-patient hospital care are exacerbated by the inadequate supply of affordable intermediate- or long-term care beds for patients who have recovered from the acute phase of their illness but still need high-quality care in bed.

Second, as noted by Peter Rogatz in 1980 in an observation certainly still true today, there is a pressing need for appropriate housing with social and support services for the elderly who cannot live entirely on their own in ordinary housing, but nevertheless do not need institutionalization of any kind. In the absence of any kind of comprehensive program to deal with it, this problem is getting worse as the population ages and as significant financing and policy changes are not forthcoming.

The third major problem concerns the mode by which most physicians taking care of patients in hospitals have traditionally been paid, as well as the influence that physicians have over hospital operations and expenditures. The individual physician traditionally has made most of the decisions on the commitment and use of hospital resources. Yet, as noted previously, it usually has been the patient or his or her insurer who pays the physician. Thus, the physician has had neither a direct financial relationship to the hospital nor any responsibility for its financial health.

A comparable situation would be if modern school boards were to provide everything necessary for education except payment of the teachers, who would then proceed to collect fees directly from the students. Indeed, this is the way teachers were paid before the educational reforms of the mid-19th century. As noted, managed care, and health care reform in general, are beginning to change some of these relationships in some hospitals in some areas of the country.

Fourth, hospitals have internal problems with vertically organized administrative structures that are not well integrated at the service levels. Also, hospitals are organized around the knowledge of their health practitioners. In many hospitals, the vertical lines of authority of the medical staff, the nursing department, and the support services meet only in the office of the director. In some cases, they never meet. This kind of separation can make it very difficult to provide integrated patient care programs in which, in order to meet patient needs, unitary direction is needed at the functional level (Jonas, 1973). This observation is as true in the first decade of the 21st century as it was in the eighth decade of the 20th century.

A fifth problem is the programmatic and sometimes philosophical isolation of many hospitals from the real health and medical problems of their communities. For example, although there are certainly exceptions, in many hospitals outpatient services have had a distinctly second-class status, preventive medicine is practiced to a minimal extent (although that situation is improving somewhat as insurers, in particular, are gradually beginning to recognize that preventive interventions can save money in the long run), home care and rehabilitation services have been treated as luxuries (although that situation is beginning to improve as well for similar reasons), community-based chronic disease control programs are undertaken only sporadically, and "mental health" services in hospitals have little to do with *community* mental health. Although change is surely occurring, some hospitals have resolutely turned inward, wishing that everyone would just go away and leave them to do their job as they see it: taking care of sick people in bed.

Sixth, as should be apparent from what has already been said in this chapter, hospitals were plunged into the era of managed care without much warning or preparation and certainly with no formal planning for its advent. A major thrust of managed care has been to reduce hospital utilization, as previously noted. These developments have led to, among other things, a flurry of hospital bankruptcies and closings, reductions in bed complements, and mergers and takeovers, as well as the formation of an ever-increasing number of "hospital networks" (Griffith, 1999, pp. 173–186). The last is a kind of formal relationship among a group of hospitals, usually with a major tertiary-care teaching hospital at its center. However, it appears that the rate of mergers and acquisitions of hospitals slowed from 1997 through 2001, following a steady increase from 1994 through 1997, and has reached a plateau of about 55 per year since 2001: in 1994 there were 92, in 1995 there were 128, in 1996 there were 163, in 1997 there were 197, in 1998 there were 137, in 1999 there were 109, in 2000 there were 84, in 2001 there were 83, in 2002 there were 56, in 2003 there were 38, in 2004 there were 59, and in 2005 there were 53 (Irving Levin Associates, 2004). "During the five-year period ended December 31, 2009, the hospital merger and acquisition market posted a total of 278 transactions in which acute-care hospitals changed hands. This activity is fairly level with 2001–2005, which saw 284 announced hospital transactions. Among the deals announced during 2005–2009, the average number of hospitals per transaction was 2.3" (Irving Levin Associates, 2010).

Certain economies of scale and divisions of labor can be achieved with such arrangements. Consider the current climate, however: no national health care program, an increasing number of uninsured and underinsured persons (Hoffman et al., 2001; Kaiser Family Foundation, 2007), and MCOs simply looking for the best deal in making their contracts with hospitals to provide services for their beneficiaries. If hospitals, especially expensive teaching hospitals, simply look to a hospital/health care network of smaller hospitals and individual providers as the means of keeping their beds filled and do not contemplate further major service reorganization that will deemphasize expensive inpatient care and enable them to close expensive beds, some of them will not be able to survive in the current economy.

There are serious obstacles in the way of even rational planners at major teaching hospitals. As George Ross Fisher said, in a review of a book on teaching hospital mergers (2001):

> Unfortunately, managed care [companies] arrived, apparently quite willing to destroy both research and tertiary

care...if that is what it takes to preserve their profitability, which mainly lies in adverse de-selection of subscribers. When a payment system that depends on selecting only well people if possible encounters a delivery system that depends on attracting only very sick people if possible, that delivery system is in trouble.

Complex problems do not have simple solutions, and there are no panaceas. Several approaches to hospital reform are available, however. For example, we can still turn to the timeless work of John Gordon Frey-mann. Freymann developed the concept of the "mission-oriented hospi-tal" (Freymann, 1974, chapter 18), which is as valid today as it was when it was conceived. However, its broad implementation would require both a system of universal financial entitlement to health services and a system for rational, national health and health services planning. How compatible such an approach would be with for-profit managed care is anybody's guess.

The mission-oriented hospital has two principal attributes: (a) Each hospital has a mission defined and continuously modified by the specific needs of the community it serves and (b) the rational planning process provides individuality and flexibility (Freymann, 1974, p. 248). Freymann recognized that:

> The word "hospital" itself presents a problem, for today it con-notes a building that houses patients. I think "hospital" could be used in a different sense to signify a dynamic complex of facilities and skilled personnel organized to provide all types of health services. (p. 247)

The mission-oriented approach would make the hospital into a health center rather than an illness center, ending what Freymann (1974) called the "tyranny of the bed." The hospital would respond to the needs of its community in a rational, planned, dynamic manner. By definition, the acute/chronic/preventive distinctions would become relics of the past.

The current administrative problems would not be resolved automati-cally by a mission-oriented approach. Rather, *they would have to be solved in order to accomplish mission orientation*. His approach demands an admin-istrative structure that is functionally decentralized to operate integrated programs requiring staff teams at the patient care level, not one that has vertically organized reporting lines separating health care providers into independent hierarchies.

This outcome might be achieved through managed care-induced hospital reorganizations, especially networking and the development of integrated delivery systems (Kongstvedt, Plocher, & Stanford, 2001). However, because mission orientation as defined by Freymann requires, at least in part, a focus on issues other than the bottom line, achieving that outcome is likely well beyond the capabilities of contemporary for-profit managed care.

Some experts have thought that the Internet might provide a solution to at least some hospitals' problems. The supremely odd couple of Ira Magaziner, who managed the ultimate political failure of the Clinton health plan of 1994, and Newt Gingrich, the chief political opponent of the plan in the House of Representatives, came together to promote this position (Cunningham, 2000). However, as Kleinke (2000), certainly no health care radical, pointed out:

> Contrary to the claims of its well-financed promoters, the Internet will not solve the administrative redundancies, economic inefficiencies, or quality problems that have plagued the U.S. health care system for decades. These phenomena are the result of economic, organizational, legal, regulatory, and cultural conflicts rooted in a health care system grown from hybrid public and private financing; cultural expectations of unlimited access to unlimited medical resources; and the use of third-party payers rewarded to constrain those expectations. The historic in-adequacy of information technology to solve health care's biggest problems is a symptom of these structural realities, not their cause. With its revolution of information access for consumers, the Internet will exacerbate the cost and utilization problems of a health care system in which patients demand more, physicians are legally and economically motivated to supply more, and public and private purchasers are expected to pay the bills. (p. 57)

Actually, this statement does much more than shoot down the Internet-as-savior, the changing-the-way-we-manipulate-information-about-what-is-in-the-bottle-without-touching-what-is-in-bottle "solution." It summarizes the health care delivery system predicament, especially those of hospitals, as it stands today.

LONG-TERM CARE: THE EXAMPLE OF NURSING HOMES[2]

"The term *long-term care* encompasses a range of supportive, rehabilitative, nursing, and palliative services provided to people—from young to old—whose capacity to perform daily activities is restricted due to chronic disease or disability" (Feldman, Nadash, & Gursen, 2005, p. 201). There is a group of long-term care institutions other than long-term hospitals that are generically called *nursing homes*. Their number has increased significantly since the 1930s.

Formerly classified according to the level of skill involved in the care they gave, beginning in 1990 all nursing homes eligible to receive federal third-party reimbursement for the care they provide were called *nursing facilities*. In 1995, there were more than 16,000 such institutions of 25 beds or more, with more than 1,750,000 beds (NCHS, 2006, Table 116). In 2009, there were fewer nursing home facilities and beds—more than 15,700 nursing homes with about 1.7 million beds. The occupancy rate of 82.2% in 2009 was lower than in 1995 (84.5%) NCHS, 2011, Table 117). The number of nursing home residents per 1,000 people has been declining since 1973–1974, when it was 58.5 per 1,000 people 65 and over; it was 43.3 per 1,000 in 1999.(NCHS, 2006, Table 101)

About two thirds of nursing homes (and two thirds of beds) are under for-profit ownership, with 26% in the voluntary sector and 8% owned by government agencies (Feldman et al., 2005, p. 217). More than half of the financial support for nursing homes comes from public funds, much of it under the Medicaid program, as Medicare provides little long-term care coverage. In 2004, Medicaid covered 44% of nursing home care in the United States (Kaiser Family Foundation, 2007).

Much of Medicaid expenditures go for the elderly (28%) and disabled (42%), although these groups comprise 11% and 14% of Medicaid enrollees, respectively (Kaiser Family Foundation, 2007). Further, a substantial portion of expenditures for the disabled and elderly is for long-term care. However, by no means are all of the people benefiting from this payment mechanism of receiving public assistance at the time they entered a nursing home (if they are institutionalized), and many had never received public assistance. In response, a number of states have instituted "asset transfer" systems. These permit people of means to transfer property and other assets to others, usually their children, so that on paper they become "poor," and thus Medicaid eligible, after some period of time following the asset transfer.

Chronic problems with the quality of long-term care provoke periodic exposés and outcries for reform (Eisen & Sloan, 1997; Pear, 2002). However because any institutional care is expensive, the long-term solution to the long-term care problem probably lies with improved home care services and significantly improved health promotion, disease prevention, and self-care programs for the rapidly increasing number of elderly persons in the United States.

AMBULATORY CARE

Ambulatory care is health care given to a person who is not a bed patient in a health care institution. The term thus covers all health services other than community health services and personal health services for the institutionalized patient. The majority of physician–patient contacts in the United States occur in an ambulatory setting. There are two principal categories of ambulatory care. The first is provided by private physicians in solo, partnership, or private group practice, on a fee-for-service basis, and by private physicians (often the same individuals) working in one of several different types of managed care arrangements, paid either on a fee-for-service or capitation basis.

The other category is care provided in a setting with an identity independent from that of the particular individual physicians working in it. This category includes hospital-based ambulatory services (e.g., clinics, emergency departments, and health promotion centers); community-based, hospital ambulatory services (e.g., outpatient surgery centers); emergency medical services systems, such as those run by police and fire departments; local public health department clinics; neighborhood health centers and community health centers; staff and group model HMOs; and organized home care services, community mental health centers, industrial health services, school health services, and prison health services. Most physicians working in one of these settings are salaried.

> About one-half of ambulatory medical care visits (48.1 percent) were made to primary care physicians in office-based practices. The rest were to medical specialists (18.4 percent) and surgical specialists (16.4 percent) in office-based practices, and to EDs (9.7 percent) and hospital outpatient departments (7.4 percent) in nonfederal general and short-stay hospitals. (NCHS, 2011)

Ambulatory Care Utilization

In 2007, there were 1.2 billion ambulatory patient visits to office-based physicians. Americans averaged 4.05 physician visits per person. Women made up 58.2% of all physician office visits, although men visited more than women for injury-related conditions in every age group under 45 years. After age 45, women made more visits than men in each age group (NCHS 2011). The rate of ambulatory care visits continues to increase:

> From 1997 through 2007, the annual number of ambulatory care visits increased by 25 percent, driven both by the aging of the population, as older persons have higher visit rates than younger persons in general, and by an increase in utilization by older persons. After adjustment for changes in the age distribution of the population between 1997 and 2007, the overall rate of visits increased by 10.6 percent, from 364.3 to 403.1 visits per 100 persons. The age-adjusted rate of visits to office-based medical specialists showed the most significant change, increasing 29.5 percent, from 56.4 visits per 100 persons in 1997 to 73.0 visits per 100 persons in 2007. (NCHS 2011)

In 2007, the most frequent primary diagnosis in the ambulatory care setting was essential hypertension (46.3 million visits or 3.9 percent of the total). Eight out of 10 of ambulatory visits (36.6 million) were in primary care offices, and they accounted for 6.3% of the 576.6 million visits in this setting. About one-fifth (19.6%) of all ambulatory care visits in 2007 were non-illness or non-injury conditions, such as routine checkups and pregnancy exams. The most frequent non-illness or non-injury condition was the checkup for infants or children, with 43.3 million visits in 2007, or 3.6% of all ambulatory care visits. Only 4 of the top 35 ambulatory care conditions in 2007 were also among the top 35 in 2006 (NCHS, 2011).

The top six specialties visited in the ambulatory setting are general and family practice (24.2%), internal medicine (17.6%), pediatrics (13.5%), obstetrics and gynecology (7.9%), ophthalmology (5.6%), and orthopedic surgery (4.3%) (NCHS, 2004, Figure 2). In 2007, the source of payment for ambulatory visits was private insurance (59% of visits), Medicare (21% of visits), and the State Children's Health Insurance Program (SCHIP) or Medicaid (15%). About 6% of visits were paid by the individual (self-pay) and the remaining visits were paid by other sources, including Worker's Compensation (NCHS, 2011).

> Visit rates for persons with no insurance for the care provided (i.e., expected payment from solely self-pay, no charge, or charity) were lowest for all three office-based settings compared with visit rates for persons with various kinds of insurance. In contrast, the visit rate to EDs for the uninsured (41.6 visits per 100 persons) was about twice the rate of persons with private insurance (19.9 visits per 100 persons). (NCHS, 2011)

See data from www.cdc.gov/nchs/data/series/sr_13/sr13_169.pdf for more information. Now we briefly discuss the various ambulatory settings other than the physician office, chief among them the hospital outpatient department.

Hospital Outpatient Departments

For a variety of reasons, most American hospitals traditionally have focused the bulk of their efforts and activities on inpatients who are acutely ill and confined to bed (Freymann, 1974, chapter 3). Hospitals also have had to deal with other types of patients, however. Most are classified as outpatients.

Hospital outpatients require either immediate treatment for an acute and sometimes serious illness or injury, or ongoing care for a more routine matter. Very often the services of the latter type are similar to those needed by patients who attend physicians' offices. In theory at least, there are two categories of hospital ambulatory services, corresponding to the two principal categories of patient needs: emergency services, provided by emergency rooms or departments (EDs), and clinic services or outpatient departments (OPDs).

In the real world, overlap between the two categories of service is increasing. Patients, hospital staff, and hospital administrations, separately and together, are sometimes confused about the differences in role and function of the two categories. All three groups sometimes have trouble deciding which patients should go where for what.

The original intended functions of hospital emergency service units were (a) to take care of acutely ill or injured people, particularly with life-threatening or potentially life-threatening problems that required immediate attention by personnel, or equipment not found in private practitioners' offices and (b) to offer prompt hospitalization if needed. Most hospitals have found it desirable or necessary (legally required in many states) to provide such services.

In the past, it was easier for hospitals to determine that emergency services should be provided than that clinic services should be. One reason for this was that insurance carriers were more likely to reimburse hospitals for emergency services than for clinic services. Under managed care, and with the steadily increasing number of Americans who have no or inadequate health insurance coverage, this situation is changing. In fact, the use of EDs for nonpreapproved, nonurgent care by MCO beneficiaries has created a major cost-containment problem for the managed care industry. In an increasing number of instances, the MCO is refusing to pay the hospital for such care (Gresenz, Studdert, Campbell, & Hensler, 2002).

Historical Background

In the 19th century, clinic service was part of the function of most hospitals serving the poor in urban areas (Freymann, 1974). By 1916, 495 hospitals had clinics, often serving a health care personnel educational function as well as a charitable one (Roemer, 1981). Indeed, many of these clinics were originally established to care for persons who for one reason or another were not being served by a public institution.

Hospital-based emergency services came into being to meet observed needs as well. For example, in 1908, the Goshen (NY) Emergency Hospital was established. Its creation was stimulated by the building of one of New York State's early trunk highways, Route 17. The road went through the center of the village of Goshen. Traffic accidents occurred with increasing frequency. Thus, a hospital was needed, and with strong local effort, it was built.[3]

In the beginning, voluntary hospital OPDs were staffed on a rotating basis by the members of the hospital medical staff working there without pay. Voluntary hospital medical staffs consisted primarily of physicians practicing privately in the community. Thus, they were much more important in setting the style for the organization of medical practice in hospital OPDs than were those of the local government hospitals, which were much more likely to rely on the services of paid medical staff. (For contemporary staffing arrangements, see later discussion.)

Hospital clinics have changed in the past 20 years. They have become more sophisticated. In many hospitals, they have been reorganized to improve their efficiency and effectiveness by providing the care that patients need rather than simply serving the functions of the hospital as it perceived them, that is, organizing hospital services to first meet the training and educational needs of medical students and house staff. Whereas the average length of inpatient stays has decreased sharply over the past 20 years, often placing financial strains on the hospital, clinic revenue as a percent of total revenue had risen to 43.5% by 2002 (Runy, 2003). As examples of the improved care being offered, many hospitals now provide longer and more flexible clinic hours and have integrated care throughout the clinic system.

Hospital Outpatient Utilization

In 2007, approximately 89 million visits were made to hospital OPDs, 30 visits per 100 persons per year (NCHS, 2011). Paralleling the general ambulatory patient utilization figures, females had higher visit rates than males. Medicaid, State Children's Health Insurance Program (SCHIP), and private indemnity insurance were the three most common payment sources. The 10 most common reasons for visits were progress visit (follow-up to previous visit), general medical exam, routine prenatal examination, cough, medication, symptoms referable to the throat, postoperative visit, hypertension, well-baby examination, and stomach pain, cramps, and spasms. Between 1994 and 2004, the increase in visit rates was greatest among people under 21 years: infants under 1 year (up by 37%), children 1 to 12 years (up by 34%), and adolescents 13 to 21 years (up by 27%). The increase in visit rate for people over 21 was smaller—about 6%.

See data from www.cdc.gov/nchs/data/series/sr_13/sr13_169.pdf for more information.

Present Hospital OPD Organization and Staffing

Although not all clinics are found in teaching hospitals (those affiliated with medical schools), most are. Given the way medical education is structured, teaching hospitals have over time found that the best way of organizing OPDs to provide opportunities for teaching and research is to have separate disease, organ, or organ system-specific clinics (Freymann, 1974, p. 255). This is still largely the case, although there has been an increase in clinics that specialize in treatment of a demographic group (e.g., women or the elderly) as well as conditions that cross disease or organ-specific boundaries (e.g., pain management clinics).

Typically, teaching hospitals have three categories of clinics: medical, surgical, and other. Medical clinics, of which a family practice unit or a general medical clinic approximating the function of the general internist may be a part, include cardiology, neurology, dermatology, allergy, and gastroenterology specialties. General surgery, orthopedics, urology, plastic surgery, and the like compose the surgical clinic group. Included in the third, catchall group are pediatrics and the pediatric subspecialties, obstetrics-gynecology and its subspecialties, and other specialties such as rehabilitation medicine.

The larger teaching hospitals often have more than 100 different specialty and subspecialty clinics. Thus, a hospital-based physician working in the usual hospital clinic organization can concentrate on diabetes, peripheral vascular disease, or stroke in his or her teaching and research. This is useful for the provider focusing on a particular disease or condition. It may also be helpful to the patient who has a single disease or problem of a rather complex or unusual nature. Difficulties may arise, however, for the patient with multiple medical problems. Such a patient's care may be divided among multiple clinics, with no one physician coordinating the care and providing an overview of the patient as a person rather than as a collection of organ systems (e.g., the cardiovascular system), or organs (e.g., the eye), or even organ components (e.g., the retina).

There are five functional categories of physician staff in teaching hospital clinics. First, it was formerly very common for the hospital's voluntary (read private) attending medical staff to draw clinic duty as part of repaying the hospital for granting admitting privileges for their private patients at no cost to themselves. This is still the case in some institutions.

Second, by the 1980s, many medical schools had become increasingly dependent for their financial support on taking a share of the income physicians earned in the clinics. The money was received primarily from third-party payers. Today, many clinics in medical school-owned teaching hospitals are staffed by medical school faculty whose work there generates both some of their own income and money for the school's general fund. The management system for dividing this income between the physicians and the institution providing the space and supporting staff is usually referred to as the *clinical practice plan*.

Third, to carry out teaching, supervisory, and research functions, a teaching hospital may assign full-time salaried inpatient physicians, usually junior staff, to the clinics. Fourth, house staff (physicians in post-medical school, graduate specialty training, including interns, residents, and fellows) usually draw significant clinic duty from time to time throughout the course of their training. Fifth, for clinics with many patient visits, hospitals may hire outside physicians exclusively to work in them on a sessional or part-time salaried basis.

All of these arrangements, in the context of the fragmented, subspecialty-focused organization of most teaching hospital clinics, create serious problems for the future development of primary care and primary care physicians. As one of the nation's experts on the subject, Fitzhugh Mullan, put it in terms that are still true today (Landy, 2001): "Medical education in the U.S. marginalizes primary care, and the current medical reimbursement system, which gives much higher compensation to specialists than to generalists, encourages medical institutions to skew treatment in favor of atomized high-tech interventions."

Some Problems Faced by Clinic Patients

The basic contradiction in hospital ambulatory services is clear. On the one hand, there are the teaching and research needs of specialty-oriented providers. On the other, there are the needs of patients with either ordinary problems or several different problems requiring the care of several specialties. For many of them, a dysfunctional disjunction of fragmented care has been created (Roemer, Kramer, & Frink, 1975). This situation is not new but has not changed since it was noted by Roemer and colleagues back in 1975. Professional recognition of the problem and recommendations for correcting it also have not changed.

In 1964, at a conference on "The Expanding Role of Ambulatory Services in Hospitals and Health Departments" held at the New York Academy of Medicine, Cecil Sheps (1965) said:

> As I sat through the sessions yesterday and today I had a persistent feeling of déjà vu. I possess a book written by Michael M. Davis and published in 1927 [*Clinics, Hospitals and Health Centers*, New York: Harper, 1927]. In it there is quoted a statement prepared in 1914 that describes the purpose of an outpatient department just as clearly as anything said at this conference: that the focus must be on the patient, that care must be organized around the patient, and that the hospital must take the community as its venue and not simply the patients who come to it. (p. 148)

An echo of this recommendation was found in John Gordon Freymann's mission-oriented hospital concept from the 1970s. A 1980s version of what Davis was talking about in 1927 and Freymann was talking about in the 1970s was called community-oriented primary care (COPC) (Dobbie, Kelly, Sylvia, & Freeman, 2006; Longlett, Kruse, & Wesley, 2001; Madison, 1983; Mullan, 1982; Mullan & Conner, 1982; Nutting, Wood, & Conner, 1985; Rhyne, Bogue, Kukulka, & Fulmer, 1998). It is still a model for which to strive. Its major elements are as follows:

- The clinical practice of comprehensive primary medical care
- The use of applied epidemiology in practice planning

- Community involvement in program planning
- The use of data gathered in practice operations in a continuous feedback loop for future program planning
- Continuing surveillance of community health status and needs

The model can be used in any medical practice, whether solo, group, or hospital-based. The principal problem COPC faces is not conceptual; the ideas have been with us for many years, and they are obviously sound. The difficulty is in implementation. To this day there are only a few institutions that are even interested in trying to approach the ideal, much less able to find the personnel and money necessary to reach it.

Hospital Emergency Services

In 2007, Americans made about 116.8 million visits to hospital emergency departments, or close to 39.4 visits per 100 persons per year (NCHS, 2011). With the exception of children under 1 year of age, persons 75 years and older had the highest annual rate of visits. African Americans had a higher visit rate (74.6 per 100 people) than did Whites (35.9 per 100 people) (NCHS, 2011). About 19.6% of all visits were for the treatment of injuries and adverse effects of medical treatment. General symptoms encompassed 15.6% of the distribution, whereas symptoms referable to the musculoskeletal system, digestive system, and respiratory system collectively encompassed 38.2% of the distribution (13.8%, 13.7%, and 10.7%, respectively; McCaig & Nawar, 2006, Table 7). From the patient perspective, the most common reasons that patients came into an ED were stomach ache, chest pain, fever, back symptoms, headache, cough, shortness of breath, vomiting, pain, lacerations and cuts, accidents, and symptoms referable to the throat (McCaig & Nawar, 2006, Table 8).

The hospital ED thus serves a variety of functions. First, it provides care to critically ill and injured patients, true emergencies. Second, in many voluntary hospitals it also serves as a secondary, well-equipped private physician's office, with more sophisticated resources than are available in a typical doctor's private office. Third, EDs are a source of patient admissions to the hospital.

A fourth role that has become increasingly important in the years since World War II is obvious from looking at the list of reasons for visits from the patients' perspective. It is the provision of care to persons who are neither injured nor critically ill, but who (a) have not seen or cannot reach their private physician, (b) find that their regular clinic is not open when needed, (c) find that their regular or covering HMO-assigned primary-care gatekeeper physician is not available, (d) are geographically out of region, or, increasingly, (e) have no insurance coverage and thus have no place else to go when they get sick (e.g., Alavy, Chung, Maggiore, Shim, & Dhuper, 2006; Moon, Laurens, Weimer, & Levy, 2005).

For virtually all patients who go to an emergency room (knowing, by the way, that the wait for service is likely to be long unless they are seriously ill or injured and that they are unlikely to be seen by a physician they have met before), for whichever reason just listed, the visit qualifies, in their mind, as an "emergency." However, from the provider perspective, things are seen rather differently. In terms that still apply, back in 1968 E. Richard Weinerman and his associates (Weinerman, 1968, p. 1040) defined three categories of patients presenting themselves to emergency units:

- Nonurgent: Condition does not require the resources of an emergency service; referral for routine medical care may or may not be needed; disorder is nonacute or minor in severity.
- Urgent: Condition requires medical attention within the period of a few hours; there is a possible danger to the patient if medically unattended; disorder is acute but not necessarily severe.
- Emergent: Condition requires immediate medical attention; time delay is harmful to patient; disorder is acute and potentially threatening to life or function.

Of course, these definitions are made from the professional perspective. Most patients do not make the kinds of distinctions health professionals make. Many patient visits to emergency rooms are for conditions that are neither urgent nor emergent from a medical viewpoint. "Nonurgent" and some "urgent" cases can overtax hospital EDs with responsibilities with which they are for the most part not ideally equipped to deal.

In the view of many analysts, the solution to the problem of the inappropriate use of the emergency room must be found outside the walls of the hospital. It must encompass an integrated system of medical care for the entire community, ensuring availability of appropriate medical care at all hours and to all classes of the population. Thus, we come back to the definitions of comprehensive primary care, to the visions of Michael Davis, John Knowles, and John Gordon Freymann, and to the concept of community-oriented primary care.

See data from www.cdc.gov/nchs/data/series/sr_13/sr13_169.pdf for more information.

Hospital Ambulatory Services Outside the Walls of the Hospital

From the 1980s onward, hospitals have been developing community-based facilities, both within their walls and at satellite sites. These facilities provide services that traditionally have required inpatient stays but, with advances in medical practice and technology, can now safely be offered on an outpatient basis (Anderson, 1990; Ermann & Gabel, 1985; Lin, Yang, Wen, & Chang. 2006; Podolsky, 1996). Such facilities include satellite

OPDs, which may separate specialty clinics as do many hospitals, or may be more like a community health center; comprehensive diagnostic centers for laboratory, x-ray, and related testing; and ambulatory surgery centers (Medical Group Management Association, 2002), where surgery that can be safely performed on an outpatient basis is done.

Ambulatory surgery centers are quickly increasing in number, and many of them are part of hospital systems. Surgeries in these settings are replacing inpatient surgeries. There were more than 5,300 ambulatory surgical centers in the United States in 2012. They perform 23 million surgeries annually, and Medicare approves them to perform more than 3,500 procedures (Ambulatory Surgery Center Association, 2012). New technologies, such as arthroscopic surgery, which allow for the use of noninvasive or minimally invasive procedures, certainly are at the center of this rapid growth. The payers of care strongly support this transformation because of the tremendous difference in charges for surgery done on an outpatient basis and that done for inpatients. Patients generally view ambulatory surgery favorably because of a better physical environment, the ease of access that many centers provide, and the overriding factor that the patients do not have to be admitted to a hospital.

Public Health Agency Clinics

In many parts of the United States, local government provides personal ambulatory health services in public hospitals, through local health departments, and in other venues. Local health departments operate an array of special clinics, focusing primarily on the prevention of disease.

Important among their services are clinics for tuberculosis control (often providing treatment as well as case finding and contact investigation services), child health (where immunizations, examinations, and education on child rearing are provided), prenatal care, sexually transmitted disease control, and certain mental health problems. In recent years, some public health agencies have broadened the scope of their services to include family planning, chronic disease detection, and general primary (disease treatment) care. Precisely how much care is provided is not known. Although there are more than 2,000 local health department units providing some kind of care, public health services are not a major factor in the overall ambulatory care picture (Association of State and Territorial Health Officials, 2006; Health Resources and Services Administration [HRSA], 2006).

The provision of personal disease treatment service by local health departments has been a subject of controversy ever since the practice began in the 19th century (Rosen, 1971; Winslow, 1929, chapter 17). Battles with the private physician sector over the role of local health departments were especially fierce during the 1920s, when some local health departments developed plans to expand their general disease treatment services

(Myers, Steinhardt, Mosley, & Cashman, 1968; Rosen, 1971; Winslow, 1929, chapter 17).

The efforts of the organized representatives of U.S. physicians to stop these developments were generally met with success. To this day, local health department personal health services are usually limited to those medical areas in which private physicians are not very interested (e.g., routine well-baby examinations), not especially competent (e.g., treatment, case finding, and contact investigation for sexually transmitted diseases and tuberculosis), or not available (e.g., primary care in underserved areas).

Lately there has been a diminution in organized medicine's opposition to the involvement of local health departments in the provision of direct medical services to the poor. Some hard-pressed urban and suburban health departments have done this, especially where access to public hospital services is limited or nonexistent.

Neighborhood and Community Health Centers

In the late 1960s and early 1970s, the neighborhood health center (NHC) movement emerged on the U.S. health care scene. The NHC was based on the concepts of full-time salaried physician staffing, multidisciplinary team health care practice, and community involvement in both policy-making and facility operations (Davis & Schoen, 1978; Zwick, 1972/1974). The movement was strongly stimulated by the federal Office of Economic Opportunity (OEO). The OEO was the lead agency for the "war on poverty" initiated by President Lyndon Johnson from 1964 through 1968.

For poor people, the NHCs sought to provide one-stop shopping for comprehensive ambulatory care—a full range of preventive and rehabilitative as well as treatment services that were affordable and of high quality. The NHCs also aimed to intervene in the cycle of poverty, by providing jobs and skills/career development opportunities for the residents of the communities they served. The movement did not meet with overwhelming success, in terms of patient visits provided. Conceptually, though, it was very important, leading to, among other things, the community-oriented primary care model mentioned earlier.

The NHC did not represent an entirely new concept in the United States. The 19th-century freestanding urban "dispensary" was an early general ambulatory care center that primarily served the poor. Although it was organized differently, it performed some functions similar to those of the modern NHC or the community health center, the NHC's successor. Health department ambulatory care programs developed during the last quarter of the 19th century had some elements that would also appear later in NHCs, such as districting and comprehensiveness (Rosen, 1971).

The experience with prepaid group practice (PPGP) in the 1930s, 1940s, and 1950s influenced the development of the NHC movement of the 1960s and 1970s (Light & Brown, 1967). With varying degrees of vigor and success, the NHCs attempted to make multidisciplinary group practice work. Along with physicians and nurses, they employed social workers, neighborhood health workers (usually people from the area served, specially trained by the NHC with a combination of basic nursing and social service skills), and sometimes lawyers, all on salary. These health care teams helped patients deal with both social and medical problems.

At the movement's peak, in the early 1970s, there were an estimated 200 NHCs nationally (Callan & Fein, 1972). In the mid-1970s, the Nixon and Ford administrations more narrowly defined the scope of the NHC program and renamed its facilities *community health centers* (CHCs). The CHCs, which included many of the original NHCs, were to concentrate on the delivery of primary care services. They were to deemphasize other NHC roles, such as providing employment opportunities and training programs, stimulating social and economic development in their communities, and concerning themselves with community-wide as well as personal health problems.

By the early 1980s, there were more than 800 CHCs serving more than 4.5 million people (Sardell, 1983), a remarkable resurgence for a program that received little publicity. By the early 1990s (Starfield, 1992), there were fewer CHCs (540), but with a total of 2,000 locations and sub-locations serving close to 6 million poor people in all 50 states, the District of Columbia, and the major U.S. territories. In 2001, President George W. Bush initiated an expansion of the CHCs. As a result, by 2006 there were more than 3,800 community and migrant worker health centers providing care for more than 14.6 million people (HRSA, 2006).

Today, "health centers" refer to all the diverse public and nonprofit organizations and programs that receive federal funding under section 330 of the Public Health Service (PHS) Act, as amended by the Health Centers Consolidated Act of 1996 (P.L. 104–299) and the Safety Net Amendments of 2002. They include Community Health Centers, Migrant Health Centers, Health Care for the Homeless Health Centers, and Primary Care Public Housing Health Centers.

Health centers are characterized by five essential elements that differentiate them from other providers:

- They must be located in or serve a high-need community, that is, "medically underserved areas" or "medically underserved populations"
- They must provide comprehensive primary care services as well as supportive services, such as, translation and transportation services that promote access to health care
- Their services must be available to all residents of their service areas, with fees adjusted upon patients' ability to pay
- They must be governed by a community board with health center patients comprising a majority of members

- They must meet other performance and accountability requirements regarding their administrative, clinical, and financial operations. (HRSA, 2012)

As of 2010, 38% of CHC patients were uninsured, and 93% had incomes below 200% of the federal poverty level (HRSA, 2010). Racial and ethnic minorities comprised 62.3% of CHC patients. In 1999, a disproportionate share had special health care needs (11% were substance abusers, 5% were homeless, and 2.5% were HIV positive). The CHCs provide a broad range of support services, including transportation, translation, health education, nutrition, and AIDS management, and have been considered by those who use them to provide high-quality care (McAlearney, 2002). Many of the CHCs were on the brink of financial insolvency in the late 1990s, but the Bush Administration initiative to expand CHCs has eased the financial difficulties of these health care providers (HRSA, 2006).

Industrial Health Service Units

A range of industrial health hazards exist, from traumatic injury to occupational exposure to harmful substances (e.g., silica, asbestos, and lead). The number of "in-plant" health units in the United States is not known, but there are thousands of them. In small plants (fewer than 100 workers), health services are ordinarily quite rudimentary. They are often limited to a first-aid kit and arrangements with some local health facility to which injured workers may be sent. Very large plants (with more than 2,500 workers) usually have some systematic in-plant health service. Customarily, it is staffed with trained industrial nurses and part-time or full-time physicians. In a few companies, in-plant health services are comprehensive, providing employees with complete medical care for all disorders, job connected or not.

The long-term trend in American industry is toward greater concentration of production in fewer large corporations. Although at one time it seemed that concentration might enhance the prospects for improving occupational health programs, in the 1980s there were actually reductions in service in many large corporations in the name of cost savings (D. Parkinson, personal communication, October 25, 1990). This situation does not appear to have improved since that time.

School Health Clinics

In 2010, there were more than 78.5 million students in primary and secondary schools, colleges, and universities, both private and public. More than 32.7 million were enrolled in primary schools and 16.6 million in secondary schools (U.S. Census Bureau, 2012, Table 1). Almost all educational institutions provide some type of organized, ambulatory health service. About half of the school health services are run by local health departments, the balance being run by boards of education, on their own or in cooperation with the local health department.

Very little disease treatment is done in school health programs. Usually carried out by school nurses, the work of most of these programs is confined to case finding and prevention for certain chronic or epidemic diseases, for example, screening for vision and hearing difficulties and providing immunizations. Referrals are made to physicians for diagnosis and treatment, should they be indicated. College and university health services are more likely to provide general diagnostic and treatment care. Some pay special attention to mental and substance abuse problems.

Home Care and Hospice

According to Strahan (1996):

> Home health care is provided to individuals and families in their place of residence to promote, maintain, or restore health or to maximize the level of independence while minimizing the effects of disability and illness, including terminal illness. These agencies are often referred to today as "hospitals without walls" because advances in technology allow dozens of complex illnesses, once treated almost exclusively in the hospital, to be treated at home.

Hospice care is defined as a program of palliative and supportive care services that provides physical, psychological, social, and spiritual care for dying persons, their families, and other loved ones. Hospice services are available in both the home and inpatient settings.

In 2010, there were 33,000 providers in the United States and 10,581 Medicare-certified home care agencies (NAHC, 2010). Total home care spending is difficult to estimate due to limitations of data sources:

> The Centers for Medicare & Medicaid Services (CMS) estimated total spending for home care to be $65 billion in 2008. These estimates do not include spending for home care services that are unavailable in the national health accounts data; for example, payments made by consumers directly to independent providers....Medicare is the largest single payer of home health care services. In 2009, Medicare spending accounted for approximately 41 percent of home health expenditures....In 2009, the home health benefit accounted for 4.2 percent of total Medicare spending ($434 billion). Nearly 37 percent was spent for hospital care, 14 percent for physician services, and nearly three percent for hospice care." (NAHC 2010)

In 2010, about 7.2 million predominantly elderly (69%), women (64%) received organized home health services (NAHC, 2010). The major diagnoses for this group, based on Medicare home health utilization data, were circulatory system diseases and heart disease (38.1%), diseases of the musculoskeletal system and connective tissue (12.6%), endocrine, nutritional, and metabolic diseases and immunity disorders (11.7%), and diabetes mellitus (10.8%) (NAHC, 2010, Table 5).

SUMMARY

The bulk of the need for medical care and for the provision of health services occurs in the ambulatory setting. In the United States, a disproportionate share of health care resources is devoted to inpatient care, both acute and long term. If, overall, health care is to be improved, this imbalance needs to be addressed. Furthermore, given the current profile of disease and disability in the United States, it is obvious that significant improvements in the health of the American people could be achieved by the widespread implementation of known health-promotive and disease-preventive measures in the ambulatory setting (U.S. Department of Health and Human Services, 2000). This is the central element of comprehensive primary care.

NOTES

1. For an extensive treatment of hospital governance issues, see Kovner & Neuhauser, (2001) and Kovner & Channing, (2001).
2. Long-term care deserves a fuller discussion than we have room for in this book. Much of this section is based on Feldman, Nadash, and Gursen (2005). The reader is referred to this source for more detail on nursing homes in particular and long-term care in general.
3. Why is this particular example chosen, one might ask? Because Dr. Jonas' grandmother happened to have been a member of that hospital's founding board of directors, and his stepmother was a long-time member of the board of its successor, Arden Hill Hospital.

REFERENCES

Agency for Healthcare Research and Quality (AHRQ). (2009a). HCUP facts & figures: Cost by diagnosis. Retrieved December 30, 2011, from www.hcup-us.ahrq.gov/reports/factsand-figures/2009/exhibit4_1.jsp

Agency for Healthcare Research and Quality (AHRQ). (2009b). Number of stays, stays per 10,000 population, and growth of the most frequent principal diagnoses for hospital Stays, 1997 and 2009. Retrieved December 30, 2011, from www.hcup-us.ahrq.gov/reports/factsand-figures/2009/exhibit2_2.jsp

Agency for Healthcare Research and Quality (AHRQ). (2011). The National Hospital Bill: The most expensive conditions, by payer, 2008. Retrieved January 1, 2012, from www.hcup-us.ahrq.gov/reports/statbriefs/sb107.pdf

Alavy, B., Chung, V., Maggiore, D., Shim, C., & Dhuper, S. (2006). Emergency department as the main source of asthma care. Journal of Asthma, 43(7), 527–532.

Ambulatory Surgery Center Association. (2012). *History.* Retrieved February 3, 2012, from www.ascassociation.org/Home

American Hospital Association (AHA). (1990). *Hospital statistics 1990–1991.* Chicago, IL: Author.

American Hospital Association (AHA). (2011a). *AHA guide, 2011.* Chicago, IL: Health Forum.

American Hospital Association (AHA). (2011b). *Hospital statistics, 2011.* Chicago, IL: Health Forum.

American Hospital Association (AHA). (2011c). *AHA environmental scan 2011.* Chicago, IL: Author.

Anderson, H. (1990, August 5). Out-patient care: A nationwide revolution. *Hospitals,* p. 28.

Andrews, M. (January 2, 2012). Hospitals are making room for alternative therapies. *Los Angeles Times.* Retrieved January 15, 2012, from http://articles.latimes.com/2012/jan/02/health/la-he-hospitals-alternative-medicine-20120102

Association of State and Territorial Health Officials (ASTHO). (2006). *Access to care.* Retrieved December 20, 2006, from www.astho.org/?template=access.html

Bernstein, N. (January 21, 2012). Chefs, butlers, marble baths: Hospitals vie for the affluent. *The New York Times.* Retrieved January 23, 2012, from http://www.nytimes.com/2012/01/22/nyregion/chefs-butlers-and-marble-baths-not-your-average-hospital-room.html

Callan, D., & Fein, O. (1972). NENA: Community control in a bind. *Health PAC Bulletin, 41*(June), 3–12.

Commission on Public General Hospitals. (1978). *The future of the "public" general hospital.* Chicago, IL: Hospital Research and Educational Trust.

Cunningham, R. (2000, November–December). Two old hands and the new new thing. *Health Affairs, 19*(6), 33–40.

Eisen, R., & Sloan, F. A. (Eds.). (1997). *Developments in health economics and public policy* (Vol. 5). New York, NY: Springer Publishing.

Davis, K., & Schoen, C. (1978). *Health and the war on poverty.* Washington, DC: Brookings Institution.

Dobbie, A., Kelly, P., Sylvia, E., & Freeman, J. (2006). Evaluating family medicine resident COPC programs: Meeting the challenge. *Family Medicine, 38*(6), 399–407.

Ermann, D., & Gabel, J. (1985). The changing face of American health care: Multi-hospital systems, emergency centers, and surgery centers. *Medical Care, 23*(15), 401–420.

Feldman, P. H., Nadash, P., & Gursen, M. D. (2005). Long term care. In A. R. Kovner & S. Jonas (Eds.), *Jonas and Kovner's health care delivery in the United States* (8th ed., pp. 274–325). New York, NY: Springer Publishing.

Felt-Lisk, S., McHugh, M., & Howell, E. (2002). Monitoring local safety-net providers: Do they have adequate capacity? *Health Affairs, 21*(5), 277–283.

Fisher, G. R. (2001). [Review of the book *Mergers*]. *Journal of the American Medical Association, 286*(24), 3132–3133.

Freymann, J. G. (1974). *The American health care system: Its genesis and trajectory.* New York, NY: Medcom.

Friedman, E. (1997). California public hospitals: The buck has stopped. *Journal of the American Medical Association, 277*(7), 577–581.

Gresenz, C. R., Studdert, D. M., Campbell, N., & Hensler, D. R. (2002). Patients in conflict with managed care: A profile of appeals in two HMOs. *Health Affairs, 21*(4), 189–196.

Griffith, J. R. (1999). *The well-managed health care organization* (4th ed.). Chicago, IL: Health Administration Press.

Hall, M. J., & Owings, M. F. (2002, June 19). *National Hospital Discharge Survey 2000.* Advance data (No. 329). Hyattsville, MD: National Center for Health Statistics.

Haugh, R. (2002). Nowhere else to turn. *Hospitals and Health Networks,* April, 44–48.

Health Resources and Services Administration (HRSA). (2006). HSS awards $10 million to expand health center services for farmworkers, homeless. *HRSA news.* Retrieved December 20, 2006, from http://archive.hrsa.gov/newsroom/news2006.htm

Health Resources and Services Administration (HRSA). (2010). *Health center data.* Retrieved January 1, 2011, from http://bphc.hrsa.gov/healthcenterdatastatistics/index.html

Health Resources and Services Administration (HRSA), Bureau of Primary Care. (2012). *What is a health center?* Retrieved February 2, 2012, from http://bphc.hrsa.gov/about/index.html

Hoffman, C., Schoen, C., Rowland, D., & Davis, K. (2001). Gaps in health coverage among working-age Americans, and the consequences. *Journal of Health Care for the Poor and Underserved, 12*(3), 272–289.

Huang, J., Silbert, J., & Regenstein, M. (2005). *America's public hospitals and health systems, 2003.* Washington, DC: National Association of Public Hospitals and Health Systems.

Institute of Medicine (IOM). (2000). *To err is human: Building a safer health system.* Washington, DC: National Academies Press.

Institute of Medicine (IOM). (2002). *Unequal treatment: Confronting racial and ethnic disparities in health care.* Washington, DC: National Academies Press.

Irving Levin Associates. (2004). *Trends and indicators in the changing health care marketplace.* Kaiser Family Foundation. Retrieved November 4, 2006, from www.kff.org/insurance/7031/ti2004-5-12.cfm?RenderForPrint=1

Irving Levin Associates (2010). *The hospital M&A market: Five-year review & outlook second edition, 2010.* Retrieved December 30, 2011, from www.levinassociates.com/sites/default/files/pdf/hospital/hospital2abstract.pdf

Jonas, S. (1973). Some thoughts on primary care: Problems in implementation. *International Journal of Health Services, 3*(2), 177.

Kaiser Family Foundation. (2007). *Health coverage and the uninsured.* Retrieved January 11, 2007, from www.kff.org/uninsured/index.cfm

Kleinke, J. D. (2000). Vaporware.com: The failed promise of the health care Internet. *Health Affairs, 19*(6), 57–71.

Knowles, J. H. (1965). The role of the hospital: The ambulatory clinic. *Bulletin of the New York Academy of Medicine, 41*(2), 68–79.

Kongstvedt, P. R., Plocher, D. W., & Stanford, J. C. (2001). Integrated health care delivery systems. In P. R. Kongstvedt (Ed.), *The managed health care handbook* (4th ed., pp. 42–71). Gaithersburg, MD: Aspen.

Kovner, A. R., & Channing, A. H. (2001). *A career guide for the health services manager* (3rd ed.). Chicago, IL: Health Administration Press.

Kovner, A. R., & Neuhauser, D. (2001). *Health services management: Readings and commentary* (7th ed.). Chicago, IL: Health Administration Press.

Landy, J. (2001, September 25). *September 25 NYC forum on the threats to primary care in the U.S.* New York, NY: Physicians for a National Health Program announcement, distributed by email.

Light, H. L., & Brown, H. J. (1967). The Gouverneur Health Services Program: An historical view. *Milbank Memorial Fund Quarterly, 45*(4), 375–390.

Lin, W. C., Yang, Y., Wen, Y. K., & Chang, C. C. (2006). Outpatient versus inpatient renal biopsy: A retrospective study. *Clinical Nephrology, 66*(1), 17–24.

Longlett, S. K., Kruse, J. E., & Wesley, R. M. (2001). Community-oriented primary care: Historical perspective. *Family Practice and the Health Care System, 14*(1), 54–63.

MacEachern, M. T. (1962). *Hospital organization and management.* Berwyn, IL: Physician's Record Co.

Madison, D. L. (1989, June 15). The interstudy edge. *Medical Benefits, 6*(11), 1.

May, E. L. (2004). Strengthening the safety net. *Healthcare Executive, 19*(1), 10–15.

McAlearney, J. S. (2002, March–April). The financial performance of community health centers, 1996–1999. *Health Affairs, 21*(2), 219–225.

McCaig, L. F., & Nawar, E. W. (2006). *National Hospital Ambulatory Medical Care Survey: 2004 Emergency department summary.* Advance data (No. 372). Hyattsville, MD: National Center for Health Statistics.

Medical Group Management Association. (2002). *Ambulatory surgery center performance survey: 2001 report*. Englewood, CO: Author.

Moon, T. D., Laurens, M. B., Weimer, S. M., & Levy, J. A. (2005). Nonemergent emergency room utilization for an inner-city pediatric population. *Pediatric Emergency Care, 21*(6), 363–366.

Mullan, F. (1982). Sounding board: Community-oriented primary care. An agenda for the 80's. *New England Journal of Medicine, 307*(17), 1076–1078.

Mullan, F., & Conner, E. (Eds.). (1982). *Community-oriented primary care—conference proceedings*. Washington, DC: National Academies Press.

Myers, B. A., Steinhardt, B. J., Mosley, M. L., & Cashman, J. W. (1968). Medicare's effects on medical care. The medical care activities of local health units. *Public Health Reports, 83*(9), 757–769.

National Association for Home Care & Hospice (NAHC). (2010). *Basic statistics about home care*. Retrieved January 1, 2011, from www.nahc.org/facts/10HC_Stats.pdf

National Center for Health Statistics (NCHS). (2006). *Health, United States, 2006*. Hyattsville, MD: U.S. Department of Health and Human Services.

National Center for Health Statistics (NCHS). (2009). *Number, rate and average length of stay for discharges from short-stay hospitals by age, region, and sex: United States, 2009*. Retrieved December 30, 2011, from www.cdc.gov/nchs/data/nhds/1general/2009gen1_agesexalos.pdf

National Center for Health Statistics (NCHS). (2010). *Health, United States, 2009*. Hyattsville, MD: U.S. Department of Health and Human Services.

National Center for Health Statistics (NCHS). (2011). *Health, United States, 2010*. Hyattsville, MD: U.S. Department of Health and Human Services.

National Center for Health Statistics (NCHS). (2011). *Ambulatory medical care utilization estimates for 2007. Vital and health statistics, 13*(169). Retrieved January 1, 2011, from www.cdc.gov/nchs/data/series/sr_13/sr13_169.pdf

Nutting, P. A., Wood, M., & Conner, E. M. (1985). Community-oriented primary care in the United States. *Journal of the American Medical Association, 253*(12), 1763–1766.

Pear, R. (2002, February 18). 9 of 10 nursing homes in U.S. lack adequate staff, a government study finds. *The New York Times*, p. A11.

Podolsky, D. (1996, August 12). Breaking down the walls. *U.S. News and World Report*, p. 61.

Prybil, L. D. (1982). Growth and impact of multiunit hospital systems. *American Journal of Hospital Pharmacy. 39*(11):1888–1891.

Rhyne, R., Bogue, R., Kukulka, G., & Fulmer, H. (Eds.). (1998). *Community-oriented primary care: Health care for the 21st century*. Washington, DC: American Public Health Association.

Roemer, M. I., & Friedman, J. W. (1971). *Doctors in hospitals*. Baltimore, MD: Johns Hopkins.

Roemer, M. I. (1981). *Ambulatory health services in America*. Gaithersburg, MD: Aspen Systems.

Roemer, R., Kramer, C., & Frink, J. E. (1975). *Planning urban health services: From jungle to system*. New York, NY: Springer Publishing.

Rogatz, P. M. (1980, January 1). Directions of health system for the new decade. *Hospitals*, p. 67.

Rosen, G. (1971). The first neighborhood health center movement: Is rise and fall. *American Journal of Public Health, 61*(8), 1620–1637.

Rosenberg, C. E. (1979). The origins of the American hospital system. *Bulletin of the New York Academy of Medicine, 55*(1), 10–21.

Runy, L. A. (2003). *Outpatient revenue on the rise…but profits don't follow*. Hospital-connect.com. Retrieved February 2, 2012, from www.hhnmag.com/hhnmag_app/jsp/articledisplay.jsp?dcrpath=AHA/PubsNewsArticle/data/0310HHN_InBox_TheDataPage&domain=HHNMAG

Sardell, A. (1983). Neighborhood health centers and community-based care: Federal policy from 1965 to 1982. *Journal of Public Health Policy, 4*(4), 484–503.

Sheps, C. G. (1965). Conference summary and the road ahead. *Bulletin of the New York Academy of Medicine, 41*(1), 146–156.

Starfield, B. (1992). *Primary care*. New York, NY: Oxford University Press.

Stern, B. J. (1946). *Medical services by government*. New York, NY: The Commonwealth Fund.

Stevens, R. (1971). *American medicine and the public interest*. New Haven, CT: Yale University Press.

Strahan, G. W. (1996, April 24). *An overview of home health and hospice care patients: 1994 National Home and Hospice Care Survey*. Advance data. Hyattsville, MD: National Center for Health Statistics.

Thrall, T. H. (1996). What PHOs know. *Hospitals and Health Networks*, September, p. 54.

U.S. Census Bureau. (2005). *Statistical abstract of the United States: 2006*. Washington, DC: U.S. Department of Commerce.

U.S. Census Bureau. (2012). *School enrollment: Enrollment status of the population 3 years old and over, by sex, age, race, hispanic origin, foreign born, and foreign-born parentage: October 2010*. Retrieved on June 4, 2012, from www.census.gov/hhes/school/data/cps/2010/tables. html

Verghese, A. (1996, November 30). My hospital, dying a slow death. *New York Times*. Retrieved from www.nytimes.com/1996/11/30/opinion/my-hospital-dying-a-slow-death.html

Weinerman, E. R. (1968). Problems and perspectives of group practice. *Bulletin of the New York Academy of Medicine [2nd Series]*, *44*, 1423.

Winslow, C. E. A. (1929). *The life of Herman Biggs*. Philadelphia, PA: Lea & Febiger.

Zwick, D. I. (1972). Some accomplishments and findings of neighborhood health centers. *Milbank Memorial Fund Quarterly*, *50*(4), 387–420.

THREE

The People Who Provide Health Care

© Artizans Entertainment Inc. By Steve Artley.

In 2009, almost 15.5 million people, about 11.1% of all civilians employed in the United States, were working in health service sites (National Center for Health Statistics [NCHS], 2011, Table 105). This was up from 12.2 million people, or 9% of all employed persons, working in health care in 2000. In 2009, about 40% of them worked in hospitals, 16% in nursing and other residential care facilities, and more than 25% in practitioner offices and clinics including those of physicians, dentists, chiropractors, optometrists, and other practitioners. Since 1970, as the number of hospitals has shrunk, there has been a gradual decline in the percentage of health care personnel working in hospitals (it stood at close to two-thirds in 1970). There have been concomitant increases in the percentages working in practitioner offices and clinics. This trend has continued into the 21st century, even though the greatest declines occurred in the latter part of the 20th century. In 2000, for example, 42.6% of health services workers were employed in hospitals, compared to 40% in 2009. The percent working in practitioner offices and clinics declined from 26% in 2000 to 25% in 2009.

The U.S. Department of Labor has identified about 700 categories of skilled health occupations. In 2009, some of the largest groups of health care professionals without a doctoral degree (e.g., MD, DO, DDS, DC) were about 2.6 million active registered nurses (RNs), 728,670 licensed practical nurses (LPNs), 217,920 emergency medical technicians and paramedics, and about 268,000 pharmacists (NCHS, 2011, Table 110).

In 2008, the American Medical Association (AMA) reported 784,199 active physicians (those with an MD degree) (NCHS, 2011, Table 107). The ratio of other health personnel to physicians reflects the complexity of the U.S. health care system. With close to 800,000 physicians in active practice, there are more than 19 other health care workers for each physician. (In 1988, there were close to 18 other health care workers for each physician. This compares to about three other health care workers per doctor in 1920 (Donabedian, Axelrod, & Wyszewianski, 1980). Most of these other personnel have skills learned through special training. Only about one-fifth is "nonhealth care"—specifically clerical, custodial, or similar personnel.

Under the laws of most states, only physicians, dentists, and a few other types of practitioners may serve patients directly, without being authorized to do so by another health professional who is licensed for independent practice. Among the other independent health professions are chiropractic, optometry, podiatry, psychotherapy, and, in some states, midwifery and physical therapy. For the most part, nurses work on the orders of physicians, although in certain circumstances, in certain states, some nurses, called "nurse practitioners" or "advanced practice nurses" (see later discussion), can work independently.

Other types of health care providers working on the orders and under at least the general supervision of physicians include clinical laboratory, x-ray, electrocardiographic, and other specialized technicians such as cardiorespiratory therapists, those who operate kidney dialysis machines, and those who work in rehabilitation services. In dentistry, one finds dental hygienists, dental technicians, and dental assistants working under the orders of dentists. Certain other health professionals (e.g., nutritionists and dietitians; physical, occupational, and speech therapists and audiologists; statisticians and statistical clerks; and medical record librarians and information technology specialists) work both under physicians' orders and, in certain circumstances, such as school or industrial settings, independently.

Many of these "other health" occupations originally developed out of the nursing profession. Today, in countries less developed than the United States, work done in the United States by a laboratory technician, physical therapist, or dietitian is often done by a nurse (and at times even by a physician). At the same time, in the United States, medical practice itself has become more and more specialized. It is interesting to note that the same phenomenon has occurred within the largest health profession, nursing. Consider, for example, the development of the nurse specialties such as operating room nurse, intensive care nurse, nurse anesthetist, nurse midwife, and nurse practitioner/advanced practice nurse. In the next two sections, we consider the two largest health professions, medicine and nursing, in more detail.

PHYSICIANS

Historical Background

The profession of medicine in America has changed dramatically over the course of history. The role, training, and expectations of pre–Revolutionary War physicians are practically unrecognizable to us today, as the following description of the profession in the 18th century attests:

> [There were] 3,500 practicing physicians in the colonies in 1775. Of these, less than 300 had received a medical degree. Only a handful had graduated from the ten-year-old Philadelphia Medical College. The remainder, mainly from the middle and southern colonies, attended the European medical schools. Admission requirements included a knowledge of the classics and a husky bankroll. By the time the graduating thesis had been written in Latin, the student had been exposed to all the latest theories that Edinburgh, London, or the Continent had to offer. Theories aplenty—but the fledgling M.S.'s returned to America without having seen a patient!

The bulk of the practicing physicians in the colonies—including all of the independent New Englanders—were apprentice-trained. Some had undergraduate degrees, while others were no more than 15 years old when starting their medical careers. Benjamin Rush noted that the only prerequisite for a "doctor's boy" was the ability to stand the sight of blood! His teacher was likely to be a prominent physician-surgeon, well qualified to guide the student through the maze of anatomy, osteology, the compounding of medicine, surgery, and the writings of Hippocrates. Toward the end of the 3- to 6-year apprenticeship, the doctor's boy was doing his own bloodletting, tooth-pulling, wound dressing, and some minor surgery. His certificate of proficiency gave the same practicing privileges as a medical student from the continent (Wilbur, 1980, p. 1).

Since then, a vast health care system has developed in the United States to facilitate the practice of the allopathic physician (MD), whose early days in America are described in the foregoing passage. This section of the chapter describes physician training and practice today.

Licensure

According to the Medical Practice Act of New York State (Article 131, Para. 6521 of the State Education Law): "The practice of the profession of medicine is...diagnosing, treating, operating or prescribing for any human disease, pain, injury, deformity or physical condition" (University of the State of New York [USNY], 1995a, p. 31).

In the United States, the medical license is granted by the states. To qualify for a medical license in New York State, for example, one must hold an MD or DO degree or its equivalent from a school meeting the state education department's requirements; have certain postgraduate (residency) practice experience; pass a medical licensure examination as designated by the department; be a citizen or resident alien; be of "good moral character;" and pay a fee (USNY, 1995a, p. 31). All states have similar requirements.

In our time, few medical school graduates enter practice before completing at least 3 years of residency training.

Private Medical Practice[1]

The primary mode of organization of physicians in the United States (and, indeed, of most of the other health care providers who are licensed to practice independently) is what is called "private practice." Traditionally, the private practitioner contracts directly with patients (although almost never in writing) to provide a set of services (usually not spelled out in any detail). In return, the practitioner is paid a fee by the patient directly or, more commonly, by a third-party payer (i.e., an entity other than the practitioner or the patient, such as a health insurance company or the Medicare program). This arrangement is appropriately called the fee-for-service system.

Among the major factors that influence what the physician in private practice may do to and for patients are the licensing laws of the state in which the physician is located, the requirements of his or her malpractice insurer, and the stipulations of the hospital to which the physician admits patients, if, indeed, he or she is a hospital staff member. Since the mid-1990s, the era of "managed care," this mode of physician organization has been changing (Bodenheimer, 1999; Dudley & Luft, 2001; Shortell, Waters, Clarke, & Budetti, 1998). Physician participation in managed care increased between 1988 and 1999, when 91% of all physicians had at least one managed care contract (up from 61%) and 49% of average practice revenue was derived from managed care (up from 23%). Participation in managed care declined, but only slightly, between 1999 and 2001 (Kaiser Family Foundation, 2002). However, it is not clear whether managed care is changing physician practice in the 21st century. Some research shows that it is having no impact on physician propensity to order services since 2000 (O'Neill & Kuder, 2005). On the other hand, some research indicates that managed care patients are less likely to see a specialist than those where there is no physician gatekeeper (Forrest et al., 2003).

Over time, the proportion of physicians hired on a salaried basis and/or working in large groups has increased. Following is the situation in

2007 for care provided in the offices of nonfederally employed physicians not in hospital outpatient clinics or emergency departments:

> Overall, 67.8 percent of visits were made to physicians who were owners of the practice. More visits, 83.0 percent, were to practices that were either owned by a physician or a group of physicians than other ownership arrangements. Over one-half of office visits (57.3 percent) were made to physicians who were part of a group practice, defined as having three or more physicians.
>
> The percentage of U.S. physicians who own their practices has declined over the past two decades. The percentage of physicians practicing in independent, solo, or small-group practices declined while the percentage of physicians practicing in larger practices increased. From 1997 to 2007, the percentage of visits to physicians who were solo practitioners decreased 21 percent. During the same period, visits to physicians who were part of a group practice with 6–10 physicians increased 46 percent.
>
> About one-fifth, or 21.1 percent of visits occurred in multispecialty practices, and 48.4 percent were to single specialty practices. The remaining 30.5 percent of office visits were to solo practitioners. (Hsiao, Cherry, Beatty, & Rechtsteiner, 2010, p. 3)

The trend toward group practice and away from physician ownership is especially true for younger physicians. Among the reasons for this mode of employment that younger physicians find attractive are receiving a regular income and comprehensive fringe benefits; the provision of medical malpractice insurance by the employer; regular hours and regular night and weekend coverage schedules; avoiding the difficulties associated with entering into private practice in many desirable living areas, many of which have an over-abundance of physicians; avoiding the high costs of starting a private practice, a particular burden to so many of today's new physicians who start professional life with a large debt accumulated during their medical training; and finally, avoiding the tribulations of office practice dealing with managed care company scrutiny.

Indeed, the era of managed care has put many physicians under a great deal of pressure. As Thomas Bodenheimer noted in an observation that is still valid in the 21st century (1999):

> As the 20th century closes, the practice of medicine in the United States faces challenges as great as it ever has. On the one hand, medical science and technology have brought unimaginable benefits to the America population. On the other hand, these advances have contributed to the escalation

of health care costs above what many people are able to pay. Physicians are caught in the middle—pressured by private and governmental purchasers of health care to keep costs down, while driven by the public and their own professional standards to do everything that might be beneficial for each patient. (p. 584)

Patterns of Practice

An important feature of medical practice organization in the United States is that most physicians see patients both on an ambulatory basis in their own offices and as hospital inpatients. (A small percentage of doctors do not have hospital appointments. How many is not known. Most of them are probably in urban areas with a surfeit of hospitals, or rural ones with none within a reasonable distance. Another small percentage belongs to the growing sub-specialty of "hospitalist," physicians who, usually working for the hospital, see only hospitalized patients; also see the later discussion.) In most other countries, physicians either see ambulatory patients only or work full time in hospitals.

In the United States, ambulatory care is the predominant setting for medical care. Most ambulatory care visits are in physician offices (83% in 2007), with the remainder provided in hospital outpatient departments and emergency departments. In 2007, 58.0% of office visits were made to primary care specialists, 22.2% to medical specialists, and the remaining 19.8% to surgical specialists (Hsiao, Cherry, Beatty, & Rechtsteiner, 2010).

During 2007, an estimated 994.3 million visits were made to physician offices in the United States, an overall rate of 335.6 visits per 100 persons. About one-third of office visits, 34.9 percent, were made to practices with all or partial electronic medical records systems, while 85.1 percent of the visits were made to practices with all or partial electronic submission of claims. From 1997 to 2007, the percentage of visits to physicians who were solo practitioners decreased 21 percent. During the same period, visits to physicians who were part of a group practice with 6–10 physicians increased 46 percent. There were an estimated 106.5 million injury- or poisoning-related office visits in 2007, representing 10.7 percent of all visits. Medications were ordered, supplied, or administered at 727.7 million office visits, accounting for 73.2 percent of all office visits. In 2007, about 2.3 billion drugs were ordered, supplied, or administered, resulting in an average of 226.3 drug mentions per 100 visits. (Hsiao, Cherry, Beatty, & Rechtsteiner, 2010, p. 1)

The unusual arrangement in America offers some significant advantages to the patient. For example, for the many conditions for which one physician is technically competent to provide both ambulatory and inpatient care, there is continuity of care. In many cases requiring surgery, the nonsurgical referring physician will participate in the pre- and postoperative phases of care in the hospital. With the advent of managed care, however, this system may be changing. Managed care emphasizes the use of the primary care physician. Most plans do not allow beneficiaries to see a specialist without seeing or at least receiving the approval of their primary care physician first (although this pattern is beginning to change; Ferris et al., 2001).

Under managed care, the primary care physician has two main functions (Bodenheimer, Lo, & Casalino, 1999; Shortell, Waters, Clarke, & Budetti, 1998).   One is to provide most of the health care that his or her patients need most of the time and coordinate the rest as a "gatekeeper" for what is best for the patient (Somers, 1983). The other, developed as the for-profit managed care industry has spread, is to act as the gatekeeper for the system, controlling the use of hospital and specialist care, at least as much for fiscal as for medical reasons.

Following the first model seems to be leading physicians in the United States to emulate a pattern based on the system in Great Britain, where primary care physicians, still called "general practitioners," see patients almost exclusively on an ambulatory basis. The specialists, although seeing patients on both an ambulatory and inpatient basis, are virtually the only ones who handle hospitalized patients.

In 1996, Wachter and Goldman coined the term *hospitalist* to describe physicians who see patients solely on an inpatient basis. As they noted (Wachter & Goldman, 1996):

> [Taking into account] the realities of managed care [in the United States] and its emphasis on efficiency . . . we anticipate the rapid growth of a new breed of physicians we call "hospitalists"— specialists in inpatient medicine—who will be responsible for managing the care of hospitalized patients in the same way that primary care physicians are responsible for managing the care of outpatients. (p. 514)

Their prediction seems to be a reality. This movement has grown in strength over the past decade. Reported advantages of the hospitalists approach include reduced patient length of stay, reduced per-case cost, decreased cost under several different risk-based payment systems, fewer inappropriate admissions through the emergency department, improved patient satisfaction, reduced readmission rates, increased admissions from remote physicians, and standardized care protocols and disease management programs (Haugh, 2002).

Six years after they published their first article on the hospitalist concept, based on a literature review of studies of the new model, Wachter and Goldman concluded (2002):

> Empirical research supports the premise that hospitalists improve inpatient [care] efficiency without harmful effects on quality or patient satisfaction.... [T]he clinical use of hospitalists is growing rapidly, and hospitalists are also assuming prominent roles as teachers, researchers, and quality leaders. The hospitalist field...seems destined to continue to grow. (p. 487)

In August 2006, Wachter said in an interview:

> We have good data that show that there are about 15,000 hospitalists in the United States today, and the forces for growth are only accelerating. It now seems likely to me that the hospitalist movement will grow to about 30,000 to 50,000 physicians, much more than previously predicted. (Wachter, 2006)

We shall see.

Medical Specialization[2]

Specialization is the most prominent feature of the organization of American medical practice. It is one of the major results of the explosion of biomedical knowledge and technology that began in the last third of the 19th century. In the arenas of complex pathophysiological states and complicated surgery, it has become ever more difficult for a physician to master in depth more than one small area of what biomedical science and technology make possible and have to offer. Thus, even within specialties, there is further subspecialization. For example, certain ophthalmic (eye) surgeons "do only retinas," and certain orthopedic surgeons "do only hips."

Whereas the high-tech specialties demand a great depth of knowledge and skill in one particular area, the specialties of family medicine, primary care pediatrics, and primary care internal medicine demand a great breadth of knowledge and competency (Starfield, 1992). It is the case that many of the nonprimary care specialties focus on a relatively narrow range of knowledge and skills, although both are developed in great depth. In one sense, then, most of the developments in medical specialization in terms of ever-narrowing focus have made the practice of medicine easier for the physician within each specialty than it is in primary care.

The knowledge-technology explosion is certainly one factor that accounts for the ever-increasing specialization of American medicine. Another is the financial incentive that is part of specialization: There has

almost always been more money to be made in the specialties than in primary care. At the same time, there has never been a health personnel planning policy in this country that might exert some external controls on the
distribution of physicians between the primary care and specialty sectors
and within each specialty sector itself.

Specialization does have its advantages for patients. The high degree of
knowledge and skill that specialists possess is beneficial to the patient who
has a problem in that particular area of specialization. However, it also
has its disadvantages. Specialists tend to focus on their specialty's organ
or organ system to the exclusion of others. Some, when facing a patient,
see only the organ of their own specialty, not the whole person first. The
patient's overall well-being may suffer if there is no professional who can
(a) see the patient as a whole person, (b) put together into one clinical
picture observations derived from a variety of patient complaints arising
from different organ systems, (c) guide the patient through an intelligent
use of the knowledge of several specialists, and (d) set up an organized
means for communication among specialists.

This is not an argument against specialization per se; the vast expansion
of medical knowledge requires such specialization, at least for a certain
proportion of the profession. It is, however, an argument for a more rational approach to the organization of specialists and a significant improvement in the provision of primary care physician services, an argument that
has a long history (Colwill, 1986; Geyman, 1986; Starfield, 1992; White,
1968). It is an argument for the "pro-patient" variant of the gatekeeper, as
originally described by Somers (1983).

Medical Education

In the United States, including Puerto Rico, there were 136 fully accredited allopathic medical schools in 2011 (Liaison Committee on Medical
Education [LCME], 2012). Allopathic (MD) medical schools in the United
States and Canada are accredited by a voluntary agency called the Liaison Committee on Medical Education (LCME). This agency is comprised
of representatives from the AMA and the Association of American Medical Colleges (AAMC) and their Canadian counterparts. There were also
26 osteopathic (DO) medical schools accredited by the American Osteopathic Association in 2011 (AOA, 2011).

All but a few medical schools are attached to a university. In the university, the medical school is invariably a separate college with its own
dean (or the equivalent), sometimes loosely linked with other health professional schools in a "health sciences center." About 60% of the medical
schools are sponsored by state governments as part of state public universities; the rest are under private auspices. All the schools have received
substantial, although primarily indirect, financial support from the federal government for many years.

Entry to U.S. medical schools usually requires a university bachelor's degree. The standard medical school program lasts another 4 years. It is termed "undergraduate" medical education even though, in the university sense, it is graduate education. This is because, in medical training, the postmedical degree, hospital-based residency experience is considered "graduate medical education." Admission to medical schools is selective (AAMC, 2011). For the class entering in 2010–2011, there were 42,742 applicants, of whom 18,665 found places, a ratio of about 2:1. The peak number of applicants was about 47,000 for the entering class of 1996. The number of applicants has been on the up-swing from 37,000 in 2002. The ratio of applicants to places fell steadily through the 1990s from a high of 2.7 in 1995–1996 (AAMC, 2006a, Table 6).

The proportion of women in medical school has been increasing since the early 1970s (AAMC, 2006a, Table 6). In 1982–1983, women accounted for about one-third of applicants and matriculants to medical school. In 2009–2010, women accounted for 47% of the entering class, and about 48% of the graduating class that entered 4 years before (AAMC, 2011).

The record for increasing the admission rates for African Americans does not match that for women. From the 1970s through 1990, the percentage of African American admissions remained unchanged at about 6%. By 1995, this number had increased to 9%. However, by 2000, it had fallen to 7.5% and was 6.6% in 2006. At the same time, Hispanic admissions remained around 7% in 2006. In 2006, Asian Americans accounted for close to one-fifth of all admissions (AAMC, 2006b, Table 8). As for graduates of medical school, among the class of 2010, about 63% were non-Hispanic white, 7% African American, 21% Asian, and 7% Hispanic or Latino. This profile of graduates represents a slight increase since 2002 in Asians (up from 19%) and Hispanics or Latinos (up from 6%), and a slight decrease in non-Hispanic Whites (down from 64%). African American medical school graduates accounted for the same percent of the 2002 graduating class as in 2010—7% (AAMC, 2011).

The ratio of full-time faculty to students is very high, much higher than in virtually any other branch of education. In fact, in medical education, the number of faculty actually exceeds the number of students, by a ratio of close to 1.77:1 (Barzansky & Etzel, 2005). This is one of the reasons medical education is so expensive (Krakower, Ganem, & Jolly, 1996). Although tuition and fees account for only about 4.0% of total medical school expenditures, it is not unusual for a student to graduate with upward of $100,000 in debt accumulated for undergraduate and medical education.

An unusual aspect of U.S. medical education is that a significant number of U.S. citizens are trained to be physicians in off-shore, for-profit medical schools, established for the purpose of providing places for at least some of those applicants to U.S. schools who cannot gain entry to them. These off-shore schools are not recognized by the LCME. A number of states, with New York in the lead (Jonas, 1981, 1984), have over the years established their own programs for certifying graduates of these programs as eligible to take the state licensing examinations, as well as the schools for the purpose of permitting their students to take clinical clerkship training in hospitals in the respective states (Monahan, 2001). This is true in the 21st century, as well.

Graduate Medical Education

In academic year 2010–2011, there were 8,887 Accreditation Council for Graduate Medical Education (ACGME) accredited residency programs in 133 specialties and subspecialties (ACGME, 2012). Nearly 24,000 physicians complete their medical training through programs of graduate medical education (GME) each year (Bureau of Health Professions, 2006). Before entering residencies and fellowships, new physicians must complete the 4 years of medical education. About 80% of physicians completing GME are graduates of U.S. medical schools, and most of those are schools of allopathic medicine, which graduate about 16,000 MDs annually. This number has been relatively stable since 1980, and the baseline projections assume that that it will remain stable through 2020. Schools of osteopathic medicine graduate approximately 3,000 DOs per year, and baseline supply projections assume this number will increase to 4,000 per year by 2020.

More than 5,000 international medical graduates (IMGs) are accepted annually to GME programs. An increasing percentage of these are U.S. citizens who graduated from medical schools in other countries. IMGs who are not U.S. citizens or permanent residents can enter GME programs under the temporary work (H) or training (J) visa programs. Those IMGs with a J visa can participate in the J-1 visa waiver program, which allows physicians to remain in the United States if they provide primary care in federally designated health professional shortage areas (HPSAs) for at least 3 years after completing their GME program.

Physician Supply

As of 2008, about 82% of the 954,224 living, presently or formerly licensed, U.S. allopathic doctors of medicine (MDs) were in active practice (NCHS, 2011, Table 107). About 25% of the active MDs received their medical training outside the United States and Canada. That is quite a remarkable percentage considering the size of and the ongoing investment in the U.S. medical education system. As Fitzhugh Mullan has pointed out (1995) in an observation that is still true, despite the output of the U.S. medical schools, physician needs in many medically underserved areas could not be met without a steady influx of so-called IMGs (both U.S. citizens and foreign nationals who have attended non-U.S. medical schools) to U.S. residency programs, especially those in hospitals situated in those same underserved areas.

Slightly more than 20,000 of the physicians active in 2002 were in federal government service, most of them in the armed forces or units of what was formerly the U.S. Public Health Service. More than 80% of the federal physicians worked in patient care services. These percentages have varied marginally since 1975. (Since 2003 census reports have merged both federal and nonfederal physicians) In 2008, about 741,000 (greater than 94%) of all physicians worked in patient care. Of those, about 75% were in office-based practice, about 15% were house staff (residents in training), and more than 10% were fully qualified physicians working full time in hospitals (NCHS, 2011, Table 107).

The slightly more than 43,000 professionally active physicians who were not engaged in patient care worked in medical teaching, administration, research, state and local health services, the pharmaceutical industry, and the like. Among the several medical specialties, the largest numbers were found in internal medicine (about 108,000), general and family practice (about 75,000), pediatrics (more than 51,000), obstetrics and gynecology (close to 34,000), and general surgery (close to 25,000).

In 2008, the overall MD physician/population ratio was 27.7 per 10,000 (Health, United States, 2011, Table 106). This is up from a post–World War II low in 1960 of 14 and from the 1988 figure of 22.6 per 10,000. There was a wide variation in physician/population ratio by geographic area. The state with the highest ratio, Massachusetts (many medical schools, given the population size), had about 44 per 10,000, whereas the state with the lowest ratio, Idaho, had just under18 per 10,000.

Although there are no known differences in health status that vary consistently with physician/population ratios, utilization of health services is generally higher in those areas that have more physicians (Eisenberg, 1986, pp. 15–17; Wennberg et al., 1996; Wennberg, Fisher, & Skinner, 2002). Among the factors influencing the amount of work physicians do are income goals, desired practice style, personal characteristics, practice setting, and standards established by clinical leadership (Eisenberg, 1986, chapter 2).

Physician Workforce Projections

In 1986, this author had this to say about the issue of physician supply (Jonas, 1986):

> At the same time that geographical distribution is quite uneven and remains a serious problem, the nation is confronting a general oversupply of physicians....This situation creates a different set of problems [from that created by the former perceived undersupply of physicians]. To determine rationally the size of the physician manpower pool, some measure of need or demand for services is necessary...but need and demand

alone cannot be the base for determining man-power [supply]. Patterns of practice vary…productivity varies…and supply affects demand….One can try to rely on the force of an economic market to [manage] the size of the pool, or one can regulate supply, or do some of both. This is, in general, what has been tried to date; it has [obviously] not been very effective. (p. 65)

And so it seemed at that time that there was an impending oversupply of physicians.

Now turn to 2002. The leading journal of health policy analysis, *Health Affairs*, devoted a good portion of its January to February 2002 issue to eight articles on the subject (see *Health Affairs*, 21[1], pp. 140–171). The lead article (Cooper, Getzen, McKee, & Laud, 2002) held that the nation was moving back to a stage of undersupply. However, that position was disputed strongly (e.g., Weiner, 2002).

The fact is the answers still are not clear. Of course, proper supply cannot be determined until demand and its relationship to supply are understood; some controls over what doctors do and do not do and what other health professionals could do just as well are established; and some arrangements for rationalizing the geographic distribution of physicians are made (see Mullan, 2002). That, however, would require a national physician supply and distribution policy and a planning program to implement it. Historically, as previously noted, neither has ever existed in the United States, despite the fact that the first national study on the issue that recommended that such a policy be created was published in 1959 (Fordham, 1980). Given our national aversion to health services planning, it is unlikely that one will be implemented in the foreseeable future.

Despite what has just been said about the total absence of organized health care services planning in the United States, forecasting is a function in which we are still engaged. Trying to forecast how many and what types of physicians are needed to meet the health care needs of the U.S. population as it grows and ages over the next several decades is a complex process. One major factor that must be considered is the trends in health care usage. Over the past 50 years, the adequacy of the future supply of physicians in the United States has been analyzed regularly. This has been done in order to provide for timely changes to be made to educate future generations of physicians efficiently and effectively. However, the changes that have been made have been the result of medical schools, and in certain cases, state governments, acting independently. Previous physician workforce planning analyses have resulted in the improvement of and changes to the medical education infrastructure, and prompted government increases in funding of medical education resources. In the 1950s and 1960s, for example, reactions to projections of physician shortages prompted U.S. medical schools to expand their programs, and immigration of physicians trained at foreign medical schools was promoted successfully to increase physician supply.

In the 1980s and 1990s, with the increase in health care costs mounting sharply, and the advent of managed health care promising greater efficiency and cost containment, there was an increased reliance on the use of primary care physicians, that is, family practitioners, pediatricians, and internists. This shift led health care analysts to forecast a surplus of specialists and a corresponding need for more generalists. This projection, however, did not take into account the public's strong response against health maintenance organizations' (HMOs)/managed care industry measures to inhibit health care usage. It also failed to consider the implications of "out-of-plan usage" by those covered under HMOs. In addition, analysis of physician supply needs was complicated by fundamental differences between the health statuses of those receiving health care from an HMO and those obtaining health care on a fee-for-service basis.

Today, there is concern about the growth of undergraduate medical education without a commensurate growth in GME, that is, residency programs. As we discussed earlier, graduates of medical school must complete a residency program in order to practice medicine. However, GME is not expanding, and this problem is being discussed by policy makers:

> There is general, but not universal, agreement that we either have or will have a shortage of physicians. All recognize that GME is the rate-limiting step in the production of practicing physicians in this country. The output of U.S. nationals who will be candidates for medical residencies is in the process of being accelerated significantly by expansion in size and number of U.S. schools offering training for the MD and DO degrees[1] and also by rapid expansion of the "off-shore" model (i.e., schools located abroad training mostly U.S. nationals for entry into the U.S. GME system). Thus, both public demand for additional physicians as well as demand from an increasing number of U.S. medical school graduates seeking residency positions will apply significant pressure for additional GME training opportunities. An interesting consequence of the projected substantial increase in demand for GME training by U.S. nationals is that availability as opposed to choice will play an increasingly important role in specialty selection. Thus, for example, if newly funded GME positions are confined to primary care, we can predict a significant increase in the numbers of U.S. nationals training in those specialties....On the other hand, public funding, which is the main source of GME support, has been effectively "capped" since the passage of the Balanced Budget Act (BBA) of 1997, and there are few signs that the political process favors provision of significant new resources. (Edelman & Romeiser, 2010, p. 149)

Physician Supply Model

In 1993 the Health Resources and Services Administration's Bureau of Health Professions (BHPr) developed the Physician Supply Model (PSM), a demographic utilization-based computerized system, to forecast the supply and specialization areas for 18 medical specialties required to maintain a high quality of physician services in the United States through 2020 (Cooper, 1995). Since 2000, the PSM has modeled physician supply needs utilizing figures obtained from the National Center for Health Statistics, the AMA, and the American Osteopathic Association regarding the supply of physicians in the workforce in a given year, the number of newly graduated medical doctors from United States and international medical schools during that year, and the depletion of that year's physician supply due to death, disability, retirement, or career change.

The PSM calculates the number of active physicians in a given year, with breakdowns by demographic characteristics including age, gender, type of medical degree (MD or DO), medical specialty, whether the medical degree was earned in the United States or internationally (USMG or IMG), and the physician's primary activity. The PSM also determines the number of full-time equivalent (FTE) physicians (where one FTE equals the average annual patient care hours per physician in the year 2000), varying by specialty.

Since calculation of PSM FTEs began in 2000, gender and age have been found to influence the estimate of FTEs, with women and older physicians tending to work fewer FTEs. Accordingly, as the population of active physicians has aged and more women have become physicians, the number of FTEs per active physician has decreased over the past several years (Bureau of Health Professions, 2006).

Physician productivity, which must be taken into account when forecasting the supply of physician services, is estimated on the basis of several factors, including the number of hours during which patient care is provided, and the number of patients seen. The PSM takes into consideration trends in the average number of hours worked and whether changes in health care delivery can alter the duration and number of patient visits, thereby affecting physician supply needs (National Center for Health Workforce Analysis, 2006). A report by the Bureau of Health Professions in 2008 had the following findings about the supply and demand for physician services:

> The baseline projections from BHPr's physician supply and requirements models suggest that overall requirements are growing faster than the FTE supply of physicians. Between 2005 and 2020, requirements are projected to grow to approximately 976,000 (22 percent), while FTE supply is projected to

grow to approximately 926,600 (14%). These projections suggest a modest, but growing, shortfall of approximately 49,000 physicians by 2020 if today's level of health care services is extrapolated to the future population.

These projections suggest supply imbalances in many medical specialties, although rebalancing residency programs to areas of greatest need will help mitigate severe imbalances. The supply of primary care physicians is growing slightly faster than demand, and this trend could help to relieve the current undersupply of primary care physicians in some Federally designated shortage areas. Approximately 7,000 additional primary care physicians are currently needed to de-designate primary care HPSAs.

The projections suggest a growing shortage of specialists, with demand growing by approximately 62,000 more physicians than will be supplied. Surgical specialties account for more than half of this shortfall, although non-surgical specialties such as cardiology and pathology show demand growing significantly faster than supply. (Bureau of Health Professions, 2008, p. 70)

NURSING[3]

Historical Background

Women have provided the basic caring function in Western health care institutions since these institutions first developed in Europe during the first millennium CE. The development of the modern nursing profession is customarily dated to 1854, when the English nurse Florence Nightingale traveled to the Russian Crimea in response to a British government mandate to improve hospital care during the Crimean War.

To accomplish this objective, the first task Nightingale needed to deal with was finding qualified nurses. The second was convincing the military physicians that the care she and her nurses proposed to provide would not spoil the soldiers by "coddling the brutes." Third, Nightingale had to show that she had special skills and knowledge that, when incorporated into the management of sick and wounded soldiers, would lead to positive outcomes that could benefit the war effort. The nursing reforms she introduced eventually reduced hospital mortality from 60% to about 1%. This did not prevent repeated attempts on the part of her male military and medical superiors to undermine the program and eliminate the nurses, despite the fact that she had been sent to the Crimea by the British government.

In the U. S. Army, in the Spanish–American War and World War I, sick and wounded soldiers suffered unnecessarily while nurses struggled for the right to provide high-quality nursing care. It was not until 1944 that nurses in the military forces were granted temporary status as officers. Only in 1947 did Congress establish permanent Army and Navy Nurse Corps (Kalisch & Kalisch, 1978).

Definition of Nursing

The definition of nursing changes as medical care changes. More than 20 years ago, nursing was defined by the American Nurses Association (ANA, 1990, p. 8) as:

> assessment, diagnosis, planning, intervention, and evaluation of human responses to health or illness; the provision of direct nursing care to individuals to restore optimum function, or to achieve a dignified death;...the provision of health counseling and education; the establishment of standards of practice for nursing care in all settings, including the development of nursing policies, procedures, and protocols for specific settings;...collaboration with other independently licensed health care professionals in case finding and the clinical management and execution of interventions identified to be appropriate in a plan of care; and the administration of medication and treatments as prescribed by those persons qualified under the provision of the [law].

In 1995, the ANA added the concept that the "authority of the profession is based on a social contract between society and the profession" (Kovner & Salsberg, 2002, p. 73). According to the Nursing Practice Act of New York State (Article 139, Para. 6902 of the State Education Law) (USNY, 1995b, p. 41):

> The practice of the profession of nursing as a registered professional nurse is defined as diagnosing and treating human responses to actual or potential health problems through such services as case finding, health teaching, health counseling, and provision of care supportive to or restorative of life and well-being, and executing medical regimens prescribed by a licensed or otherwise legally authorized physician or dentist. A nursing regimen shall be consistent with and not vary [from] existing medical regimen.

Furthermore, the act states (Para. 6901) (USNY, 1995b, p. 41):

> "Diagnosing" in the context of nursing practice means the identification of and discrimination between physical and psychosocial signs and symptoms essential to effective execution and management of the nursing regimen. Such diagnostic privilege is distinct from medical diagnosis. "Treating" means selection and performance of those therapeutic measures essential to the effective execution and management of the nursing regimen, and execution of any prescribed medical regimen. "Human responses" means those signs, symptoms and processes which denote the individual's interaction with an actual or potential health problem.

According to the ANA (1995, p. 8), the areas of concern include care and self-care processes; physiological and pathophysiological processes in areas ranging from rest and sleep to nutrition and sexuality; physical and emotional comfort, discomfort, and pain; emotional difficulties; decision and choice making; perceptual orientation; relationships and role performance; and social policies. Nurturing is basic to all nursing functions.

Nursing is currently defined by the American Nurses Association (ANA, 2011, 2003) as follows: "Nursing is the protection, promotion, and optimization of health and abilities, prevention of illness and injury, alleviation of suffering through the diagnosis and treatment of human response, and advocacy in the care of individuals, families, communities, and populations" (ANA, 2003, pp. 25–26).

The essential features of professional nursing are considered to be:

- Provision of a caring relationship that facilitates health and healing
- Attention to the range of human experiences and responses to health and illness within the physical and social environments

- Integration of objective data with knowledge gained from an appreciation of the patient's or group's subjective experience
- Application of scientific knowledge to the processes of diagnosis and treatment through the use of judgment and critical thinking
- Advancement of professional nursing knowledge through scholarly inquiry
- Influence on social and public policy to promote social justice

This definition emphasizes the current importance of understanding the patient's social context, promoting social justice, and advancing scholarship for the practice of nursing. Although these activities may always have been understood to be important to nursing practice, the current definition makes their importance explicit.

Categories of Nurses and Nursing Education

Nurses comprise the largest group of health professionals. There were about 2,600,000 active RNs in the United States in 2009 (NCHS, 2011, Table 110). Close to 1,300,000 of them had associate degrees or hospital-based nursing school diplomas, about 731,200 had baccalaureate degrees, and almost 235,000 had graduate degrees. The RN/population ratio was about 860 per 100,000 in 2010 (Kaiser Family Foundation, 2010). The heterogeneity of the U.S. health care system has created a need for nurses in many different types of service. In 2008, about 62% of all RNs worked in hospitals (ANA, 2010). An increasing number work in ambulatory care facilities—10% in 2008. The balance work primarily in nursing homes for the chronically ill, public health agencies, schools, industrial clinics, nursing education, private medical or dental offices, and other private duty positions.

There are three major groups of nurses: RNs, LPNs, and nurses' aides. RNs have the highest level of education, the most responsibility under the states' nurse practice acts, and the most authority. Generally, LPNs and aides function under the supervision of an RN. "Registration" in nursing was originally a voluntary function of the nursing profession. It now means licensure by the states, at a significantly higher level of responsibility and authority than that accorded to the "licensed practical" nurse. To be an RN, one must have a high school diploma and a diploma from a hospital-based program or a Bachelor of Science in Nursing (BSN) degree from a college or university, or, since 1952, an associate degree in nursing (ADN) from a 2-year college program. An increasingly prevalent accelerated nursing program enables those with degrees in other fields to change to a nursing career. There are also traditional master's and doctoral programs for RNs. The master's degree in nursing (MSN) is the preferred preparation for nursing leaders and advanced practice registered nurse (APRNs) preparation is preferred for positions with prescriptive and diagnostic authority. These programs are designed and expected to advance the professional practice of nursing, meet expected workforce shortages, as well as provide better employment opportunities for individuals.

Currently, there are more than 840 baccalaureate programs in the United States. Total enrollment in all nursing programs leading to a baccalaureate degree was 208,784 in 2009, a 9.6% increase from 2008. The landmark report, *The Future of Nursing*, was released by the Institute of Medicine (IOM) in 2010. The report recommends that at least 80% of the nursing workforce hold a baccalaureate degree or higher by 2020, compared to the current 50% (IOM, 2010). It also recommends doubling the number of nurses with a doctorate by 2020. The report emphasized the need for education:

> This report offers recommendations that collectively serve as a blueprint to (1) ensure that nurses can practice to the full extent of their education and training, (2) improve nursing education, (3) provide opportunities for nurses to assume leadership positions and to serve as full partners in health care redesign and improvement efforts, and (4) improve data collection for workforce planning and policy making. (IOM, 2010)

Compared to the BSN programs, the 2-year programs leading to an ADN focus more on technical skills than theory, and they are often used as a stepping stone to the BSN. The diploma path is a 2- to 3-year experience, and it is usually hospital-based. There are about 100 diploma programs at present. Most utilize local colleges for nonnursing courses. Graduates of all three types of programs are eligible through state licensing exams to become RNs.

There are more than 330 master's degree programs accredited by the Commission on Collegiate Nursing Education (CCNE) or the National League of Nursing Accrediting Commission (NLNAC). There is a wide variety of master's degree programs including the Master of Science degree in nursing (MSN), the Master of Nursing degree (MN), the Master of Science degree with a major in nursing (MS), and the Master of Arts degree with a major in nursing (MA).

Advancing from the RN to the MSN usually takes about 3 years. "The number of RN to MSN programs has more than doubled within the past 15 years, from 70 programs in 1994 to 173 programs today. According to American Association of Colleges of Nursing's (AACN) 2010 survey of nursing schools, 32 new RN to MSN programs are in the planning stages" (AACN, 2011a). Proceeding from an RN to a BSN takes 1 to 2 years. There are more than 600 RN-to-BSN programs nationwide. "Enrollment in RN to BSN programs is increasing in response to calls for a more highly educated nursing workforce. From 2009 to 2010, enrollments increased by 21.6% or by 13,468 students, marking the eighth consecutive year of increases in RN to BSN programs" (AACN, 2011a).

The fastest growing nursing education programs are the practice and research-based doctoral programs with enrollment, up more than 20% in 2009. They include the Doctor of Nursing Practice (DNP), Doctor of Philosophy in Nursing (PhD), and Doctor of Nursing Science (DNSc), which prepare individuals for faculty roles, advanced practice clinical careers, and careers as research scientists. DNP programs totaled 120 in 2009, with an additional 161 programs in planning stages. Research-oriented doctoral programs totaled 120 with 8 in the planning stages in 2009. Total enrollment in 2009 in research-focused doctoral programs was 4,177 and practice-focused doctoral programs was 5,165 (AACN, 2011b).

LPNs, also called licensed vocational nurses, may or may not have completed high school before entering a 12- to 18-month training program. LPN programs are operated by a variety of institutions, including hospitals, adult schools, junior colleges, and technical schools. Like RNs, LPNs must pass a state-supervised examination to become licensed, but their work requires a significantly lower level of skill and knowledge than does that of the RN.

The education of the nurses' aides group is highly variable. Some aides take a formal educational program. For others, training is primarily on the job. In the work setting, the mix of RNs, LPNs, and aides is determined by the nature of patient care provided, government regulation, budget, and available personnel. In certain states, financial incentives have been provided to encourage facilities such as nursing homes to employ better qualified nursing staff, following findings that doing so improved the quality of patient care (Wunderlich, Sloan, & Davis, 1996).

From Nursing Shortage to Nursing Oversupply, and Back Again

Like the supply of physicians, over time the supply of nurses has rarely been in tune with either the real or the perceived need. Nursing shortages have occurred periodically in the United States (Aiken, 1982). One shortage in the early 1950s led to the formalization of LPN training and the requirements previously mentioned. In the early 1990s, another shortage appeared to be on the horizon (Aiken & Mullinix, 1987; Secretary's Commission on Nursing, 1988). In 1990, the U.S. Department of Health and Human Services estimated the nursing shortage to be about 200,000 (Moses, 1992). It predicted shortages of about 350,000 in the year 2000, 520,000 in 2010, and 875,000 in 2020.

In 1988, the RN position vacancy rate in hospitals was over 11%. Nevertheless, nursing school enrollments were actually declining, and minority recruitment was lagging. However, one striking feature of the nursing profession is that a significant number of its members of working age were not employed in nursing. If half of the approximately 400,000 RNs not working in nursing in 1990 (Moses, 1992) had been employed, there would have been no nursing shortage. In the 1980s, authorities on the subject cited many reasons to account for this employment gap (Igelhart, 1987). Among the reasons were low salaries (the average starting salary for a staff nurse in 1988 was $25,000), limited chances for significant increases in pay over the life of a career (the average maximum salary for a head nurse in 1988 was $45,000), poor working conditions (high-tech work creates much stress, and shift work is a serious problem), poor professional image, and greater career opportunities for women.

Among steps suggested to solve the nursing shortage at that time were more creative solutions to the nights-and-weekends shifts problem, giving nurses more control over their own work, expanding nurse participation in hospital decision making, improving continuing professional education, restructuring the work of the nurse, and developing better career ladders for nurses (Helmer & McKnight, 1989).

Another key factor in the nursing shortage (especially given the fact that so many nurses of working age were not employed in nursing) was the doctor–nurse relationship and what was wrong with it from the nurses' point of view (Stein, Watts & Howell, 1990). As Aiken and Mullinix pointed out in 1987, "Much of the dissatisfaction of nurses with hospital practice is related to the absence of satisfying professional relationships with physicians" (p. 645). At the center of the nursing shortage, then, remained the need to change the rules of the "doctor–nurse game" (Stein, Watts, & Howell, 1990), the source of much of the dissatisfaction noted by Aiken and Mullinix. After all, not all of those 400,000 RNs who in 1990 were not in nursing chose to leave the profession simply because they were burned out, too old, having children, wanted to stay at home, or thought some other line of work would be better.

Suddenly the nurse supply situation seemed to change. What a difference managed care seemed to make (Lumsdon, 1995). There were both closures and size shrinkages of hospitals. By the mid-1990s, not only was there no longer a nursing shortage, but nurse layoffs were occurring in certain areas of the country (Rosenthal, 1996). The University of California's Pew Center for the Health Professions (CHP, 1999) predicted that 200,000 to 300,000 hospital nurse positions could be eliminated by the year 2000. Suddenly, a vast surplus appeared to be on the horizon. Regardless of what the true situation was, however, as with physician supply, no comprehensive national planning was occurring to deal with the supply, distribution, and role and function of either the existing nurse pool or the nursing education system.

But then, the situation changed rapidly once again. The new nursing shortage appeared as quickly as had the apparent oversupply of the mid-1990s. Once again, the predictions of future severe nursing shortages made in the late 1980s seemed to be at least somewhat on target. In 2001, the American Hospital Association (AHA) reported that for hospitals alone there were about 126,000 RN vacancies (Parker, 2002). But this time, the shortage problem went beyond just nurses.

A *New York Times* headline reported "Worker Shortage in Health Fields Worst in Decades" (Steinhauer, 2000). The president of the AHA, Dick Davidson (2001), proclaimed: "The single greatest challenge for hospitals today and in the future is the recruitment and retention of high quality staff across many disciplines." According to data compiled by the AHA, the reasons for these shortages echoed those of earlier times (Selvam, 2001). In 2004, the AACN published the "Nursing Shortage Fact Sheet," which documents the continued shortage of nurses in the United States. For example, the number of first-time candidates for the National Council Licensure Examination for Registered Nurses (NCLEX-RN®) declined significantly from 1995 to 2003 for BSNs, ADNs, and diploma nurses. The overall decline for all categories was 96,438 to 76,618 (AACN, 2004).

In 2011, the AACN was still concerned about a nursing shortage, citing numerous statistics that suggest a looming shortage. For example,

On April 1, 2011, the U.S. Bureau of Labor Statistics (BLS) reported that the healthcare sector of the economy is continuing to grow, despite significant job losses in recent months in nearly all major industries. Hospitals, long-term care facilities, and other ambulatory care settings added 37,000 new jobs in March 2011, the biggest monthly increase recorded by any employment sector. As the largest segment of the healthcare workforce, RNs likely will be recruited to fill many of these new positions. The BLS confirmed that 283,000 jobs have been added in the healthcare sector within the last year. (AACN, 2011c)

One important issue for job satisfaction and retention among nurses is hours worked. The working hours of RNs in hospitals have changed. The use of extended work shifts and overtime has escalated as hospitals cope with a shortage of RNs.

While systematic national data on trends in the number of hours worked per day by nurses are lacking, anecdotal reports suggest that hospital staff nurses are working long hours with few breaks and often little time for recovery between shifts. Scheduled shifts may be eight, twelve, or even sixteen hours long and may not follow the traditional pattern of day, evening, and night shifts. (Rogers, Hwang, Scott, Aiken, & Dinges, 2004, p. 202)

Another issue is the nurse-to-patient ratio. In 1999, California became the first and only state—at this point—to set a minimum nurse-to-patient ratio. The California hospitals and the California Healthcare Association have fought the law on the basis of cost, other performance activities, and the nursing shortage. The governor issued an emergency regulation to void the law, but the California Superior Court voided the governor's order. To deal with the nursing shortage, hospitals have used a variety of tactics including competitive compensation and the use of temporary staff. However, hospitals are unsure whether they can maintain or meet future needs and the increased costs associated with these tactics (May, Bazzoli, & Gerland, 2006).

Both long working hours and high nurse-to-patient ratios are a concern from a patient safety perspective. According to a 1997 outcome study covering 6 million discharges from 800 hospitals in 11 states (Needleman, Buerhaus, Mattke, Stewart, & Zelevinsky, 2002), "[A] higher proportion of hours of nursing care provided by RNs and a greater number of hours of care by RNs per day are associated with better care for hospitalized patients." Nurses are justifiably concerned about patient safety and their own well-being. For example, a study conducted for AFT Healthcare, a union, found that nurses view understaffing as a serious problem for nurse burnout and the quality of care that patients receive:

> Not surprisingly, nurses perceive a serious staffing shortfall. Fully three in five (61%) hospital nurses say the nurses at their hospital are responsible for too many patients, whereas only 2% believe that the nurses at their hospital could safely provide care for more patients.... Fully four in five (82%) hospital nurses support legislation that would establish a maximum number of patients that nurses can be required to care for at one time, with 57% strongly favoring and 25% somewhat favoring such legislation. Just 13% say they are opposed.... (Hart & Research Associates, 2003)

A third looming issue is that of worker protection for nurses. In 2006, the National Labor Relations Board exempted RNs from union membership if they have certain kinds of supervisory duties. In the majority decision, the board's three Republicans adopted a broad definition of *supervisor*, which included those who assigned others to location, shift, or significant tasks, such as a nurse overseeing a shift who might assign another nurse to a particular patient.

The board's majority ruled that workers should be considered supervisors, exempt from union membership, if they oversaw another employee and could be held accountable for that subordinate's performance. The board's majority also ruled that workers could be considered supervisors if supervisory duties were only 10% to 15% of their total work time. In dissenting, the board's two Democrats said, "Today's decision threatens to create a new class of workers under federal labor law: workers who have neither the genuine prerogatives of management, nor the statutory rights of ordinary employees" (Greenhouse, 2006).

At the beginning of the new millennium, at least some members of all health care occupations have been found to be dissatisfied with their current working conditions. For example, 40% or more of hospital employees other than physicians wanted better pay, a better work environment, better benefits, and more advancement opportunities. One-third of all health care employees were disappointed both in physician leadership and in the quality of institutional management and supervision. The problems for nurses in particular, however, seemed not to be new, except that they appeared to be getting worse (Steinbrook, 2002). As Steinbrook put it, "Nursing is an embattled profession" (p. 1757).

A particularly chilling fact reflecting on the nursing shortage and its projected future was that in 2004 only 16.6% of RNs were under the age of 35, compared to 40.5% in 1980. Further, the percentage of nurses over 54 years of age was 25.5% in 2004, compared to only 17.1% in 1980 (Bureau of Health Professions, 2005). One possible solution to the nursing shortage was summed up in a cartoon that appeared in the American Hospital Association's journal, *Hospitals and Health Networks* (March 2002). In it, a doctor is introducing a patient in a hospital bed to a robot. In so doing, he says: "Meet Nurse X-2002. She [sic] will be handling your recovery. If you have any questions, call Radio Shack."

Nurses in Expanded Roles

The scope of nurse practice has expanded since the days of Florence Nightingale. Each expansion first occurred along the route of on-the-job experience and training. Only later would such developments be formalized into an educational program. Thus, for example, the first public health nurses, who appeared during World War I; the first maternal and child health nurses, who also came on the scene in the early 1920s; the first nurse anesthetists, nurse midwives, clinical nurse specialists; and, ultimately, nurse practitioners were all first prepared outside of any formal educational system.

In each instance, the initial informal efforts to create a new arena for nursing were followed by the establishment of standards, formal curricula in approved programs, and, more recently, the preparation for advanced levels through master's and doctoral degree programs in universities. The development of each new form of and forum for nursing was also accompanied by a serious struggle for acceptance, especially within the medical profession. This was especially true if the new form was or could be taken to be in economic competition with physicians.

Over time, the acceptance of new roles for nurses as first demonstrated in practice has led to continuing changes in nursing practice laws across the country. For example, in well-defined primary care practice, an in-depth review of research carried out in the 1970s found no differences between the quality of care provided by qualified nurses and that provided by physicians (Record, 1981). This finding has been confirmed more recently (Mundinger et al., 2000). Properly prepared nurses in advanced practice, the nurse practitioners or advanced practice nurses, can provide primary ambulatory care, normal pregnancy care and delivery, and routine anesthesia at least as well as physicians (Mundinger, 2002).

In 1988, New York State, following the lead of a number of other states, formalized the nurse-practitioner role in its education law, to wit (New York State Education Department, 2005, para. 6902[3]):

> The practice of registered professional nursing by a nurse practitioner...may include the diagnosis of illness and physical conditions and the performance of therapeutic and corrective measures...in collaboration with a licensed physician...provided such services are performed in accordance with a written practice agreement and written practice protocols. The written practice agreement shall include explicit provisions for the resolution of any disagreement between the collaborating physician and the nurse practitioner regarding...diagnosis or treatment...within the scope of practice of both. To the extent the practice agreement does not so provide, then the collaborating physician's diagnosis or treatment shall prevail.

This sort of legislation opened the door for truly expanded nurse practice. It is proving to be a boon to patients, especially in such areas as primary care and chronic/multiple disease management, prevention, and early detection (Mundinger, 2002).

The number of Advanced Practice Nurses (APRNs)—RNs with specialized training and advanced degrees—has risen from about 30,000 in 1990 to about 140,000 in 2010 (American Academy of Nurse Practitioners, 2010). APRN is the title used to encompass those nurses who have masters or doctoral degrees with specialty education and often certification that confers prescriptive authority. The growth of the APRN profession is linked to numerous factors. A major one is the decline in the number of doctors choosing primary care as their specialty, a trend that is expected to continue. From 1998 to 2005, medical school surveys showed that the percentage of 3rd-year residents intending to pursue careers in general internal medicine went from 54% to 20%. Many new doctors are choosing more lucrative specialties, in part because of the debt they incur during medical school, and less time-demanding ones with more regular hours as well. The supply of family practice physicians is falling just as the Baby Boomer population is aging and their need for medical care is rising. APRNs in many cases can and do fill this need. APRNs can perform many of the duties of primary care doctors, such as performing physical exams;

diagnosing and treating common health problems; prescribing medications (from a specified list); ordering and interpreting x-rays; providing prenatal care, family planning services, and gynecological exams; and giving immunizations. In addition, APRNs are considered to be less rushed and more holistic in their approach to patients, factors increasing patient satisfaction.

Some states allow APRNs to practice more independently and comprehensively than others. In these terms, in 2002 the following states were considered the best environments to practice as an APRN: New Mexico, Arizona, Iowa, Oregon, Montana, Maine, and Washington. The least favorable, most restrictive, states were Alabama, Virginia, Georgia, and South Carolina (National Center for Health Workforce Analysis, 2002).

PHYSICIAN ASSISTANTS

The health profession of physician assistant (PA) has developed in the United States since the Vietnam War (1965–1973). The early development of the PA profession occurred just as the Vietnam War was getting under way; it received a big boost from the return of Vietnam-veteran medical corpsmen. One can only speculate whether or not the PA profession would have been more than a blip on the radar screen of the history of health services had there been no Vietnam War. Had the PA profession not developed as it did, would the profession of nurse practitioner become more prominent in the United States? But the war did occur, and whether or not the two are integrally related, the PA profession has become an established U.S. health services profession.

By the mid-1980s, the PA profession had become a complex and multifaceted one (Schafft & Cawley, 1987). According to Schafft and Cawley (1987, p. 6), the PA's role involves:

- Approaching a patient of any age group in any setting to elicit a detailed and accurate history, perform an appropriate physical examination, delineate problems, and record and present patient data
- Analyzing health status data obtained via interview, examination, and laboratory diagnostic studies and delineating health care problems in consultation with the physician
- Formulating, implementing, and monitoring an individualized treatment or management plan for a patient in consultation with the physician
- Instructing and counseling patients regarding compliance with the prescribed therapeutic regimen, normal growth and development, family planning, emotional problems of daily living, and health maintenance
- Performing routine procedures essential to managing simple conditions produced by infection or trauma, assisting in the management of more

complex illness and injury, and initiating evaluations and therapeutic procedures in response to life-threatening situations

By the mid-1990s, it was estimated that PAs "can perform 80% of the routine functions of a primary-care physician's practice" and "are widely accepted by patients" (American Academy of Physician Assistants [AAPA], 1996).

From its beginnings, the PA profession was conceived as an extension of the profession of medicine. Unlike nursing, it was not meant to be another separate profession. In each state, PA licensure is provided for under the medical practice act rather than under a separate law, as is the case with nursing. Although the gender balance within the PA profession has changed over the years to approximately 50:50 (AAPA, 1996), in the beginning, it was predominantly male. For these reasons, many of the power issues that cloud the relationship between physicians and nurses have not appeared.

This status is reflected in the AAPA definition of a PA (AAPA, 2006):

> Physician assistants are health care professionals licensed to practice medicine with physician supervision.... As part of their comprehensive responsibilities, PAs conduct physical exams, diagnose and treat illnesses, order and interpret tests, counsel on preventive health care, assist in surgery, and in virtually all states can write prescriptions. Within the physician–PA relationship, physician assistants exercise autonomy in medical decision making and provide a broad range of diagnostic and therapeutic services. A PA's practice may also include education, research, and administrative services.

In 2011, there were more than 159 PA training programs (AAPA, 2011). Most of them were offered through medical schools, teaching hospitals, or schools of the allied health professions in 4-year colleges. In 2011, there were about 481,000 certified PAs in the United States.

Although in the early days most PAs worked in primary care, by the 1980s, specialization became common. In 1996, about half of the PA population worked in family practice (37.2% of the total), general internal medicine, general pediatrics, and obstetrics/gynecology; another 22% were in surgery; and close to 10% in emergency medicine, with the balance in the other specialties. Some PAs work for individual physicians, but most are employed in hospitals, clinics, group practices, and other organized health care settings. As noted earlier, like nurse practitioners, for the same kinds of patients, PAs provide care that is comparable in quality to that provided by physicians. Listed as the best environment to practice as a PA are North Carolina, Oregon, and Montana. The most restrictive states to practice are Mississippi, New Jersey, Virginia, District of Columbia, and Ohio (National Center for Health Workforce Analysis, 2002).

OTHER HEALTH CARE PROFESSIONS AND OCCUPATIONS

There are many other categories of health worker that provide them. In mental health centers, for example, the staff includes psychologists, psychiatric social workers and nurses, and other support staff, in addition to psychiatrists. Community outreach workers are a new type of health care worker trained in recent years by certain ambulatory care programs, both general and mental.

In local health department centers, public health nurses are the mainstay of the clinics that focus on preventive services. These nurses work with part-time physicians who are otherwise mainly in private practice. Other personnel in public health clinics include health educators, nutritionists and dietitians, and sexually transmitted disease investigators. Besides the personnel staffing the clinics, public health agencies employ sanitarians, statisticians, community health educators with specialized skills, and family planning counselors.

In sum, the health personnel picture in the Unites States is complex. On the technical side, it is highly developed, and many patients greatly benefit from the availability of so many different health care personnel with so much detailed education, training, and experience. There are gaps and overlaps, however, and maldistribution by geographic area and differing levels of patient access to care are significant problems.

PRIMARY CARE AND ITS PROVIDERS

© Cartoonist Group. By Steve Kelley.

Much of the health care workforce provides primary care. Members of all health care occupations participate in primary care, including physicians, nurses, PAs, and so forth. In this section, we discuss primary care—what it is, its purpose, and its role in health care delivery in the United States.

Primary care and ambulatory care go together like apple pie and ice cream. This is so even though not all primary care is delivered in an ambulatory setting, nor is all ambulatory care primary care. Nevertheless, because they are in most instances closely associated, they will be covered in the same chapter.

As noted in Chapter 1, by sheer volume, primary health care services are predominant in the health care delivery system but primary care has proved challenging to define precisely. Over the years, many definitions have been offered. One such normative definition is the following (Jonas, 1973):

> Primary care is medical attention to the great majority of ills. It should be provided continuously over a significant period of time by the same appropriately trained individual (or team) who is sympathetic, understanding, knowledgeable and equipped, who is as capable of keeping people well as he is of returning them to health when they fall ill. (p. 177)

Unfortunately, to this day the coordination of preventive and curative services occurs less often than it should in much of American medical practice (McGinnis, Williams-Russo, & Knickman, 2002; Stange, Woolf, & Gjeltma, 2002).

In 1977, the Institute of Medicine reviewed 33 different definitions of the term *primary care* (Ruby, 1977). Its summary definition from 1978, both normative and descriptive, was the following (Eisenberg, 1997):

> [Primary care is] the provision of integrated, accessible health care services by clinicians who are accountable for addressing a large majority of personal health needs, developing a sustained partnership with patients, and practicing in the context of family and community. (p. 615)

In 1996, Barbara Starfield provided one normative definition, covering both what primary care is and, in the best of all possible worlds, what it ought to be:

> Primary care is the means by which the two goals of a health services system—optimization of health and equity in distributing resources—are balanced. It is the basic level of care provided equally to everyone. It addresses the most common problems in the community by providing preventive, curative,

and rehabilitative services to maximize health and well-being. It integrates care when more than one health problem exists, and deals with the context in which illness exists and influences people's responses to their health problems. It is care that organizes and rationalizes the deployment of all resources, basic as well as specialized, directed at promoting, maintaining, and improving health. (p. 1365)

In 1997, Eric Cassell, expressing a career-long concern for the personal and interpersonal aspects of medical practice, addressed a different kind of "balance" in offering his own "ought to be" definition of primary care (Geiger, 1997):

[Primary care is] careful history taking…artfully enhanced by skillful questioning at every point in the illness…supplemented by discerning scrutiny of patients' presentation to the world, behavior, mood and feelings, environment and context…plus the physical examination, supplemented by the mediated investigations offered by modern tests and imaging. (p. 1637)

For achieving the best in primary care (and, indeed, for all of medicine), as Kerr White (1968/1973), anticipating Cassell, so splendidly put it:

One wants to avoid the confusion inherent in the encounter between the patient who implicitly says to the doctor, "I hope you treat what I've got" and the physician who implicitly says to the patient, "I hope you've got what I treat." (p. 362)

According to many authorities, the ideal primary care environment is one that provides classic "comprehensive care" (Reader & Soave, 1976). In terms that still apply, John Knowles (1965) defined the latter at a conference held in 1964:

Comprehensive medicine in this [ambulatory care] context means the coordination of all the various caring elements in the community with those of the medical profession by a team of individuals representing all disciplines, with all the techniques and resources available to the physician and his patient. The aim of these individuals would be to provide total care—somatic, psychic, and social—to those in need, and to study and research the expanding social and economic problems of medical care with the intent of improving the organization and provision of health services. (p. 73)

The concept of community-oriented primary care (COPC) was developed back in the 1980s (Madison, 1983; Mullan, 1982; Mullan & Conner, 1982; Nutting, Wood, & Conner, 1985). It grew out of the concept of comprehensive care as defined by Knowles (1965). According to Rhyne, Cashman, and Kantrowitz (1998):

> COPC is a process by which a defined population's health problems are systematically identified and addressed. Ideally, it combines principles of primary care, epidemiology, and public health.... [It] could [also] be called community-responsive health care, community-based primary care, or something else. The process is the important element. The community is a partner at every step. (p. 2)

These are all ideal or, at least in part, normative definitions of primary and comprehensive care. In functional terms, however, primary care is that care which most people need, and use, most of the time, for most of their health and illness concerns.

Functions

The primary feature of *comprehensive* primary care is its integrating role in medical practice. In the past, when nearly all medical services were rendered by a family's general practitioner, coordination was almost automatic. Today, a primary care doctor or team can still provide most of the care that is necessary most of the time. But in the context of modern medical knowledge and technology, organization and planning for such a practice must be undertaken.

Medical complications or new problems at times will require the expertise of others. Coordination of care can be ensured if the primary provider assesses the situation correctly, helps the patient with a proper referral, then integrates the outcome of the referral into the patient's ongoing care (Bodenheimer, Lo, & Casalino, 1999). This important function of the primary provider prevents fragmentation of care and the hit-or-miss nature of patient self-referral to specialists and promotes comprehensive care, for the patient as a whole person, not merely a set of parts.

The term *gatekeeper* was originally applied to this function by Anne Somers (1983). In the still-applicable sense that Somers used the term, the *gatekeeper* function of the primary care practitioner can only benefit the patient. In the managed care era, however, the term gatekeeper has taken on a different meaning in describing the main function of the primary care physician: to monitor, regulate, and control the use of medical and related services by managed care organizations'(MCO) patients. Thus, a fiscal responsibility has now been added to the task list of the primary care physician (Alexander, Hall, & Lantos, 2006; Shortell, Waters, Clarke,

& Budetti, 1998). In this version, the gatekeeper function as carried out may not always be to the patient's benefit.

Under managed care, primary responsibilities that the physician may have to the payer for the patient's care may on occasion conflict with the responsibility the physician has for the care of the patient. In some MCOs, for example, managed care physicians receive monetary bonuses for holding down utilization of services by their patients (Alexander et al., 2006). As Bodenheimer and colleagues noted (1999):

> Primary care gatekeeping [in MCO terms], in which the goal of the primary care physician (PCP) is to reduce patient referrals to specialists and thereby reduce costs, is not an adequate system in which to practice medicine. However, returning to the pre–managed care model of uncoordinated open access to specialists is a poor solution. The primary care model should be retained, but PCPs should be transformed from gatekeepers into coordinators of care, in which the goal of the PCP is to integrate both primary and specialty care to improve quality. (p. 2045)

In contrast to the situation in many other countries, the primary care relationship in the United States traditionally has not ended at the hospital admitting office. Instead, primary care physicians have provided a good deal of the inpatient care. Most board-certified family practitioners, general internists, and general pediatricians in this country have hospital admitting privileges.

In most other industrialized nations, primary care physicians work only in ambulatory care offices and health centers. Specialists provide inpatient and hospital clinic care. However, with the growth of managed care in the United States, the development of the hospitalist model is occurring. It remains to be seen how far this development will go.

Historical Background

Thinking about primary care in conceptual terms has hardly been confined to recent decades (Roemer, 1975, 1981; Roemer, Kramer, & Frink, 1975). Nor has its implementation been without its early champions in the United States. As far back as the 1930s, primary care received a strong endorsement from the Committee on the Costs of Medical Care and, in the intervening years, from many other authorities (Somers, 1983). In Great Britain, the concept goes back at least as far as the 1920 Dawson report on the structure of health services (Sidel & Sidel, 1983).

Despite these recommendations, in the United States, as physician specialization and subspecialization increased dramatically in the period following World War II, much of the ambulatory care provided in private offices and groups and in hospital outpatient departments became highly fragmented (Freymann, 1974). The need to restore continuity and coordination was recognized in the 1960s and led to a revitalization of the primary care concept (Institute of Medicine, 1978).

Many of the health services entities called *neighborhood health centers* that developed in the 1960s and 1970s fostered the primary care approach, as did many of the original health maintenance organizations developed in the 1970s and 1980s. Nevertheless, in the 1990s, it was still the case that most people in the United States did not have access to comprehensive primary care, even with (or perhaps because of) the advent of for-profit managed care (Starfield, 1996). There is no reason to believe that this situation has changed for the better in the 21st century. For instance, a report on primary care access in Texas deems the situation a crisis (Stoneham, Banning, Kroll, & Young, 2004).

Primary Care Workforce

In the ideal primary care setting, an appropriately trained health professional or team provides most of the preventive and curative care for an individual or family over a significant period of time. In the late 1960s, a task list for the ideal primary care system and primary care provider was developed, one that is still valid (Committee on Medical Schools, 1968, p. 753):

- Assessment of total patient needs before these are categorized by specialty
- Elaboration of a plan for meeting those needs in the order of their importance
- Determination of who shall meet the defined needs—physicians (generalist or specialist), nonphysician members of the health care team, or social agencies
- Follow-up to see that needs are met
- Provision of such care in a continuous, coordinated, and comprehensive manner
- Attention at each step to the personal, social, and family dimensions of the patient's problem
- Provision of health maintenance and disease prevention at the same level of importance as the provision of cure and rehabilitation

This description of functions shows that primary care is not simply a collection of services. Above all it is a state of mind, to wit (Committee on Medical Schools, 1968):

> The primary-care physician must be capable of establishing a profile of the total needs of the patient and his family. This

evaluation should include social, economic, and psychological details as well as the more strictly "medical" aspects. He [sic] must know what resources are available for meeting those needs. He should then define a plan of care, deciding which parts are to be carried out by himself and which by others. The plan should have a long-range dimension. It should be understandable to the patient and his family, and it should include a follow-up on whether indicated measures have been undertaken and whether they have been effective. (p. 74)

Today, both the task list and state-of-mind requirements apply as well to primary care nurse practitioners and PAs as to primary care physicians.

Among physicians, primary care is provided variously by family practitioners (prepared to deliver primary care services to entire families), general pediatricians, specialists in general internal medicine, and for many women of child-bearing age, obstetrician-gynecologists. As noted previously, it has now been shown that nurse practitioners/advanced practice nurses (Mundinger, 2002) and physicians' assistants can provide primary care for most patients that is at least equal in quality to that provided by physicians. It is thus likely that the debate over who should be doing what to whom in primary care will continue for many years to come.

Primary Care and the Health Care Delivery System

Some observers believe that the level and quality of primary care provision serve as good markers for the quality of a nation's health care delivery system as a whole (Davis, Schoenbaum, & Audet, 2005). Concerning the variation in primary care quality among nations, Starfield (1996) has noted:

First, countries with better primary care tend to be countries that strive toward equity in distribution of health services and toward more equitable income distributions. Apparently, a commitment to social equity goes along with a commitment to equity in the distribution of health care resources. Second, it is not the number of primary care physicians, or even the ratio of primary care physicians to specialists, that accounts for the differential effects of the health services across those countries. Rather, the differences are a result of how the resources are distributed, whether or not they are organized to achieve the functions of primary care, and whether they clearly specify the roles and interrelationships between primary care and specialist physicians. (p. 1365)

As stated at the outset of this section, primary care goes with ambulatory care as ice cream goes with apple pie (neither of which is unhealthy if eaten only occasionally). Historically, there is movement in the right direction. Much remains to be done.

CONCLUSIONS

Paralleling the expected growth in health care in the next decade (National Center for Health Workforce Analysis, 2003), health occupations are projected to be leading sources of new jobs and job growth in the next decade (Martiniano & Moore, 2006):

> Health continues to be the fastest growing employment sector in the country. Between 2004 and 2014, the health sector is projected to grow by more than 27% compared to less than 12% for all other employment sectors. Within health care, jobs in home health care and offices of health practitioners, particularly physician offices, are projected to grow the fastest. The health occupations projected to add the most new jobs between 2004 and 2014 are registered nurses, home health aides, orderlies, and personal and home care aides. In addition, many of these occupations will need more recruits to fill vacancies created by retirements or other departures. Demand for other health professions including medicine, pharmacy, and dentistry are also expected to grow. Given the growing demand for health care workers in a variety of occupations and professions, current health workforce shortages are not only expected to persist, but to worsen. (pp. 2,3)

Health care employment is expected to make up a larger portion of total U.S. employment by 2014 than in the past. In 1994, a little more than 8% of U.S. jobs were in the health sector, and this increased to 9% in 2004 and is projected to rise to 10% by 2014.

Home health care and offices of health practitioners are expected to grow faster than all other health care settings, with an average annual growth rate of 5.4% and 3.2%, respectively. In comparison, the expected average annual growth rate for the entire economy is 1.2% over the same period. Employment in offices of health practitioners is expected to grow by nearly 37% between 2004 and 2014. This represents more than one-third of the total projected growth in health sector employment. Physician and dental offices are projected to add nearly 760,000 and more than 240,000 jobs, respectively.

Seventeen health occupations ranked in the top 30 fastest growing occupations, with 7 ranking in the top 10 and 15 ranking in the top 20.

The number of PAs is expected to increase by 50%, medical assistants by 52%, home health aides by 56%, physical therapist assistants by 44%, physical therapists by 37%, and medical scientists by 34%.

Nursing is one of the 30 occupations expected to provide the greatest number of new jobs. Nursing is projected to add 703,000 new jobs over the period. An additional 500,000 new RNs will be required to replace RNs leaving the occupation, bringing the total number of RNs needed to fill new and existing jobs to 1.2 million.

The health occupations will continue to be leading sources of jobs for Americans in the coming years because of projected growth in health care. Many of these jobs are well-paying and/or offer health benefits. The professionals who work in the health care sector should continue to be highly valued by the society at large, and by the persons who directly receive their services.

NOTES

1. Data on physicians are available from two publications of the American Medical Association: *Physician Socioeconomic Statistics* and *Physician Characteristics and Distribution in the U.S.*
2. A particularly detailed history of the development of specialization in American medical practice is presented by Rosemary Stevens in her still-relevant history, *American Medicine and the Public Interest* (New Haven, CT: Yale University Press, 1971).
3. For more discussion on nursing, see Kovner and Salsberg (2002) and the Springer series, *Advanced Practice Nursing.*

REFERENCES

Accreditation Council for Graduate Medical Education (ACGME). 2012. *The ACGME at a glance.* Retrieved January 3, 2012, from www.acgme.org/acWebsite/newsRoom/newsRm_acGlance.asp

Aiken, L. H. (Ed.). (1982). *Nursing in the 1980's: Crises, opportunities, challenges.* Philadelphia, PA: Lippincott.

Aiken, L. H., & Mullinix, C. F. (1987). The nurse shortage. Myth or reality? *New England Journal of Medicine, 317*(10), 645.

Alexander, G. C., Hall, M. A., & Lantos, J. D. (2006). Rethinking professional ethics in the cost-sharing era. *American Journal of Bioethics, 6*(4), W17–W22.

American Academy of Nurse Practitioners. (2010). *Frequently asked questions.* Retrieved November 29, 2006, from www.aanp.org/AANPCMS2/ResearchEducation/EducationPageOne/Continuing+Education/CEFAQ.htm

American Academy of Physician Assistants (AAPA). (1996). *Information on the physician assistant profession.* Alexandria, VA: Author.

American Academy of Physician Assistants (AAPA). (2006). *Information about PAs and the PA profession.* Retrieved November 29, 2006, from www.aapa.org/the_pa_profession/what_is_a_pa.aspx

American Academy of Physician Assistants (AAPA). (2011). *Quick facts.* Retrieved December 31, 2011, from www.aapa.org/the_pa_profession/quick_facts.aspx

American Association of Colleges of Nursing (AACN). (2004). *Nursing shortage fact sheet.* Retrieved November 4, 2006, from www.aacn.nche.edu/media-relations/fact-sheets

American Association of Colleges of Nursing (AACN). (2011a). *Degree completion programs for registered nurses: RN to master's degree and RN to baccalaureate programs.* Retrieved December 31, 2011, from www.aacn.nche.edu/media-relations/fact-sheets/degree-completion-programs

American Association of Colleges of Nursing (AACN). (2011b). *New AACN data show growth in doctoral nursing programs.* Retrieved December 31, 2011, from www.aacn.nche.edu/news/articles/2010/enrollchanges

American Association of Colleges of Nursing (AACN). (2011c). *Nursing shortage.* Retrieved December 31, 2011, from www.aacn.nche.edu/media-relations/fact-sheets/nursing-shortage

American Association of Medical Colleges (AAMC). (2006a). *Data warehouse: Table 6; applicants, accepted applicants, and matriculants by sex, 1995–2006.* Retrieved November 20th, 2006, from www.aamc.org/data/facts

American Association of Medical Colleges (AAMC). (2006b). *Data warehouse: Table 8; Hispanic ethnicity and non-Hispanic race by acceptance status, 2004–2006.* Retrieved November 29th, 2006, from www.aamc.org/data/facts

American Association of Medical Colleges (AAMC). (2011). *Data warehouse: Table 29: Total U.S. medical school graduates by race and ethnicity within sex, 2002–2011.* Retrieved June 4, 2012, from https://www.aamc.org/download/147312/data/table29-gradsraceeth0211.pdf

American Association of Medical Colleges (AAMC). (2012). *U.S. medical school applicants and students 1982–83 to 2010–2012.* Retrieved June 4, 2012, from https://www.aamc.org/download/153708/data/charts1982to2012.pdf

American Nurses Association (ANA). (1990). *Suggested state legislation: Nursing Practice Act, Nursing Disciplinary Diversion Act, Prescriptive Authority Act.* Kansas City, MO: Author.

American Nurses Association (ANA). (1995). *Nursing's social policy statement.* Kansas City, MO: Author.

American Nurses Association (ANA). (2003). *Nursing's social policy statement* (2nd ed.). Silver Spring, MD: Nursebooks.org.

American Nurses Association (ANA). (2010). *Nursing: Scope and standards of practice* (2nd ed.). Silver Spring, MD: NursesBooks.org.

American Nurses Association (ANA). (2011). *What is nursing?* Retrieved December 31, 2011, from www.nursingworld.org/EspeciallyForYou/What-is-Nursing

American Osteopathic Association (AOA). (2011). *Colleges of osteopathic medicine.* Retrieved January 3, 2012, from www.osteopathic.org/inside-aoa/about/affiliates/Pages/osteopathic-medical-schools.aspx

Barzansky, B., & Etzel, S. I. (2005). Educational programs in U.S. medical schools, 2004–2005. *Journal of the American Medical Association, 294*(9), 1068–1074.

Bodenheimer, T. (1999). Physicians and the changing medical marketplace. *New England Journal of Medicine, 340*(7), 584–588.

Bodenheimer, T., Lo, B., & Casalino, L. (1999). Primary care physicians should be coordinators, not gatekeepers. *Journal of the American Medical Association, 281*(21), 2045–2049.

Bureau of Health Professions, Health Resources and Services Administration. (2005). *The registered nurse population: National sample survey of registered nurses, March 2004.* Retrieved February 4, 2012, from http://bhpr.hrsa.gov/healthworkforce/rnsurveys/rnsurveyfinal.pdf (now 2008)

Bureau of Health Professions, Health Resources and Services Administration. (2006). *Physician supply and demand: Projections to 2020.* Retrieved February 3, 2012, from http://bhpr.hrsa.gov/healthworkforce/reports/physwfissues.pdf

Bureau of Health Professions, Health Resources and Services Administration. (2008). *The physician workforce: Projections and research into current issues affecting supply and demand.* Retrieved December 31, 2011, from http://bhpr.hrsa.gov/healthworkforce/reports/physwfissues.pdf

Center for the Health Professions (CHP). (1999, Winter). Primary care tries to find its footing in the new century. *Front and Center, 3*(6), 1.

Colwill, J. M. (1986). Education of the primary physician: A time for reconsideration? *Journal of the American Medical Association, 255*(19), 2643–2644.

Committee on Medical Schools of the Association of American Medical Colleges in Relation to Training for Family Practice. (1968). Planning for comprehensive and continuing care of patients through education. *Journal of Medical Education, 43*(6), 751–759.

Cooper, R. A. (1995). Perspectives on the physician workforce to the year 2020. *Journal of the American Medical Association, 274*(19), 1534–1543.

Cooper, R. A., Getzen, T. E., McKee, H. J., & Laud, P. (2002). Economic and demographic trends signal an impending physician shortage. *Health Affairs, 21*(1), 140.

Davidson, D. (2001, August 6). A message. *AHA News* (Suppl.), p. 1.

Davis, K., Schoenbaum, S. C., & Audet, A. M. (2005). A 2020 vision of patient-centered primary care. *Journal of General Internal Medicine, 20*(10), 953–957.

Donabedian, A., Axelrod, S. A., & Wyszewianski, L. (1980). *Medical care chartbook* (7th ed.). Ann Arbor, MI: AUPHA Press.

Dudley, R. A., & Luft, H. S. (2001). Managed care in transition. *New England Journal of Medicine, 344*(14), 1087–1092.

Edelman, N. E., & Romeiser, J. (2010). Financing of graduate medical education. In *Ensuring an effective physician workforce for America*. Chaired by M. E. Johns. Proceedings. Association of Academic Health Centers, October, 2010, Atlanta, GA.

Eisenberg, J. M. (1986). *Doctors' decisions and the cost of medical care*. Ann Arbor, MI: Health Administration Press.

Eisenberg, J. (1997). [Review of the book *Primary care—America's health in a new era*]. *New England Journal of Medicine, 336*(22), 1615.

Ferris, T. G., Chang, Y., Blumenthal, D., & Pearson, S. D. (2001). Leaving gatekeeping behind—effects of opening access to specialists for adults in a health maintenance organization. *New England Journal of Medicine, 345*(18), 1312–1317.

Fordham, C. C. (1980). The Bane Report revisited. *Journal of the American Medical Association, 244*(4), 354–357.

Forrest, C. B., Nutting, P., Werner, J. J., Starfield, B., von Schrader, S., & Rohde, C. (2003). Managed health plan effects on the specialty referral process: Results from the Ambulatory Sentinel Practice Network referral study. *Medical Care, 41*(2), 242–253.

Freymann, J. G. (1974). *The American health care system: Its genesis and trajectory*. New York, NY: Medcom.

Geiger, H. J. (1997). [Review of the book *Doctoring: The nature of primary care medicine*.] *New England Journal of Medicine, 337*(22), 1637.

Geyman, J. P. (1986). Training primary care physicians for the 21st century. *Journal of the American Medical Association, 255*(19), 2631–2635.

Greenhouse, S. (2006, October 4). Board redefines rules for union exemption. *The New York Times*. Retrieved from www.nytimes.com/2006/10/04/washington/04labor.html?pagewanted=all

Hart, P. D., & Research Associates. (2003). *Patient-to-nurse staffing ratios: Perspectives from hospital nurses*. Washington, DC: AFT Healthcare.

Haugh, R. (2002, January). Finance: Patience required. *Hospitals and Health Networks*, p. 18.

Helmer, F. T., & McKnight, P. (1989). Management strategies to minimize nursing turnover. *Health Care Management Review, 14*(1), 73.

Hsiao, C. J., Cherry, D. K., Beatty, P. C., & Rechtsteiner, E. A. (2010). National Hospital Ambulatory Medical Care Survey: 2007 summary. *National Health Statistics Reports, 27*. Hyattsville, MD: National Center for Health Statistics.

Igelhart, J. K. (1987). Problems facing the nursing profession. *New England Journal of Medicine, 317*(10), 646.

Institute of Medicine. (1978). *A manpower policy for primary health care*. Washington, DC: National Academy of Sciences.

Institute of Medicine (IOM). (2010). *The future of nursing: Leading change, advancing health.* Washington, DC: National Academies Press.

Jonas, S. (1973). Some thoughts on primary care: Problems in implementation. *International Journal of Health Services, 3*(2), 177.

Jonas, S. (1981). Sounding boards. State approval of foreign medical schools: Ensuring the quality of the training of the students and graduates from foreign medical school entering New York State. *New England Journal of Medicine, 305*(1), 45.

Jonas, S. (1984). The historical and theoretical basis for the New York State Board of Regents' policy concerning U.S. foreign medical graduates. *New York State Journal of Medicine, 84*(7), 345–347.

Jonas, S. (1986). Health manpower. In S. Jonas (Ed.), *Health care delivery in the United States* (3rd ed., pp. 54–89). New York, NY: Springer Publishing.

Kaiser Family Foundation. (2002, May). *Trends and indicators in the changing health care marketplace, 2002* (Exhibit 6.1, p. 64). Retrieved January 3, 2011, from www.kff.org/insurance/7031/print-sec6.cfm

Kaiser Family Foundation. (2010). *Registered nurses per 100,000 population, 2010. StateHealthFacts.org.* Retrieved December 31, 2011, from www.statehealthfacts.org/comparemaptable.jsp?cat=8&ind=439

Kalisch, P. A., & Kalisch, B. J. (1978). *The advance of American nursing.* Boston, MA: Little, Brown.

Knowles, J. H. (1965). The role of the hospital: The ambulatory clinic. *Bulletin of the New York Academy of Medicine, 41*(2), 68–79.

Kovner, C. T., & Salsberg, E. S. (2002). The health care workforce. In A. R. Kovner & S. Jonas (Eds.), *Jonas and Kovner's health care delivery in the United States* (7th ed., pp. 68–106). New York, NY: Springer Publishing.

Krakower, J. Y., Ganem, J. L., & Jolly, P. (1996). Review of US medical school finances, 1994–1995. *Journal of the American Medical Association, 276*(9), 720–724.

Liaison Committee on Medical Education (LCME). (2012). *Directory of accredited medical education programs.* Retrieved January 3, 2012, from www.lcme.org/directry.htm

Lumsdon, K. (1995, December 5). Faded glory. *Hospitals and Health Networks,* p. 31.

Madison, D. L. (1983). The case for community-oriented primary care. *Journal of the American Medical Association, 249,* 1279–1282.

Martiniano, R., & Moore, J. (2006). *Health care employment projections: An analysis of bureau of labor statistics occupational projections: 2004–2014.* Retrieved February 19, 2007, from http://chws.albany.edu

May, J. H., Bazzoli, G. J., & Gerland, A. M. (2006). Hospitals' responses to nurse staffing shortages. *Health Affairs—Web Exclusive,* pp. w316–w323. Retrieved February 3, 2012, from http://content.healthaffairs.org/cgi/content/abstract/25/4/W316

McGinnis, J. M., Williams-Russo, P., & Knickman, J. R. (2002, March–April). The case for more active policy attention to health promotion. *Health Affairs, 21*(2), 78–93.

Monahan, T. J. (2001). New York State evaluation of foreign medical schools: An update. *Journal of Medical Licensure and Discipline, 87,* 154.

Moses, E. B. (1992). *The registered nurse population: Findings from the National Sample Survey of Registered Nurses.* Rockville, MD: U.S. Dept. of Health & Human Services, Bureau of Health Professions, Division of Nursing.

Mullan, F. (1982). Sounding board: Community-oriented primary care. An agenda for the 80's. *New England Journal of Medicine, 307*(17), 1076–1078.

Mullan, F., & Conner, E. (Eds.). (1982). *Community-oriented primary care—Conference proceedings.* Washington, DC: National Academies Press.

Mullan, F. (1995). Beware of medical quick fixes. *Public Health Reports, 110*(6), 668–673.

Mullan, F. (2002). Perspective: Some thoughts on the white-follows-green law. *Health Affairs, 21*(1), 158–159.

Mundinger, M. O. (2002). Perspective: Through a different looking glass. *Health Affairs, 21*(1), 162–164.

Mundinger, M. O., Kane, R. L., Lenz, E. L., Totten, A. M., Tsai, W. Y., Cleary, P. D., . . . Shelanski, M. L. (2000). Primary care outcomes in patients treated by nurse practitioners or physicians: A randomized trial. *Journal of the American Medical Association, 283*(1), 59–68.

National Center for Health Statistics (NCHS). (2011). *Health, United States, 2010.* Hyattsville, MD: U.S. Department of Health and Human Services.

National Center for Health Workforce Analysis, Bureau of Health Professions, Health Resources and Services Administration. (2002). *A comparison of changes in the professional practice of nurse practitioners, physician assistants, and certified nurse midwives: 1992–2000.* Retrieved February 3, 2012, from http://bhpr.hrsa.gov/healthworkforce/reports/comparechange19922000.pdf

National Center for Health Workforce Analysis, Bureau of Health Professions, Health Resources and Services Administration. (2003). *Changing demographics and the implications for physicians, nurses, and other health workers.* Retrieved February 3, 2012, from   www.nachc.com/client/documents/clinical/Clinical_Workforce_Changing_Demographics.pdf

National Center for Health Workforce Analysis, Bureau of Health Professions, Health Resources and Services Administration. (2006). *The physician workforce: Projections and research into current issues affecting supply and demand.* Retrieved February 3, 2012, from http://bhpr.hrsa.gov/healthworkforce/reports/physwfissues.pdf

Needleman, J., Buerhaus, P., Mattke, S., Stewart, M. & Zelevinsky, K. (2002). Nurse-staffing levels and the quality of care in hospitals. *New England Journal of Medicine, 346*(22), 1715.

New York State Education Department, Office of the Professions. (2005). *Education law (Article 139, Nursing).* Retrieved February 3, 2011, from www.op.nysed.gov/prof/nurse/article139.htm

Nutting, P. A., Wood, M., & Conner, E. M. (1985). Community-oriented primary care in the United States. *Journal of the American Medical Association, 253*(12), 1763–1766.

O'Neill, L., & Kuder, J. (2005). Explaining variation in physician practice patterns and their propensities to recommend services. *Medical Care Research Review, 62*(3), 339–357.

Parker, C. (2002, October 1). Nursing shortage, working conditions, intertwined at Congressional hearing. *AHA News,* p. 1.

Record, J. C. (1981). *Staffing primary care in 1990: Physician replacement and cost savings.* New York, NY: Springer Publishing.

Reader, G. G., & Soave, R. (1976, Fall). Comprehensive care revisited. *Milbank Memorial Fund Quarterly: Health and Society,* p. 391.

Rhyne, R., Cashman, S., & Kantrowitz, M. (1998). An introduction to community-oriented primary care (COPC). In R. Rhyne, R. Bogue, G. Kukulka, & H. Fulmer (Eds.), *Community-oriented primary care: Health care for the 21st century* (pp. 2–31). Washington, DC: American Public Health Association.

Roemer, M. I. (1975, March 1). From poor beginnings, the growth of primary care. *Hospitals,* p. 38.

Roemer, M. I. (1981). *Ambulatory health services in America.* Gaithersburg, MD: Aspen Systems.

Roemer, R., Kramer, C., & Frink, J. E. (1975). *Planning urban health services: From jungle to system.* New York, NY: Springer Publishing.

Rogers, A. E., Hwang, W. T., Scott, L. D., Aiken, L. H., & Dinges, D. F. (2004). The working hours of hospital staff nurses and patient safety. *Health Affairs, 23*(4), 202–212.

Rosenthal, E. (1996, August 19). Once in big demand, nurses are targets for hospital cuts. *The New York Times.* New York and Region. News, A. 16.

Ruby, G. (1977). *Definitions of primary care* [Staff paper]. Washington, DC: Institute of Medicine.

Schafft, G. E., & Cawley, J. F. (1987). *The physician assistant*. Rockville, MD: Aspen.

Secretary's Commission on Nursing. (1988). *Final report*. Washington, DC: U.S. Department of Health and Human Services.

Selvam, A. (2001, April). The state of the health care workforce. *Hospitals and Health Networks, 75*(4), 40.

Shortell, S. M., Waters, T. M., Clarke, K. W. B., & Budetti, P. P. (1998). Physicians as double agents. *Journal of the American Medical Association, 280*(12), 1102–1108.

Sidel, V. W., & Sidel, R. (1983). *A healthy state* (Rev. ed.). New York, NY: Pantheon.

Somers, A. R. (1983). And who shall be the gatekeeper? The role of the primary physician in the health care delivery system. *Inquiry, 20*(4), 301–313.

Stange, K. C., Woolf, S. H., & Gjeltma, K. (2002). One minute for prevention: the power of leveraging to fulfill the promise of health behavior counseling. *American Journal of Preventive Medicine, 22*(4), 320–323.

Starfield, B. (1992). *Primary care*. New York, NY: Oxford University Press.

Stein, L. I., Watts, D. T., & Howell, T. (1990). The doctor-nurse game revisited. *New England Journal of Medicine, 322*(8), 546.

Starfield, B. (1996). Public health and primary care: A framework for proposed linkages. *American Journal of Public Health, 86*(10), 1365–1369.

Steinbrook, R. (2002). Nursing in the crossfire. *New England Journal of Medicine, 346*(22), 1757–1766.

Steinhauer, J. (2000, December 25). Worker shortage in health fields worst in decades. *The New York Times*, p. 1.

Stoneham, L., Banning, T., Kroll, C., & Young, J. (2004). *Fading away: Access to primary care: Flirting with disaster*. Primary Care Coalition. Retrieved December 20, 2006, from www.tafp.org/advocacy/FadingAway.pdf

University of the State of New York (USNY). (1995a). *Medicine handbook*. Albany, NY: New York State Education Department.

University of the State of New York (USNY). (1995b). *Nursing handbook*. Albany, NY: New York State Education Department.

Wachter, R. M. (2006, August). The hospitalist field a decade later. *Internal medicine world report*. Retrieved November 4, 2006, from www.hcplive.com/primary-care/publications/internal-medicine-world-report

Wachter, R. M., & Goldman, L. (1996). The emerging role of "Hospitalists" in the American health care system. *New England Journal of Medicine, 335*(7), 514–517.

Wachter, R. M., & Goldman, L. (2002). The hospitalist movement 5 years later. *Journal of the American Medical Association, 287*(4), 487–494.

Weiner, J. P. (2002). A shortage of physicians or a surplus of assumptions? *Health Affairs, 21*(1), 160–162.

Wennberg, J. E. & Members of the Dartmouth Atlas of Health Care Working Group. (1996). *The Dartmouth atlas of health care*. Chicago, IL: American Hospital Publishing.

Wennberg, J. E., Fisher, E. S., & Skinner, J. S. (2002). Geography and the debate over Medicare reform. *Health Affairs* (Suppl. Web Exclusive), pp. W96–W114. Retrieved February 19, 2007, from http://content.healthaffairs.org/cgi/content/abstract/hlthaff.w2.96

White, K. L. (1968, January). Organization and delivery of personal health services—public policy issues. *Milbank Memorial Fund Quarterly*. [Reprinted in J. B. McKinlay (Ed.), *Politics and law in health care policy*. New York: Prodist, 1973.]

Wilbur, C. K. (1980). *Revolutionary medicine, 1700–1800*. New York, NY: Chelsea House.

Wunderlich, G. S., Sloan, F. A., & Davis, S. (Eds.). (1996). *Nursing staff in hospitals and nursing homes: Is it adequate?* Washington, DC: National Academies Press.

FOUR

Government and the Health Care System

TOP U.S. THREATS IN...

1991   2001   2011

© Cagle Cartoons, Inc. By Cameron Cardow.

As noted in Chapter 1, the U.S. government operates neither the health care delivery system nor the health services financing system in anything close to their entirety. In fact, in the United States, government is less involved with the provision of health care (in contrast to the payment for health services, with which it is heavily involved) than in any other industrialized country in the world.

Perhaps the most important reason for this difference is the political and economic strength of the private medical, hospital, insurance company, and now managed care sectors of the health services economy and their opposition to what they term "government control and interference." In the view of these and other stakeholders, the health care sector in the United States is already the most regulated of all economic sectors. Additionally, they argue that numerous rules contradict or duplicate others. It is commonly cited that there are more than 130,000 pages of rules and instructions for the Medicare and Medicaid programs and it is commonly claimed that meeting the regulatory demands of all the relevant agencies requires up to an hour of paperwork for every hour of patient care provided (American Hospital Association, 2001).

There are, of course, exceptions to this rule of dominance by the private sector. These include certain select areas of the health care delivery system that are not profitable or are technically difficult to deal with, such as care of the sick poor, care of the mentally ill, care of special, distant population groups, such as Native Americans living on reservations, providing payment for both short- and long-term care of the elderly, and infectious disease control and other personal public health services. Therefore, as restricted as the U.S. government's role is compared with that found in other nations, in terms of dollars spent (see Chapter 5), its role still looms rather large and thus deserves our attention.

> The one hundred thirty thousand pages of Medicare regulations stifle provider innovation. We know that because conservative politicians such as Newt Gingrich tell us this every chance they get. The evidence? A decade ago, the estimable Mayo Clinic added up the pages; who, after all, doesn't believe the Mayo Clinic? This nugget, demonstrating regulation run amok, even made it into the talking points that candidate George Bush used against Al Gore in one of their 2000 debates, although Bush managed to mangle the details.
> The only problem is that the number 130,000 is wrong—not just a little wrong, but about 127,500 pages wrong. I know this because as a senior political appointee at the Centers for Medicare and Medicaid Services (CMS), I was selected to defend the number in a congressional hearing. In fact, most of what Mayo counted as pages of regulations were newsletters, non-precedential payment appeal decisions, and other assorted tidbits, many going back fifteen years. Medicare-related? Yes. Regulations? Not even close. (Berenson, 2007)

The burden of clinical documentation and clerical duties has been widely discussed across settings. A 2006 survey of internal medicine residents and program directors reported spending 4 hours daily on documentation; only 38.9% reported spending this amount of time in direct patient contact. The majority of residents (56.5%) and program directors (63.0%) believed that feedback on documentation occurred less than 50% of the time. Program directors were more likely than residents to view feedback on documentation as highly important (73.2% vs. 58.6%) (Oxentenko, West, Popkave, Weinberger, & Kolars 2010).

HISTORICAL BACKGROUND

The government's role in U.S. health care has developed and expanded gradually over a long period of time. In his preface to a seminal book on government medical services of the 1940s by Stern (1946), Smillie, one of the first medical sociologists (as was Stern) and a noted public health authority of the day, said:

> Our forefathers certainly had no concept of responsibility of the Federal Government, nor of the state government, for health protection of the people. This was solely a local governmental responsibility. When Benjamin Franklin wrote "Health is Wealth" in the Farmers' Almanac, he was saying that health was a commodity to be bought, to be sold, to be conserved, or to be wasted. But he considered that health conservation was the responsibility of the individual, not of government. The local community was responsible only for the protection of its citizens against the hazards of community life. Thus government responsibility for health protection consisted of (a) promotion of sanitation and (b) communicable disease control. The Federal Constitution, as well as the Constitutions of most of the states, contains no reference or intimation of a federal or state function in medical care. The care of the sick poor was a local community responsibility from earliest pioneer days. This activity was assumed first by voluntary philanthropy; later, it was transferred, and became an official governmental obligation. (p. xiii)

Professor Stern (1946) continued that line of thinking in the introduction to his book:

> Government action in the field has traditionally been limited to the care of the indigent and has been dominated in its scope and administration by the restraining influences of the parochial poor laws. Gradually, and especially after the passage of the Social Security Act and during [World War II], government medical care has increasingly been furnished to some nonindigent groups. New patterns of government medical care are being formulated and the role of local, state, and federal governments in the field is changing.... The attitudes of the medical profession and of the public toward government medical programs will determine whether these resources are to be used progressively to distribute more medical care of higher quality to the American people. (pp. 4,5)

What a contemporary ring this last sentence has, even though it was written more than 60 years ago. Even without any kind of national health system, government at all jurisdictional levels in the United States was much more heavily involved in the health care delivery system in both degree and kind in 2007 than it was in 1946. Consider, for example, such initiatives as Medicare and Medicaid, government regulation of spending and payment and the environment, the development and approval of pharmaceuticals, and support of biomedical research and health professions education, as well as traditional public health services and care for the poor in certain jurisdictions. Particularly in the last regard, certain characteristics have remained unchanged. They are most significant. To quote Smillie again (Stern, 1946):

> Practically all governmental procedures in medical care stem from the original local community responsibility for the care of the sick poor, and many of our great municipal hospitals, clinics, and health services of today still bear the stigma of pauperism. (p. xiv)

By the term *medical care*, Smillie meant what we have often referred to as *personal health services* or *direct health care delivery*.

What has been termed the *pauper stigma*, signifying that "poor equals bad" and that poverty is the fault of the poor, is still attached to much government activity in direct health care delivery (although certain health department services have managed to escape the taint). It is rooted in the Protestant work ethic, which held people directly accountable for their state in life. The legal implementation of that ethic goes back at least as far as the Elizabethan Poor Laws in England (de Schweinitz, 1943/1961).

Although, in our society today, some may accept socioeconomic explanations as to why some people are well off and others are destitute, the attitudes of many toward the proper role of government in health care are still colored by old values and prejudices toward the poor and people of color (Jonas, 1986; still the case 20 years later). Additionally, the health status of the latter groups is different from that of the nation as a whole (as noted throughout this book). For example, one study (Geronimus, Bound, Waidmann, Hillemeier, & Burns, 1996) reported in 1996 that

> When they were compared with the nationwide age-standardized annual death rates for whites, the death rates for both sexes in each of the [studied] poverty areas were excessive, especially among blacks.... Boys in Harlem [a predominantly African American district in New York City] who reached the age of 15 had a 37 percent chance of surviving to the age of 65; for girls the likelihood was 65 percent. (p. 1552)

And a more recent study by Geronimus and colleagues (Geronimus, Hicken, Keene, & Bound, 2006) found:

> ...evidence that racial inequalities in health exist across a range of biological systems among adults and are not explained by

racial differences in poverty. The weathering effects of living in a race-conscious society may be greatest among those Blacks most likely to engage in high effort coping. (p. 826)

A broader application of this finding is that of Michael Marmot (2002): "Income is related to health in three ways: through the gross national product of countries, the income of individuals, and the income inequalities among rich nations and among geographic areas" (p. 31).

Many questions remain about the role of government in health today, some of which have resonated for decades. In his preface to the landmark report of the Institute of Medicine's Committee on the Future of Public Health, Remington (Institute of Medicine [IOM], 1988) summarized these well in terms that, for better or worse, still apply:

But what is the most appropriate nature of that governmental presence? How should government's role relate to that of the private sector? How should governmental responsibility for public health be apportioned among local, state, and federal levels? Should government be the health care provider of last resort or does it have a greater responsibility? Should public health consist only of a necessary residuum of activities not met by private providers? How should governmental activities directed toward the maintenance of an environment conducive to health be apportioned among various agencies? But above all, just what is public health? What does it include and what does it exclude? Based on an appropriate definition, what kinds of programs and agencies should be constructed to meet the needs and demands of the public, which is often resistant to an increasing role, or at least an increasing cost, of government? (pp. v,vi)

These questions have yet to be answered definitively for the United States. The public debate about the role of government in health care sharply diminished in intensity following the defeat of the Clinton health plan, but made its way back onto the national political agenda following the election of Barack Obama in 2008, which resulted in the Patient Protection and Affordable Care Act (PPACA) signed into law on March 23, 2010.

This is not to say that there were not calls "to do something" at the governmental level, both in the delivery of personal health services (IOM, 2001) as there have been throughout the 20th century, and in dealing with the nonmedical determinants of health (Lurie, 2002; McGinniss, Williams-Russo, & Knickman, 2002). Although early in the new millennium there was little political resonance for these concerns, given especially the power of the for-profit sector's political lobby, that situation may be changing as we move through the second decade of the new century.

THE CONSTITUTIONAL BASIS OF GOVERNMENT AUTHORITY IN HEALTH CARE

It is argued that a very significant role for government in health care delivery is justified by the amount of money government spends on it. This says nothing about the calls for major reforms that could be undertaken by no agency other than government that echo down to us from the early 1930s and resonate in many voices today. But such a role has a constitutional basis as well.

To understand government operations in the health care delivery system, it is essential to understand the structure of the government itself.[1] A basic principle of the U.S. Constitution is that sovereign power is to be shared between the federal and state governments, a principle called federalism. At its heart, the U.S. Constitution is an agreement among the original 13 states to delegate some of their inherent powers to a federal government, on behalf, not of themselves as separately sovereign entities, but of, as the Preamble to the Constitution says, "the people of the United States." As part of this agreement, in the Tenth Amendment to the Constitution, the states explicitly reserved to themselves the rest of the power: "The powers not delegated to the United States by the Constitution, nor prohibited by it to the states, are reserved to the states respectively, or to the people."

Because it is not explicitly mentioned in the Constitution, among the powers reserved to the states is the "police power." It is the latter that forms the basis of the states' role in health (Mustard, 1945, pp. 17–21). As Grad (2005) points out:

> In the states, government authority to regulate for the protection of public health and to provide health services is based on the "police power"—that is, the power to provide for the health, safety, and welfare of the people. It is not necessary that this power be expressly stated, because it is a plenary power that every sovereign government has, simply by virtue of being a sovereign government. For purposes of the police power, the state governments—which antedate the federal government—are sovereign governments.... [T]he exercise of the police power is really what government is about. It defines the very purpose of government. (p. 11)

Among the states' other inherent powers are those of delegation of their own authority. The states used this power to create a third tier of government, local government. Most states have delegated some of their own health powers to that tier. The constitutional basis of the federal government's health authority is found in the powers to tax and spend to provide for the general welfare, and regulate interstate and foreign commerce (see the Preamble and Article 1, Section 8 of the Constitution) (Grad, 2005, pp. 11–15).

The other basic constitutional principle affecting health and health services is *separation of powers*. The Constitution divides the sovereign power of the federal government among three branches of government: executive, legislative, and judicial. Under separation of powers, each branch of the federal government has its own authority and responsibility, spelled out in the Constitution. Furthermore, the Constitution spells out curbs on the powers of each branch, exercised by the other two. This arrangement is called the *system of checks and balances*.

One very important check on the power of both the federal legislative and executive branches, *judicial review* of the constitutionality of their actions, is not found in the Constitution, however. It was established early in the 19th century by the third Chief Justice of the Supreme Court, John Marshall, and his colleagues on the bench. It has become an accepted part of the U.S. constitutional system only because the other two branches have granted the Court that authority in practice and have followed its determinations.

In organizing themselves, the state governments have followed fairly closely the tripartite form of government established under the U.S. Constitution, with checks and balances and separation of powers. At the tertiary level of government, the boundaries between the branches at times become blurred, however. For example, in some suburban and rural areas, the local chief executive officer presides over the local legislative body. Nevertheless, in most U.S. jurisdictions, separation of powers is a major principle of government.

THE HEALTH CARE FUNCTIONS OF GOVERNMENT

The Legislative Branch

At each level of government, federal, state, and local, each of the three branches of government has responsibility and authority for health and health services. Legislatures create the laws that establish the means to safeguard the public's health, in matters ranging from the assurance of a pure water supply to protecting the health of workers in their places of employment. The legislatures also enact the legal framework within which the health care delivery system functions, determining which individuals and institutions are authorized to deliver what services to which persons under what conditions and requirements.

In the past, legislatures have imposed certain requirements for planning and development on the system, although in most jurisdictions that function has been minimized or has disappeared entirely. If the government is to participate in health care financing (see Chapter 5), directly deliver services, or support research efforts, the legislature must first establish the legal authority for those programs.

The Judiciary

The judiciary generally supports the work of the other two branches of government. The judicial branches at the three levels of government have important powers relating to health and health services. In the criminal law arena, working in concert with the law enforcement arms of the executive branches, under the authority granted to them by their respective legislatures, they can try apprehended transgressors of the criminal law and determine punishment for those successfully prosecuted. For example, although it is a state legislature that creates the licensing law for physicians and the executive branch that administers it, it is the judicial system that determines the guilt or innocence of a person charged with "practicing medicine without a license." The criminal justice system also plays a vital role in safeguarding the public's health. For example, it enforces sanitary protection and pollution control legislation, with criminal sanctions if necessary.

In the civil arena, the judicial system handles disputes arising from the provision of health services, for example, through the process of malpractice litigation. The judicial system adjudicates contract cases arising from health care system disputes, such as those between providers or patients, on one side, and a managed care organization (MCO) on the other. It protects the rights of individuals under the due process and equal protection clauses of the Fifth and Fourteenth Amendments to the Constitution. Together, then, the judicial and executive branches form the civil and criminal justice systems, at the federal, state, and local levels.

The Executive Branch

In common parlance, the term *government in health care* refers to the executive branch that delivers health care services, drafts and enforces provider/payer regulations, and administers financing programs, not the legislature that creates the programs or regulatory authority, nor the courts that settle disputes arising under the laws and adjudicates violations of them. Therefore, in the remainder of this chapter the term *government* refers to the executive branch of government.

Provision of Personal Health Services

At the federal level, personal health services are provided, for the most part, to *categories of persons*: members of the uniformed services and their families, Native Americans, and military veterans, for example. State governments provide personal health services, for the most part, to *persons who have specific diseases*, such as mental illness and tuberculosis. Local governments' personal health services are *stratified by class*. Generally, they are for the poor. There are occasional overlaps, for example, governments at all levels provide health services for prisoners; one category of person.

Provision of Community Health Services

Government at all levels is the major provider of the traditional community-wide "public health" services, such as pure water supply and sanitary sewage disposal, food and drug inspection and regulation, communicable disease control (e.g., immunization and the control of sexually transmitted diseases), vital statistics, environmental regulation and protection, and public health laboratory work.

Certain community health activities are shared with the private sector. For example, in public health education, voluntary agencies such as the American Cancer Society and the American Heart Association are important participants. Private refuse companies do much of the solid waste collection and, in certain states, supply the water. Private organizations such as the Sierra Club and the Natural Resources Defense Council are active in environmental protection. Private institutions also play a vital role in health sciences education and research.

Health Services Financing

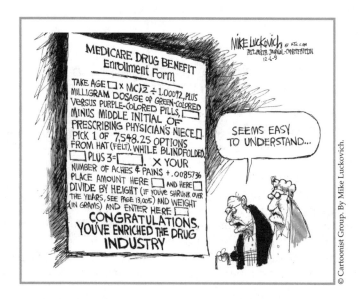

© Cartoonist Group. By Mike Luckovich.

As will be described in more detail in Chapter 5, government participates in the financing system in three ways. First, it pays for the operation of its own programs, both personal and community. It does this directly, for example, through the federal government's Veterans Affairs hospital system or a municipal hospital serving primarily the poor. It also does this indirectly, for example, through the federal government's provision of grants to state governments to help pay for personal care in state mental hospitals and for the operation of the state's public health agencies at the community level. The states, in turn, indirectly support local government public health activities by providing money for that purpose.

Second, through grants and contracts to nongovernmental agencies (and, in certain cases, other governmental agencies), governments support other types of health-related programs, for example, in biomedical research and medical education. Third, and this is by far the major role of government in financing, under such programs as Medicare and Medicaid, governments pay providers for the delivery of care to patients. As will be discussed in greater detail in Chapter 5, federal, state, and local public funds accounted for about 47% of national health expenditures in 2010, up from 42% in 1980 and 38% in 1970 (NCHS, 2011, Table 122). Between 2008 and 2009, a general trend toward greater federal, than state and local, spending is evident:

> Shares of total national health spending financed by businesses (21 percent), households (28 percent), governments (44 percent), and other private sponsors (7 percent) have remained relatively steady over time. Between 2008 and 2009, however, the federal government share increased significantly (from 24 to 27 percent), while the state and local government share declined (from 17 to 16 percent). (CMS, 2009)

THE FEDERAL GOVERNMENT AND THE PROVISION OF HEALTH SERVICES

Many federal agencies are involved in the delivery of personal and community health services. The U.S. Department of Health and Human Services (DHHS) is the most important federal actor in health and health care. Including its social service functions, as of 2011, the department operated more than 300 different programs (DHHS, 2011). There are two other federal agencies with major health services responsibilities: the Department of Veterans Affairs (VA) and Department of Defense (DOD). Other federal agencies with significant health-related responsibilities include the Department of Agriculture (nutrition policy, meat and poultry inspection, food stamps), the Environmental Protection Agency, and the Department of Labor (administering the Occupational Safety and Health Act).

Department of Health and Human Services

In 2011, the mission of the DHHS, as stated on its website (2011), was: "[to protect] the health of all Americans and [provide] essential human services, especially for those who are least able to help themselves."

This stood in contrast with the more explicit mission for the department, as stated under the previous administration, which was to

> protect and promote the health, social and economic well-being of all Americans and in particular those least able to help themselves—children, the elderly, persons with disabilities, and the disadvantaged—by helping them and their families develop and maintain healthy, productive, and independent lives. (DHHS, 1996)

As of 2011, the DHHS had 11 major operating divisions. (Until March 31, 1995, the Social Security Administration had been part of the DHHS. On April 1, 1995, it became an independent agency.) All are concerned with health in one way or another.

Many of these operating divisions are part of the Public Health Service (PHS), which has a long and proud history, dating back to a 1798 act that created the Marine Hospital Service (Mustard, 1945, pp. 23–81; Schmeckebier, 1923, chapter 1; Stern, 1946, pp. 145–154). In 1878, Congress added foreign quarantine responsibilities to the work of the Marine Hospital Service. This led in 1889 to the development of a quasimilitary personnel system (the Commissioned Corps of the PHS). The corps was made up largely of career medical people, commanded (only symbolically in recent years) by the Surgeon General of the United States.

The PHS continued to gain responsibilities over time. Following the end of World War II, it grew rapidly, with the passage of the Hospital Survey and Construction (Hill-Burton) Act of 1946; the major expansion of the National Institutes of Health (NIH); the creation of the Communicable Disease Center in Atlanta (now the Centers for Disease Control and Prevention); and the development of drug abuse control, mental retardation, and mental health centers and comprehensive health planning activities, among others. Since 1996, the PHS has existed in name only. It is no longer an operating administrative entity. However, 8 of the 11 operating divisions that comprise the DHHS are still considered the PHS.

Collectively, the 11 operating divisions of the DHHS carry out a variety of functions: regulation, direct provision of personal and community health services, provision of financial support for a variety of health services through grants and contracts, direct biomedical research, and provision of the principal federal support of biomedical research in nongovernmental agencies. A brief description of these divisions follows.

National Institutes of Health (NIH)

Through its multiple institutes, such as the National Cancer Institute and the National Heart, Lung, and Blood Institute, the NIH is responsible for supporting and carrying out biomedical research. Its primary mission focuses on basic biomedical research at the organ-system, tissue, cellular, and subcellular levels. NIH has its own (intramural) research program on its campus in Bethesda, Maryland, and provides funds for research at many other institutions around the country through (extramural) grants and contracts. NIH also fosters research by supporting training, resource development, and construction.

Food and Drug Administration

The task of the Food and Drug Administration (FDA) is to protect the public against food, drug, and medical device and product hazards and to ensure drug potency and effectiveness. Thus, the FDA regulates prescription drugs and over-the-counter medications, biological products, and human blood and its derivatives. The focus is on the assurance of the efficacy and safety of a product before marketing and on the assurance of continuing quality after approval. Medical devices are regulated in a similar manner. Radiological equipment is also regulated, the goals being to control radiation exposure to the public as well as to ensure efficacy.

The regulatory programs of the FDA, especially those focusing on the efficacy and safety of drugs and medical devices, are sometimes controversial. Industry spokespeople maintain that the entry of useful drugs to the market is at times unnecessarily delayed by a lengthy and expensive approval process. Supporters of that process recall, for example, the thalidomide disaster. Nevertheless, in the mid-1990s, the FDA did manage to introduce internal reforms, significantly speeding up the drug review process (MacPherson, 1996).

Even so, there has been continued controversy over the FDA regulatory process since that time. For example, in 2005, Senators Samuel Brownback (R-KS) and James Inhofe (R-OK) introduced the Access, Compassion, Care and Ethics for Seriously Ill Patients Act (S. 1956), which would make it easier for seriously ill patients to receive drugs that are not yet fully approved (GovTrack.US, 2006). In 2005, Senators Charles Grassley (D-IO) and Christopher Dodd (D-CT) introduced the Food and Drug Administration Safety Act of 2005 (S. 930), which established the Center for Postmarket Drug Evaluation and Research to address the problems of adverse drug effects after a drug has gone to market (Library of Congress, 2006). Neither of these bills passed. In October 2011, Representative Michael Rogers (R-MI) introduced R. 3214: Food and Drug Administration Mission Reform Act of 2011, which proposes revisions to the FDA mission that address issues of regulation. For example, the bill proposes that the following language be included in the FDA mission statement:

(G) Ensures that regulations are accessible, consistent, transparent, written in plain language, and easy to understand;
(H) Measures, and seeks to improve, the actual results of regulatory requirements; and
(I) incorporates a patient-focused benefit-risk framework that accounts for varying degrees of risk tolerance, including for people living with a life-impacting chronic disease or disability. (GovTrack.US, 2011)

The Rogers bill, as of this writing of the book, was in the early stages of consideration.

Centers for Disease Control and Prevention

The Centers for Disease Control and Prevention (CDC) is the national public health agency primarily responsible for prevention efforts. Its programs are aimed at preventing and controlling disease and personal injury, directing foreign and interstate quarantine operations, developing programs for health education and health promotion, improving the performance of clinical laboratories, and developing the standards necessary to ensure safe and healthful working conditions for all working people. Through the National Center for Health Statistics, the CDC collects and publishes a variety of vital health and health services data. It maintains the nation's reference laboratories and supports laboratory training programs.

Indian Health Service

The Indian Health Service (IHS) provides health care for about 2 million Native Americans and Alaska Natives who live on or near Indian reservations. In 2011, there were 50,349 inpatient admissions, 11.8 million outpatient visits, and 3.56 million dental services provided. Health services provided include hospital, ambulatory, preventive, and rehabilitative care and community sanitation. The Indian Health Service has a system of 28 hospitals, 58 health centers, 31 health stations, and 5 school health centers. In addition, tribal facilities include 17 hospitals, 235 health centers, 166 Alaska Village Clinics, 92 health stations, and 28 school health centers (IHS, 2011).

Health Resources and Services Administration

The Health Resources and Services Administration (HRSA) runs the direct service programs of the DHHS for "medically needy" persons. Primarily through community and migrant health centers serving more than 19 million people and more than 77 million patient visits in 1,124 organizations across more than 8,100 service sites, HRSA supports efforts to increase the number and diversity of health care professionals caring for the underserved and vulnerable. These include low-income populations, the uninsured, those with limited English proficiency, migrant and seasonal farmworkers, individuals and families experiencing homelessness, and those living in public housing (HRSA, 2011).

Substance Abuse and Mental Health Services Administration

The Substance Abuse and Mental Health Services Administration (SAMHSA) works to improve the quality and availability of substance abuse prevention, addiction treatment, and mental health service; conducts clinical and biomedical research in its own laboratories; provides funding to the states to support mental health services and substance abuse programs; funds extramural research, research training, and prevention programs through grants and contracts; monitors substance abuse; and supports innovative treatment and prevention projects nationwide.

Agency for Healthcare Research and Quality

The Agency for Healthcare Research and Quality (AHRQ) "supports research on health care systems, health care quality and cost issues, access to health care, and effectiveness of medical treatments. It provides evidence-based information on health care outcomes and quality of care" (DHHS, 2011). It is designed to improve the quality of health care, reduce its cost, improve patients' safety, address medical errors, and broaden access to essential services.

Other Federal Departments

Many other federal departments have some health services responsibilities, as previously noted. Several are discussed here.

The Department of Veterans Affairs (VA) provides many services to veterans (VA, 2011). After military service, the U.S. veteran becomes entitled to a remarkably broad range of health services through a health care subsystem, the precise equivalent of which is not found in any other nation in the world. This fact is doubtless related on the one hand to the lack of a national health insurance program for the general population and on the other to the political power of the veterans' organizations.

A veteran is defined as anyone who served 90 days or more in an armed service, but a veteran must have received an honorable or general discharge in order to be automatically eligible. The specific rules covering health care eligibility for the many classes of veterans are complex. They may be reviewed in detail on the VA website. A financial means test for certain classes was introduced by the Bush administration in 2003. The number of patients with service-connected disabilities treated in Veterans

Affairs hospitals has been dropping over time, although with the advent of the Iraq war it is now again on the increase.

The VA owns the largest centrally directed hospital and clinic system in the United States (VA, 2011). In 2011, the VA health care system included 152 VA Hospitals, with at least one in each state, as well as in Puerto Rico and the District of Columbia. The VA operates more than 807 ambulatory care and community-based outpatient clinics and 288 Veterans Centers. VA health care facilities provide a broad spectrum of medical, surgical, and rehabilitative care. There are 8.34 million people enrolled in the VA Health Care System, up from 7.7 million in 2005. In 2010, there were 75.6 million outpatient visits, up from 57.5 million in 2005, and 679,000 inpatient admissions up from 587,000 in 2005.

There is a major shift under way from a primary focus on inpatient care to one on outpatient services, health promotion and disease prevention, and easier access to the system.

The Department of Defense (DOD) oversees the health services of the various branches of the military through the Military Health System. Each of the armed forces—the Army, Navy, Air Force, and Marines—has its own network of health facilities: hospitals, clinics, and field posts (Assistant Secretary of Defense, 1990, 1996, and the website). All DOD health personnel are members of the military and salaried according to their military ranks (without relation to the specific services they render). The same basic structure prevails in times of war or peace. Health promotion and disease prevention are emphasized and integrated with the delivery of treatment services.

Through both its own facilities and contracting arrangements with civilian providers, DOD provides health services to members of the armed forces, their dependents, surviving dependents of service people killed while on active duty, and military retirees and their dependents. Servicemen and women are eligible for retirement benefits after a minimum of 20 years of service. The health services part of that package is paid in addition to the VA benefits for which they may be eligible.

An unusual aspect of military medical departments is that they are charged not only with providing a full range of direct health services but also with providing for the environmental health and protection of their military communities. This unification of administrative responsibility for personal and community preventive and treatment services is rarely found elsewhere in the U.S. health care delivery system.

The U.S. Department of Agriculture (USDA) oversees the Food Safety Inspection Service (FSIS); the Food and Nutrition Service (FNS), which includes the Women, Infants, and Children (WIC) nutritional program, school breakfast and lunch programs, and the Food Stamp program, which helps poor people to buy food; the Center for Nutrition Policy and Promotion (CNPP), which, in cooperation with the DHHS, periodically issues dietary guidelines for the nation; the Animal and Plant Health Inspection Service (APHIS); and the Rural Utilities Service (RUS), which includes telemedicine programs. The USDA conducts research on the nutrient composition of foods, food consumption, and nutritional requirements. The FSIS and APHIS are operated in cooperation with the FDA (USDA, 2006).

Focusing on preventive activities in the workplace, the Occupational Safety and Health Administration (OSHA) is part of the Department of Labor. OSHA uses criteria developed by the National Institute for Occupational Safety and Health (NIOSH), part of the CDC, to set national standards for occupational safety and health (Brock & Tyson, 1985). Since 1970, workplace fatalities have been reduced by more than 65% and occupational injury and illness rates have declined by 67%. At the same time, U.S. employment has almost doubled. Worker deaths in America are down—from about 38 worker deaths a day in 1970 to 12 a day in 2010. Worker injuries and illnesses are also down—from 10.9 incidents per 100 workers in 1972 to fewer than 4 per 100 in 2010 (OSHA, 2011).

The major responsibilities of OSHA are to develop workplace health and safety standards, to enforce and gain compliance with the standards, to engage in education and training, to help the states in occupational safety and health matters (26 states have their own occupational safety and health programs), and to aid business in meeting OSHA requirements (OSHA, 2011). There are a few industries that are not covered by OSHA. For example, the health and safety of miners is the province of the Bureau of Mines in the Department of the Interior.

The Environmental Protection Agency (EPA) is an independent unit of the federal government created during the Nixon administration that was elevated to cabinet-level status during the Clinton administration (EPA, 2006). It has major responsibilities for the control of air and water quality and pollution, solid waste disposal, pesticide contamination, radiation hazards, and toxic substances (EPA, 1988, 1989, and the website). The EPA conducts research on air, water, and land pollution control technology and the effects of pollution on humans, develops criteria and issues national standards for pollutants, and enforces compliance with these standards.

STATE GOVERNMENTS' ROLE IN HEALTH SERVICES

At the state level many different agencies are involved in health services. For example, in most states, departments other than the health department provide two of the important health-related functions managed primarily by the states: mental illness treatment services and Medicaid operations. Furthermore, the licensing authority for health personnel sometimes resides in the education department, vocational rehabilitation is often found in a special agency, occupational health in the labor department, environmental protection in a separate department, and school health with local boards of education. Most states also have a board of health, usually appointed by the governor, which has varying administrative, policy, and advisory functions.

In the 1920s, political struggles with private practitioners led to a limitation of service responsibilities for both the state and local health departments. Haven Emerson, a leading public health official of the time, defined the "Basic Six" services appropriate for departments of public health: vital statistics, public health laboratories, communicable disease control, environmental sanitation, maternal and child health, and public health education (Wilson & Neuhauser, 1976, p. 204).

Some time ago, the Association of State and Territorial Health Officials (ASTHO) defined a state health program as

> [a] set of identifiable services organized to solve health related problems or to meet specific health or health related needs, provided to or on behalf of the public, by or under the direction of an organizational entity in a State Health Agency [SHA], and for which reasonably accurate estimates of expenditures can be made. (ASTHO, 1980, p. vii)

Using this definition, ASTHO identified six program areas for SHAs: "personal health, environmental health, health resources, laboratory, general administration and services, and funds to local health departments not allocated to program areas" (ASTHO, 1980, p. 9). Although the number has stayed the same, in some states the content of the work has expanded well beyond that covered by the "Basic Six" (Dandoy, 1996). In 2012, the ASTHO General Policy on Public Health (ASTHO, 2012) stated:

> Public health is what we, as a society, do collectively to assure living conditions in which people can be healthy. Federal, state, territorial, and local governmental agencies working with public and private entities comprise the nation's public health system. Collectively, the system prevents disease, injury, and disability; protects against environmental hazards; promotes physical and mental health; responds to disasters and emerging diseases; and ensures access to health care services.
>
> Within this broader public health system, governmental public health—composed of federal, state, and local health agencies—occupies an exceptional and fundamental role. It is uniquely accountable to the public and elected representatives for the responsible use of tax dollars that fund its activities. The U.S. Constitution reserves to the states the primary authority and legal responsibility to protect the health of the population within their borders. Still, no single component of the government's public health system can function to maximum effectiveness without the other two.

The governmental public health system is successful if it fulfills its unique federal, state, territorial, and local roles and effectively collaborates with government agencies and the private sector.

Of note in this most recent ASTHO policy statement is the emphasis on evidence-based public health, that is, holding the public health system accountable for implementing sound practice and evidence-based methods that address public health problems effectively and efficiently.

Since World War II, as the health care delivery system has become vastly more complex, there have been an increasing number of public health and health services interests requiring protection. In response, governments have vastly expanded the responsibilities of both state and local departments of health and other health-related governmental agencies. Those responsibilities now include, for example, regulation and quality assurance for physicians, hospitals, other provider agencies and groups (including institutional licensure) planning (what there is of it), ever more complex environmental protection functions and, of course, regulation of payers.

As noted earlier, it is interesting just how much government regulation of the health care system there is in the United States, well beyond that found in other countries. This is precisely because there is no national health system, so in order to provide some modicum of financial, as well as health care quality protection to the public, the various players must be regulated. As also noted previously, state and local health-related activities outside the health departments have expanded, as well.

Health Statistics

Among the oldest of public health functions is the collection and analysis of vital and health statistics. Data on births, deaths, marriages, and divorces (the "vital" statistics), and incidence of the several reportable (primarily infectious) diseases, are collected by the local health authorities and forwarded to the state level. There they are codified and analyzed, often by various demographic characteristics, such as age, gender, marital status, ethnicity, and geographic location. Each state then forwards its collected data to the National Center for Health Statistics of the CDC for further analysis and publication.

Licensing

Licensing is a basic government function in health care. The licensing process for individual practitioners first establishes minimum standards for qualification. It then applies those standards to applicants to determine who may and who may not deliver what kinds of health services. Licensing of health care institutions sets minimum standards for each facility and their personnel as a group, applies the standards, and determines whether the institution may operate.

The licensing authority is one of the most significant of the health powers residing with the states. The manner in which it is used is a major determinant of the character of the health care delivery system. The medical licensing system is particularly significant in that regard. Because no one can practice medicine without a license, the system has given physicians tight control over the central product of the health care delivery system, medical services. By exercising this control, physicians have largely determined the structure of the health care delivery system: how it is organized, the types and functions of the institutions, and the powers of the several categories of personnel who work in it—until, that is, the advent of the MCOs, which took major control of many physicians' purse strings.

LOCAL GOVERNMENTS' ROLE IN HEALTH SERVICES

A local health department (LHD) is a unit of either state or local government focusing exclusively on a "substate" geographic area, usually well-defined and considered by virtually any observer to be "local" in nature—a county, city, town, parish, or village. A current link to descriptions of local health departments nationally, as well as to descriptions of most of the major units, boards, and associations in health care, may be found at http://healthguideusa.org/local_health_departments.htm.

There is wide variation in the activities and services offered by local health departments. The activities and services most frequently offered directly by local health departments are the provision of adult immunizations (88% of departments), communicable and infectious disease surveillance (88% of departments), provision of child immunizations (86% of departments), tuberculosis screening (81% of departments), inspection of food service establishments (77% of departments), environmental health surveillance (75% of departments), food safety education (74% of departments), tuberculosis treatment (72% of departments), tobacco use prevention (70% of departments), and school and daycare inspection (68% of departments). The availability of the services varies by the size of the population served. For example, 79% of departments serving populations smaller than 25,000 people offer child immunization services, while 93% of departments serving more than 500,000 people do so. That the local health department does not provide a service either directly or through contract does not necessarily indicate that those services are not publically available within a jurisdiction. In some cases, another local government agency, a state agency, or a nongovernment organization (NGO) may provide the service. Following is a brief description of some of the common public health services and programs at the local level (NACCHO, 2009; 2010).

Public Health Contributions

State and local public health services, and indeed federal services, face many problems. The current state of affairs is still best summarized by the Committee on the Future of Public Health, which published its report in 1988 (IOM, 1988):

> Many of the major improvements in the health of the American people have been accomplished through public health measures.... But the public has come to take the success of public health for granted.... [T]his nation has lost sight of its public health goals and has allowed the system of public health activities to fall into disarray. Public health is what we, as a society, do collectively to assure the conditions in which people can be healthy.... [M]any problems demonstrate the need to protect the nation's health through effective, organized, and sustained effort by the public sector.... The current state of our abilities for effective public health action...is cause for national concern.... [W]e have slackened our public health vigilance nationally, and the health of the public is unnecessarily threatened as a result.... Successes as great as those of the past are still possible, but not without public concern and concerted action to restore America's public health capacity. This [report] envisions the future of public health, analyzes the current situation and how it developed, and presents a plan of action that will, in the committee's judgment, provide a solid foundation for a strong public health capability throughout the nation. (pp. 1,2)

The committee's report is commended to those readers who are concerned with the future of public health in the United States. These observations are certainly still valid. If anything, the situation has gotten worse, as witnessed by the disorganized response to the 2001 anthrax outbreak.

CONCLUSIONS

Although government is heavily involved in health and health care in the United States, politics and the economic system significantly limit the degree of that involvement. Government provides the legal underpinning for the system through the licensing laws. It regulates the financial workings of the system and its quality of care. It also regulates the causes of potential environmental and occupational hazardous exposures and the possible responses to them. In addition, government is a direct financier and a direct provider of service. It is preeminent in community health services and plays an important role in supporting health sciences education and research.

Most health care providers of both the individual and corporate variety recognize (often grudgingly) the reality that government is already heavily involved in the health care system. As noted, they welcome participation in certain critical areas: licensing; care of the mentally ill, the tubercular, and the poor; and community health services. However, it is likely that the questions about the proper role of government in health for our country today, summarized so well by Remington at the beginning of this chapter, cannot be fruitfully resolved until the place and the power of the private health services provider sector in the health care delivery system as a whole are redefined.

NOTE

1. The *Public Health Law Manual* by Grad (2005), *Health and the Law* by Christoffel (1982), and "The Legal Basis for Public Health" by Richards and Rathbun, chapter 4 in Scutchfield and Keck's *Principles of Public Health Practice* (1996), are valuable guides to the legal basis of government activity in health care and to the many legal procedures involved in the enforcement of public health law.

REFERENCES

American Hospital Association (AHA). (2001). *Patients or paperwork? The regulatory burden facing America's hospitals.* Chicago, IL: AHA. Retrieved December 15, 2006, from www.aha.org/aha/content/2001/pdf/FinalPaperworkReport.pdf

Assistant Secretary of Defense for Health Affairs. (1990, June). *Report on the reorganization of military health care.* Washington, DC: Author.

Assistant Secretary of Defense for Health Affairs. (1996). *Office of the assistant secretary for health affairs.* Washington, DC: Author.

Association of State and Territorial Health Officials (ASTHO). (1980). *Comprehensive national public health programs, of state and territorial health agencies, fiscal year 1978.* Silver Springs, MD: Author.

Association of State and Territorial Health Officials (ASTHO). (2012). *ASTHO general policy on public health.* Retrieved on June 4, 2012, from www.astho.org/Display/AssetDisplay.aspx?id=160

Berenson, R. A. (2007). Separating fact from fiction: A new role for Health Affairs. *Health Affairs, 26*(7), 1528–1530.

Brock, W. E., & Tyson, P. R. (1985). *All about OSHA.* Washington, DC: U.S. Government Printing Office.

Centers for Medicare and Medicaid Services (CMS). (2009). *NHE fact sheet.* Retrieved January 1, 2011, from www.cms.gov/NationalHealthExpendData/25_NHE_Fact_Sheet.asp#TopOfPage

Dandoy, S. (1996). The state public health department. In F.D. & C.W. Keck (Eds.), *Principles of public health practice.* Albany, NY: Delmar.

de Schweinitz, K. (1943). *England's road to social security.* New York, NY. (Reprinted, A. S. Barnes, 1961.)

Environmental Protection Agency (EPA). (1988). *Environmental progress and challenges: EPA's update.* Washington, DC: U.S. Government Printing Office.

Environmental Protection Agency (EPA). (1989). *Your guide to the United States environmental protection agency.* Washington, DC: EPA Office of Public Affairs.

Environmental Protection Agency (EPA). (2006). *About EPA*. Retrieved December 15, 2006, from www.epa.gov/epahome/aboutepa.htm

Geronimus, A. T., Bound, J., Waidmann, T. A., Hillemeier, M. M., & Burns, P. B. (1996). Excess mortality among Blacks and Whites in the United States. *New England Journal of Medicine*, *335*(21), 1552–1558.

Geronimus, A. T., Hicken, M., Keene, D., & Bound, J. (2006). "Weathering" and age patterns of allostatic load scores among Blacks and Whites in the United States. *American Journal of Public Health*, *96*(5), 826–833.

GovTrack.US. (2006). *109th U.S. Congress (2005–2006), S. 1956[109]: ACCESS Act*. Retrieved January 7, 2007, from www.govtrack.us/congress/bill.xpd?bill=s109–1956

GovTrack.US. (2011). *112th U.S. Congress (2011–2012), H.R. 3214: Food and Drug Administration Mission Reform Act of 2011*. Retrieved January 7, 2012, from www.govtrack.us/congress/bill.xpd?bill=h112–3214

Grad, F. (2005). *The public health law manual* (3rd ed.). Washington, DC: American Public Health Association.

Health Resources and Services Administration (HRSA). (2011). *Health center data*. Retrieved January 1, 2011, from http://bphc.hrsa.gov/healthcenterdatastatistics/index.html

Indian Health Services (IHS). (2011). *IHS fact sheets*. Retrieved January 1, 2011, from www.ihs.gov/PublicAffairs/IHSBrochure/Profile.asp

Institute of Medicine (IOM). (1988). *The future of public health*. Washington, DC: National Academies Press.

Institute of Medicine (IOM). (2001). *Crossing the quality chasm: A new health system for the 21st century*. Washington, DC: National Academies Press.

Jonas, S. (1986). On homelessness and the American way. *American Journal of Public Health*, *76*(9), 1084–1086.

Library of Congress. (2006). *Food and Drug Administration Safety Act of 2005 (introduced in Senate)*. Retrieved January 7, 2007, from http://thomas.loc.gov

Lurie, N. (2002). What the federal government can do about the non-medical determinants of health. *Health Affairs*, *21*(2), 94–106.

MacPherson, P. (1996). The FDA just says yes. *Hospitals and Health Networks*, *70*(10), 34–36, 38.

Marmot, M. (2002). The influence of income on health: The views of an epidemiologist. *Health Affairs*, *21*(2), 31–46.

McGinnis, J. M., Williams-Russo, P., & Knickman, J. R. (2002). The case for more active policy attention to health promotion. *Health Affairs*, *21*(2), 78–93.

Mustard, H. S. (1945). *Government in public health*. New York, NY: Commonwealth Fund.

National Association of County and City Health Officials (NACCHO). (2009). *2008 National profile of local health departments*. Washington, DC: Author.

National Association of County and City Health Officials (NACCHO). (2010). *The local health department workforce: Findings from the 2008 national profile of local health departments*. Washington, DC: Author.

National Center for Health Statistics (NCHS). (2011). *Health, United States, 2010: With special feature on death and dying*. Hyattsville, MD: U.S. Department of Health and Human Services.

Occupational Safety and Health Administration (OSHA). (2011). *Commonly used statistics*. Retrieved January 1, 2011, from www.osha.gov/oshstats/commonstats.html

Oxentenko, A. S., West, C. P., Popkave, C., Weinberger, S. E., & Kolars, J. C. (2010). Time spent on clinical documentation: A survey of internal medicine residents and program directors. *Archives of Internal Medicine*, *170*(4), 377–380.

Richards, E. P., & Rathbun, K. C. (1996). The legal basis of public health. In F. D. Scutchfield & C. W. Keck (Eds.), *Principles of public health practice*. Albany, NY: Delmar.

Schmeckebier, L. F. (1923). *The public health service*. Baltimore, MD: Johns Hopkins University Press.

Scutchfield, F. D., & Keck, C. W. (Eds.). (1996). *Principles of public health practice.* Albany, NY: Delmar.

Stern, B. J. (1946). *Medical services by government: Local, state and federal.* New York, NY: Commonwealth Fund.

U.S. Department of Agriculture (USDA). (2006). *An overview.* Retrieved January 5, 2007, from www.usda.gov

U.S. Department of Health and Human Services (DHHS). (1996). *Mission statement.* Retrieved June 4, 2012, from http://govinfo.library.unt.edu/npr/library/nprrpt/annrpt/vp-rpt96/appendix/hhs.html

U.S. Department of Health and Human Services (DHHS). (2011). *HHS home.* Retrieved January 1, 2011, from www.hhs.gov

U.S. Department of Veterans Affairs (VA). (2011). *Statistics at a glance.* Retrieved January 1, 2011, from www.va.gov/vetdata/docs/quickfacts/Homepage-slideshow.pdf

Wilson, F. A., & Neuhauser, D. (1976). *Health services in the United States.* Cambridge, MA: Ballinger.

Financing the Health Care System

Health care is like no other sector of the economy. In his seminal 1963 article, "Uncertainty and the Welfare Economics of Medical Care," Kenneth Arrow identified these differences as uncertainty, asymmetries of information, and nonmarketability of risks inherent in medicine and medical practice. Even after a millennium of observation and study, our knowledge about the human body, disease, and medicine is very much incomplete. In addition, whereas the physician nearly always has more medical knowledge, patients generally know more about their own history, so there is usually a significant information asymmetry between patient and provider.

Economists refer to situations where an individual's behavior changes when he or she is able to shift the risks of decisions to others as moral hazard. If an accident costs a person $2,000 but insurance pays $1,500, the insured person has less incentive to avoid the accident than if the insurance paid only $500. While some may argue that this doesn't apply to one's health, clearly people who defer medical treatment until they end up in an emergency department and the need for programs that reward people for preventive and wellness activities are instances of people making decisions both worse financially and for their health when others bear the risk.

Financing health care is a tension among the ethics and values we place on human life, the asymmetries of information, and uncertainty about care wrapped in nonmarketable risks. The implication is that the health care market would collapse if entirely governed by market forces, even though the health care sector exists within a general market economy. At some level, health care competes for resources (e.g., workers, supporting goods and services) against the production of food, the construction of homes, the creation of movies, and the seemingly infinite number of other goods and services that a nation of 300 million people and associated businesses consume. At some level, providing resources for an additional surgeon to perform cardiac surgeries means that fewer houses can be constructed or that the quality or quantity of food produced will be diminished. Within the health care sector itself, tradeoffs are also made: Money spent on a magnetic resonance imaging (MRI) machine is money not spent on additional doctors, money spent on research is money not spent on providing care, and money spent researching one disease is money not spent on another. Thus, financing health care in the United States is a complex matter of workarounds, redundancies, and contradictions. Furthermore, because the United States lacks a single national health care payment system, how the money is paid to the providers of health care has become very complicated (Igelhart, 1999a).

This chapter describes the basics of health care financing and the system that handles its functions: how much money is spent on health care in the United States, where the money comes from, what the money is spent on, and how the money is paid to health care providers.

Throughout this chapter, please refer to Table 5.1, which displays total National Health Expenditures (NHEs), per capita amounts, percent distribution, and average annual percent growth for selected years from 1960 to 2010 (CMS, 2012a, Table 1). Table 5.2 displays national health consumption by source of funds for selected years from 1960 to 2009, and Table 5.3 displays NHE by type of expenditure for selected years from 1960 to 2009 (CMS, 2012b).

HOW MUCH IS SPENT

Health care spending has increased in the United States every year since 1960 in both absolute and relative terms (see Table 5.1). Between 1980 and 2009, per capita spending on health care increased by more than a factor of 7. In 1980 health care expenditures accounted for only 9.2% of the GDP, in contrast to 17.6% of the GDP in 2009. During the 1980s, the annual rate of increase in health care expenditures was constantly in the double-digit range, even when inflation and the GDP growth rates were not. Why this happened is a matter of much controversy.

Starting in the 1990s, with the advent of managed care and its downward pressure on both physician and hospital usage, a brake was put on health care cost increases, at least for several years: the rates of increase from 1970 through 1990 had been over 10% per year (see Table 5.1). By 1993, the rate of increase had fallen to 8.4%, and from 1997 through 1998 it was a little under 6%. In 1999, the rate of increase began an upward trend, going from 6.5% to 9.5% in 2002. Starting in 2003, NHE growth rates slowed every year through 2009, when spending grew at only 4%.

Nonetheless, since gross domestic product (GDP) declined by 1.7% in 2009, health care spending increased from 16.6% to 17.6% of GDP[1]. That figure is about 46% higher than the percentage of the GDP spent by the country with the next highest spending rate—the Netherlands—and over 50% higher than Germany (OECD, 2011). Germany has a comprehensive national health insurance program. In fact, it is the oldest such program in the world. Only when housing, household operation, and residential investment (not a common grouping) are combined into a supercategory (i.e., "Shelter") is there any larger spending category (U.S. Bureau of Economic Analysis, 2011). In 2004, 13.5 million people were employed in health care—13.1 million were wage and salary workers and about 411,000 were self-employed (U.S. Bureau of Labor Statistics, 2006). In 2008, the number of wage and salary workers increased 9% to 14.3 million (U.S. Bureau of Labor Statistics, 2011).

A considerable part of the constant upward trend in health care spending in the United States has been caused by factors other than simple utilization, such as the ever-intensifying use of expensive technology-based diagnostic and procedural interventions, especially at the beginning and the end of life (Franks, Clancy, & Nutting, 1992; Meier & Morrison, 2002). In "The Growth in Cost Per Case Explains Far More of U.S. Health Spending Increases Than Rising Disease Prevalence," Roehrig and Rousseau (2011) show that three-quarters of the increase in real per capita health spending was attributable to growth in cost per case. Thus, it remains to be seen how long the increase in expenditure rate will remain at a relatively modest level (although still above the general rate of inflation), or whether it will return to its previously astronomical (double-digit) levels, as in the 1970s and 1980s.

WHERE THE MONEY COMES FROM, WITHIN THE SYSTEM

In the United States, health care is paid by some combination of the patient, the provider, and a third-party payer. Money paid directly by the patient for health care costs is referred to as "out-of-pocket." *Charity care* and *forgiven debts* are the terms providers use when they have borne the

Table 5.1 Total National Health Expenditures, Per Capita Amounts, Percent Distribution, and Average Annual Percent Growth for Selected Years from 1960 to 2009

Item	1960	1970	1980	1990	1993	1997	1998	1999
Billions of Dollars								
National Health Expenditures	$27.3	$74.8	$255.7	$724.0	$921.3	$1,142.4	$1,208.6	$1,286.8
Health Consumption Expenditure	24.8	67	235.6	675.3	860.1	1,070.2	1,128.5	1,200.0
Personal Health care	23.3	63.1	217.1	616.6	781	974.5	1,028.3	1,088.8
Admin and Net Cost of PHI	1.1	2.6	12	38.7	52.3	60.9	62.7	70.5
Public Health	0.4	1.4	6.4	20	26.8	34.8	37.5	40.7
Investment	2.6	7.8	20.1	48.7	61.2	72.2	80.1	86.8
Millions								
U.S. Population[a]	186	210	230	254	263	274	277	280
Billions of Dollars								
Gross Domestic Product[b]	$526	$1,038	$2,788	$5,801	$6,667	$8,332	$8,794	$9,354
Per Capita Amount in Dollars								
National Health Expenditures	$147	$356	$1,110	$2,853	$3,502	$4,166	$4,362	$4,599
Health Consumption Expenditure	133	319	1,022	2,661	3,269	3,902	4,073	4,289
Personal Health care	125	300	942	2,430	2,969	3,553	3,712	3,891
Admin and Net Cost of PHI	6	12	52	153	199	222	226	252
Public Health	2	6	28	79	102	127	135	146
Investment	14	37	87	192	233	263	289	310
Percent Distribution								
National Health Expenditures	100	100	100	100	100	100	100	100
Health Consumption Expenditure	90.6	89.6	92.1	93.3	93.4	93.7	93.4	93.3
Personal Health care	85.4	84.3	84.9	85.2	84.8	85.3	85.1	84.6
Admin and Net Cost of PHI	3.9	3.5	4.7	5.4	5.7	5.3	5.2	5.5
Public Health	1.4	1.8	2.5	2.8	2.9	3	3.1	3.2
Investment	9.4	10.4	7.9	6.7	6.6	6.3	6.6	6.7
Percent of Gross Domestic Product								
National Health Expenditures	5.2	7.2	9.2	12.5	13.8	13.7	13.7	13.8
Average Annual Percent Growth From Previous Year Shown								
National Health Expenditures		10.6	13.1	11	8.4	5.5	5.8	6.5
Health Consumption Expenditure		10.5	13.4	11.1	8.4	5.6	5.4	6.3
Personal Health Care		10.4	13.2	11	8.2	5.7	5.5	5.9
Admin and Net Cost of PHI		9.4	16.4	12.4	10.6	3.9	3	12.3
Public Health		13.8	16.9	12	10.2	6.8	7.5	8.8
Investment		11.7	10	9.2	7.9	4.2	11	8.4
U.S. Population[a]		1.2	0.9	1	1.2	1	1	1
Gross Domestic Product[b]		7	10.4	7.6	4.8	5.7	5.5	6.4

[a]Census resident-based population less armed forces overseas and population of outlying areas.
Source: U.S. Bureau of the Census.
[b]U.S. Department of Commerce, Bureau of Economic Analysis.
Note: Numbers and percents may not add to totals because of rounding. Dollar amounts shown are in current dollars.
Source: Centers for Medicare and Medicaid Services (2012a; 2012b), Office of the Actuary, National Health Statistics Group; U.S. Department of Commerce, Bureau of Economic Analysis; and U.S. Bureau of the Census.

2000	2001	2002	2003	2004	2005	2006	2007	2008	2009
$1,378.0	$1,495.3	$1,637.0	$1,772.2	$1,894.7	$2,021.0	$2,152.1	$2,283.5	$2,391.4	$2,486.3
1,288.5	1,401.4	1,531.6	1,658.2	1,772.9	1,890.3	2,016.9	2,135.1	2,234.2	2,330.1
1,164.4	1,264.1	1,371.6	1,479.0	1,585.0	1,692.6	1,798.8	1,904.3	1,997.2	2,089.9
81.1	89.8	108.1	125.5	133.9	141.6	155.5	162	164	163
43	47.5	51.9	53.7	54	56.2	62.6	68.8	72.9	77.2
89.6	94	105.4	114	121.8	130.7	135.2	148.4	157.2	156.2
283	285	288	291	293	296	299	302	305	307
$9,952	$10,286	$10,642	$11,142	$11,868	$12,638	$13,399	$14,062	$14,369	$14,119
$4,878	$5,240	$5,682	$6,098	$6,458	$6,827	$7,198	$7,561	$7,845	$8,086
4,561	4,911	5,316	5,706	6,043	6,385	6,746	7,069	7,329	7,578
4,122	4,430	4,761	5,089	5,402	5,717	6,016	6,305	6,552	6,797
287	315	375	432	456	478	520	536	538	530
152	166	180	185	184	190	209	228	239	251
317	329	366	392	415	441	452	491	516	508
100	100	100	100	100	100	100	100	100	100
93.5	93.7	93.6	93.6	93.6	93.5	93.7	93.5	93.4	93.7
84.5	84.5	83.8	83.5	83.7	83.7	83.6	83.4	83.5	84.1
5.9	6	6.6	7.1	7.1	7	7.2	7.1	6.9	6.6
3.1	3.2	3.2	3	2.8	2.8	2.9	3	3.1	3.1
6.5	6.3	6.4	6.4	6.4	6.5	6.3	6.5	6.6	6.3
13.8	14.5	15.4	15.9	16	16	16.1	16.2	16.6	17.6
7.1	8.5	9.5	8.3	6.9	6.7	6.5	6.1	4.7	4
7.4	8.8	9.3	8.3	6.9	6.6	6.7	5.9	4.6	4.3
6.9	8.6	8.5	7.8	7.2	6.8	6.3	5.9	4.9	4.6
15.1	10.7	20.4	16.1	6.7	5.7	9.9	4.2	1.3	-0.6
5.5	10.4	9.2	3.6	0.5	4.1	11.4	9.9	6	5.9
3.1	4.9	12.2	8.2	6.8	7.3	3.4	9.8	6	-0.6
1	1	1	0.9	0.9	0.9	1	1	0.9	0.9
6.4	3.4	3.5	4.7	6.5	6.5	6	4.9	2.2	-1.7

cost of providing care. Anyone responsible for payment of a health care cost other than the patient (or the patient's family) or the provider is a third-party payer. Third-party payers include the patient's or their relative's employer, private insurance or managed-care organization (MCO) engaged by the patient or another party, charity organizations, and federal, state, and local governments. In many cases, several of these parties—patient, provider, and third-party payers—come together to pay a single bill. To use a typical example, a child might visit a pediatrician who would then receive a small "copay" from the mother ("out-of-pocket") during the visit. Then the pediatrician's office would bill a private insurance firm (perhaps an MCO contracted by the father's employer), which would pay some or the remainder of the bill. If the pediatrician is not fully reimbursed by the third-party payer, he or she would absorb the unpaid balance as charity care or forgiven debts. Very complicated relationships can enjoin three or more payers.

In the United States, payers are generally categorized as private or public. Within the private sector, private health insurance companies and out-of-pocket expenditures are primary. Within the public sector, federal, state, and local governments all provide funding for health care. The public sector may act as a provider of services or as a third-party payer. For example, some health care programs are operated and paid for directly by the government: the federal Department of Veterans Affairs health care system, state mental hospitals, and public general hospitals operated by local governments. These are all supported mainly by tax revenues. On the other hand, the Medicare program acts as a third-party payer in that it does not provide services, but only the money to pay for health services supplied by hospitals, physicians, and others.

Traditionally, for many patients, health care has been provided under a direct, private (usually unwritten) contract between themselves and the provider of care. But that care is usually paid for by a third-party payer as defined previously. This system has been further complicated by the development of managed care. Patient care is still paid for by a third party, but the patient now has a written contract with the MCO, not the physician, describing in detail what care he or she will be entitled to under what circumstances, delivered by whom, in return for the payment made to the MCO, usually by the patient's employer. This written contract with the payer replaces the old unwritten contract with the provider. Among other things, this change in contract type has had a major impact on just who is ultimately in charge of patient care decisions.

Private Health Insurance

The history of private health insurers[2] and the rise of managed care are discussed in more detail in Chapter 7, whereas the current and historical financial involvement of the private health insurers will be briefly examined here. The salient feature of private insurance in the United States is that most people obtain it through their employer (or spouse's or parent's employer). One can almost say that employers (and employees, through their contributions to health insurance premiums) are the true payers in this case and that private insurance companies are the administrators of payments. Outside of employer-sponsored plans, private health insurance can be difficult to obtain because of the inherent problems of moral hazard and asymmetries of information discussed earlier. For example, a "Standard Individual (not part of a group plan) Point of Service" insurance plan to cover a family starts at more than $4,500 per month with some options exceeding $8,000 per month in New York County, even though the benefits are not more generous than a typical employer plan, which would cost far less to the same family (NYSDFS, 2012).

About 64% of Americans have some type of private health insurance coverage (U.S. Census Bureau, 2011, Table 155). This is a decrease from 73% in 1990. Generally speaking, insurance companies are either for-profit or non-profit. BlueCross BlueShield (BCBS) has been a major private health insurer since 1929. According to the BlueCross BlueShield Association by 2010 there were 38 affiliates throughout the United States and 100,000 persons enrolled system-wide. In 2005, BlueCross BlueShield launched two programs aimed at increasing information transparency among providers, consumers, and employers—Blue Health Intelligence (BHI) and Blue Distinctions (BCBS, 2012).

Originally, BCBS was entirely nonprofit, although a move to convert to for-profit status began for some BCBS companies in the mid-1990s (Cunningham & Sherlock, 2002). The commercial insurance companies such as Metropolitan Life and Aetna, either independently or in partnership with an MCO, have always operated on a for-profit basis only. Some of their surplus of income over expenditures is paid to the owners of the company as profit.

The private sector—through health insurance companies, out-of-pocket payments, and other sources—paid for about 51% of national health care consumption in 2009, down from about 60% in 1990. Private health insurance companies alone paid for about 34% of national health care consumption in 2009. In 1970, this percentage had been about 23% and then slowly started to rise until it reached 34% in 1990, after which it stayed roughly constant (see Table 5.2).

Out-of-Pocket Expenditures

Out-of-pocket expenditures include direct payments to providers for noninsured services, extra payments to providers of insurance-covered or managed care-covered services that bill at an amount higher than the insurance/managed care company pays for that service, and deductibles and coinsurance on health insurance/managed care benefits.

A deductible is a flat amount; for example, $200 per individual or $500 per family, that a health care beneficiary must pay out-of-pocket before the insurance company will begin paying for any health services received during some time period (usually a calendar year). Coinsurance is a share for example, 20% of the payment for each service covered by insurance for which the beneficiary is responsible.

Under managed care, beneficiaries receiving health services from a provider of their choice within the plan (a so-called point-of-service arrangement) or out-of-plan entirely will usually pay for some or all of the excess charges out-of-pocket. Today, however, there are an increasing number of "luxury" MCO plans, available at an extra cost above that normally borne by the beneficiary's employer. They provide for unfettered patient choice of physician, without prior authorization and without additional payment beyond the usual deductible or coinsurance.

Out-of-pocket expenditures accounted for about 13% of national health care consumption in 2009. This is down from over 16% in 2000, nearly 25% in 1980, and over 50% in 1960 (see Table 5.2).

Government Spending

Government spending has accounted for an increasing proportion of the health care dollar since 1960 (see Table 5.3). At that time, 5 years before Congress enacted the Medicare and Medicaid programs, the government's share was about 23% of the total. By 1970, it was 37% and by 1980 it was almost 42%. In 2009, local, state, and federal programs covered about 49% of national health care consumption. The vast majority is through the Medicare and Medicaid programs (see Table 5.2).

Medicare[3]

The first national social insurance program to finance medical care in the United States was established by Congress in 1965 as part of President Lyndon Johnson's "Great Society" program. Called Medicare, it is authorized by Title XVIII of the Social Security Act (Hoffman, Schoen, & Rowland, 2001; Igelhart, 1999c; Moon, 2001). Originally, it provided payment for some health services for persons 65 years of age and older who were eligible for Social Security or Railroad Retirement benefits, whether they took them or not. In 1973, its coverage was broadened to include those permanently disabled workers and their dependents who were eligible for old age, survivors', and disability insurance under Social Security, as well as persons with end-stage renal disease.

Medicare has four parts: hospital insurance (Part A), which also covers skilled nursing facility care on a very limited basis, as well as hospice and home health care; supplementary medical insurance (Part B), which covers physician and certain other health professional services, hospital outpatient care, and certain other services; Medicare + Choice (Part C), which permits Medicare beneficiaries to enroll in MCOs; and Medicare Prescription Drug Coverage (Part D), which was designed to lower the

Table 5.2   National Health Consumption by Source of Funds for Selected Years from 1960 to 2009

ROW LABELS	SUM OF 2009	SUM OF 2000	SUM OF 1990	SUM OF 1980	SUM OF 1970	SUM OF 1960
Medicare/ Medicaid/ CHIP	$887,348	$427,856	$183,843	$63,420	$12,962	$0
Medicaid (Title XIX)	$373,941	$200,481	$73,661	$26,033	$5,290	$0
Federal	$246,984	$116,918	$42,607	$14,521	$2,842	$0
State and Local	$126,957	$83,563	$31,054	$11,511	$2,447	$0
Medicare	$502,289	$224,360	$110,182	$37,387	$7,673	$0
Federal	$502,289	$224,360	$110,182	$37,387	$7,673	$0
Total CHIP (Title XIX and Title XXI)	$11,118	$3,015	$0	$0	$0	$0
Federal	$7,822	$2,100	$0	$0	$0	$0
State and Local	$3,296	$916	$0	$0	$0	$0
Private Health Insurance	$801,190	$458,191	$233,944	$69,048	$15,428	$5,780
Out-of-Pocket	$299,345	$202,117	$138,795	$58,414	$24,982	$13,038
Other Federal/ State/Local	$176,709	$96,354	$67,034	$28,824	$10,612	$5,218
Other Private	$88,259	$60,941	$31,724	$9,430	$1,700	$374
Public Health Activity (Gov't)	$77,213	$43,000	$19,996	$6,445	$1,356	$371
Grand Total	$2,330,064	$1,288,459	$675,336	$235,581	$67,040	$24,780

Source: Adapted from CMS (2012b).

costs of prescription medication for Medicare beneficiaries. Medicare Part A is funded primarily from Social Security taxes, whereas about two-thirds of Part B is funded from general revenues, with the balance coming from enrollee premium payments. Medicare prescription drug coverage is funded through premiums.

Medicare is operated by the Centers for Medicare and Medicaid Services (CMS, formerly called the Health Care Financing Administration) of the U.S. Department of Health and Human Services. Its administrative costs are remarkably low compared to those of the private health insurance sector, ranging from 1% to 2% (Hoffman, Klees, & Curtis, 2000, p. 11).

Medicare Part D, which was part of the Medicare Prescription Drug Improvement and Modernization Act (MMA) of 2003, began on January 1, 2006. Part D provides eligible patients with prescription drug benefits,

Table 5.3   National Health Expenditure by Type of Expenditure for Selected Years from 1960 to 2009

TYPE OF EXPENDITURE	SUM OF 2009	SUM OF 2000	SUM OF 1990	SUM OF 1980	SUM OF 1970	SUM OF 1960
Hospital Care	$759,074	$415,530	$250,439	$100,517	$27,168	$8,985
Physician and Clinical	$505,888	$290,019	$158,950	$47,715	$14,337	$5,640
Prescription Drugs	$249,904	$120,897	$40,290	$12,049	$5,497	$2,676
Nursing Home and Home Health Care	$205,234	$117,545	$57,457	$17,648	$4,253	$867
Administration (Government and Private)	$162,989	$81,064	$38,741	$12,033	$2,626	$1,067
Research and Investment	$156,230	$89,564	$48,687	$20,103	$7,783	$2,566
Other Health, Residential, and Personal Care	$122,623	$64,703	$24,322	$8,507	$1,331	$451
Dental Services	$102,222	$62,012	$31,521	$13,333	$4,675	$1,964
Other Medical Products	$78,137	$56,676	$36,211	$13,855	$5,072	$2,366
Public Health Activity	$77,213	$43,000	$19,996	$6,445	$1,356	$371
Other Professional Services	$66,781	$37,015	$17,408	$3,478	$726	$392
Grand Total	$2,486,293	$1,378,023	$724,023	$255,683	$74,823	$27,346

Source: Adapted from CMS (2012b).

designed to reduce the cost of medications. Coverage is provided through private entities, both stand-alone prescription drug plans (PDPs) and the more comprehensive Medicare Advantage (MA) plans. The financial risk of the program is shared by both private entities and the government.

Enrollment into Medicare Part D is voluntary for those who did not previously receive drug coverage through Medicaid. The population subset that is eligible for both Medicaid and Medicare is known as "dual eligibles." Before 2006, their drug coverage was provided by the Medicaid program. In the beginning, beneficiaries had the option to choose which plan best suited their needs. Later, they were automatically enrolled in what the government decided was the appropriate plan.

For those not covered under dual-eligible status, there is a monthly premium, estimated to be $35 in 2006. This premium is in addition to the annual premium for Medicare Part B (about $420). Under the plan's current structure, there is a $250 deductible to be paid by the individual. After the deductible is paid, Medicare pays 75% of prescription drug costs, up to $2,250 in total drug costs. Between $2,250 and $5,100, Medicare Part D provides no coverage. This gap in coverage is known as the "doughnut hole." After the gap, Medicare pays 95% of drug costs. In every category, the individual is expected to pay the remaining portion of costs, either out-of-pocket or through additional private insurance coverage. The deductibles, premiums, and limits will increase annually (Burns, Glaun, & Lipschutz, 2005).

Most Medicare beneficiaries use providers of their choice. Physicians are paid on a fee-for-service basis, according to a fee schedule constructed on the so-called resource-based relative value system (RBRVS). In the mid-1980s, it replaced the old inflation-stimulating "usual and customary fee" system. Because the "usual and customary fees" were set by the physicians themselves, the inflation factor was built in.

Unfortunately, as payments to physicians began to decline in the early 2000s as a result of the federal Balanced Budget Amendment (BBA) of 1998, an increasing number of physicians refused to accept Medicare fees as payment in full. In this instance, the physician sees only those Medicare patients who agree to accept responsibility for the total charges and then submit the bill to the Medicare program to obtain whatever reimbursement they can.

Hospitals are reimbursed on an episode-of-care basis, the amount of payment for each case determined by a formula based on a fiscal construct called the Diagnosis-Related Group (DRG), one form of the prospective payment system (PPS). Managed care was introduced into the Medicare program in the mid-1990s (Himmelstein & Woolhandler, 2001, chapter 5; Zarabozo, Taylor, & Hicks, 1996). However, MCOs claimed that Medicare reimbursement levels were too low (Moon, 2001), and, as a result, they dumped almost 1 million beneficiaries on January 1, 2001.

In 2009, total Medicare expenditures were over $502 billion (see Table 5.2), covering some of the health care costs for about 46 million enrollees, up from $224 billion for almost 40 million beneficiaries in 2000. In 1998, although about 75% of Medicare enrollees incurred some expenses, about 50% of the total paid for care went to only 6% of beneficiaries who received care (Hoffman et al., 2001, pp. 32, 93). Medicare financed 32% of all spending for hospital care and 22% of physician services costs (Hoffman et al., 2001, Tables 2 and 3). As noted by Meier and Morrison (2002), "In 2002, 50 percent of deaths of Medicare beneficiaries occurred in hospitals, often after stays in intensive care units, visits to multiple physicians in the months before death, and enormous expenditures for treatments intended to prolong life" (p. 1087).

Looking toward the mid-21st century, the Medicare program is seriously in need of rescue and reform (Igelhart, 1999c; Moon, 2001). The "baby boomers"—those people born in the immediate post–World War II era—became eligible for Medicare starting in 2010, whereas the number of working people available to finance the system through the payroll tax that presently supports it will, in relative terms, continue to decline. Medicare covers that part of the population that requires the most medical services (i.e., the elderly), but it is financed narrowly by the limited payroll tax.

Medicaid

Along with Medicare, Congress created the Medicaid program in 1965, authorized by Title XIX of the Social Security Act (Hoffman et al., 2001; Igelhart, 1999b; Rosenbaum, 2002). Medicaid is a needs-based program that provides coverage for some health services for some of the poor on a "means-tested" basis. Therefore, to receive Medicaid coverage, unlike Medicare coverage, a person must apply for it. Also, in contrast to Medicare, the Medicaid program then applies a series of income-level determinations to each applicant, thus "testing their means." Only those persons whose incomes and other assets fall below a certain level as specified by law or regulation (varying from state to state) are declared eligible for coverage.

Medicaid is supported by federal and state tax levy funds and is administered by the states. Each state program is distinct and unique. Therefore, benefits and coverage vary widely from state to state. Like Medicare, Medicaid generally reimburses providers on a fee-for-service/episode-of-care basis, although in the mid-1990s managed care was introduced into the Medicaid program, as it was to Medicare, and each year the proportion of fee-for-service beneficiaries has been declining.

Title XIX, as amended, requires a state to provide a set of 14 services in order to be eligible to receive federal funds for its program, with a very complicated set of requirements governing just who may be considered eligible for Medicaid and who may not. The 1996 Welfare Reform Act has had a major impact on Medicaid because of its elimination of the Aid to Families with Dependent Children (AFDC) program; the principal welfare program in the United States since the time of the New Deal.

A combination of low income eligibility requirements and low fees paid to providers (many of whom have therefore chosen not to participate) has led to very limited coverage in many states. A few of the wealthier states now provide Medicaid coverage for the *medically indigent*. These are persons in an income range deemed not to be low enough to qualify them by income, but low enough to make paying for health services a heavy burden.

Some states (e.g., New York) allow elderly persons with assets to divest themselves of those assets by passing them on to their children over a period of time. They can thus artificially "spend down" (by this divestiture to family members) to the stipulated Medicaid-eligible income and assets levels without actually spending the money to pay for care. Of course, this means that the taxpayers of the state pick up the costs of care of a person otherwise ineligible for Medicaid.

It is interesting to note that in 2007, whereas 50% of Medicaid beneficiaries were children and 25% were nonelderly, nondisabled adults (most of them the mothers of the covered children), about 67% of all Medicaid expenditures were for the benefit of the aged (25%) and the disabled (42%) (Kaiser Family Foundation, 2010). Eligible elderly accounted for 10% of Medicaid beneficiaries, and eligible disabled accounted for 15%. In 2009, Medicaid covered about 16% of all personal health care spending, with over 50 million people receiving some kind of Medicaid coverage (see Table 5.2).

Children's Health Insurance Program

Created as the State Children's Health Insurance Program (SCHIP) by the Clinton Administration's Balanced Budget Act (BBA) of 1997, the Children's Health Insurance Program provides health coverage for uninsured children who are not eligible for Medicaid. It is jointly financed by the federal and state governments and administered by the states. Within broad federal guidelines, each state determines the design of its program, eligibility groups, benefit packages, payment levels for coverage, and administrative and operating procedures. SCHIP provides a capped amount of funds to states on a matching basis for federal fiscal years (FY) 1998 through 2007. Federal payments to states are based on state expenditures under approved plans. "Though an optional program, all states expanded coverage under SCHIP, with an estimated 6.7 million children and 700,000 adults enrolled in SCHIP at some point during 2006" (Urban Institute, 2010).

Other Government Programs

Among other major government health programs are, at the federal level, those offered through the Department of Defense, the Department of Veterans Affairs, and the National Institutes of Health (the federal government's major biomedical research arm); at the state level, the state public health and mental hospital services; and, at the local level, the local public general hospitals and local public health services.

These government programs are paid for primarily with broad-based tax levy funds. Together, they consume a relatively small proportion of the national health care budget. For example, in 2009, national expenditures on public health services accounted for about 3.1% of the total (see Table 5.1). By way of comparison, payments for program administration and the net cost of private insurance (administration and profit) together were more than twice as much as expenditures for public health services.

Changes in Government Health Programs
Due to the Obama Health Plan

The Patient Protection and Affordable Care Act of 2010 will be discussed in Chapter 8. However, it will bring changes to the government programs discussed here. For one, it will effect a major expansion of Medicaid, beginning in 2014. Further, it will change some of the reimbursement aspects of Medicare. Also, it will expand care for children:

> Health reform is expected to have a number of positive effects on the lives of children age 18 and under. More children are expected to have health insurance coverage under reform, which in turn should increase their receipt of needed health care and ultimately improve their health and functioning. The single most important way that the estimated seven to eight million uninsured children will gain coverage under health care reform is likely to be through increases in coverage through Medicaid and the Children's Health Insurance Program (CHIP) among the children who are already eligible for coverage under those two programs. (Kenney & Pelletier, 2010)

WHERE THE MONEY GOES

NHE are calculated by the CMS, Office of the Actuary, National Health Statistics Group (CMS, 2011a). NHE comprise the following two major categories: (a) Health Consumption and (b) Investments, a category made up of Research and Structures and Equipment. Most expenditures fall within Health Consumption, and most of these are for personal health care (hospital care; physician and other professional services including dentistry; nursing home and home health care; and medical products including prescription drugs and durable medical equipment). Complementary and alternative medicine (CAM) is included under Other Professional and Personal Health Care Services, and vitamins, supplements, and minerals are included under Other Medical Products. The other two categories within Health Consumption are: (a) Government Administration and Net Cost of Private Health Insurance; and (b) Government Public Health Activities. NHE does not include expenditures for a much broader definition of health care that might include (nonmedically supervised) dieting and weight loss, health and fitness clubs, sporting goods and related recreation, and healthy foods.

How does the United States spend its health care dollars? In 2009, 93.7% of NHE were for Health Consumption, while the remaining 6.4%

was directed to research and investment. Within Health Consumption about 90% paid for Personal Health Care, 7% for Government Administration and Net Cost of Private Health Insurance, and about 3% for Government Public Health Activities. Of the major groups within Personal Health Care, hospital care accounted for 31% of NHE, physician and clinical services for 20%, prescriptions drugs 10%, and nursing home and home health care accounted for 8% (see Table 5.1 and Figure 5.1).

How are NHE allocated by health condition and characteristics of patients? Through its Medical Expenditure Panel Survey (MEPS) program, the Agency for Healthcare Research and Quality (AHRQ) maintains the most complete source of data on the cost and use of health care and health insurance coverage.[4] Through large-scale surveys of families and individuals, their medical providers (doctors, hospitals, pharmacies, etc.), and employers across the United States, MEPS collects data on the specific health services that Americans use, how frequently they use them, the cost of these services, and how they are paid for, as well as data on the cost, scope, and breadth of health insurance held by and available to U.S. workers (AHRQ, 2012).

Ranked by expenditure, in 2008 the top 12 diseases or conditions accounted for 54% of MEPS-captured spending (Center for Financing,

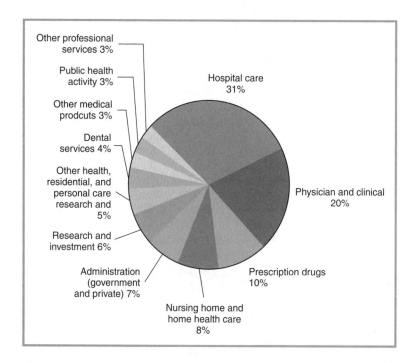

Figure 5.1 National health expenditures, 2009.

Access, and Cost Trends, 2008). It should be emphasized that different (e.g., broader or narrower) categorizations of disease may produce different rankings (see Figure 5.2).

Figure 5.3 charts expenditures by age and sex in 2008 and confirms what many would expect: older people use more health care than younger people, on average. For men, expenditures drop after age 18, while it starts to rise for women. Then after age 35, expenditures start to rise for men,

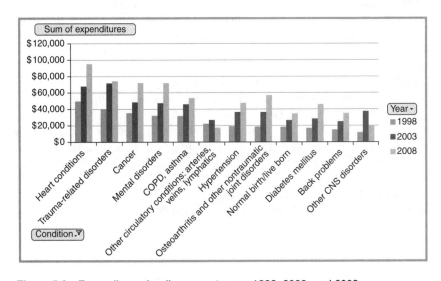

Figure 5.2   Expenditures by disease category, 1998, 2003, and 2008.

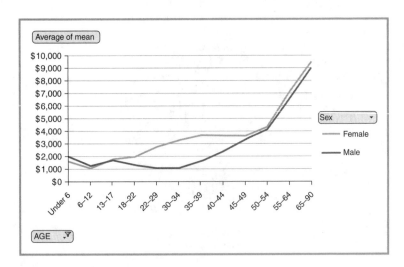

Figure 5.3   Mean medical expenditures by age and sex, 2008.

Source: Adapted from Agency for Healthcare Research and Quality (2012).

catching up to women by 49, after which expenditures for both men and women start to rise rapidly with age.

Figure 5.4 indicates that health care spending is highly concentrated in the population. In 2002, half the population accounted for only 3% of total health care spending. Five percent of people accounted for 49% of spending and 1% accounted for 22% of expenditures (Stanton & Rutherford, 2006). Or, to put it another way, for every $100 spent by someone in the bottom half, someone in the top 1% spent more than $35,000.

Roughly a quarter of this small group remained in the top 1% of health care expenditures in 2003, and clearly, 75% did not.[5] Of the people who were in the top half of expenditures in 2002, most remained in the top half the following year (see Figure 5.5). Mirroring this, most of the people who were in the bottom half of expenditures in 2002 remained in the bottom half the following year. The implication is that there is both a strong chronic and episodic utilization of health care. High or low use in one year is a strong predictor of similar use in the next. However, even over short periods of time, a sizable segment of the population moves between percentiles.

Although numerous studies advise of the relatively significant resources spent during the last year of life—and even more during the last 6 months—Ezekiel J. Emanuel and Linda L. Emanuel (1994) argue:

> Cost savings due to changes in practice at the end of life are not likely to be substantial. The amount that might be saved by reducing the use of aggressive life-sustaining interventions for dying patients is at most 3.3 percent of total national health care expenditures.

They also assert that these savings "would not restrain the rate of growth in health care spending over time. Instead, this amount represents a fraction of the increase due to inflation in health care costs and less than (the amount) needed to cover the uninsured population" (p. 543). Accepting

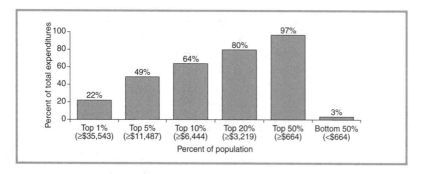

Figure 5.4   Concentration of expenditures, 2002.

Source: Reprinted with permission from Cohen & Yu (2006).

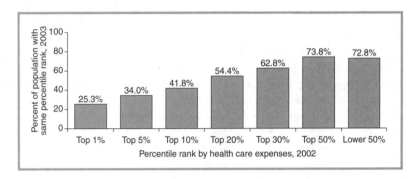

Figure 5.5   Persistence in the level of health care expenditures, U.S. civilian non-institutionalized population, 2005 to 2006.

Source: Reprinted with permission from Cohen & Yu (2006).

this, we cannot assume that less aggressive care at the end of life will solve the financial problems of the health care system.

HOW THE MONEY IS PAID: PROVIDERS, PAYERS, AND PAYMENTS

Provider Payment Approaches

In the health care market, professional services from physicians, therapists, dentists, and so forth accounted for 27% of NHE in 2009. These providers are also considered to drive the utilization of much of the remainder of NHE, including hospital care, nursing home and home health care, prescription drugs, and medical equipment, devices, and supplies. Prescription drugs and other medical products are also markets with their own dynamics, but this discussion focuses on how the services of health care providers and institutions (e.g., hospitals, nursing homes) are paid.

In general, there are six payment modes that people and organizations use to buy and sell services. These are cost/cost-plus, hourly or time and materials, fee-for-service, fixed-price, capitation, and value. We will discuss each in relationship to the provision of personal health care services.

Cost/Cost-Plus

Reimbursement is how hospitals describe payment received for services they have already provided. Under a cost payment method, the organization providing the service tracks all costs associated with each customer and then asks to be paid that amount. This is similar to how an employee might be reimbursed for expenses incurred during a business trip. The employee would offer receipts for plane fare, hotel, food, and other allowable items and then expect to receive exactly that amount in return. An indemnity plan is one under which the covered party is reimbursed for all expenses he or she incurs.

An organization is often paid on a cost-plus basis (so-called because a contract specifies that the organization will be reimbursed for actual costs plus an additional percentage of those costs). The cost-plus method provides an additional margin out of which the providing organization can generate profit after any nonproject expenses are paid.

In practice, no independent entity can be paid in a cost-only manner. Of course, a profit-generating organization will never survive under a pure cost-only reimbursement model, but even nonprofits need more than cost reimbursement to survive. Under any contract there are nonreimbursable expenses, and every significant organization has expenses that are not specific to one project. The margin allowed on the cost-plus project is what an organization draws from to pay these expenses.

Some people like cost-plus contracts because they provide high levels of transparency and seem to limit profits. However, there are drawbacks. These bills are often so detailed that the payer can understand only the bottom line.[6] In practice, what is reimbursable, as well as ceilings and thresholds on the amounts, must be set. Accounting for utilization of shares of resources can be complicated, and approaches must be agreed on. In addition, cost-plus contracting does not reward the organization, in this case the health care provider, for either better quality or finding new ways to provide services more cheaply. In a true cost-plus system, the contract penalizes the providing organization for cutting costs.

Time and Materials

The hourly payment method, common in service industries, is often referred to as *time and materials*. In this case, a provider would be charged a fixed hourly rate covering all the costs except agreed-on materials, which would be billed as incurred. For example, a residential electrician might pass along all costs for fixtures and breakers and charge $85 per hour for his time, which then must cover his vehicle, all his tools, any assistants he might employ, and so forth. Time and materials tends to be the system of choice in cases where the scope of work is not clear to either party. Per diem (by the day) reimbursement remains a very common payment method for hospitals (Kaiser Family Foundation, 2002). Although such a system encourages the hospital to work hard to minimize overhead expenses, payers will always worry that the hospital is not looking for ways to increase efficiency.

Fee-for-Service

The fee-for-service method is common when the scope of work is clear to both sides. It is the oldest form of payment for health services and the predominant system of paying physicians, dentists, and private providers in the Other Professional Services category of the NHE. For example, a dentist will typically have a set price for a cleaning and checkup. If additional services are needed, those will be performed at essentially published prices. In such a system, the risk of inefficiency is borne by the provider and the risk of bad advice is borne by the customer. Whether a root canal requires 1 hour or 2 hours to perform and whether or not a root canal is the best use of the patient's money, the dentist receives the same payment. The local market and the dentist's reputation drive the rates he or she can charge.

According to some observers (Jonas, 1978; Roemer, 1962), in the past this piecework system was a major cause of many of the observed problems in the health care delivery system. Although the patient's risk that he or she overpays for a service is reduced, such systems do not reward the providers for better quality service. Nor do they reward the provider for steering the patient toward more efficient services. A frequent complaint is that preventive medicine is completely ignored (Lown, 1998; Medical Reform Group of Ontario, 1980).

Fixed-Price

A service is called *productized* when it can be marketed or sold as a commodity, which implies that a fixed price will buy a known quantity of that service. Critically, the known quantity is a customer-centric outcome (or in the case of health care, treatment of a disease or condition on a per-episode basis). This can be compared with the provider-centric fee-for-service system, which focuses on what the provider does, whereas a fixed-price, productized approach is nominally focused on the condition presented by the patient.

The PPS was adopted for Medicare by the federal government in 1983 for Medicare Part A benefits (i.e., payments to hospitals) as a way to control costs. It can be seen as forcing productization on the hospitals—at least with respect to the patients covered by Medicare. With PPS, the hospital is paid a predetermined rate for each Medicare patient based on the patient's presenting condition. Each patient is classified into a DRG, a preset list created by the CMS. Except for certain extremely high-cost patients, the hospital receives a flat rate for the DRG, regardless of the volume of actual services provided to a patient.

In such a system the provider is rewarded for how efficiently the patient is treated. Quality is emphasized to the extent that it affects the efficiency of the treatments for the initial diagnosis. The negative side of this type of system is that it intrinsically rewards providers who exaggerate the reported severity of the diagnosis, because disease classification determines the amount of payment that will be received. Since patients are classified by the same organizations that treat them, there can be what is called "up-coding." Also, providers are rewarded for attracting or seeking healthier patients (who otherwise tend to heal faster than sicker ones) and preventive medicine tends to remain a low priority.

Capitation

Capitation is a fixed prepayment per person to the health care provider for an agreed-on array of services. The payment is the same no matter how many services or what type of services each patient actually gets. In theory, such a system encourages the selection of the least expensive treatments as well as promotes services likely to result in the lowest overall cost during the contract period. However, such a system has no reinforcement for promoting the long-term health of the patient. With capitation, providers are likely to be rewarded for enrolling patients least likely to consume many health services, that is, the healthy.

One can also see *global budgeting* (a payment method common to government-run facilities) as a simplified form of capitation—one with only one payer. The provider receives a global budget, which must cover all costs of treatment needed by the eligible population. This is the common way of paying for Veterans Administration hospitals, state mental hospitals, and local health department clinics. In practice, a global budget model tends to resemble the cost model, as the budgets are often negotiated starting with the previous year's cost, and those in operational control are not usually rewarded for coming in under budget (in bureaucracies, coming in under budget is taken as a sign that the budget was set too high).

Value

Not frequently seen in health care services, *value-based compensation* is the payment model in which the performing organization is rewarded for the value delivered. Value-based systems are most often used when the value is easy to measure and indisputable. For example, personal injury lawyers often offer their services purely for a contingency fee because the value of the lawsuit proceeds is easy to measure.

One of the assumptions of market theory is that the buyer, in this case, the patient, has a sense of the value of what he or she is buying. As Arrow pointed out in 1963, the uncertainties surrounding medicine make it difficult for providers to know the real value of what they are providing and even more difficult for the patient, who is almost certainly at an information disadvantage relative to the provider. On the other hand, if patients started paying for care according to how much it was worth to them economically, the system would tend toward valuing the lives of wealthier people more highly, which most people would find unethical. Finally, in an emergency situation, a patient may not be able to value care until after the care is provided.

Risk Transfer and Good Intentions

The different payment models can be arranged along a continuum representing the financial risk borne by the buyer and the risk borne by the provider. If the payment model with which the patient pays is different from the payment model under which the provider operates (as is possible in a system with third-party payers such as the current U.S. health system), then the possible combinations can be represented as a matrix (see Figure 5.6).

With each combination, any risk not borne by the provider or patient is borne by the third-party payer. One could expect a third-party payer to

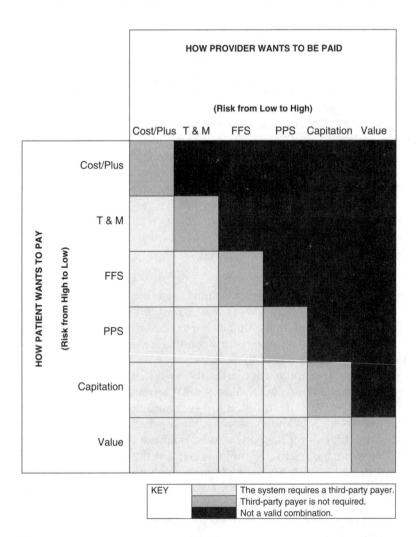

FIGURE 5.6 Provider and patient risk matrix.

react to this risk by excluding people or conditions, rejecting charges, capping fees, or otherwise capping coverage and raising premiums.

On the other hand, even when the payment methods match (e.g., the patient and the provider operate under a fee-for-service contract), either side may wish to use an intermediary. The introduction of health savings accounts (HSAs) has essentially created an opening for a different type of institution in health care that starts to resemble something like American Express as opposed to United Health. So one sees banks—experts in low-risk, high-volume transactions such as managing payments for product purchases—entering the health care market.

It should be noted that how we pay for health care has both short-term and long-term implications. The system of payment affects how the principals act in the system today, but also who and where the principals are tomorrow. There is no shortage of physicians in training who vie for residencies in dermatology or cosmetic surgery, but pediatrics is always in need. A simple capitation system will encourage physicians (and other providers) toward healthier patients. Similarly, a system rewarding outcomes may encourage physicians away from riskier cases. The challenge of rewarding for process consistency is that nearly all best practices are contraindicated in some populations.

Third-Party Payers

Insurance (Risk Management)

Who should pay for health care? As important as how we pay for health care is who controls the payments. Although ultimately all costs of health care are borne by the people, how the money gets from the people to the providers of goods (antibiotics, vitamins, wheelchairs, etc.) and services (physicians, hospitals, chiropractors) shapes the system. A system where people purchase directly from the providers, just as they purchase cars and hire mechanics, will be very different from one in which the people give their money to the government, which then maintains a health care system much like all governments maintain a military.

Although most people do not need very much health care in a given year, any significant health care incident is likely to be very expensive. Severe illness can easily cost tens of thousands of dollars, and heroic measures (e.g., trauma and organ transplants) can easily cost in the hundreds of thousands of dollars. Some rare conditions can even cost into the millions of dollars to treat (Thomas, 2006; Zhang, 2006). A health care condition requiring $500,000 in treatment would exceed the lifetime income of most people and would be financially devastating for all but a small percent of the population.

As noted earlier, whereas a significant number of people retain their health expenditure rank from year to year, a sizeable number do not.

Therefore, most people desire some sort of insurance to protect themselves against wild swings in health care costs. As Glied (2001) pointed out, people do not buy health insurance to insure their health, but rather to insure their ability to pay for (and obtain) health care in the event that their health status changes. Historically, health insurance was intended to cover major medical events (Dranove & Millenson, 2006).

Matching Different Provider and Patient Payment Approaches

The real motivation for having third-party payers is to bridge the gap between how people want to pay for health care and how third-party payers want to be paid. Although there is little need for a third-party payer in a case where a person wants to pay a fixed monthly amount for health care to a provider who is paid on a capitation basis and offers the entire range of medical services, in reality people do not usually have this option.

More often, people obtain their health care from a variety of providers who may be operating under any one of those aforementioned models, and quite often an individual provider will offer services under multiple and differing charging models. A third-party payer adds value by converting a stream of monthly payments into a stream of service-driven or ailment-driven payments to providers.

Maintaining a Network of Providers

To maintain this conversion, the third-party payer maintains a network of providers with which it has negotiated contracts. These contracts detail which payment models will be used and what rates will be used, as well as other details common to commercial contracts.

Price and Provider Expertise

With the most extensive databases of patient visits, especially over time, third-party payers have the benefit of expertise. The databases of third-party payers are a wellspring of information for longitudinal studies and better understanding of treatment options. Third-party payers deal with an array of providers daily. They know the going rate for a wide variety of procedures and consultations across geographic regions and quality tiers. They can conduct quantitative quality studies more easily than any other organization. Therefore, it is third-party payers who have the best chance of predicting which providers will offer a good outcome.

CONCLUSIONS

The United States spends more on health care than any other country in the world, both on a gross basis and on a per capita basis. Further, the United States has a uniquely complex financing and payment system (as demonstrated by the information in this chapter). As some have assessed, we creakily crank dollars through the system, which requires enormous amounts of eligibility determination, benefit checking, coinsurance/deductible calculation/billing/collection, preutilization authorization, utilization review, and so on (Himmelstein & Woolhandler, 2001). Mountains of paperwork are created, astronomical voice and fax/telephone costs are incurred, and untold amounts of computer time and space are used. Huge numbers of staff are required to carry out these activities.

In addition to the high cost of administration, the U.S. health care system still leaves many people without health insurance and, therefore, with reduced access to health care. In 2009, more than 50 million Americans had no health care coverage of any kind (U.S. Census Bureau, 2011, Table 155). This lack of health insurance has many negative consequences, ranging from personal anxiety, to increased use of emergency rooms (often meaning that care was deferred past the point where it might have been routine—and cheap—to where it was complex and expensive, with the delay leading to avoidable complications), to growing personal bankruptcy rates (Hoffman et al., 2001). This is projected to change under the Patient Protection and Affordable Care Act passed under President Obama in 2010. See Chapter 8 for a discussion.

In the next chapter, we discuss the performance—quality, equity, and efficiency—of the complex system that we have developed for providing health care in the United States. This is followed by chapters on the history of attempts to reform the system and projections about the future.

NOTES

1. Like all elements of the GDP, unpaid work is not counted. This is particularly significant in health care because most medical symptoms are self-diagnosed and treated (Dean, 1981). Additionally, it is very common for people to receive care from family and loved ones in the course of mild illness. When people stay home from work because of illness, the GDP is reduced. On the other hand, if those same people were taken care of by a paid caregiver, the GDP would increase.

2. A comprehensive overview of private health insurance is Gary Claxton's "How Private Insurance Works: A Primer," available from the Kaiser Family Foundation's website, www.kff.org.

3. An ongoing series of reports on, and guides to, the Medicare system are available from Medpac, the Medicare Payment Advisory Commission to the U.S. Congress, at www.medpac.gov.

4. The expenditures included in the MEPS survey are a subset of those included in the Personal Health Care component of the NHE. Although the sample of U.S. civilian non-institutionalized population surveyed in the Household Component of MEPS represents 98% of the U.S. population, the nature of the population excluded from the MEPS sample is such that they are likely to have very different health care expenditures. In addition, the NHE includes expenditures on nonpatient services (gift shops, cafeterias, etc.) as well as other expenditures not counted by MEPS (e.g., nonprescription nondurable goods

and CAM services). In 1996, the expenditures of MEPS Household Component made up about 60% of the Personal Health Care component of National Health Expenditures, and in 2003, MEPS accounted for $895.5 billion or slightly less than 62% of the estimated $1,446 billion spent on Personal Health Care. The authors strongly recommend that anyone planning to use either NHE or MEPS data for analysis or decision-making should supplement their understanding of the inclusions, exclusions, and limitations of such data with the article "Reconciling Medical Expenditure Estimates From the MEPS and the NHA," by Selden and colleagues (Selden et al., 2001).

5. The MEPS data also indicate that of the people who dropped out of the top percentiles of 2002, only a small percentage can be explained by death, institutionalization, or ineligibility in the following year (Cohen & Yu, 2006).

6. In health care, a cottage industry has formed around the interpretation of medical bills. For fees ranging between $50 and $250 per hour, *claims assistance* professionals or *health care advocates* will decipher bills, challenge errors, and negotiate discounts (Francis, 2006; Whitehouse, 2006).

REFERENCES

Agency for Healthcare Research and Quality (AHRQ). (2012). *Medical expenditure panel survey background.* Retrieved June 6, 2012, from http://meps.ahrq.gov/mepsweb/about_meps/survey_back.jsp

Agency for Healthcare Research and Quality (AHRQ). (2012). *Medical expenditure panel survey household component data.* 2008 Full Year Person-Level File. Released December 2010. (Generated using MEPSnet/HC). Retrieved June 6, 2012, from http://meps.ahrq.gov/mepsweb/data_stats/download_data_files.jsp

Arrow, K. J. (1963). Uncertainty and the welfare economics of medical care. *American Economic Review, 53*(5), 941–973.

Blue Cross Blue Shield Association (BCBS). (2012). *About the Blue Cross and Blue Shield Association.* Retrieved June 6, 2012, from http://www.bcbs.com/about-the-association

Burns, B., Glaun, K., & Lipschutz, D. (2005). *Consumers face inadequate protections concerning Medicare Part D. Enrollment and/or disenrollment problems.* California Health Advocates. Retrieved March 31, 2007, from www.cahealthadvocates.org/_pdf/advocacy/2006/Brief_Inadequate_P5.pdf

Center for Financing, Access, and Cost Trends. (2008). *Total expenses for conditions by site of service: United States, 2003: Medical expenditure panel survey component data.* Rockville, MD: Agency for Healthcare Research and Quality.

Centers for Medicare and Medicaid Services (CMS). (2012a). *NHE web tables.* Retrieved June 6, 2012, from https://www.cms.gov/Research-Statistics-Data-and-Systems/Statistics-Trends-and-Reports/NationalHealthExpendData/downloads/tables.pdf

Centers for Medicare and Medicaid Services (CMS). (2012b). *National health expenditures by type of service and source of funds, CY 1960–2009.* Retrieved January 2, 2012, from www.cms.gov/NationalHealthExpendData/downloads/nhe2009.zip

Cohen, S. B., & Yu, W. (2006). *The persistence in the level of health expenditures over time: Estimates for the U.S. population, 2002–2003* (Statistical Brief No. 124). Rockville, MD: Agency for Healthcare Research and Quality.

Cunningham, R., & Sherlock, D. B. (2002). Bounceback: Blues thrive as markets cool toward HMOs. *Health Affairs, 21*(1), 24–38.

Dean, K. (1981). Self-care responses to illness: A selected review. *Social Science & Medicine [A], 15*(5), 673–687.

Dranove, D., & Millenson, M. L. (2006). Medical bankruptcy: Myth versus fact. *Health Affairs, 25*(2), w74–w83.

Emanuel, E. J., & Emanuel, L. L. (1994). The economics of dying. The illusion of cost savings at the end of life. *New England Journal of Medicine, 330*(8), 540–544.

Francis, T. (2006, March 20). Escape from claims hell. *Wall Street Journal.*

Franks, P., Clancy, C. M., & Nutting, P. A. (1992). Gatekeeping revisited—protecting patients from overtreatment. *New England Journal of Medicine, 327*(6), 424–429.

Glied, S. A. (2001). Health insurance and market failure since Arrow. *Journal of Health Politics, Policy and Law, 26*(5), 957–965.

Himmelstein, D. U., & Woolhandler, S. (2001). *Bleeding the patient: The consequences of corporate health care.* Monroe, ME: Common Courage Press.

Hoffman, C., Schoen C., Rowland, D., & Davis, K. (2001). Gaps in health coverage among working-age Americans and the consequences. *Journal of Health Care for the Poor and Underserved, 12*(3), 272–289.

Hoffman, E. D., Klees, B. S., & Curtis, C. A. (2000). Overview of the Medicare and Medicaid programs. *Health Care Financing Review, Medicare and Medicaid Statistical Supplement,* 1–348.

Igelhart, J. K. (1999a). The American health care system: Expenditures. *New England Journal of Medicine, 340*(1), 70–76.

Igelhart, J. K. (1999b). The American health care system: Medicaid. *New England Journal of Medicine, 340*(5), 403–408.

Igelhart, J. K. (1999c). The American health care system: Medicare. *New England Journal of Medicine, 340*(4), 327–332.

Jonas, S. (1978). *Medical mystery: The training of doctors in the United States.* New York, NY: W.W. Norton.

Kaiser Family Foundation. (2010). *The Medicaid program at a glance.* Retrieved June 6, 2012, from http://www.kff.org/medicaid/upload/7235-04.pdf

Kaiser Family Foundation. (2002). *Trends and indicators in the changing health care marketplace. Section 6: Trends in health plan and provider relationships.* Retrieved March 1, 2007, from www.kff.org/insurance/7031/ti2004–6-set.cfm

Kenney, G. M., & Pelletier, J. (2010). *How will the Patient Protection and Affordable Care Act of 2010 affect children?* Washington, DC: Urban Institute. Retrieved January 29, 2012, from www.urban.org/uploadedpdf/412129-PPACA-affect-children.pdf

Lown, B. (1998). Physicians need to fight the business model of medicine. *Hippocrates, 12*(5), 25–28.

Medical Reform Group of Ontario. (1980). *The crisis in health care.* Toronto, Canada: Author.

Meier, D. E., & Morrison, R. S. (2002). Autonomy reconsidered. *New England Journal of Medicine, 346*(14), 1061–1066.

Moon, M. (2001). Health policy 2001: Medicare. *New England Journal of Medicine, 344*(12), 928–931.

New York State Department of Financial Services (NYSDFS). (2012). *Premium rates for standard individual health plans, January 2012.* Retrieved January 29, 2012, from www.dfs.ny.gov/insurance/hmorates/html/hmonewyo.htm

Organisation for Economic Cooperation and Development (OECD). (2011). *OECD Health Data 2011.* Retrieved January 2, 2011, from www.oecd.org/document/16/0,3343,en_264 9_34631_2085200_1_1_1_1,00.html

Roehrig, C. S., & Rousseau, D. M. (2011). The growth in cost per case explains far more of U.S. health spending increases than rising disease prevalence. *Health Affairs, 3*(9), 1657–1663.

Roemer, M. I. (1962, Spring). On paying the doctor and the implications of different methods. *Journal of Health and Human Behavior, 3*(1), 4–14.

Rosenbaum, S. (2002). Health policy report: Medicaid. *New England Journal of Medicine, 346*(8), 635–640.

Schroeder, S. A. (2001). Prospects for expanding health insurance coverage. *New England Journal of Medicine, 344*(11), 847–852.

Selden, T. M., Levit, K. R., Cohen, J. W., Zuvekas, S. H., Moeller, J. F., McKusick, D., & Arnett, A. H. (2001). Reconciling medical expenditure estimates from the MEPS and the NHA, 1996. *Health Care Financing Review, 23*(1), 161–178.

Stanton, M. W., & Rutherford, M. K. (2006). *The high concentration of U.S. health care expenditures*. Research in Action (Issue 19). Rockville, MD: Agency for Healthcare Research and Quality.

Thomas, R. (2006, November 23). Million dollar man: Life slowly returning to normal after struggle with tick bite. *Decatur (IL) Daily*.

Urban Institute. (2010). *State Children's Health Insurance Program (SCHIP)*. Retrieved January 29, 2012, from www.urban.org/health_policy/medicaid/medicaid-and-schip.cfm

U.S. Bureau of Economic Analysis. (2011). *Table 2.5.5. Personal consumption expenditures by type of expenditure*. Washington, DC: Bureau of Economics Analysis, U.S. Department of Commerce.

U.S. Bureau of Labor Statistics. (2006). Health care (NAICS 62, except 624). In *Career Guide to Industries, 2006–07 Edition* (pp. 231–237). Washington, DC: Bureau of Labor Statistics, U.S. Department of Labor.

U.S. Bureau of Labor Statistics. (2011). Healthcare. In *Career Guide to Industries, 2010–11 Edition*. Washington, DC: Bureau of Labor Statistics, U.S. Department of Labor. Retrieved January 2, 2012, from www.bls.gov/oco/cg/cgs035.htm

U.S. Census Bureau. (2011). *Statistical Abstract of the United States: 2012*. Washington, DC: U.S. Department of Commerce.

Whitehouse, K. (2006, January 1). How to fight overcharges. *Wall Street Journal*.

Zarabozo, C., Taylor, C., & Hicks, J. (1996). Medicaid managed care: Numbers and trends. *Health Care Financing Review, 17*(3), 243–246.

Zhang, J. (2006, December 5). Amid fight for life, a victim of lupus fights for insurance. *Wall Street Journal*.

SIX

Health Care System Performance

"You needn't worry about confidentiality. Your medical records were carefully transferred to computer and accidently trashed."

©Artizans Entertainment Inc. By Chris Wildt.

Participating in the evaluation of our health care system's performance is an increasingly important function of health care professionals. Whether you are entering the health care field to provide direct care to patients as a nurse, therapist, physician, or other clinician, or to assume a role in the management of a health care organization—be it a hospital, nursing home, health insurance company, or other organization—you must be aware of the significant efforts and potential consequences of the activities related to evaluating the performance of the health care system. These efforts will affect your day-to-day work as well as the future of your profession.

Health care systems are generally evaluated on three criteria: (a) quality of health care; (b) equity of health care; and (c) efficiency of health care (Aday, Begley, Lairson, & Balkrishnan, 2004; Aday, Begley, Lairson, & Slater, 1993). Health care performance may be assessed at the micro level—for physician practices, hospitals, or other health care settings—or at the macro level—for regions, states, and nations. For example, at the micro level, we may be interested in the quality of health care at a specific hospital, ambulatory surgery center, or physician practice. At the macro level, we may want to know about the quality of health care available in our state compared to other states. We can evaluate performance against several types of referents. We can use a "gold standard" to determine whether we have achieved the recognized "best" possible performance. We can use our own previous performance as a "benchmark" to determine whether we have improved over time. We can use a "benchmark" from another entity to determine whether we are doing as well as or better than an appropriate referent—provider practice, hospital, region, state, or nation.

In this chapter, we discuss each of the indicators of health care performance—quality, equity, and efficiency. We conclude the chapter with a discussion of the importance of data and information systems for evaluating performance in health care.

QUALITY OF HEALTH CARE

Using the model originally developed by Dr. Avedis Donabedian, health care quality is assessed in terms of structure, process, and outcomes (Donabedian, 1980–1985). "Structure...is meant to designate the conditions under which care is provided" (Donabedian, 2003, p. 46). It includes material resources, such as facilities and equipment; human resources, such as number and qualities of professional and support personnel providing health care; and organizational characteristics, such as (for individual facilities such as hospitals) nonprofit status, academic affiliation, and governing structure. Examples of structure-oriented questions are: What is the nurse-to-patient ratio on a hospital floor? What is the age of the facility? What proportion of a hospital's patients do not have insurance, are receiving Medicaid, or are covered by Medicare? Are the physicians in a practice salaried employees or paid on a fee-for-service basis?

Process "is taken to mean the activities that constitute health care—including diagnosis, treatment, rehabilitation, prevention, and patient education—usually carried out by professional personnel, but also including other contributions to care, particularly by patients and their families" (Donabedian, 2003, p. 46). For example, a study of health care process might ask the following questions: Is infection control policy followed by the hospital staff? How long does it take for the primary care physician to receive the test results needed for diagnosis? How does the treating physician transmit information about a drug's side effects to the patient? What is the waiting time in the emergency room? How much time does a physician spend with a patient, on average, for an annual physical? What is the standard practice among the physician staff for treating a particular health condition, such as acute myocardial infarction or stroke?

Structure and process influence the outcomes, or effectiveness, of health care. For example, each of the structure- and process-oriented issues just mentioned may lead to poor health care outcomes, but they are not outcomes in themselves. Outcomes "are taken to mean changes (desirable or undesirable) in individuals and populations that can be attributed to health care" (Donabedian, 2003, p. 46). Generally speaking, there are two types of outcomes used to assess the quality of health care systems: (a) the outcomes of persons who have received care, that is, patients; and (b) population health outcomes, that is, the outcomes of both people who have and people who have not received health care. We will begin with population health outcomes and then consider the health outcomes of patients.

Population Health Outcomes

Health outcomes can be measured at the population level and used to evaluate the quality of a health care system (Kindig, 1997). Population health indicators include population mortality and morbidity rates. These are used in macro-level performance evaluations of regions, states, and nations. We assume the impact of health care on these rates even though we are not directly measuring use of health care among the population considered. If, for example, a disease-specific mortality rate is higher in one region than another, we assume that the health care system has not been optimal in the region with the higher mortality rate.

Historically, population health indicators have been age-adjusted death rates, disease-specific death rates, life expectancy, time lost to premature death, and infant mortality rate (IMR).[1] The United Nations International Children's Emergency Fund (UNICEF) defines IMR as the probability of dying between birth and exactly 1 year of age (UNICEF, 2006). This rate is expressed per 1,000 live births per year. IMR is an important measure that indicates the well-being of infants, children, and pregnant women, as it is associated with maternal health, quality and access to care, and public health in a given population.

Life expectancy is defined by the World Health Organization (WHO) as the number of years of life that can be expected on average in a given population. By using the life expectancy within that population, the time lost to premature death, also called years of potential life lost (YPLL), can be calculated. YPLL is the difference between actual age at death and expected age at death. It illustrates that the more premature a death, the greater the loss of life (WHO, 2012a).

A more recent concept of population health takes into account quality of life. Healthy life expectancy (HALE) at birth is defined by WHO as the "average number of years that a person can expect to live in 'full health' by taking into account years lived in less than full health due to disease and/or injury" (WHO, 2012a). HALE is a measure that combines length and quality of life into a single estimate that indicates years of life that can be expected in a specified state of health (Kindig, 1997, p. 45). Other health-adjusted life expectancy measures are quality-adjusted life years (QALY), which emphasizes the individual's perceived health status as the indicator of quality of life; disability-adjusted life years (DALY), which combines mortality and disability measures; and years of healthy life (YHL), which combines perceived health and disability activity limitation measures from the National Health Interview Survey (Kindig, 1997).

Mortality rate is the number of deaths in a given population per year (WHO, 2012a). The *age-adjusted mortality rate* takes into account the population's age distribution when calculating mortality rate. Using a statistical method that "standardizes" the target population to a reference population, this measure is commonly used when comparing mortality rates across different populations.

Next, we will briefly consider the quality of the U.S. health care system based on population health indicators.

Life Expectancy and Age-Adjusted Mortality

Life expectancy can be used as a health care assessment measure in at least two ways. First, we can compare the life expectancy in one society to life expectancy in another. Second, we can compare life expectancies among subgroups within one society. In both cases, life expectancy rates indicate that the United States has a problem.

First, we consider life expectancy in the United States compared to other nations. In 2004, WHO comparisons of 13 peer countries indicated that the United States ranked 10th of 13 in life expectancy at birth for males, and 12th of 13 in life expectancy at birth for females (WHO, 2012b). These peer countries are Australia, Belgium, Canada, Denmark, Finland, France, Germany, Japan, the Netherlands, Spain, Sweden, the United Kingdom, and the United States.

Next, we examine life expectancy among subgroups within the United States. There are significant differences between population subgroups (Adler et al., 1993; Adler & Rehkopf, 2008; Institute of Medicine, 2003; Pappas et al., 1993). In 2002, the projected life expectancy at birth for U.S. residents was 77.3 years (U.S. Census Bureau, 2005, Table 96). For men, it was 74.5 years; for women, 79.9 years. These numbers were all improved from those observed in 1990, respectively, 75.4, 71.8, and 78.8.

However, in 2002, as in all previous years, there was a marked difference in life expectancy at birth by race: 75.1 for White males, and 68.8 for African American males (U.S. Census Bureau, 2005, Table 98). Similarly, White females had a life expectancy at birth of 80.3, compared to 75.6 for African American females. In 2002, the age-adjusted death rate was 8.5 per 1,000 population, 10.1 for males, and 7.2 for females (U.S. Census Bureau, 2005, Table 99). (Age adjustment statistically accounts for the fact that life expectancy from birth is shorter for males than for females.) Again, this was an improvement over 1990, when the age-adjusted death rate was 9.4 per 1,000 population, 12.0 for males, and 7.5 for females. Yet the age-adjusted death rate for White males in 2002 was 9.9 per 1,000 population, and for African American males it was 13.4 (U.S. Census Bureau, 2005, Table 99). White females had an age-adjusted mortality rate of 7.0 compared to that of African American females with 9.0. The difference in life expectancy and mortality between Whites and African Americans is thought in part to reflect differences in standard of living, as well as access to health services (Geiger, 1996; Institute of Medicine, 2003; Schwartz et al., 1990).

Quality-of-Life Adjusted Measure

The WHO (2012b) comparisons of the United States to the same 12 peer countries indicate, once again, that the U.S. population is not as healthy as we would expect. In 2002, HALE at birth for males was 67.2 years in the United States, the lowest ranked country of the 13. Japan was ranked first (72.3 years). For HALE at birth for females, the United States was ranked 12th of 13 in 2002. In 2002, the age-standardized DALY per 100,000 population for all causes of death was higher in the United States than in any of its 12 peer countries (12,781/100,000 population). The next highest DALY was 10,878/100,000 population in Belgium.

Infant, Neonatal, and Maternal Mortality

Comparison of IMRs in the United States to the same 12 peer countries also indicates a problem in the United States. In 2004, the U.S. IMR was 6.0 per 1,000 live births (WHO, 2012b). Although this rate is low, it is the highest of the 13 peer countries. In 2000, neonatal mortality was also highest in the United States (5 per 1,000 live births), compared to its peer countries, and maternal mortality was third highest (14 maternal deaths per 100,000 live births).

The subgroup comparison of infant mortality within the United States also indicates problems. The difference in the IMR in the United States between Whites and African Americans is striking. In 2002, it was 5.8 for Whites and 13.8 for African Americans (U.S. Census Bureau, 2005, Table 105). The African American IMR has been at least double that for Whites since 1915, when the rate was first recorded as 99.9 per thousand overall (Grove & Hetzel, 1968).

Clinical Outcomes

Health outcomes that are specific to the persons who receive care are often called clinical outcomes. We frequently use the following outcome measures in studies of health care quality among patients: readmission to the hospital after a surgical procedure; functional capacity after medical intervention; long-term pain and discomfort after medical treatment; infection acquired during a hospital stay (nosocomial); 5-year mortality rates among patients treated for cancer, heart disease, or other diseases; development of comorbidities after medical therapy; and satisfaction of the patient with the outcomes of health care treatment. Clinical outcomes research is the term given to studies that focus on the persons who receive care (patients) and the outcomes of their treatment.

Following is a discussion of health care quality at the micro level of clinical outcomes. We examine two aspects related to micro-level evaluation of health care quality: clinical effectiveness and patient safety.

Clinical Effectiveness

A major concept used in defining the quality of health care in the present era is the evaluation of its *effectiveness*, that is, whether the care produces the desired or intended result. This term is synonymous with *efficacy*. Assessing the effectiveness, or efficacy, of health care at the micro level of physician practices, hospitals, and other health care settings is becoming increasingly evidence-based, that is, based on scientifically valid, empirical research. One of the best and most well-known definitions of evidence-based medicine is from an article in the *British Medical Journal* (Sackett, Rosenberg, Gray, Haynes, & Richardson, 1996):

> Evidence based medicine is the conscientious, explicit, and judicious use of current best evidence in making decisions about the care of individual patients. The practice of evidence based medicine means integrating individual clinical expertise with the best available external clinical evidence from systematic research. (p. 71)

Thus, the standards against which quality is measured are based on clinical research. Clinical outcomes research is the foundation of quality improvement efforts at the micro level. Beginning in the last decade of the 20th century, and funded by the Agency for Healthcare Research and Quality (AHRQ), the Centers for Disease Control and Prevention (CDC), the National Institutes of Health (NIH), and other organizations, researchers have continually generated, updated, and published the results of clinical outcomes studies.

These studies have then been synthesized by experts in the field, and the synthesized results are translated into clinical practice guidelines (or alternatively, clinical practice protocols). A standard definition of clinical practice guidelines was developed by Field and Lohr (1992): "systematically developed statements to assist practitioner and patient decisions about appropriate healthcare for specific clinical circumstances."

Clinical practice guidelines are published by government agencies, such as the Preventive Services Task Force, and voluntary agencies, such as the medical specialty societies and the disease-specific advocacy organizations such as the American Cancer Society. Each set of practice guidelines or protocols is the result of the distillation of the evidence provided by hundreds of studies. Performance assessment and the development of evidence-based "best practices" focuses on the quality of care in clinical settings such as hospitals, ambulatory care centers, and nursing homes, for categories of disease conditions, such as heart disease, infectious diseases, diabetes, or asthma.

The following abstract from a study by Carson, McDonagh, and Peterson (2006) is an example of a clinical outcomes study. It compares the effectiveness of different atypical antipsychotic drugs for people with dementia:

Although the Food and Drug Administration (FDA) has not approved atypical antipsychotics for use in patients with dementia, they are commonly prescribed in this population. Recent concerns about increased risk of cerebrovascular events and mortality have led to warnings. A systematic review was conducted to assess the benefits and harms of atypical antipsychotics when used in patients with behavioral and psychological symptoms of dementia. Electronic searches (through March 2005) of the Cochrane Library, Medline, Embase, and PsycINFO were supplemented with hand searches of reference lists, dossiers submitted by pharmaceutical companies, and a review of the FDA Website and industry-sponsored results database. Using predetermined criteria, each study was assessed for inclusion, and data about study design, population, interventions, and outcomes were abstracted. An overall quality rating (good, fair, or poor) was assigned based on internal validity. The evidence for olanzapine and risperidone supports their effectiveness compared with placebo. Short-term adverse events were similar to placebo. Risperidone had no advantage over haloperidol on efficacy measures in the better-quality studies. Risperidone had an advantage over haloperidol on some measures of extrapyramidal symptoms. Evidence for the other atypical antipsychotics is too limited to assess efficacy and safety. Trials were short term and conducted in highly selected populations. The potential for increased risk of cerebrovascular adverse events and mortality is a serious concern. To make judgments about when the benefits of atypical antipsychotics outweigh the potential harms, clinicians need more information. Additional data from existing trials and more complete reporting of trial results could provide this information. (p. 354)

The study used as an example here is typical of evidence-based research, where the results are suggestive but inconclusive, and therefore, the implications for clinical guidelines are not certain. However, evidence-based medicine uses the results of many such studies to determine the clinical efficacy of a set of clinical practices (that is, clinical guidelines or protocols) in order to overcome the limitations of a single study.

Although clinical practice guidelines are sometimes deridingly referred to as "cookbook medicine," they are proliferating and increasingly used by insurers and other payers to evaluate the quality of medical care provided to patients.

Patient Safety

Another aspect of health care quality is patient safety. The patient safety movement of the 1990s led to a great deal of interest in improving the quality of health care delivery through the application of methods borrowed from other industries and pioneered by Deming. Deming was an American statistician, considered the father of the modern quality assurance movement. He developed his system following the end of World War II. Unable to get a hearing in this country, he went to Japan. His methods, designated *Statistical Process Control* (SPC) and *Total Quality Management* (TQM), strongly influenced the rebirth and eventual massive expansion of Japanese industry post–World War II. *Patient safety* has been defined by the Institute of Medicine (2000) as "freedom from accidental injury; ensuring patient safety involves the establishment of operational systems and processes that minimize the likelihood of errors and maximizes the likelihood of intercepting them when they occur" (p. 211). Therefore, patient safety encompasses all events and situations that result in accidental harm to patients including medication errors, surgical mistakes, falls, improper use of medical devices, and nosocomial infection.

The Institute of Medicine report, *To Err Is Human* (2000), has played a major role in bringing national attention to the issue of patient safety.

> The Report converted an issue of gradually growing professional awareness over a great deal of time to one of substantial public concern in a manner and pace unprecedented in modern experience with matters of healthcare quality. The epidemiologic finding that more than 1 million injuries and nearly 100,000 deaths occur in the United States annually as a result of mistakes in medical care came from studies nearly a decade old. But this was new information for the public, and it resonated strongly. (Leape, Berwick, & Bates, 2002, p. 501)

To Err Is Human brought a new perspective to health care quality assurance by supporting the importation of industrial quality improvement practices into health care settings. Using Charles Perrow's analysis of the Three Mile Island accident (Perrow, 1984) as a model, the report advocates a systems approach to health care improvement in order to understand and modify the conditions that contribute to errors. The authors conclude (Institute of Medicine, 2000):

> The application of human factors in other industries has successfully reduced errors. Health care has to look at medical error not as a special case of medicine, but as a special case of error, and to apply the theory and approaches already used in other fields to reduce errors and improve reliability. (p. 66)

There are many excellent books on the application of health improvement methods to health care including the classic by Berwick and his colleagues (Berwick, Gladfrey, & Roessner, 1990) and the more recent by Dlugacz and his colleagues (Dlugacz, Restifo, & Greenwood, 2004). A number of organizations provide training in quality improvement methods. Hospitals that have applied these quality improvement methods have reported significant success in improving safety (e.g., Van den Heuvel, Bogers, Does, van Dijk, & Berg, 2006).

A Health Care Quality Improvement Example

Nosocomial Infections

In this section, we will examine in detail one health care delivery problem that has been the focus of a great deal of concern in recent years: hospital-acquired infections. Hospital-acquired infections have been identified by the CDC as a major health problem in the United States. Also called *nosocomial infections*, these are infections that were not present or incubating in the patient at the time of admission to the hospital. Infections that occur 72 hours after hospital admission are considered nosocomial.

Preventing the occurrence of hospital-acquired infections is a challenging job. The microorganisms that cause infection are ubiquitous in hospitals. In addition, hospitals inadvertently assist infective microorganisms to enter and multiply freely in a human host. For example, the abundance of couriers in hospitals makes it easier for infective microbes to reach susceptible humans. Every staff member—maintenance, cleaning, and food service; laboratory, imaging, and other technician; nurse, aide, physician, and resident—is a possible carrier. In the course of performing their jobs, hospital staff members move from patient to patient, potentially exposing them to pathogens acquired from prior contact with contaminated persons, surfaces, and equipment.

A single lapse in infection control protocol on a single day by just one of the many people who comes into contact with a patient during a hospitalization may result in that patient's exposure to an infective agent. Further, the chance that infection control procedures will not be followed increases if hospitals are understaffed, as many are today. If infective microorganisms reach a patient, routine hospital procedures provide them with new pathways into the body. Treatment with antibiotics can further exacerbate the problem by increasing antimicrobial resistance among the organisms that cause hospital-acquired infections. It is difficult not to conclude that hospital staff members seeking to prevent patient infection are at a disadvantage compared to their microscopic companions that cause infection.

We will discuss (a) the magnitude of the nosocomial infection problem; (b) how we presently attempt to prevent nosocomial infections; (c) why the current approach to preventing nosocomial infections is not as successful as it should be; (d) what initiatives have been undertaken by the major stakeholders to address the problem; and (e) recommendations for achieving additional improvement.

What Is the Magnitude of the Nosocomial Infection Problem?

The figures currently cited by nearly every author writing on the topic are about 2 million patients affected annually by nosocomial infections, resulting in about 80,000 deaths and adding at least $5 billion to U.S. health care costs every year (e.g., Institute of Medicine, 2000). These figures were estimated from a few studies conducted in the 1990s (Institute of Medicine, 2000), and they are difficult to confirm because we lack uniform, consistently collected data from all U.S. hospitals regarding their infection rates. This lack of data inhibits our ability to compare infection rates for hospitals, regions, and states and track infection rates over time. Therefore, we cannot answers questions such as the following: Which hospitals, states, or regions are doing better than others? How much better are some hospitals, states, or regions doing than others? How much has the nosocomial infection rate in the United States changed over time? Is the U.S. rate generally going up or down?

However, even without infection rates that are comparable across hospitals, states, regions, and time, there are several reasons to conclude that the present situation is not satisfactory. The primary evidence comes from the magnitude of nosocomial infection rates that are reported in studies conducted by individual hospitals or hospital systems and the National Nosocomial Infection Surveillance (NNIS) System. Although there is no standard infection rate that is held up as the "gold standard," other industries would not accept the failure rates that hospitals accept in terms of nosocomial infections. In other industries, the goal for errors that are as costly as nosocomial infections and that can be fatal or disabling would be close to zero. Yet, the evidence we have about nosocomial infection rates indicates that they are much higher than desirable, given the potential of these infections to cause death or disability and to raise hospital costs substantially (CDC, 1996, 2001; Richards et al., 2001).

In addition, evidence of a high and increasing rate of antimicrobial resistance among the major infective organisms indicates poor overall control of nosocomial infections. Bacteria, fungi, and even viruses can become resistant to drugs. However, bacteria cause most of the drug-resistant problems in hospitals. The development of antimicrobial resistance is largely associated with antibiotic overuse or misuse, and the rapid increase in the number and prevalence of resistant pathogens over the past two decades can be attributed in part to the fact that an estimated 50% of all antibiotics currently prescribed are either the wrong drug or the wrong dose, or taken for the wrong duration (U.S. Congress, 1995). Primary prevention of nosocomial infections would reduce the use of antimicrobials and, therefore, would have a positive impact on the development of antimicrobial resistance (CDC, 1996, 2001; Richards et al., 2001).

How Do We Attempt to Prevent Nosocomial Infections Now?

Infection control programs are the foundation of efforts to prevent hospital-acquired infections. They have their origin in the nosocomial *Staphylococcus aureus* infection outbreaks of the 1950s and the subsequent recommendation of the American Hospital Association to include infection surveillance as a regular hospital function (Haley et al., 1985). The interest in preventing hospital-acquired infections led to the development of Infection Control Guidelines. Between 1974 and 1983, the Study on the Efficacy of Nosocomial Infection Control (SENIC) established the scientific basis for infection control programs. The SENIC project and the massive number of clinical research studies that followed have been the basis for evidence-based recommendations about how to prevent nosocomial infections.

Today, the professional infection control organizations, particularly the Association for Professionals in Infection Control and Epidemiology (APIC), the Society for Healthcare Epidemiology of America (SHEA), the Surgical Infection Society, and the CDC's Division of Healthcare Quality Promotion and Hospital Infection Control Practices Advisory Committee (HICPAC) (CDC, 2006b, 2012a, 2012b), continually generate, update, and publish Infection Control Guidelines based on expert review, assessment and synthesis of current research, and integration of new findings. Thus, the Infection Control Guidelines are evidence-based, having been distilled from the research on each infection control area. The guidelines reflect the current state of knowledge about infective agents—detection, prevention of their transmission, and treatment—derived from research in the basic and clinical sciences. The guidelines are based on evidence from thousands of scientific studies.

Some of the areas for which guidelines have been developed are surgical site infections (Mangram et al., 1999), intravascular catheter-related infections (CDC, 2002a), construction and environmental risks (Bartley & 1997 and 1999 APIC Guidelines Committee, 2000; CDC, 2003), isolation pre-cautions (Garner, 1996), disinfection and sterilization (Rutala & 1994 and 1996 APIC Guidelines Committee, 1996; Rutala & Weber, 2001), health care–associated pneumonia (CDC, 2004), nosocomial transmission of methicillin-resistant *S. aureus* (MRSA) and vancomycin-resistant *Entero-coccus* (VRE) (HICPAC, 1995; Muto et al., 2003), emerging antimicrobial resistance (Houghton, 2002; Shlaes et al., 1997), hand hygiene (CDC, 2002b), blood-borne pathogens (OSHA, 1991), surveillance (CDC, 1999), and employee health policies (Bolyard et al., 1998).

Why Is the Current Approach Not as Successful as it Should Be?

There are two major reasons for our current lack of success in control-ling nosocomial infections: (a) Infection Control Guidelines are not fully implemented and (b) acceptance within the health care community that a large proportion of nosocomial infections are not "preventable." Each issue is briefly discussed next.

Research suggests that when hospitals fully implement the Infection Control Guidelines, the rate of nosocomial infection falls dramatically, in some cases to the desired level of close to zero. We know that the Infec-tion Control Guidelines have dramatically reduced nosocomial infection rates when they have been fully implemented, for instance within indi-vidual hospitals and in some European countries (e.g., IHI, 2006; Muto et al., 2003). Therefore, improving compliance with the guidelines should be remarkably effective in reducing the nosocomial infections in U.S. hospitals.

However, whereas a great deal of effort is, and has been, expended on developing the Infection Control Guidelines and training infection control professionals, less effort has been devoted to ensuring that the Infection Control Guidelines are implemented, fully and appropriately, in each U.S. hospital (e.g., Goldsteen, Goldsteen, Gladwin, & Jefferson, 2004). This is the hard part. Within hospitals, competing priorities, declining budgets, and entrenched behaviors and beliefs about infection control have inhib-ited the implementation of practices that research has shown prevent noso-comial infections. However, hospitals that have attempted to reduce their nosocomial infection rates have demonstrated that two key programmatic elements can overcome these problems: (a) application of quality improve-ment methods borrowed from other industries and (b) institutional will. These ingredients must be present if change is to occur and be sustained.

In addition to ensuring that the Infection Control Guidelines are fully implemented, clinical and technological breakthroughs can lead to improvement of the guidelines. The current Infection Control Guidelines pertain to what are considered "preventable" infections. At present, the CDC estimates that a minimum of 33% of all nosocomial infections are preventable (Weinstein, 1998). A review of studies by Harbarth, Sax, and

Gastmeier (2003) concluded that 20% of infections are preventable. In both cases, the proportion of infection considered preventable is quite low. However, new technologies and new discoveries in the basic sciences of genetics, microbiology, biochemistry, and so forth will undoubtedly have a tremendous impact on our ability to detect and prevent transmission of infectious disease organisms in hospital settings. They will be used to improve the Infection Control Guidelines and increase the proportion of nosocomial infections that are considered "preventable."

What Initiatives Have the Major Stakeholders Undertaken to Address the Problem?

Many relatively new initiatives are underway to facilitate infection control excellence among U.S. hospitals. They are the result of the patient safety movement discussed earlier, as well as increased public attention to the problem of nosocomial infections, particularly because of media coverage. These initiatives are:

- Strengthening oversight of Infection Control Programs by The Joint Commission (formerly the Joint Commission on Accreditation of Healthcare Organizations or JCAHO), the major accrediting body for health care organizations, and other health care accrediting organizations
- Providing process-oriented infection control performance information to consumers and purchasers
  - National Quality Forum
  - Leapfrog Group
- Providing hospital-level, nosocomial infection rates to consumers and purchasers
  - State Public Disclosure Legislation
  - Consumers Union Public Disclosure Initiative
- Providing quality improvement expertise to individual hospitals
  - Private efforts, most notably by the Institute for Healthcare Improvement (IHI)
  - Public efforts led by the CDC
- Developing clinical and technical breakthroughs in the prevention of nosocomial infections

The first four types of initiatives are aimed at ensuring full implementation of the Infection Control Guidelines. Of these, strengthening Joint Commission oversight of Infection Control Programs, providing process-oriented infection control performance information to consumers and purchasers, and providing hospital-level nosocomial infection rates to consumers and purchasers will have an impact on institutional will, via external pressures for change. Each of these initiatives has the potential to motivate hospital leadership to give nosocomial infection control priority within the organization because of its possible adverse impact on a hospital. The fourth type of initiative—providing quality improvement expertise to individual hospitals—assists hospitals to respond to external pressures for better nosocomial infection control via training in the quality improvement methods that have been shown to be effective in bringing about organizational excellence. The fifth type of initiative focuses on the other main thrust of efforts to prevent nosocomial infections: that is, improving the Infection Control Guidelines themselves through clinical and technical advances.

What Additional Improvement Efforts Are Needed?

- Despite current, significant efforts, there is still much that must be done to prevent hospital-acquired infections in terms of (a) ensuring that the Infection Control Guidelines are fully implemented in all U.S. hospitals and (b) advancing clinical and technical breakthroughs that will improve the Infection Control Guidelines themselves. Following are activities that would contribute to the prevention of hospital-acquired infections without duplicating the current efforts of major infection control stakeholders.
- Develop support for a system to collect outcomes data (nosocomial infection rates) from all U.S. hospitals and disclose these data to external stakeholders
- Develop cost benefit information to justify expenditures and guide allocations for Infection Control Programs
- Study the impact of public disclosure legislation
- Identify internal barriers to implementing infection control practices and develop appropriate measures to address these barriers
- Develop nonproprietary software to improve infection surveillance in hospitals
- Develop more Model Infection Control programs, with greater visibility for them
- Fund research on clinical and technological breakthroughs to improve infection control guidelines
- Improve the training and education of all health care workers at all levels in infection control, with continuing education and ongoing evaluation of clinical performance at the bedside.

Organizations With Major Influence on Health Care Quality

The following section describes the efforts of public and private organizations to improve the quality of health care in the United States. These efforts are increasingly collaborative. Many businesses that pay for the health care of their employees have banded together. Public initiatives are increasingly coordinated. And, private–public partnerships have developed. However, it is difficult to say which organizations are the most influential. Clearly, The Joint Commission and the Centers for Medicare and Medicaid Services (CMS), as one of the largest payers of health care services in the country, are extremely influential. However, private organizations and other public agencies have very important roles, as well. The impact of these significant efforts on the quality of U.S. health care is yet to be determined.

The Joint Commission and Other Health Care Accrediting Organizations

Though they are private entities, the accrediting organizations have a great deal of direct and indirect influence on quality assurance and improvement in health care. This is particularly true because of the relationship between the CMS certification process and accreditation by a CMS-approved accrediting organization:

> In order for a healthcare organization to participate in and receive payment from the Medicare or Medicaid programs, it must be certified as complying with the Conditions of Participation (CoP), or standards, set forth in federal regulations. This certification is based on a survey conducted by a state agency on behalf of the Centers for Medicare & Medicaid Services (CMS). However, if a national accrediting organization, such as the Joint Commission, has and enforces standards that meet the federal Conditions of Participation, CMS may grant the accrediting organization "deeming" authority and "deem" each accredited health care organization as meeting the Medicare and Medicaid certification requirements. The healthcare organization would have "deemed status" and would not be subject to the Medicare survey and certification process. (American Society for Healthcare Engineering [ASHE], 2012)

The Conditions of Participation (CoPs) and Conditions for Coverage (CfCs) set by CMS are standards that CMS considers essential for improving quality and protecting the health and safety of Medicare and Medicaid beneficiaries. Through its approval process, CMS tries to ensure that the standards of approved accrediting organizations meet or exceed the Medicare standards set forth in the CoPs and the CfCs (CMS, 2012).

The Joint Commission (2012) is the oldest and largest health care accrediting organization in the country, accrediting nearly 19,000 health care organizations in the United States, including general, psychiatric, children's, and rehabilitation hospitals; critical access hospitals; home care organizations; nursing homes and other long-term care facilities; behavioral health care organizations; ambulatory care providers; and independent or freestanding clinical laboratories.

The Joint Commission aims to provide standards for high-quality care that will ensure both patient and staff safety. Accreditation is designed to ensure quality care, maintain infection control, and help reduce the occurrence of medical errors. The performance measurement tools used by The Joint Commission have developed over the years. For example, in 1986, The Joint Commission (then JCAHO) developed the Indicator Measurement System (IMS). It had six sets of performance measures, for perioperative care, obstetrical care, trauma care, oncology care, infection control, and medication use. This system was not implemented, but it set the stage for the current ORYX initiative, which is based on multiple measurement systems. As described by The Joint Commission (2012), the ORYX system

> Integrates outcomes and other performance measurement data into the accreditation process. ORYX measurement requirements are intended to support Joint Commission accredited organizations in their quality improvement efforts. Performance measures are essential to the credibility of any modern evaluation activity for health care organizations. In 2010, The Joint Commission categorized its performance measures into accountability and non-accountability measures. This approach places more emphasis on an organization's performance on accountability measures—quality measures that meet four criteria designed to identify measures that produce the greatest positive impact on patient outcomes when hospitals demonstrate improvement: research, proximity, accuracy and adverse effects. Non-accountability measures (for example, providing smoking cessation advice) are more suitable for secondary uses, such as exploration or learning within individual health care organizations, and are good advice in terms of appropriate patient care. Going forward, The Joint Commission will only adopt accountability measures for its ORYX program.

The principal objective of measurement activities, including ORYX, is to create the technical infrastructures within health care organizations and also The Joint Commission to support performance measurement and improvement in the health care system (The Joint Commission, 2012). Other CMS-approved, but much smaller, accrediting bodies for hospitals are the American Osteopathic Association's Healthcare Facilities Accreditation Program and DNV Healthcare, which were approved in 2008. The Accreditation Association for Ambulatory Health Care, the American Association for Accreditation of Ambulatory Surgery Facilities, and the Accreditation Commission for Health Care are CMS-approved for non-hospital health care settings including ambulatory surgery centers and hospices (CMS, 2012).

Federal Agencies

The major federal government agencies that focus on ensuring and improving the quality of health care are described next. Each of these agencies has been discussed previously in Chapters 5 and 6, but the following discussion focuses on their role in ensuring quality and evaluating health systems performance.

Centers for Medicare and Medicaid Services. The CMS is a federal agency within the U.S. Department of Health and Human Services. (Until 2001 it was known as the Health Care Financing Administration or HCFA.) CMS has several offices and initiatives that focus on improving the quality of health care, including the Office of Clinical Standards and Quality, the Quality Initiatives, and the Medicare Health Outcomes Survey. Because Medicare and Medicaid pay for so much health care in the United States, their ability to influence quality throughout the health care system is enormous.

> The Office of Clinical Standards and Quality (OCSQ) serves as the focal point for all quality, clinical and medical science issues and policies for CMS programs.... It coordinates quality-related activities with outside organizations. OCSQ also monitors the quality of Medicare and Medicaid programs and evaluates the success of interventions. (CMS, 2007a)

The overall goal of the Quality Initiative (QI) is to improve the quality of services of Medicare and Medicaid recipients through methods of provider accountability and public disclosure. The QI was launched nationally in 2002 with the Nursing Home Quality Initiative (NHQI) and expanded in 2003 with the Home Health Quality Initiative (HHQI) and the Hospital Quality Initiative (HQI). In 2004, the Physician Focused Quality Initiative, which includes the Doctor's Office Quality Project, was developed. In 2004, the QI was expanded to officially include kidney dialysis facilities. The End Stage Renal Disease (ESRD) QI promotes ongoing CMS strategies to improve the quality of care provided to ESRD patients. In 2006, CMS launched the Physician Voluntary Reporting Program (CMS, 2007b). In 2009, CMS estimated that almost all settings covered by Medicare were covered by quality measures (CMS, 2009).

CMS, in collaboration with the National Committee for Quality Assurance (NCQA), launched the Medicare Health Outcomes Survey (HOS) in 1998 to study the outcomes of Medicare managed care. The Medicare HOS is being used as part of the effectiveness of care component of the Health Plan Employer Data and Information Set (HEDIS). The HOS measure includes physical and mental health outcomes and risk adjustment techniques. In addition to health outcomes measures, the HOS is used to collect the Urinary Incontinence in Older Adults and Physical Activity in Older Adults HEDIS measures (CMS, 2007c).

Agency for Healthcare Research and Quality. The AHRQ is the division of the U.S. Department of Health and Human Services charged with coordinating, conducting, and supporting research, demonstrations, and evaluations related to the measurement and improvement of health care quality. The AHRQ mission is "to improve the quality, safety, efficiency, and effectiveness of health care for all Americans" (AHRQ, 2007a). AHRQ is charged with disseminating scientific findings about clinical practice guidelines and facilitating public access to information on the quality of health care. AHRQ research provides evidence-based information on health care outcomes; quality; and health care cost, use, and access. The information helps health care decision makers—patients and clinicians, health system leaders, purchasers, and policymakers—make more informed decisions and improves the quality of health care services. Beginning in 2005, AHRQ's "research agenda reflected a shift to emphasize the translation of research into practice" (AHRQ, 2007b). Nearly 80% of AHRQ's annual budget of approximately $300 million is awarded as grants and contracts to researchers at universities and other research institutions across the country through its evidence-based practice centers and the National Quality Measures Clearinghouse (AHRQ, 2007c,d). Researchers are funded to conduct systematic, comprehensive analyses and syntheses of the scientific literature and to develop reports and technology assessments based on the research-supported evidence (i.e., clinical practice guidelines). To ensure that report findings are translated into improvements in clinical practice, AHRQ enlists partners such as specialty societies and health systems, which use the findings of evidence-based practice centers to develop tools and materials that will improve the quality of care.

Centers for Disease Control and Prevention. The CDC is the nation's primary government agency for developing disease prevention and control initiatives and health promotion and education activities. In terms of health care quality, it has a particularly important role in the control of nosocomial infection. The Division of Healthcare Quality Promotion (DHQP) undertakes initiatives in conjunction with other CDC divisions, such as the National Center for Infectious Diseases, when appropriate. The DHQP is charged with protecting patients and health care personnel and promoting safety, quality, and value in the health care delivery system (CDC, 2005a, 2012a). Among the DHQP priorities are the following:

- Measuring, validating, interpreting, and responding to data relevant to health care outcomes, health care-associated infections/antimicrobial resistance, related adverse events, and medical errors among patients and health care personnel. This priority is primarily addressed through the NNIS system discussed previously in this chapter

- Investigating and responding to outbreaks and emerging antimicrobial-resistant pathogens and infections among patients or associated with the health care environment
- Identifying and evaluating the efficacy of interventions designed to prevent health care–associated infections or antimicrobial resistance, related adverse events, and medical errors
- Promoting clinical microbiology laboratory quality

The CDC provides extensive information on infection control guidelines, infectious disease outbreak management, antimicrobial resistance, laboratory practice, sterilization and disinfection, and surveillance. The CDC further offers advice and consultation to health care providers or regional health departments on matters relating to infection control. It also operates a free rapid notification system through which time-sensitive e-mail messages about important health care events (e.g., outbreaks, product recalls) and publications (e.g., new health care guidelines) are sent to persons active in the prevention of health care–acquired infections and antimicrobial resistance.

The CDC's Healthcare Infection Control Practices Advisory Committee (HICPAC) is a federal advisory committee made up of 14 external infection control experts who provide advice and guidance to the CDC regarding the practice of health care infection control, strategies for surveillance, and prevention and control of health care–associated infections in U.S. health care facilities. One of the primary functions of the committee is to issue recommendations for preventing and controlling health care–associated infections in the form of guidelines, resolutions, and informal communications. HICPAC has issued practice guidelines on the following subjects: environmental infection control in health care settings; hand hygiene in health care settings; intravascular device–related infections; surgical site infections; isolation precautions; nosocomial pneumonia; and catheter-associated urinary tract infection.

Along with the Get Smart for Healthcare: Know when Antibiotics Work Campaign, the CDC has an Interagency Task Force on antimicrobial resistance, which partners with hospitals, state and local health departments, medical and professional associations, health insurers, private industry, continuing medical education organizations, and other health agencies to promote universal adoption of several practice recommendations concerning infection prevention, effective diagnosis and treatment, wise antimicrobial use, and transmission prevention designed to prevent antimicrobial resistance among patients. As part of this campaign, the CDC provides clinicians with information for preventing antimicrobial resistance among specific patient populations (e.g., surgical, children), including fact sheets listing the particular steps that should be taken to prevent resistant infections in targeted populations and materials for distribution to patients with tips on infection prevention.

National Institutes of Health. The NIH are a primary source of funding for medical and behavioral research in the United States. An agency under the federal Department of Health and Human Services, the NIH funds a broad array of extramural projects, grants, contracts, and cooperative agreements conducted primarily by universities, hospitals, and other research institutions. Much of the patient-oriented research includes studies into the development of new technologies, human disease mechanisms, therapeutic interventions, and clinical trials. Other clinical research includes epidemiological and behavioral studies, outcomes research, and health services research. The NIH is the source of much funding for clinical outcomes studies that are used for evidence-based medicine and clinical practice guidelines.

Public/Private Partnerships and Private Initiatives

There are also a number of private initiative or private–public partnerships providing health care performance information to consumers and purchasers. Both the consumers and the purchasers of hospital services, such as insurance companies and the Medicare program, have a vital interest in the quality of those services. However, until fairly recently, consumers and purchasers had very limited ability to evaluate the quality of a hospital's performance in any aspect of care. Now, two organizations—the National Quality Forum (NQF) and the Leapfrog Group—are attempting to rectify this problem by developing standard measures of hospital quality and disseminating information about hospital performance to purchasers and consumers. The effectiveness of providing consumers and payers with information about health care quality is controversial and untested, as yet.

National Quality Forum. The NQF is a nonprofit organization created to improve the quality of American health care by: building consensus on national priorities and goals for performance improvement, endorsing national consensus standards for measuring and publicly reporting on performance, and promoting the attainment of national goals through education and outreach programs (National Quality Forum, 2012). Established in 1999 as a partnership between public and private stakeholders, the NQF aims to promote health care quality improvement by developing the intellectual framework for nationally standardized performance measures and quality data reporting so that individual hospitals and health systems can be compared. The NQF encourages the use of standardized measures by consumers and stakeholders within the health care system. However, it should be noted that the NQF has no authority to implement its standards, although payers of hospital services such as insurance companies and the Medicare program can demand compliance with their standards.

The NQF enjoys broad participation from health care consumer advocacy groups, public and private purchasers, health care professionals, employers, provider organizations, health plans, accrediting bodies, organized labor, and organizations involved in health care research and quality improvement. The organization is governed by a 27-member board of directors representing consumers, purchasers, providers, insurers, health services experts, and representatives from the CMS and the AHRQ. Currently, there are more than 200 member organizations active in the NQF.

The NQF seeks not only to promote new guidelines, standards, and quality measures to rectify serious and pervasive quality deficiencies, but also to reconcile the redundant and often incompatible guidelines, standards, and reporting measures offered by various organizations and agencies dedicated to health care quality improvement. The NQF consensus process was developed pursuant to and in accordance with the National Technology Transfer Act of 1995 (U.S. Office of Management and Budget Circular A-119). This means that NQF endorsement of hospital performance measures and standards confers on them the special legal status of *voluntary consensus standards*. This status makes NQF-endorsed recommendations more easily adopted for use by Medicare, Medicaid, and other federally funded health care programs; that is, federal health care programs can require hospitals to adopt NQF recommendations in order to qualify for federal insurance programs.

The NQF has issued reports endorsing a set of quality measures and endorsing patient safety practices. The measures are designed to provide consumers, providers, purchasers, and quality improvement professionals the tools to evaluate and compare the quality of care in hospitals across the nation using a standard set of measures. The goal is to make data on these performance measures publicly available and thus enable performance-based decisions about hospital selection, create incentives for hospital performance improvement, enhance value-based purchasing, and generally stimulate the improvement of health care.

The Leapfrog Group. The Leapfrog Group (2012) is a member-supported program aimed at mobilizing employer purchasing power to alert America's health industry that big leaps in health care safety, quality, and customer value will be recognized and rewarded. It was established in 2000 to:

> reward hospitals for advances in patient safety and quality and to educate employees, retirees, and families about the importance of hospitals' efforts in this area. Leapfrog purchasers provide health benefits to more than 34 million Americans and spend billions on healthcare annually.

Leapfrog was founded by the Business Roundtable, and its funding comes from its members. Leapfrog aims to give consumers information on hospital quality so that they are able to make more informed hospital choices and to mobilize employer health care purchasing power to improve patient safety. Focusing on quality of care issues relevant to urban area hospitals, the group works with medical quality improvement experts to identify problems and propose solutions believed to improve hospital patient care.

The Leapfrog Group's strategy is to recommend a set of safety practices, and then survey hospitals regarding the practice areas targeted. For each recommended practice, the hospital is rated on the following scale: fully implemented recommended practice, good progress in implementation, good early stage in implementation, willing to report but does not meet criteria for good early stage, and did not disclose. Leapfrog collects and makes publicly available comparative hospital ratings based on implementation of the recommended practices. This information is available through the HealthGrades website and through the Leapfrog Group website (http://www.leapfroggroup.org/cp).

The Leapfrog Group encourages health care purchasers to provide incentives to hospitals that implement and report on the recommended practices. Incentives such as increased patient volume, price variation based on performance, and public recognition are expected to encourage hospitals to adopt Leapfrog's recommendations. The Leapfrog Group further encourages corporate purchasers who utilize health plans as intermediaries to hold the health plans accountable for ensuring application of Leapfrog standards.

The Leapfrog Group Safe Practices Score was based initially on the NQF's Safe Practices for Better Healthcare: A Consensus Report. Since that initial report, Leapfrog has utilized NQF updated reports to keep current. The most recent version of the report endorsed 34 practices that should be universally used in applicable clinical care settings to reduce the risk of harm to patients. There are practices aimed at: leadership and teamwork; preventing illness and infections; creating and sustaining a culture of safety; at matching care needs to service capability; improving information transfer and communication; improving medication management, health care associated–infections, and specific care processes. Included in the 34 practices are two of the original three Leapfrog Leaps: Computerized Physician Order Entry and ICU Physician Staffing. After completion of the Leapfrog hospital survey, each hospital's relative ranking, compared with other hospitals, is displayed on the Leapfrog website, along with their results for the initial three Leaps and other measurement areas. In the 2011 Hospital Survey, Leapfrog scored hospitals' progress on 17 of the 34 NQF Safe Practice areas for a total of 737 points. Each practice area was assigned an individual weight, which was factored into the overall score. Hospitals were then ranked by quartiles.

Institute for Healthcare Improvement. A number of private organizations provide expertise and leadership to hospitals that voluntarily aim to improve their quality of health care. Foremost among these organizations is the Institute for Healthcare Improvement (IHI). The IHI is a not-for-profit organization with a mission to improve health by focusing on a set of goals adapted from the Institute of Medicine's six improvement aims for the health care system: safety, effectiveness, patient centeredness, timeliness, efficiency, and equity (IHI, 2012). IHI attempts to bring change by identifying gaps; helping the public to understand and demand the improvement that is needed and possible; spreading improvement knowledge across the globe; and providing methods, tools, and other supports, largely through partnerships, for thousands of health care organizations to turn knowledge into improved results. IHI initiates and supports innovation efforts, so as to discover, cultivate, and demonstrate the feasibility of new, more capable designs. In terms of health care quality improvement, the IHI orientation is the Deming model of continuous quality improvement. The IHI focus is on innovation, R&D, and the creation of new solutions to old problems. In recent years, their research has been directed at transforming entire systems through redesign of all major care processes. This work was ultimately manifested in the 100,000 Lives Campaign and 5 Million Lives Campaign, in which IHI spread best practice changes to thousands of hospitals through the United States, and created a national network for improvement focused on reducing needless deaths and preventing harm from care.

Legislative Initiatives

In addition to the federal, private, and private–public efforts just discussed, state legislatures have become involved in quality health care issues. For example, several states have passed or have pending legislation that mandates hospitals to disclose their infection rates to the public. The rationale behind these initiatives is that hospitals will improve their Infection Control Programs if threatened by the loss of patients or purchasers to competitors that seem to have better infection control performance than their own. ("Sunlight is the best disinfectant.")

Pennsylvania and Illinois were leaders in this area. Following widely publicized investigative series on preventable deaths attributable to nosocomial infection in the *Chicago Tribune* and the *Pittsburgh Tribune-Review*, Illinois and Pennsylvania instituted policies requiring hospitals to report data on nosocomial infections to oversight agencies and adopted plans to make comparative data on infection rates available to the public. These states were the first to require systematic, ongoing reporting on nosocomial infection data.

The Illinois and Pennsylvania initiatives fall within a clear consumer choice model for addressing nosocomial infections. Rather than compelling hospitals to adopt new infection control practices, the legislation works by publicly disclosing infection rates, which proponents assert will better enable consumers to make appropriate health care decisions as well as provide a market incentive for health care providers to improve infection control in their facilities. Both the Illinois legislation (Hospital Report Card Act) and the new reporting rules promulgated by the Pennsylvania Health Care Cost Containment Council went into effect on January 1, 2004. After the Illinois and Pennsylvania programs were adopted, Missouri and Florida also passed laws instituting nosocomial infection reporting requirements. Finally, a piece of federal legislation titled "The Patient Safety and Quality Improvement Act" was enacted in 2005 (White House, 2005). This legislation created a voluntary, confidential medical errors reporting database and had widespread support from representatives of the health care industry at the time of signing.

Whereas consumer advocates support programs that require public disclosure of quality information such as infection rates, the hospital industry regularly opposes such programs, expressing concern that publicizing quality data will lead to increased tort litigation against providers. It is unclear as of the writing of this book what effects these legislative initiatives will have on the quality of health care. Also, another problem with the "consumer choice" approach is that, in most cases, consumers do not have a choice. Their doctor tells them what hospital they are going to, or there is only one hospital that is accessible anyway. Furthermore, most people on their way to a hospital are sick enough that they do not want to stop to evaluate their choices and could not do much with the information anyway. They just want to be admitted and taken care of.

EQUITY OF HEALTH CARE

Equity is the second criterion used to evaluate the performance of health care systems.

Equity or distributive justice is concerned with the fair allocation of benefits and burdens among those who are deserving of care and those who are in a position to pay for it—the two groups may or may not be the same (Aday et al., 1993, p. 120).

We are concerned about inequities in access to health care as well as inequities in the quality of health care—as measured and evaluated by standards established for structure, process, and outcomes. We use disparities in access and quality of health care to indicate inequity.

The factors that are consistently associated with inequities in health care access and quality are socioeconomic status (SES), race and ethnicity, and geographic location. We find in study after study that people with low income, low education, and low-status occupations; people belonging to minority racial and ethnic groups, particularly African American and Hispanic; and people who live in rural areas or inner cities are more likely to have poor access to care and poor-quality health care (Institute of Medicine, 2003).

Equity and the Quality of Health Care

Is the distribution of quality health care equitable in the United States? An examination of disparities in quality of care suggests that it is not (Fiscella, Franks, Gold, & Clancy, 2000). For example, lower SES is associated with receiving fewer Papanicolaou tests, mammograms, childhood and adult influenza immunizations, and diabetic eye exams. Lower SES is also associated with late enrollment in prenatal care and lower quality ambulatory and hospital care. Racial and ethnic status is linked to quality of care received. Elderly African Americans receive fewer preventive medicine procedures when compared with elderly Whites. African Americans, in general, receive less intensive hospital care, and Hispanic women receive fewer medical procedures and preventive measures as compared to Whites. African Americans have also been found to have higher rates of end-stage diabetic conditions such as amputations, indicating poor-quality ambulatory care.

However, a recent study by the RAND Corporation (Asch et al., 2006) suggests that inequities in health care quality may not be as important as deficiencies in the overall level of quality in the United States. In the RAND study, health care quality differed little between people in different socioeconomic, racial, ethnic, and geographic groups. Rather, the researchers found that health care was mediocre for all groups, equally. The study suggests that disparities in quality of care may be closing, but the overall quality of health care for all Americans needs much improvement. The discrepancy between the RAND study findings and those of previous research had not been resolved at the time this book was written, but it is an important issue that should generate a great deal of research in the future.

Equity and Access to Health Care

Is access to health care equitable in the United States? Here the evidence is quite clear. People without health insurance (or with poor health insurance) have much reduced access to health care. As we have discussed, the United States finances health care through a mixed system, based largely on employer-based health insurance and the public insurance programs for the elderly and disabled (Medicare) and the poor (Medicaid). This patchwork system leaves 46.1 million people without health insurance (U.S. Census Bureau, 2006). Millions more are underinsured, that is, they do not have comprehensive coverage. This can mean high deductibles and copays and limited coverage for a variety of health care services, including mental health services, medical equipment, and preventive care (Lee & Tollen, 2002).

The health care access problems of the uninsured are well documented. The uninsured are much less likely to have a "usual place to go" for medical care. If they have a usual place for health care, they are less likely than insured persons to have a physician's office as their site of care. Uninsured adults are more likely to use "safety net" providers such as community health centers, emergency rooms, and public health or free clinics as their usual place for health care. They are less likely than the insured person to see the same health care provider each time they obtain health care. They are more likely to report that they do not get needed health care, and they have fewer ambulatory care visits. Research has shown that uninsured persons are significantly more likely to delay seeking health care. Lack of health insurance has been found to be significantly related to the failure to fill a recommended prescription, and it is found that medications, even when filled, are not taken as directed, but saved or spread out over a longer than prescribed period of time to save money (Kaiser Family Foundation, 2002).

Not all Americans have the same probability of being uninsured. National surveys have consistently found that age, SES, race, and ethnicity are predictors of being uninsured or underinsured. The majority of the uninsured and underinsured are employed. Typically, 18- to 34-year-olds are the least likely to have health insurance, either because they cannot afford it or because they choose not to be insured, preferring to spend that money on something else. People who have had only a high school education or less schooling are more likely to be uninsured. A higher percentage of Hispanics and African Americans are uninsured compared to non-Hispanic Whites. Foreign-born noncitizens rank the highest of all in rate of being uninsured (Jonas & Kovner, 2005; Kaiser Family Foundation, 2006).

Another factor leading to inequities in access to health care is geographic location. People who live in rural America and those who live in inner cities have reduced access to health care, even if they have health insurance. These areas often lack health care resources, including physicians and other health care providers and facilities, particularly easy-to-reach, comprehensive hospitals. Rural residents generally face a greater financial burden for obtaining care than do urban and suburban residents, and mental health services can be scarce (Reschovsky & Staiti, 2005). Rural areas tend to attract fewer doctors than urban areas. Even though 20% of Americans live in rural areas, only 9% of U.S. physicians practice in rural areas (AHRQ, 2005).

The problem of equity, in both access to and quality of health care, is well known, and there have been efforts to remedy the problem starting early in the 20th century when reformers began to focus on securing universal health care coverage in the United States. The history of the efforts to correct the inequities in the U.S. health care system is described at length in Chapter 8—"Health Care Reform."

EFFICIENCY OF HEALTH CARE

Efficiency is the third criterion for judging a health care system. "Efficiency requires that we produce the combination of goods and services with the highest attainable total value, given our limited resources and technology" (Aday et al., 1993, p. 73). Efficiency is either allocative or production. Allocative efficiency concerns attaining the most valued mix of health care services. Production efficiency refers to producing a given level of health care services at minimum cost. As an example, an allocative efficiency issue is how much to invest in preventive versus curative medical services, whereas a production efficiency issue might concern whether and when to substitute relatively low-cost nurses for higher-cost physicians in the provision of health care services.

At the micro level of physician practices, hospitals, and other health care settings, efficiency is assessed using (a) production functions and (b) cost-effectiveness, cost-benefit, and related cost-utility analysis (Aday et al., 1993). These analyses are used to determine, for example, which of two equally effective treatments should be recommended to clinicians. If both are effective, the goal of efficiency suggests that the least expensive treatment is preferable. These kinds of decisions are increasingly made by health care payers. For example, the Commonwealth Fund newsletter (March 2006) reports:

> Washington State's Health Care Authority, which coordinates the Prescription Drug Program for the state's Medicaid, public employee, and worker compensation programs, is using an integrated approach to value-based pharmaceutical purchasing. The evidence-based drug review process involves a thorough analysis of quality and effectiveness before applying cost considerations. The process, which includes an evidence-based preferred drug list and supplemental rebates from pharmaceutical manufacturers, is producing savings of about $20 million each year to the state—over 5 percent of its Medicaid fee-for-service drug spending—and about $40 million in combined state–federal spending.

At the macro level, efficiency analysis is based on comparisons between regions, states, and nations. Often we use international comparisons of health care systems (Aday et al., 1993). We can use WHO statistics and the Commonwealth Fund to contrast the United States with peer nations including Australia, Canada, France, Germany, Japan, New Zealand, Norway, the Netherlands, Switzerland, Sweden, and the United Kingdom on numerous indicators of cost and available health care resources. In 2010, the United States was ranked first in proportion of its gross domestic product spent on health services (16.2%) and ranked first in per capita total expenditures on health care. At the average exchange rate in U.S. dollars, per capita expenditure was $7,290 in the United States, compared to $3,837 in the Netherlands, the country ranked first in overall health system performance (Davis, Schoen, & Stremikis, 2010). The United States was ranked second to last in physicians per 1,000 population, and last in number of physician visits per capita. The United States ranked in the bottom of the percent who believe if they became seriously ill, they would be confident they could afford the care they needed. Overall, the United States ranks last on mortality amenable to health care, last on infant mortality, and second to last on health life expectancy at age 60. Primary care physician survey data also suggests the United States is lagging in adoption of national policies that promote primary care, quality improvement, and information technology. The United States is spending more per capita on health care and providing fewer basic health care resources relative to other countries. Further, the U.S. rankings on various measures of mortality discussed previously in this chapter (see "Population Health Outcomes") suggest that the U.S. health care system is not efficient, because our rankings on life expectancy, quality-of-life adjusted life expectancy, infant mortality, and other mortality rates are consistently lower than those of peer nations spending less on health care.

A NATIONAL SCORECARD

There is increasing interest in evaluating the performance of the U.S. health care system comprehensively, rather than piece by piece. One substantial effort is that of the Commonwealth Fund (Commonwealth Fund, 2011; Schoen et al., 2006). They have developed a scorecard that evaluates the U.S. health care system on quality, access, equity, and efficiency by comparing national scores to benchmarks. This macro-level evaluation of the health care system uses 42 performance indicators, many of which are composites, some of which are old and others newly developed for the scorecard. There are five broad domains: health outcomes, quality, access, efficiency, and equity. Within the domain of quality, there are four subdomains: effectiveness, coordination of care, safety, and patient-centered, timely care. The benchmarks generally reflect the performance of top-performing groups, but not "perfection." The scorecard compares U.S. average performance with benchmarks drawn from the top 10 percent of U.S. states, regions, health plans, and hospitals or other providers, as well as from the top-performing countries. If average U.S. performance came close to the top rates achieved here at home or abroad, then average scores would approach the maximum of 100.

The 2011 scorecard finds that the United States as a whole scores only 64, compared with 67 in 2006 and 65 in 2008—well below the benchmarks.

The scorecard combines many old indicators of health system performance with new ones, but the story it tells is familiar. Based on the data presented in this chapter, it is quite clear that the U.S. health care system could use improvement. The benefit of the scorecard is that it has assembled multiple measures, has quantified them on the same scale, and can provide a composite score, which we can use now as a benchmark for improvement efforts. The authors conclude:

> The overall picture that emerges from the scorecard is one of missed opportunities and room for improvement. Despite high expenditures, the United States lags behind other countries on indicators of mortality and healthy life expectancy. Within the United States, there is often a substantial spread between the top and bottom groups of states, hospitals, or health plans as well as wide gaps between the national average and top rates. As a result, the U.S. performance relative to benchmarks averages near 50 for efficiency to 70 for healthy lives, quality, access, and equity, for an overall average score of 66 across the main domains of performance. On multiple indicators, the United States would need to improve its performance by 50 percent or more to reach benchmark countries, regions, states, hospitals, health plans, or targets. (Schoen et al., 2006, p. w472)

DATA AND INFORMATION TECHNOLOGY

Every major organization with an interest in health care performance recognizes the need for better data in order to benchmark the current situation and then determine if improvements have occurred in quality; access and equity; and cost and efficiency. These organizations include the payers for health care such as the Medicaid and Medicare programs and private health insurance companies; providers of health care including hospitals; private foundations such as the Robert Wood Johnson Foundation with a focus on health policy; the public–private partnerships such as the National Quality Forum and JCAHO; and many consumer groups such as Consumers Union, which has an interest in nosocomial infection control. It is generally agreed, as Hanrahan and his colleagues write, "Proper functioning of health care systems requires an advanced health information network that supports clinical care, personal health management, population health, and research. But this infrastructure does not yet exist in the United States" (Hanrahan, Foldy, Barthell, & Wood, 2006, p. 16).

The health information systems needed to evaluate performance are both internal to health care organizations and external between health care organizations. The latter are called regional health information organizations or RHIOs. The electronic medical record (EMR) or electronic health record (EHR) is one of the basic sources of data for internal health information systems, as well as for RHIOs, but both types of systems will include other data as well. These systems will be used to: (a) conduct clinical outcomes studies; (b) measure population health outcomes, such as morbidity and mortality rates for regions, states, and the nation; (c) design and evaluate interventions to improve clinical practice; and (d) increase access, equity, and efficiency.

"Ok ...nurse...tweet all my followers, I'm about to make a thoracic incision."

Office of the National Coordinator for Health Information Technology

Perhaps the most influential health information initiative is that of the Office of the National Coordinator for Health Information Technology (ONC) located in the U.S. Department of Health and Human Services. The ONC has four sequential goals: informing clinicians, interconnecting clinicians, personalizing health care, and improving population health (U.S. Department of Health and Human Services, 2006). The ONC initiative in health information includes a great deal of private-sector reliance on developing communication standards, software, hardware, and training for those who will use the system.

Informing Clinicians

Although using EHRs promotes quality and efficiency in health care settings, few health care organizations and practices in the United States have computerized their medical records as of the writing of this book.

Acceptance is growing, and many hospitals, in particular, have or are obtaining electronic medical record systems. However, most small practices still use paper records exclusively. The ONC has identified several reasons for the slow adoption of EHRs among health care organizations and practices, including the cost of hardware, software, and training and disruption of the present workflow. Therefore, one goal of the ONC is to arrange for the investment in EHRs to be shared between clinicians and others in the health care system. The office is exploring financial and nonfinancial incentives for investors. Second, the ONC will certify EHR software vendors to help clinicians choose vendors with standard products. Third, the ONC will develop a strategy to provide access to EHRs in rural and underserved areas.

Interconnecting Clinicians

The ONC initiative is patient record based, and the second goal of the initiative is to provide access to patient health information in any health care setting, any place in the United States:

> The current practice of using separate paper files for one patient in multiple clinical settings is limiting and can compromise the quality of health-care received. Conversion to an EHR system is necessary but not sufficient to solve the portability problem. That's because each clinician or medical practice may purchase an EHR system from different vendors, which may not be compatible with one another. Unless EHR systems can communicate, they are simply islands of data where patient information does not flow seamlessly from one clinical setting to the next. Without clinicians' ability to exchange information with one another electronically, whether it is across town or across the country, patients' information may not be readily available when and where it is needed. To remedy this, an interoperable system based upon a common architecture must be developed. Patient records would then be available electronically virtually anywhere in the country.

The ONC strategy to create a national health care information network that can be accessed by any health care provider is to foster the development of RHIOs; develop a common set of communication standards to be used by the RHIOs through a National Health Information Network (NHIN); and apply the same standards as developed for the private health care sector to government health care.

Personalizing Health Care

The ONC's third goal is to equip patients to participate actively in their own health care and in health care decision making through the development of a national health information system.

Innovations in technology are emerging to give patients electronic access to their health record and the ability to gather specific information tailored to their illnesses, chronic conditions and health characteristics. Widespread adoption of these innovations, via a concept known as a Personal Health Record (PHR), will revolutionize consumer health care decision-making.

The ONC's strategy for facilitating patient participation in their own health care involves promoting the use of PHRs, stimulating informed consumer choice, and encouraging the use of telehealth systems to improve the quality and cost-effectiveness of health care in rural and underserved areas.

The PHR is an electronic application through which individuals can maintain and manage their health information (and that of others for whom they are authorized) in a private, secure, and confidential environment....For example, a PHR can be used to effectively synthesize an abundance of health information and tailor it to a patient's specific needs.

In order to stimulate informed consumer choice, the ONC supports providing patients or potential patients with information about the quality of their health care providers and organizations and the clinical effectiveness of treatments. The ONC supports and will promote "efforts in the federal government and elsewhere to develop useful clinical performance measures in hospitals, nursing homes, home health agencies and other settings of care."

Population Health

The fourth goal of the ONC is to improve population health through the use of the proposed national health care information system. The ONC supports the use of the system to unify public health surveillance; streamline quality and health status monitoring of populations; and accelerate the rate at which scientific discoveries in medicine are disseminated into medical practice.

By knitting together a unified network of surveillance systems from hospital organizations, physician practices, public health agencies and other sources of incoming data on medical threats, public health professionals will have the relevant information they need to react early or issue preventive measures.

A Health Information Example: National Healthcare Safety Network

The CDC developed an Internet-based data collection and information retrieval system called the National Healthcare Safety Network (NHSN) that became available in 2005. This network is an expansion and enhancement of current surveillance and monitoring capabilities, and once implemented will replace three existing CDC surveillance systems: NNIS, the National Surveillance System for Health Care Workers, and the Dialysis Surveillance Network (CDC, 2005b).

The goal is to create a common interface web-based system for accumulating, exchanging, and integrating relevant information and resources among stake-holders, in an effort to support local efforts to promote patient safety. The two main aspects of the network are reporting of adverse events—including nosocomial infections—and disseminating information on preventing such events. Ultimately, the CDC aims to work with other public health agencies to create a national system integrating data from a variety of surveillance systems into a national aggregate data repository through which health care providers and federal, state, and private stakeholders can exchange data and retrieve information. In the beginning, however, the system will be restricted to providers submitting data in the areas currently covered by the three systems identified earlier, with the CDC acting as the central repository.

Participation

A major benefit of the proposed system will be the collection of data that essentially have been unavailable, as CDC surveillance systems have been focused on a limited number of facilities and procedures. In the current NNIS system, membership is restricted to only approximately 315 hospitals. Participating hospitals must also meet certain thresholds of bed number and size of infection control staff. Under the NSHN, all bonafide health care delivery entities (participants in the Centers for Medicare and Medicaid Services, members of the American Hospital Association, and Veterans Administration stations) whose practice generates relevant data will be encouraged to participate. Nationwide implementation of the system will be phased in, first being available to existing CDC surveillance participants, then to their affiliates, and finally to all health care entities. Nationwide availability of the system was expected sometime in 2006.

Surveillance and Data Collection

The system will be divided into various adverse event modules, including device-associated adverse events, procedure-associated adverse events, and medication-associated adverse events. The infection data collected will be similar to that collected through the NNIS, but with important differences.

Device-Associated Module. Currently, in the intensive care unit and high-risk nursery components of the NNIS system, data are collected on incidence rates and distributions for infections at all sites. In the NHSN system, infection data will initially only be collected for central-line associated bloodstream infections, catheter-associated urinary tract infections, ventilator-associated pneumonia, and infections related to dialysis treatments. Although data on fewer infection sites will be collected under the new system, surveillance will not be limited to the ICU and HRN only. Facilities may also choose to collect and report device-associated infection data for specialty care units, other wards, long-term care facilities, and home therapy. This will provide further flexibility in selecting the event and population under surveillance so that facilities may better tailor surveillance activities to their particular needs.

Procedure-Associated Module. Data will be collected on in and outpatients undergoing NHSN-defined operative procedures. Under NSHN, seven more categories of procedure are covered than under NNIS, and whereas in the NNIS system only information on surgical site infections is collected, under the NSHN information on other surgical complications will also be collected. Further, the data collection protocols being designed for the NSHN will allow for more robust information on infections in surgical patients, including the ability to link bloodstream infections, pneumonia, and urinary tract infections occurring after an operative procedure to the procedure and the ability to monitor—by type of operation—procedure-associated pneumonia regardless of whether a ventilator is used.

Medication-Associated Module. Antimicrobial resistance and antibiotic prescription monitoring will remain essentially unchanged in the transition from current surveillance activities to the NSHN.

Data Analysis and Feedback

The web-based system and central data repository being designed for the NSHN will allow participants to share data in a timely manner between users and public health agencies as well as among users (e.g., a multihospital system). The system will include data analysis wizards and statistical calculators, which will allow facilities (or groups of facilities) to generate custom reports, line lists, tables, graphs, and control charts easily. The ready availability of customizable internal and comparative analysis of infection rates is designed to facilitate the ability of health care providers to engage in continuous performance improvement.

The system will also include a repository of prevention tools, lessons learned, and best practices. It is also designed to provide automatic feedback including alerts for selected adverse events or near misses, identifying sentinel events that require an immediate response and need for root cause analysis, and identifying unusual events that might signal a preventable threat to patient safety.

CONCLUSIONS

We have discussed health care system performance from the perspective of three recognized criteria: (a) quality of health care, (b) equity of health care, and (c) efficiency of health care. Of the three, we have spent the most time on the quality of health care, mainly because over the past 20 years an increasingly large effort has developed to measure and improve quality at the micro-level. Evaluations of clinical effectiveness and patient safety are based on empirical studies that provide evidence about best practices and are the foundation of clinical practice guidelines. These studies have been well funded, and the practice guidelines that have resulted are increasingly used to evaluate the performance of health care providers—individual providers and organizations. Public as well as private organizations are involved in this effort.

Equity in access to and quality of health care, although not a major focus of this chapter, is a major concern to policy makers in the United States. Our history is replete with attempts to make our system equitable by extending health care coverage to all Americans. This history is detailed in the final chapter, but no attempts have been completely successful. The efficiency of the health care system is another area that, although important, has received less attention in this chapter. However, many of the QIs are driven by an equal interest: making our system more efficient.

Finally, we have briefly touched on the importance of data for evaluating health care performance. In the area of health information, there is tremendous activity, partially driven by improvements in the technological capability to computerize information. The electronic medical record will be the standard very shortly for all health care providers—individual and institutional—and the digitizing of this information and other information about patients will follow. Again, this development will have a significant impact on the way care is delivered and how easily it is able to be evaluated. Thus, health information systems, too, will affect the work and future of all health professionals.

NOTE

1. All of these statistics from WHO and UNICEF were the most recently published as of the writing of this book.

REFERENCES

Aday, L. A., Begley, C. E., Lairson, D. R., & Balkrishnan, R. (2004). *Evaluating the healthcare system: Effectiveness, efficiency, and equity.* Chicago. IL: Health Administration Press.

Aday, L. A., Begley, C. E., Lairson, D. R., & Slater, C. H. (1993). *Evaluating the medical care system: Effectiveness, efficiency, and equity.* Ann Arbor, MI: Health Administration Press.

Adler, N. E., Boyce, T., Chesney, M. A., Folkman, S., & Syme, S. L. (1993). Socioeconomic inequalities in health: No easy solution. *Journal of the American Medical Association, 269*(24), 3140–3145.

Adler, N. E., & Rehkopf, D. H. (2008). U.S. disparities in health: Descriptions, causes, and mechanisms. *Annual Review of Public Health, 29,* 235–252.

Agency for Healthcare Research and Quality (AHRQ). (2005, May). *Health care disparities in rural areas: Selected findings from the 2004 National Healthcare Disparities Report.*

Retrieved November 1, 2006, from http://archive.ahrq.gov/research/ruraldisp/ruraldispar.htm

Agency for Healthcare Research and Quality (AHRQ). (2007a). *Mission and budget.* Retrieved February 27, 2007, from www.ahrq.gov/about/budgtix.htm

Agency for Healthcare Research and Quality (AHRQ). (2007b). *AHRQ annual highlights, 2005.* Retrieved February 27, 2007, from www.ahrq.gov/about/highlt05.htm

Agency for Healthcare Research and Quality (AHRQ). (2007c). *Evidence-based practice centers.* Retrieved February 27, 2007, from www.ahrq.gov/clinic/epc

Agency for Healthcare Research and Quality (AHRQ). (2007d). *National quality measures clearinghouse.* Retrieved February 27, 2007, from www.qualitymeasures.ahrq.gov

American Society for Healthcare Engineering of the American Hospital Association (ASHE). (2012). *Deemed status.* Retrieved June 5, 2012, from www.ashe.org/advocacy/organizations/TJC/deemedstatus.html

Asch, S. M., Kerr, E. A., Keesey, J., Adams, J. L., Setodji, C. M., Malik, S., & McGlynn, E. A. (2006). Who is at greatest risk for receiving poor-quality health care? *New England Journal of Medicine, 354*(11), 1147–1156.

Bartley, J. M., & 1997 and 1999 APIC Guidelines Committee. (2000). APIC state-of-the-art report: The role of infection control during construction in health care facilities. *American Journal of Infection Control, 28*(2), 156–169.

Berwick, D. M., Gladfrey, A. B., & Roessner, J. (1990). *Curing health care: New strategies for quality improvement.* San Francisco, CA: Jossey-Bass.

Bolyard, E. A., Tablan, O. C., Williams, W. W., Pearson, M. L., Shapiro, C. N., & Deitchmann, S. D. (1998). Guideline for infection control in health care personnel, 1998. *Infection Control and Hospital Epidemiology, 19*(6), 407–463.

Carson, S., McDonagh, M., & Peterson, K. (2006). A systematic review of the efficacy and safety of atypical antipsychotics in patients with psychological and behavioral symptoms of dementia. *Journal of the American Geriatric Society, 54*(2), 354–361.

Centers for Disease Control and Prevention (CDC), Division of Healthcare Quality Promotion. (2005a). *About the division of healthcare quality promotion (DHQP).* Retrieved March 31, 2007, from www.cdc.gov/ncezid/dhqp

Centers for Disease Control and Prevention (CDC), Division of Healthcare Quality Promotion. (2005b). *National healthcare safety network.* Retrieved December 23, 2006, from www.cdc.gov/nhsn

Centers for Disease Control and Prevention (CDC), NNIS System. (1996). National Nosocomial Infection Surveillance (NNIS) report, data summary from October 1986–April 1996. *American Journal of Infection Control, 24*(5), 380–388.

Centers for Disease Control and Prevention (CDC), NNIS System. (1999). National Nosocomial Infections Surveillance (NNIS) System report, data summary from January 1990–May 1999, issued June 1999. *American Journal of Infection Control, 27*(6), 520–532.

Centers for Disease Control and Prevention (CDC), NNIS System. (2001). National Nosocomial Infections Surveillance (NNIS) report, data summary from January 1992–June 2001. *American Journal of Infection Control, 29*(6), 404–421.

Centers for Disease Control and Prevention (CDC). (2002a). Guidelines for the prevention of intravascular catheter-related infections. *Morbidity and Mortality Weekly Report, 51,* 1–29.

Centers for Disease Control and Prevention (CDC). (2002b). Guideline for hand hygiene in health-care settings: Recommendations of the Healthcare Infection Control Practices Advisory Committee and the HICPAC/SHEA/APIC/IDSA/Hand Hygiene Task Force. *Morbidity and Mortality Weekly Report, 51,* 1–45.

Centers for Disease Control and Prevention (CDC). (2003). Guidelines for environmental infection control in health-care facilities: Recommendations of CDC and the Healthcare Infection Control Practices Advisory Committee (HIC-PAC). *Morbidity and Mortality Weekly Report, 52,* 1–48.

Centers for Disease Control and Prevention (CDC). (2004). Guidelines for preventing health-care-associated pneumonia, 2003: Recommendations of CDC and the Healthcare

Infection Control Practices Advisory Committee (HICPAC). *Morbidity and Mortality Weekly Report, 53*, 1–23.

Centers for Disease Control and Prevention (CDC). (2012a). *Implementing and improving stewardship efforts.* Retrieved January 26, 2012, from www.cdc.gov/getsmart/healthcare

Centers for Disease Control and Prevention (CDC). (2012b). *Healthcare infection control practices advisory committee (HICPAC).* Retrieved January 26, 2012, from www.cdc.gov/hicpac/roster.html

Centers for Medicare and Medicaid Services (CMS). (2007a). *Office of clinical standards and quality.* Retrieved February 26, 2007, from www.cms.gov/CMSLeadership/11_Office_OCSQ.asp

Centers for Medicare and Medicaid Services (CMS). (2007b). *Quality initiatives: Overview.* Retrieved February 26, 2007, from www.cms.hhs.gov/QualityInitiativesGenInfo

Centers for Medicare and Medicaid Services (CMS). (2007c). *Health outcomes survey: Overview.* Retrieved February 26, 2007, from www.cms.hhs.gov/HOS

Centers for Medicare and Medicaid Services (CMS). (2009). *Roadmap for quality measurement in the traditional Medicare fee-for-service program.* Retrieved June 5, 2012, from https://www.cms.gov/Medicare/Quality-Initiatives-Patient-Assessment-Instruments/QualityInitiativesGenInfo/Downloads/QualityMeasurementRoadmap_OEA1-16_508.pdf

Centers for Medicare and Medicaid Services (CMS). (2012). *Conditions for coverage (CfCs) & conditions of participations (CoPs).* Retrieved June 5, 2012, from www.cms.gov/Regulations-and-Guidance/Legislation/CFCsAndCoPs/index.html

Commonwealth Fund. (2006, March). Washington State: An integrated approach to evidence-based drug purchasing. *Commonwealth Fund Newsletter.* New York, NY: Author.

Commonwealth Fund. (2011, October). *Why not the best? The national scorecard on U.S. health system performance, 2011.* Retrieved January 26, 2012, from www.commonwealthfund.org/~/media/Files/Publications/Fund%20Report/2011/Oct/1500_WNTB_Natl_Scorecard_2011_web.pdf

Davis, K., Schoen, C., & Stremikis, K. (2010). *Mirror, mirror on the wall: How the performance of the U.S. health care system compares internationally.* Commonwealth Fund. Retrieved January 26, 2012, from www.commonwealthfund.org/~/media/Files/Publications/Fund%20Report/2010/Jun/1400_Davis_Mirror_Mirror_on_the_wall_2010.pdf

Dlugacz, Y. D., Restifo, A., & Greenwood, A. (2004). *The quality handbook for health care organizations.* San Francisco, CA: Jossey-Bass.

Donabedian, A. (2003). *An Introduction to quality assurance in health care.* Oxford, UK: Oxford University Press.

Donabedian, A. (1980–1985). *Explorations in quality assessment and monitoring. Vol. I: The definition of quality and approaches to its measurement; Vol. II: The criteria and standards of quality; Vol. III: The methods and findings of quality assessment and monitoring—An illustrated analysis.* Ann Arbor, MI: Health Administration Press.

Field, M. J., & Lohr, K. N. (Eds.). (1992). *Guidelines for clinical practice: From development to use.* Washington, DC: National Academies Press.

Fiscella, K., Franks, P., Gold, M. R., & Clancy, C. M. (2000). Inequality in quality: Addressing socioeconomic, racial, and ethnic disparities in health care. *Journal of the American Medical Association, 283*(19), 2579–2584.

Garner, J. S. (1996). Guideline for isolation precautions in hospitals. *American Journal of Infection Control, 24*(1), 24–52.

Geiger, J. (1996). Race and health care—An American dilemma? *New England Journal of Medicine, 335*(11), 815–816.

Goldsteen, K., Goldsteen, R. L., Gladwin, C. J., & Jefferson, J. A. (2004). *Saving lives by eliminating hospital-acquired infections* (Report prepared for the Long Island Community Foundation, Jericho, New York).

Grove, R. D., & Hetzel, A. M. (1968). *Vital statistics rates in the United States: 1940–1960.* Washington, DC: National Center for Health Statistics.

Haley, R. W., Culver, D. H., White J. W., Morgan, W. M., Emori, T. G., Munn, V. P., & Hooton, T. M. (1985). The efficacy of infection surveillance and control programs in preventing nosocomial infections in U.S. hospitals. *American Journal of Epidemiology, 121*(2), 182–205.

Hanrahan, L. P., Foldy, S., Barthell, E. N., & Wood, S. (2006). Medical informatics in population health: Building Wisconsin's strategic framework for health information technology. *Wisconsin Medical Journal, 105*(1), 16–20.

Harbarth, S., Sax, H., & Gastmeier, P. (2003). The preventable proportion of nosocomial infections: An overview of published reports. *Journal of Hospital Infection, 54*(4), 258–266.

Hospital Infection Control Practices Advisory Committee (HICPAC). (1995). Recommendations for preventing the spread of vancomycin resistance: Recommendations of the Hospital Infection Control Practices Advisory Committee (HICPAC). *American Journal of Infection Control, 23*(2), 87–94.

Houghton, D. (2002). Antimicrobial resistance in the intensive care unit: Understanding the problem. *AACN Clinical Issues, 13*, 410–420.

Institute for Healthcare Improvement (IHI). (2012). *About us*. Retrieved January 26, 2012, from www.ihi.org/ihi/about

Institute of Medicine (IOM). (2000). *To err is human: Building a safer health system*. Washington, DC: National Academies Press.

Institute of Medicine (IOM). (2003). *Unequal treatment: Confronting racial and ethnic disparities in health care*. Washington, DC: National Academies Press.

Jonas, S., & Kovner, A. R. (2005). *Health care delivery in the United States* (8th ed.). New York, NY: Springer Publishing.

Kaiser Family Foundation. (2002, May). *Sicker and poorer: The consequences of being uninsured*. Retrieved November 1, 2006, from www.kff.org/uninsured/upload/Full-Report.pdf

Kaiser Family Foundation. (2006, August). *Medicaid and the uninsured: Who are the uninsured? A consistent profile among national surveys*. Retrieved November 1, 2006, from www.kff.org/uninsured/upload/7553.pdf

Kindig, D. A. (1997). *Purchasing population health: Paying for results*. Ann Arbor, MI: University of Michigan Press.

Leape, L. L., Berwick, D. M., & Bates, D. W. (2002). What practices will most improve safety? *Journal of the American Medical Association, 288*(4), 501–507.

Leapfrog Group. (2012). *Mission statement*. Retrieved January 26, 2012, from www.leapfroggroup.org/about_us

Lee, J. S., & Tollen, L. (2002). How low can you go? The impact of reduced benefits and increased cost sharing. *Health Affairs* [Web Exclusive, pp. w229–w241]. Retrieved February 27, 2007, from http://content.healthaffairs.org/cgi/content/full/hlthaff.w2.229v1/DC1

Mangram, A. J., Horan, T. C., Pearson, M. L., Silver, L. C., & Jarvis, W. R. (1999). Guideline for prevention of surgical site infection, 1999. *Infection Control and Hospital Epidemiology, 20*(4), 250–278.

Muto, C. A., Jernigan, J. A., Ostrowsky, B. E., Richet, H. M., Jarvis, W. R., Boyce, J. M., & Farr, B. M. (2003). SHEA Guideline for preventing nosocomial transmission of multidrug-resistant strains of *Staphylococcus aureus* and *Enterococcus*. *Infection Control and Hospital Epidemiology, 24*(5), 362–386.

National Quality Forum (NQF). (2012). *About NQF*. Retrieved June 5, 2012, from www.qualityforum.org/About_NQF/About_NQF.aspx

Occupational Safety and Health Administration (OSHA). (1991). *Bloodborne pathogens standard: 29 CFR 1910.1030*. Washington, DC: U.S. Government Printing Office.

Pappas, G., Queen, S., Hadden, W., & Fisher, G. (1993). The increasing disparity in mortality between socioeconomic groups in the United States, 1960 and 1986. *New England Journal of Medicine, 329*(15), 1139.

Perrow, C. (1984). *Normal accidents*. New York, NY: Basic Books.

Reschovsky, J. D., & Staiti, A. B. (2005). Access and quality: Does rural America lag behind? *Health Affairs, 24*(4), 1128–1139.

Richards, C., Emori, T. G., Edwards, J., Fridkin, S., Tolson, J., & Gaynes, R. (2001). Characteristics of hospitals and infection control professionals participating in the National Nosocomial Infection Surveillance System 1999. *American Journal of Infection Control, 29*(6), 400–403.

Rutala, W. A., & 1994–1996 APIC Guidelines Committee. (1996). APIC guideline for selection and use of disinfectants. *American Journal of Infection Control, 24*(4), 313–342.

Rutala, W. A., & Weber, D. J. (2001). New disinfection and sterilization methods. *Emerging Infectious Diseases, 7*(2), 348–353.

Sackett, D. L., Rosenberg, W. M. C., Gray, J. A. M., Haynes, R. B., & Richardson, W. S. (1996). Evidence based medicine: What it is and what it isn't. *British Medical Journal, 312*(7023), 71–72.

Schwartz, E., Kofie, V. Y., Rivo, M., & Tuckson, R. V. (1990). Black/White comparisons of deaths preventable by medical interventions. *International Journal of Epidemiology, 19*(3), 591–598.

Shlaes, D. M., Gerding, D. N., John, J. F., Craig, W. A., Bornstein, D. L., Duncan, R. A.,...Watanakunakorn, C. (1997). Society for Healthcare Epidemiology of America and Infectious Diseases Society of America Joint Committee on the Prevention of Antimicrobial Resistance: Guidelines for the prevention of antimicrobial resistance in hospitals. *Infection Control and Hospital Epidemiology, 18*(4), 275–291.

The Joint Commission. (2012). *Facts about The Joint Commission.* Retrieved June 5, 2012, from www.jointcommission.org/facts_about_the_joint_commission

UNICEF. (2006). *Definitions: Basic indicators.* Retrieved December 22, 2006, from www.unicef.org/infobycountry/stats_popup1.html

U.S. Census Bureau. (2005). *Statistical abstract of the United States: 2006.* Washington, DC: U.S. Department of Commerce.

U.S. Census Bureau. (2006, August). *Income, poverty and health insurance coverage in the United States: 2005.* Washington, DC: U.S. Department of Commerce.

U.S. Congress, Office of Technology Assessment. (1995). *Impacts of antibiotic-resistant bacteria.* Washington, DC: U.S. Government Printing Office. OTA-H-269.

U.S. Department of Health and Human Services, Office of the National Coordinator for Health Information Technology. (2006). *Goals of strategic framework.* Retrieved October 31, 2006, from www.hhs.gov/healthit/goals.html

Van Den Heuvel, J., Bogers, A. J. J., Does, R. J. M. M., van Dijk, S. F., & Berg, M. (2006). Quality management: does it pay off? *Quality Management in Health Care, 15*(3), 137–149.

Weinstein, R. A. (1998). Nosocomial infection update. *Emerging Infectious Diseases, 4*(3), 416–420.

White House. (2005). *President signs Patient Safety and Quality Improvement Act of 2005.* Retrieved January 26, 2012, from http://georgewbush-whitehouse.archives.gov/news/releases/2005/07/20050729.html

World Health Organization (WHO). (2012a). *World health statistics.* Retrieved January 26, 2012, from www.who.int/gho/publications/world_health_statistics/2011/en/index.html

World Health Organization (WHO). (2012b). *Life tables for WHO member states.* Retrieved January 26, 2012, from www.who.int/healthinfo/statistics/mortality_life_tables/en

SEVEN

History of Change: From Prepaid Group Medical Practice to Managed Care

During the 20th century, health care delivery grew from a cottage industry to a corporate enterprise. When the 20th century opened, doctors were mostly solo practitioners, hospitals were single, independent entities, long-term care for the elderly was largely home-based, and pharmaceutical and medical device manufacturing was small business—a minor part of the American economy that accommodated individual patients and physicians. As of 2008, health care spending accounted for 16.2% of the gross domestic product (GDP) (National Center for Health Statistics [NCHS], 2011, Table 122), compared to 5.2% in 1960 and even less in 1900 (Goldman & McGlynn, 2005). Today, health care spending is the largest single sector in the American economy (Goldman & McGlynn, 2005). Long-term care for the elderly is largely provided by either privately or publicly held companies, with two-thirds of nursing homes being proprietary (Stevenson, Grabowski, Bramson, 2009; GAO, 2010). In our time, the pharmaceutical industry is a multibillion dollar corporate enterprise that attracts foreign capital and is described in the language of the venture-capitalist:

> Since the mid-90's the industry has been undergoing a consolidation period. Mergers involving many large and medium size companies have been common in this period. The success of the stock market has made large amounts of capital available at reasonable rates for borrowing or for raising equity. The companies involved in the mergers are biotech companies, who develop products based on living cells. Also involved are companies who have developed new technology in unlocking the genetic makeup of humans.
>
> Many foreign companies have been entering the United States market because of its uncontrolled pricing structure, rapid approval processes, private and public insurance reimbursement policies and government support for basic research. Additionally, the industry enjoys many tax benefits not available in other countries, although the benefits are narrowing. (IRS, 2012)

This chapter and the next describes the evolution of two aspects of the health care delivery system in the United States that have resulted from the growth discussed above—organization and financing. They are linked, certainly, each trend having an effect on the other. Both are intimately tied to the cost of health care and an overall desire among policy makers and health care payers to reduce, or at least contain, costs. The organizational changes described in this chapter have also been prompted by the wish to improve the efficiency of health care delivery and the coordination of care. The financing changes discussed in the next chapter are described in terms of "health care reform." The calls for health care reform throughout the 20th century and into the 21st century have largely had two bases: cost containment and improved access to health care.

We begin with the organizational changes in health care delivery over the past century.

GROUP MEDICAL PRACTICE

Modern managed care, the current endpoint of the evolution of health care delivery organization, may be said to have evolved from prepaid multispecialty group medical practice, a form of physician organization that began in this country about a century ago (Fox, 1996; MacColl, 1966;

Mayer & Mayer, 1985). Over time, group medical practice has slowly and gradually become the most common organizational form, changing from solo physician practice. Detailed data on physician profiles and socioeconomic characteristics are found in an annual publication of the American Medical Association, *Physician Characteristics and Distribution in the United States*.

Group medical practice has taken various shapes: private fee-for-service, single or multispecialty group practice; prepaid multispecialty group practice; the health maintenance organization (HMO), including the independent practice association; and the newer forms of physician association that have appeared as managed care (MC) has grown and developed. Other than in the single-specialty variant of private fee-for-service group practice, virtually all groups in the other forms are of the multispecialty variety. At least five elements of medical practice can be shared in one way or another by a group of physicians: space, supporting staff, practice income, practice expenditures, and medical work. Many of the numerous possible permutations and combinations of these elements appear in various forms throughout the U.S. health care delivery system.

Physicians in Group Practice

The American Medical Association (1996) has defined *group medical practice* as:

> The provision of health care services by three or more physicians who are formally organized as a legal entity in which business and clinical facilities, records, and personnel are shared. Income from medical services provided by the group are treated as receipts of the group and distributed according to some prearranged plan. (p. 1)

The definition that appears in *Managed Health Care Simplified: A Glossary of Terms* (Austrin, 1999, p. 90), is very similar to this one.

Private Group Medical Practice

Private fee-for-service medical groups may be single specialty or multispecialty. Single-specialty groups are common in surgery and the surgical subspecialties (e.g., urology and orthopedics), obstetrics and gynecology, anesthesia, and radiology and are found in increasing numbers in family practice, internal medicine, pediatrics, and the medical subspecialties (e.g., cardiology and neurology) as well. There are some private fee-for-service multispecialty groups, but these are less common.

The major advantages of private group medical practice for physicians are cost sharing for space and supporting staff and services, the ability to engage allied health personnel to an extent usually not feasible for the solo practitioner, the sharing of coverage responsibilities for nights and week-ends, the ability to readily take vacations and attend academic meetings without having to make special coverage arrangements each time, and ready access to informal consultations when faced with a difficult diagnostic or therapeutic problem.

Prepaid Group Practice

Prepaid group practice (PGP) first appeared on a very limited basis in the 1890s (MacColl, 1966; Mayer & Mayer, 1985). It took two revolutionary steps forward in how physicians organized for practice. First was the payment to the physicians of a flat fee on a regular basis on behalf of each potential patient to guarantee medical coverage for that person during some specified time period, usually a year. This fee was paid whether or not medical services were used and regardless of how much medical service was used. The practice of paying a flat fee to a physician to provide a stipulated range of services for a patient for a given time period, regardless of how much or how little care the patient needs or uses, came to be known as *capitation* (now one of the two senses in which the term is used).

Organizationally, the payment for medical care in advance of any use contrasted PGP and its system of provider payment with *indemnity health insurance*. As described earlier, indemnity health insurance was the type of insurance traditionally provided by both BlueCross BlueShield and the commercial insurance companies before the advent of managed care (Tufts Health Care Institute, 2006): "Insurance that reimburses an individual for fees paid for medical services after they are performed. Payments may be made to the patient or directly to the providers, on a retrospective, fee-for-service basis."

Indemnity health insurance was commonly used in both fee-for-service private medical practice and item-of-service hospital reimbursement. However, those sources of care are not employed by, contracted to, or owned by the insurer. The insurer simply pays the freight, according to some agreed-to schedule; the financial responsibility (or risk) for the health care provided is born by the insurer.

Under the indemnity system, beneficiaries (in most cases, the beneficiaries' employers) pay sums (usually called premiums) to the insurance companies, which in turn pay the providers for the care used by the beneficiaries. Under indemnity insurance, payment is made on a fee-for-service or item-of-service basis, after the fact (or *retrospectively*). There are usually some personal payments (*deductibles* and *coinsurance*) that the beneficiaries must make themselves, as well as specified limits in dollars and units/types of service that are covered by the insurance package. This was the traditional type of insurance provided by both BlueCross BlueShield and the commercial insurance companies, before the advent of managed care.

It was commonly used in both fee-for-service private medical practice and item-of-service hospital reimbursement.

Historical Background

The two principal modern organizational pioneers in this field were the Health Insurance Plan (HIP) in New York City and Kaiser-Permanente on the West Coast (MacColl, 1966; Smits, 2002, pp. 290–292). Both were founded during the Great Depression of the 1930s. They entered periods of significant growth after World War II. As had their much smaller, much poorer predecessors in the early 20th century, they encountered much resistance from "organized medicine," that is, the American Medical Association and the state and county medical societies.

The resistance was based primarily on an antipathy to the ways in which these groups paid their physicians. One method was straight salary. The other was capitation, described earlier. Both methods were antithetical to the fee-for-service, piecework system that they were to replace.

Organized medicine also did not like the idea of providing medical care under contracts negotiated between groups of physicians and groups of patients. Organized medicine always claimed that their opposition to cap-itation and contracts had nothing to do with money, but with principle. It "distorted incentives," "made the doctor a wage slave," "interfered with medical judgment," "put a corporation between the physician and the patient," and "removed the symbol (the private fee) of the special relation-ship between doctor and patient." (It would do well to remember the old adage, "When they say 'it's not the money,' it's the money.") As both man-aged care and capitation spread as the preferred managed care mecha-nism for paying physicians, in part the outcomes that organized medicine so feared did come to pass. However, because the primary engineers of this change were the politically well-connected powers in the insurance industry rather than a small number of poorly connected political "do-gooders" of an earlier era, the medical profession found itself unable to resist the changes. It was indeed not coincidental that, in the 1990s, physi-cian incomes began to decline ("The Squeeze," 1996), at least for the time being.

Forms of Prepaid Group Practice

There are two major forms of PGP. In the *staff model*, the physicians work directly for the PGP organization on a salaried basis. HIP provided the classic example of the staff model PGP. In the *group model*, the physicians join together to form their own company. It in turn contracts to provide medical services with the financing and administrative entity that in turn sells the prepaid health care coverage package to beneficiaries or their employers. In this case, the physicians' group company pays its individual members, either on a salary or on a capitation basis. Kaiser-Permanente was the classic example of the group model PGP.

The Advantages of Classic Prepaid Group Practice

As George Silver (1963) and William MacColl (1966) noted back in the 1960s, there are many potential advantages of PGP. For the physicians, they include the opportunity to share knowledge and responsibility, the establishment of a rational division of labor between generalist and specialist, improved quality of care, regularly allotted time for continuing medical education, a regular work schedule, guaranteed (although not necessarily high) income, a fringe benefit package including malpractice insurance, better access to ancillary personnel and services, and freedom from concerns with the business aspects of medical practice.

For the patients, the advantages include no or low charges at time of service, one-stop shopping for 24-hour, 7-day service, continuity of care, and protection against unnecessary hospitalization and surgery. The primary disadvantages for patients center around the possible development of a clinic atmosphere, loss of choice of physician and hospital, delays in receiving service, locational inconvenience, and impersonality.

Typically, the most serious problem with PGP has been that such practices do not often achieve their significant potential for improving medicine. E. Richard Weinerman, an early advocate of PGP, reviewed the experience in 1968. He was quite disappointed with what he found. His observations, although made a long time ago, still apply to many current HMOs and other managed care organization (MCOs). Many of the organizational advantages for the physicians have been implemented, but clinical medicine often remains largely a matter for individual, rather than true group, practice. "Group conferences," Weinerman (1968) said, "medical audits and informal office consultations are, in my experience, more common in the descriptive literature than in daily practice" (p. 1423). He concluded:

> Perhaps most disappointing has been the hesitation on the part of most medical groups to effect changes in the "way of life" of the medical team itself. This would involve acceptance by the group as a whole of collective responsibility for the health of its patients or members...would mean actively reaching out into the community for...early detection...[and] identification and special protection for those at specific risk of disease...[and] would imply particular concern for those patients who do not use the service....It implies as much concern with rapport as with diagnostic labels, as much with education as prescription. (p. 1429)

In our era, an addition to the Weinerman conception of group practice would be a clear focus on the health of the public it served, as well as on that of each of its individual members (Koplan & Harris, 2000; Levi, 2000).

Just as with Weinerman's observations in the 1960s, early reflection on the reality of buzz phrases describing the supposed advantages of managed care—"physician–patient partnership," "putting prevention into practice," "make use of community resources," and "work from the epidemiology of the practice"—was that they were likely to be "more common in the descriptive literature than in daily practice." Today there is still no evidence that, with an occasional exception, much progress has been made along these lines in the intervening years since Weinerman made his somewhat acerbic comments.

HEALTH MAINTENANCE ORGANIZATIONS

From Prepaid Group Practice to Health Maintenance Organization

The trail from PGP to managed care was blazed in part by the health services entities known as HMOs. (Recall that HMO is sometimes used to mean all of the MCO forms, but they are really distinct) The HMO movement was originally sponsored by the first Nixon administration (1969–1973). President Nixon was interested in the idea because it had been shown that PGP could save significant amounts of money, primarily by reducing hospitalization rates (Roemer & Shonick, 1973). Although the organizational form produced the desired outcomes, there happened to be two problems with using the name *prepaid group practice* to describe what the Nixon administration wanted to do.

First was the label itself. It happened that, in attacking the institution of PGP over the years, organized medicine had liberally red-baited it. That was hardly something a president who had first come to national prominence at the height of the post–World War II McCarthyite anticommunist hysteria would want to be associated with. Second, the developer of the HMO concept, Paul Ellwood, had in mind not only PGP but also prepaid individual practice, first known as the "foundation for medical care," later as the independent practice association (IPA; see later discussion).

Although only in the latter stages of development did PGP take on financial and operational responsibility for hospital, as well as ambulatory care, the whole inpatient/outpatient package was built into the HMO concept from the beginning, for reasons of cost containment if nothing else. Thus, a new name for the old entity with significant new elements had to be found. The name that Ellwood himself came up with was HMO.

Definitions of HMO

A simple definition of the term *HMO* was provided by Shouldice (1991):

> An HMO is defined as any organization, either for-profit or nonprofit, that accepts responsibility for providing and delivering a predetermined set of comprehensive health maintenance and treatment services to a voluntarily enrolled population for a pre-negotiated and fixed periodic premium payment. [In short], HMOs are organizations that insure groups of individuals against the costs of medical services and also provide those medical services. (pp. 13, 449)

This is similar to the definition of PGP presented earlier, except that group practice per se is not specified (see also Austrin, 1999, pp. 95,96). Luft identified the characteristics of HMOs in 1980 as follows:

1. The organization assumes contractual responsibility to provide or arrange for a package of health care services, at a minimum, hospital care and physician services. The HMO assumes a set of legal obligations, set forth in a written contract that also specifies the premium to be paid for that provision.
2. The organized delivery system serves an enrolled and defined population, with enrollment required for a specified minimum period of time.
3. HMO members are enrolled on a voluntary basis.
4. The HMO receives a fixed, periodic payment, independent of the volume of services provided to each enrollee, from the firm or agency paying for the coverage for that enrollee. This is a capitated (patient-service) payment, as opposed to a capitated (provider) payment.
5. The provider/financing organization assumes financial risk (i.e., of a financial loss should the accumulated capitation payments not cover the cost of providing the contracted for services to all of the enrollees).

Today, the National Center for Health Statistics (NCHS, 2007) defines HMOs as follows:

> An HMO is a health care system that assumes or shares both the financial risks and the delivery risks associated with providing comprehensive medical services to a voluntarily enrolled population in a particular geographic area, usually in return for a fixed, prepaid fee. Pure HMO enrollees use only the prepaid capitated health services of the HMO panel of medical care providers. Open-ended HMO enrollees use the prepaid HMO health services but, in addition, may receive medical care from providers who are not part of the HMO panel. There is usually

a substantial deductible, copayment, or coinsurance associated
with use of nonpanel providers.

Additional complexities arise that must be taken into account (Barton,
1999; Dudley & Luft, 2001). First, in certain locales, there is competition
for patients among two or more HMOs. Thus, an HMO does not necessarily serve a defined population in a defined geographic area. Second,
the enrollment profile of any one HMO is now constantly changing as
employers and, in cases where employees have multiple-choice options,
beneficiaries move from one HMO to another. (Medicare beneficiaries
electing to use an HMO under Medicare+Choice may change membership each month if they so choose.)

Third, for certain beneficiaries, membership in a given HMO is not necessarily voluntary: Some employers offer only one health service option
to their employees or make one HMO more desirable than other plans
through financial and other incentives to the employee. In this case, if the
employee wants to take advantage of an offered health care benefit, he or
she can use only an HMO (rather than a traditional fee-for-service provider), and it must be the HMO that the employer selects. Fourth, unless
one adopts a very broad definition of *medical group practice*, many HMOs
cannot be characterized as one.

Complicating the picture even further, certain entirely new organizational forms have arisen over the past 20 years. It was the increasing number of permutations and combinations of the various organizational forms
that led Professor Kodner to his "when you've seen one, you've seen one"
conclusion. It would seem to be more apt than ever in the middle of the
first decade of the 21st century.

Indeed, in the 1990s in addition to the newer definition of the HMO, a
newer typology of HMO, and then managed care forms, was developed.
The HMO typology, stemming originally from the early 1970s, reflected
the adaptation of PGP to the HMO model and the addition to it of the independent practice association form (Austrin, 1999; Barton, 1999, Table 2.1;
Shouldice, 1991, pp. 96ff). The following definitions are from the National
Center for Health Statistics (2007):

1. *Staff model.* "A type of closed-panel HMO (where patients can receive
   services only through a limited number of providers) in which physicians are employees of the HMO. The providers see members in the
   HMO's own facilities."
2. *Group model.* "An HMO that contracts with a single multi-specialty
   medical group to provide care to the HMO's membership. The group
   practice may work exclusively with the HMO, or it may provide services to non-HMO patients as well. The HMO pays the medical group
   a negotiated per capita rate, which the group distributes among its physicians, usually on a salaried basis."

3. *Independent practice association (IPA).* "A type of healthcare provider organization composed of a group of independent practicing physicians who maintain their own offices and band together for the purpose of contracting their services to HMOs, Preferred Provider Organizations (PPO), and insurance companies. An IPA may contract with and provide services to both HMO and non-HMO plan participants." The physicians remain in their offices, which they own and in which they see HMO enrollees. There is no group practice at any level of abstraction and no pooling of either medical or ancillary service resources. The physicians may be paid on either a capitation or fee-for-service basis by the IPA central organization.

4. *Network model.* "An HMO model that contracts with multiple physician groups to provide services to HMO members; may involve large single and multi-specialty groups."

5. *Mixed.* "An HMO that combines features of more than one HMO model."

One major difference between group and staff model HMOs, on the one hand, and IPAs, on the other, is that the former have *closed* medical staffs; that is, the HMO or medical group has full control over its members, whereas, in most cases, any physician who can meet the (usually minimal) membership qualifications can join an IPA, at his or her option. It should be noted that, although for the most part any physician can join any IPA, the IPA medical manager usually has the power to "deselect" any physician who does not abide by the IPA's rules and procedures. Just as there are limitations in using and applying the original definition of an HMO, by the end of the 1990s there were some still newer organizational forms that the earlier HMO typology did not cover (Barton, 1999, Table 2.1). We review some of these forms later, in the section on managed care.

HMOs Entering the 1990s and Into the 21st Century

Among the developments that were undertaken by HMOs as they prepared to meet the challenges of the 21st century were the following:

- The introduction of point of service plans, allowing members to use non-plan providers by paying an additional fee. The point of service (POS) plan (NCHS, 2007) "allows members to choose to receive services from a participating or nonparticipating network provider, usually with a financial disincentive for going outside the network. More of a product than an organization, POS plans can be offered by HMOs, PPOs, or self-insured employers."
- Increasing cooperation between HMOs and major health insurers such as BlueCross BlueShield.
- Acceptance of workers' compensation cases.

- Expansion of health promotion/disease prevention, work site safety, and employees' assistance programs. (The original function of Employee Assistance Programs [EAPs] was to serve employees with addictive behavior problems. Some have expanded their work well beyond that arena.)

Also becoming more common is the network model, a hybrid form that usually has at its center an HMO, commonly of the IPA type, then points of service (Hagland, 1996). It allows HMO patients to go outside of plan to providers of their choice. These providers are then paid on an indemnity basis, with the patient bearing a significant deductible/coinsurance burden. The increase in the availability of point of service plans has continued in response to patient demands. Of course, only those persons who can afford the cost of such plans, or who work for employers who can, are able to take advantage of such plans.

MANAGED CARE

©Cartoonist Group. By Bob and Tom Thaves.

Historical Background

Managed care has been controversial since it became a common organizational form of delivery of health services. For example, in October 1996, *Consumer Reports* magazine ("Can HMOs Help," 1996) noted: "The public didn't vote for managed care. Nor did its representatives in Congress. Yet HMOs are swiftly reshaping the way Americans get their health care." At about the same time, C. Everett Koop (1996), the Surgeon General of the United States under President Ronald Reagan, observed:

> The biggest surprise in the past two years has been the rapid growth of a system known as managed care. Millions of Americans have been shifted into health-maintenance organizations, dramatically restructuring the financing and delivery of health care. The original impetus for managed care came from physicians who wanted the freedom to treat their patients without

being worried about whether they could pay for each visit, test, or procedure. In the early HMOs, cost containment was an unexpected benefit, not a primary purpose.... But now the rapidly proliferating HMOs—most of them investor-owned and for profit—seem to be interested firstly in managing costs and only secondarily in maintaining health. (p. 69)

Strictly speaking, the term HMO refers to just one of the organizational forms that is covered by the terms managed care (MC) and managed care organization (MCO). Historically, the introduction of the term *HMO* preceded that of the terms MC and MCO by some time. The first, when used under its strict definition, describes one particular set of health services organizations. The latter two have a broader meaning.

In the common health care system parlance of today, however, it happens that the terms are often used interchangeably, as in the 16-year-old *Consumer Reports* quote. Nevertheless, in this chapter, HMO refers to a specific health care delivery organizational form, whereas MC and MCO are used to refer to the whole group of organizational forms subsumed under the generic term *managed care*, described later. In other quotations in this chapter, the reader may well find the terms used interchangeably, as in the preceding quote.

As the MCO system continued to haphazardly restructure the U.S. health care delivery system, Koop's last observation framed the central question concerning the managed care revolution. As Dennis Kodner (personal communication, 1996), H. Jack Geiger (1997), Thomas Bodenheimer and colleagues (Bodenheimer, Lo, & Casalino, 1999), and the screenwriter Ilene Chaiken (2002) have also put that question (and no one of more recent vintage has put it any better): Is this revolution about managed *cost* (and potential profits), or about managed *care* (and potential improvements in the quality of medical care)?

In 1996 *Consumer Reports* ("Can HMOs Help," 1996) observed further:

Many HMOs do offer high-quality treatment. But many people who join an HMO give up a lot: the ability to choose where and how they are treated; long-standing relationships with their [present] doctors, who might not be part of the HMO; convenient access to care; and sometimes, care that is essential to their health.

In 2001, Dudley and Luft (2001) noted:

Patients have had mixed reactions to managed care; they like the low co-payments and reduced paperwork but view some managed care practices as emphasizing cost control over quality. In fact, there is widespread concern among the public, physicians, and legislators about the effect of managed care on the quality of care. (p. 1087)

Also in 2001, a survey done by the Kaiser Family Foundation and the Harvard School of Public Health put it quite succinctly: "Americans' perceptions of the managed care industry have been substantially more negative over the past several years [than they were previously], but there has been little change recently."

Looking at the situation from a broader perspective raised other issues regarding managed care. MC did not, nor by its very nature can it, solve many of the major problems faced by the health care delivery system: the marked geographic maldistribution of facilities and personnel; the serious imbalances within the medical profession between specialists and generalists and a probable oversupply of physicians in toto with an undersupply of primary care specialists; a growing shortage of registered nurses and other specialized hospital personnel; the severe lack of emphasis on both personal prevention and public health; a medical focus on the uncommon but glamorous as contrasted with the common but mundane; an overemphasis on the use of technology and drugs in diagnosis and treatment as contrasted with the use of interpersonal communication and the enhancement of self-efficacy for health; and significant deficits in health sciences education and biomedical research policy and practice in relation to public health and health care service needs. It is in this context, then, that we proceed with our examination of managed care.

Definition of Managed Care

The definition of MC is undergoing constant change. Several of the principal definitions that have appeared over time are presented next. Just as MC itself has evolved from the HMO, so have the definitions of MC evolved from the definitions of HMO.

Looking at the situation from the perspective of the primary purchaser of health care cost coverage (most often the employer), rather than from that of either the provider or the patient, an early observer of the MC phenomenon, Peter Fox (1990), wrote:

> "Managed care"...broadly defined, encompasses any measure that, from the perspective of the purchaser of health care, favorably affects the price of services, the site at which the services are received, or their utilization. As such, it represents a continuum—from plans that, for example, do no more than require prior authorization of inpatient stays, to the staff model HMO that employs its doctors and assumes risk for delivering a comprehensive benefit package. Ideally managed care should not simply seek to reduce costs; rather, it should strive to maximize value, which includes a concern with quality and access. (p. 1)

222 Jonas' Introduction to the U.S. Health Care System

Barton (1999) offered a succinct definition of managed care: "In managed care, both patient utilization and provider practices are managed by an entity that has fiduciary interest in the interactions between them" (p. 26). Austrin (1999) went on to offer a normative definition:

> Managed care [is a] system that uses financial incentives and management controls to direct patients to providers who are responsible for giving appropriate, cost-effective care.... [M] anaged care systems are intended to control the cost of health care by emphasizing prevention, early intervention and outpatient care. (p. 1118)

The common techniques that MCOs (and, indeed, HMOs before them) use to control expenditures are *precertification* for hospital admission and the use of many diagnostic and therapeutic interventions, and what is called *case management*. Under precertification, the responsible physician obtains from some central office of the MCO the permission to proceed along a certain medical line of investigation and treatment before actually proceeding to do so. Case management is keeping close track of what is happening to hospitalized patients and making sure that their care and discharge planning follow along preset lines as indicated by the admitting diagnosis, unless there are very good medical reasons to deviate from them.

There are a number of different forms of MCOs (Barton, 1999, pp. 31–41). The range can be seen as a continuum, beginning with managed indemnity (adding some elements of cost control, precertification, and case management to indemnity insurance) and ending with the integrated delivery system (IDS) (see later discussion). The most common of these forms are:

- Health maintenance organization (HMO, as previously covered)
- Preferred provider organization (PPO). "A PPO is a type of medical plan where coverage is provided to participants through a network of selected health care providers (such as hospitals and physicians). The enrollees may go outside the network, but they would pay a greater percentage of the cost of coverage than within the network" (NCHS, 2007). These are groups of independent providers (usually private practitioners or private medical groups) that have contracted with an insurer to provide named services at fixed fees. (Unlike most IPAs, the PPO does not focus on the provision of primary care or comprehensive care, but is used more commonly for physicians providing specialty diagnostic and therapeutic procedures.) The fees are set below the prevailing market rate. The insurer's beneficiaries are given a list of the preferred providers. Although the patients do not have to choose a provider from the list, they are guaranteed that if they do so, there will be no or low copayments. The advantage to the insurer is cost saving; to the provider, it is a guarantee of work.

- Exclusive provider organization (EPO): similar to the PPO, except that the beneficiary must choose a physician on the insurer's list if he or she is to receive any reimbursement for the costs of care
- Independent practice association (IPA, previously covered)
- Independent practice organization (IPO): similar to an IPA, but whereas in the IPA the physicians deal with one insurer, in an IPO an organized group of independently practicing physicians accepts patients and payments from more than one insurer
- Physician hospital organization/combined provider organization (PHO/CPO): a variant of the PPO/EPO/IPA/IPO concept that is organized by a hospital and/or its medical staff. There are many possible combinations of insurance mechanisms, administrative forms, benefit packages, use of copayment, and means of physician and institutional reimbursement. They are usually formed to provide a hospital and its medical staff the opportunity to band together to negotiate favorable rates with payers.
- Point of service plans (POS, previously covered)

More Questions, More Definitional Complications

In addition to the more complex typology, there are other characteristics that must be taken into account in understanding the field of managed care. Welch and his colleagues (1990) set forth several questions that are still to this day relevant, the answers to which help improve understanding of the complexity that is MC.

1. Do the physicians in a given MCO see MCO patients only, or do they have a mixed practice?
2. Is there an organizational "middle tier" that might process payment, carry out case management and utilization review, handle quality assurance, and possibly offer office management services to physicians in an IPA, standing between the MCO that has the contractual obligation to provide the services to its enrollees and the individual and institutional providers of those services?
3. Is there a "withhold" in the payment arrangement with the physicians? Is physician payment withheld until it is clear that certain performance standards, primarily focused on utilization and cost containment, have been met, usually over the course of a year?

Hornbook and Goodman (1991) added two important defining questions, also still quite valid:

1. Is there vertical integration between physicians and institutions? If so, how much (see later discussion, "Integrated Delivery Systems")?
2. Is the ownership for-profit or not-for-profit?

Finally, one can consider these additional questions in characterizing MCOs:

1. What is the size of the risk pool?
2. How many providers belong to the MCO?
3. Do individual providers themselves accept financial risks, and do they routinely buy reinsurance against the possibility that one of their patients might unavoidably require very expensive care for a very serious illness?
4. How does one characterize MCOs serving special needs populations (e.g., the mentally ill, patients with acquired immunodeficiency syndrome, and drug abusers), Medicare populations, and Medicaid populations?
5. Suppose a PPO accepts risk and engages in a contract for total care provision. Is it then an MCO?

Despite the complexity of the MCO definition and typology, however, it appears advisable not to get caught up in their minuscule details, unless one is engaged in MC research or responsible for planning an MCO to be successful in a particular market. After all is said and done, there are still four major groups of MCOs: staff-model HMOs; group-model HMOs; IPAs of various sorts; and an expanding category of "others," such as PPOs, PHOs, and networks.

Why Managed Care Developed When It Did

There are several explanations for the relatively sudden development of managed care. One is that, in the mid-1980s, private corporations figured out how they could appropriate for themselves the monetary surpluses generated by the U.S. health care delivery system that had typically gone to physicians, especially those in procedure-focused specialties. The medium was a cost-containment intervention called utilization review (UR).

UR had been introduced in the early days of Medicare. It was an attempt to get control of the major and continuing cost increases generated by the "usual and customary fee" system for paying physicians that the American Medical Association had extracted from the Johnson administration as its price for peacefully going along with the introduction of Medicare. It happens that medicine has a peculiar market for its services. Unlike most markets, in which the buyer generates the demand, in medicine, utilization of almost any service other than emergency care or a routine office visit is almost always provider, not patient, generated.

In this environment, the original open-ended Medicare reimbursement system invited both physician-created "demand," and thus the potential for overuse, and a gradual upward spiral in those "usual and customary fees" set by the physicians themselves. UR looked at and evaluated what physicians were actually doing in terms of the provision of diagnostic and treatment services and hospital utilization for their patients. It was thus one way to try to bring that system and its attendant steadily increasing expenditures under some kind of control.

The way UR was used in Medicare, as an after-the-fact review, was not particularly successful in achieving its announced objectives of utilization and cost containment. Other systems, such as diagnosis-related groups (DRGs), were eventually put in its place. But in dealing with physicians, private health care corporations learned from this example that if they instituted before-the-fact review, the so-called management of care, and required preuse approval, they could reduce utilization significantly. And that they have been able to do.

Although shortages may develop in the future, at least in the procedure-oriented specialties, there is presently an apparent oversupply of physicians. This is the product, at least in part, of the absolute refusal of the U.S. medical establishment to engage in any sort of physician supply planning. Given hospital occupancy rates, there is certainly a remaining financial burden resulting from the massive overbuilding of hospitals after World War II into the 1980s. (This state of affairs is the product of the very strong resistance of the U.S. hospital industry to any kind of meaningful facilities or services planning.) In this context, for-profit MCOs have been able to institute preauthorization UR on a massive scale, driving down both utilization and prices in the face of facilities and personnel oversupply. At the same time, they have been able to reap handsome profits for themselves and provide handsome incomes for their top executives (Kleinke, 2001, chapter 3).

It was this institution of physician-generated utilization controls that made it possible for the for-profit health services sector to enter the arena of the direct provision of care. For the most part, for-profit health services corporations had been standing outside of the central business of health care, the provision of physician services, until the 1990s. They had been content with pharmaceuticals, hospital supply, nursing homes, and some hospitals. But when presented with the opportunity to take some significant proportion of the excess income that was being generated by the physicians from them and arrogate it to themselves, they took it.

Managed Care Today

As of 2006, 93% of working Americans not on Medicare who had health insurance were enrolled in an MCO of some type through their employer (Kaiser Family Foundation, 2006, Chart 8). The percentage of employees in an indemnity plan had declined from 73% in 1988 to 3% in 2006. The period of steepest decline was 1988 through 1996, when the indemnity plans declined to 27% of workers. The PPO has become the most frequent type of HIP for insured workers (60% in 2006). Growth in HMO membership plateaued in 1998 and began to decline slightly in 2000 (Draper, Hurley, & Short, 2004).

Although about 98% of large employers (200+ employees) offered health care benefits, only about 48% of very small employers (3–9 workers) and 73% of small employers (10–24 workers) did so (Kaiser Family Foundation, 2006, Exhibit 2.2). It is noteworthy that the overall insured rate dropped from 69% in 2000 to 61% in 2006, because of a decline in the number of the smallest firms to offer health insurance to their employees. Additionally, whereas more than 29% of the "jumbo" firms (5,000+ workers) offered a choice of plans, fewer than 10% of small employers (3–199 workers) did so (Kaiser Family Foundation, 2006, Exhibit 4.1). Also of note is that the percentage of jumbo firms offering only one plan increased from 7% in 2000 to 29% in 2006.

INTEGRATED DELIVERY SYSTEM (IDS)

What is called the IDS is becoming a visible and important element of managed care, whether it has an insurance function or not. As an outcome of the gradual disappearance of traditional fee-for-service private practice, in some areas the boundaries that previously existed between physicians and hospitals are gradually disappearing, too.

A still valid definition of the IDS was offered by Kongstvedt, Plocher, and Stanford (2001): "IDSs may be described as falling into three broad categories: systems in which only the physicians are integrated, systems in which the physicians are integrated with facilities (hospitals and ancillary sites), and systems that include the insurance functions" (p. 46).

In the past, according to Kodner (personal communication with Jonas, September–December 1996), "Hospitals had doctors; doctors had patients." Now, increasingly, as the various forms of managed care spread and take over the health care delivery system, it is the payers or the insurance, risk-assuming side of the MCO that has the patients, with both the doctors and the hospitals providing the health care services for the MCO—and its patients. Presenting in part a normative definition, that is, what they would have liked IDSs to be, not necessarily what they all are, Stephen Shortell and colleagues (1994) defined the IDS as "[a] network of health care organizations that provides and/or arranges a coordinated continuum of care to a defined population, and is willing to be held clinically and fiscally responsible for the outcomes and health status of that population" [p. 46].

In the view expressed by Shortell and colleagues, the IDS would be an essential element in creating their "ideal health care system" (Shortell et al., 1999, p. 8), having, in summary, the following features:

1. Serves a defined population
2. Provides a defined set of services/benefits

3. Integrates services, administratively and clinically, and has an integrated information system covering all of the services offered
4. For the most part, payments to providers are made on a capitated basis
5. Will have hospital beds and one or more long-term care services such as a nursing home or a home health agency
6. Will pool the funds coming in from several sources
7. Will have a shared mission, philosophy, and vision
8. Will have centralized and joint planning and management
9. Will provide an organized continuum of care, through health care teams

In short, the ideal IDS would provide the type of coordinated, continuous, comprehensive, available, acceptable, and accessible care that was envisioned in the landmark Dawson Report—which was issued in the United Kingdom in 1920 (Sidel & Sidel, 1983, p. 152), which was described in the final report of the U.S. Committee on the Costs of Medical Care in 1932, and which reappeared in the original bills for what became the Regional Medical Program and Comprehensive Health Planning Acts of 1965 (before, that is, they were gutted in response to pressure from the American Medical Association). The question in the United States still is, can this sort of care be provided in a system that has a primary focus on either physician or corporate incomes/profit accumulation?

SOME POLICY ISSUES IN MANAGED CARE

In the mid-1990s, a longtime observer of the managed care scene laid out a list of what he thought would and should happen under MC over the next 10 years (Kodner, personal communication with Jonas, 1996):

1. An increase in the practice of population-based care
2. An increase in the use of physician/nonphysician team care
3. The development of highly sophisticated medical, health, and management information systems (MIS)
4. The return of physician control
5. Increased public sector enrollment: Medicare/Medicaid
6. "Carve-outs" (health services sectors set outside the managed care system), for example, mental health, substance abuse, and high-cost subspecialty care
7. Increased insurance company ownership of MCOs and decline in insurance company involvement in indemnity insurance
8. Decline of both group and staff model plans with a concomitant rise in other forms, such as the IDS

  9. Competition among MCOs on the basis of quality
 10. Going from managed cost to managed care

A similar list was developed by Barton (1999, p. 31), who also added rationalization of resource use, greater accountability, more disease prevention and health maintenance, and improved quality. The list by Shortell and his colleagues (1999) is also similar. However, 17 years later, we see that the emphasis on quality and population health has not occurred as completely as predicted.

Luft (2003) has described the problem of defining managed care and, therefore, of evaluating MCOs on quality, access, and cost:

> The collection of health plans commonly referred to as "managed care" has come to include an astonishing variety of forms. Although a few are tightly integrated prepaid group practices, a much larger number reflect the complex mixes of associations of clinicians and institutions into provider groups and insurers that face myriad, sometimes conflicting, incentives and employ widely disparate information systems. Managed care plans also differ in the mix of prepaid and fee-for-service patients they enroll and the associated payor sources with which they must interact.
>
>   Given this heterogeneity, it is difficult to meaningfully compare the quality of managed care plans as a group to fee-for-service plans or to assess the relative performance among types of managed care plans. (p. 1373)

Therefore, the controversy that has followed the rise of managed care regarding its ability to meet our health care goals continues today and opinion is mostly unfavorable. For example, we still question the effect of managed care on the doctor–patient relationship. Does managed care harm the relationship between physician and patient? There is evidence brought to bear on both sides of the argument (e.g., Alexander & Lantos, 2006; Light, 2006).

Further research may resolve this issue and others related to the desirability of managed care. However, the continual change of MCOs in response to critics—both consumers and providers—poses difficulties in obtaining convincing answers. Managed care has changed dramatically in response to its critics. Thus, for example, Rand Health (2005) put forward two nearly polar opposite explanations for the failure of HMO enrollment to drop in the late 1990s and early 2000s following much reported consumer disfavor with managed care: (a) Many consumers were more satisfied with their HMOs than had been thought; and (b) many HMOs relaxed their cost containment restrictions in order to avoid losing market share.

For-Profit Versus Not-for-Profit

Much of the controversy surrounding managed care concerns profit-making and its compatibility with the provision of quality, efficient, and accessible health care. A prediction of the effects of managed care as it has evolved made by health policy analyst Victor Fuchs (2002) was rather more grim:

> The announcement that most of the nation's biggest insurers—Aetna, CIGNA, Humana, the United Health Group, and Well-Point Health Network—will be introducing a new kind of health plan during the next year or two signals the beginning of a new era in health insurance in the United States. These plans feature a complicated menu of premiums, co-payments, and deductibles that will add impetus to the trend of employers offering a defined [monetary] contribution for health benefits....One of their major effects will be to shift the burden of health care costs from employees who use little care to those who use more. Thus, the new plans will be another nail in the coffin of health insurance as a form of social insurance. (p. 1822)

As Randel and colleagues (2001) put it, in terms that still apply:

> The growth of managed care in the United States has been paralleled by a rising tide of anti–managed care sentiment. The "managed care problem" is understood generally as the need to protect individuals against large companies that care more about their bottom line than about people. (p. 44)

As noted in the quote from Koop (certainly no radical reformer) at the beginning of this chapter, it is the question of for-profit versus not-for-profit health care, not just MC. It is the question of whether having the health care delivery system become a major profit center for corporate America (the insurance industry) is healthy (in a variety of senses) for America and Americans. It is the issue at the center of virtually every other health care issue related not only to managed care but to the future of the health care delivery system as a whole.

The question is not a moral one. It is a functional one. Can a profit-making system and the so-called free market solve the myriad problems of the U.S. health care delivery system, as spelled out earlier in this chapter and elsewhere in this book? Because the focus of a for-profit system must be on profits, by definition, and because the solution of so many of the problems not only cannot generate profits but also would cost considerable sums of money, the answer would appear to be no. Therefore, we turn to a consideration of health care reform.

REFERENCES

Alexander, G. C., & Lantos, J. D. (2006). The doctor–patient relationship in the post–managed care era. *American Journal of Bioethics, 6*(1), 29–33.

American Medical Association (AMA). (1996). *Medical groups in the U.S.—A survey of practice characteristics.* Chicago, IL: Author.

Austrin, M. S. (1999). *Managed health care simplified: A glossary of terms.* Albany, NY: Delmar.

Barton, P. L. (1999). The health services delivery system: Managed care. In *Managed care essentials: A book of readings.* Chicago, IL: Health Administration Press.

Bodenheimer, T., Lo, B., & Casalino, L. (1999). Primary care physicians should be coordinators, not gatekeepers. *Journal of the American Medical Association, 281*(21), 2045–2049.

Can HMOs help solve the health-care crisis? (1996, October). *Consumer Reports,* p. 28.

Chaiken, I. (2002, May 26). Damaged care [Television broadcast]. Showtime.

Draper, D. A., Hurley, R. E., & Short, A. C. (2004). Medicaid managed care: The last bastion of the HMO. *Health Affairs, 23*(2), 155–167.

Dudley, R. A., & Luft, H. S. (2001). Health policy, 2001: Managed care in transition. *New England Journal of Medicine, 344*(14), 1087–1092.

Fox, P. D. (1990). Foreword: Overview of managed care trends. In *The insider's guide to managed care* (pp. 1–12). Washington, DC: National Health Lawyers Association.

Fox, P. D. (2001). An overview of managed care. In P. R. Kongstvedt (Ed.), *The managed health care handbook* (pp. 3–16). Gaithersburg, MD: Aspen.

Fuchs, V. R. (2002). Sounding board: What's ahead for health insurance in the United States? *New England Journal of Medicine, 346*(23), 1822–1824.

Geiger, H. J. (1997). Doctoring: The nature of primary care medicine [Book review]. *New England Journal of Medicine, 337*(22), 1637.

Goldman, D. P., & McGlynn, E. A. (2005). *U.S. health care: Facts about cost, access, and quality.* Santa Monica, CA: Rand Corporation.

Hagland, M. (1996, September). Point-of-service: Staying alive. *Hospitals and Health Networks,* p. 58.

Internal Revenue Service (IRS). (2012). *Pharmaceutical industry overview–Trends.* Retrieved January 15, 2012, from www.irs.gov/businesses/article/0,,id=169580,00.html

Kaiser Family Foundation. (2006). *Employer health benefits, 2006 Annual survey.* Menlo Park, CA: Author.

Kaiser Family Foundation/Harvard School of Public Health. (2001). *National survey on consumer experience with and attitudes toward health plans.* Retrieved August 2001 from www.kkf.org.

Kleinke, J. D. (2001). *Oxymorons: The myth of a U.S. health care system.* San Francisco, CA: Jossey-Bass.

Kodner, D. (1996, September–December). *Managed Care* [A course]. New York University.

Kongstvedt, P. R., Plocher, D. W., & Stanford, J. C. (2001). Integrated health care delivery systems. In P. R. Kongstvedt (Ed.), *The managed health care handbook* (pp. 42–72). Gaithersburg, MD: Aspen.

Koop, C. E. (1996, Fall). Manage with care [Special issue]. *Time,* p. 69.

Koplan, J. P., & Harris, J. R. (2000). Not-so-strange bedfellows: Public health and managed care. *American Journal of Public Health, 90*(12), 1824–1826.

Levi, J. (2000). Managed care and public health. *American Journal of Public Health, 90*(12), 1823–1824.

Light, D. W. (2006). Be clear about managed care to get clear about doctor–patient relations. *American Journal of Bioethics, 6*(1), 38–41.

Luft, H. S. (1980). Assessing the evidence on HMO performance. *Milbank Memorial Fund Quarterly, Health and Society, 58*(4), 5015–5036.

Luft, H. S. (2003). Measuring quality in modern managed care. *Health Services Research, 38*(6, part 1), 1373–1378.

MacColl, W. A. (1966). *Group practice and the prepayment of medical care.* Washington, DC: Public Affairs Press.

Mayer, T. R., & Mayer, G. G. (1985). HMOs: Origins and development. *New England Journal of Medicine, 312*(9), 590–594.

National Center for Health Statistics (NCHS). (2007). *NCHS definitions.* Retrieved January 7, 2007, from www.cdc.gov/nchs/datawh/nchsdefs/list.htm

National Center for Health Statistics (NCHS). (2011). *Health, United States, 2010: With special feature on death and dying.* Hyattsville, MD: U.S. Department of Health and Human Services.

Rand Health. (2005). *The managed care backlash: Did consumers vote with their feet?* (Fact Sheet RB9121).

Randel, L., Pearson, S. D., Sabin, J. E., Hyams, T., & Emanual, E. J. (2001). How managed care can be ethical. *Health Affairs, 20*(4), 435–436.

Roemer, M. I., & Shonick, W. (1973). HMO performance: The recent evidence. *Milbank Memorial Fund Quarterly, Health and Society, 51*(3), 271–317.

Shortell, S. M., Gillies, R. M., & Anderson, D. A. (1994). The new world of managed care: Creating organized delivery systems. *Health Affairs, 13*(5), 46–64.

Shortell, S. M., Gillies, R. M., Anderson, D. A., Erickson, K. M., & Mitchell, J. B. (1999). Working toward an ideal system. In *Managed care essentials: A book of readings.* Chicago, IL: Health Administration Press.

Shouldice, R. G. (1991). *Introduction to managed care.* Arlington, VA: Information Resources Press.

Sidel, V. W., & Sidel, R. (1983). *A healthy state* (Rev. ed.). New York, NY: Pantheon Books.

Silver, G. A. (1963). Group practice—what it is. *Medical Care, 1,* 94.

Smits, H. L. (2002). Managed care. In A.R. Kovner & S. Jonas (Eds.), *Health care delivery in the United States* (7th ed., pp. 289–314). New York, NY: Springer Publishing.

The Squeeze: Managed care's effect on physician earnings. (1996, November). *On Managed Care, 1*(1), 1.

Stevenson, D., Grabowski, D., & Bramson, J. (2009). *Nursing home ownership trends and their impact on quality of care.* Washington, DC: U.S. Department of Health and Human Services.

Tufts Health Care Institute. (2006) *Managed care glossary.* Retrieved December 17, 2006, from www.thci.org/other resources/glossarymc.html

U.S. Government Accountability Office (GAO). (2010). *Nursing homes: Complexity of private investment purchases demonstrates need for CMS to improve the usability and completeness of ownership data.* Retrieved January 15, 2012, from www.gao.gov/assets/320/310573.pdf

Weinerman, E. R. (1968). Problems and perspectives of group practice. *Bulletin of the New York Academy of Medicine* (2nd Series). *44,* 1423.

Welch, W. P., Hillman, A. L., & Pauly, M. V. (1990). Toward new typologies for HMOs. *Milbank Memorial Fund Quarterly, 68*(2), 221–243.

EIGHT

History of Change: Health Care Reform

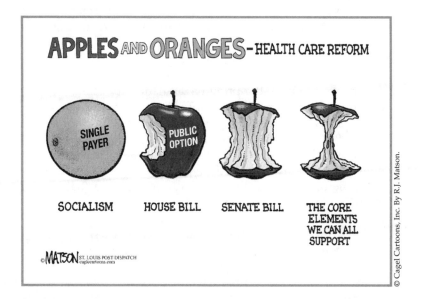

Problems with the U.S. health care system, particularly cost and access, are not new and have not gone unnoticed. Much of the criticisms of the past are just as applicable today. As far back as 1932, the findings of the first comprehensive study of health care in the United States were summarized in these terms:

> The problem of providing satisfactory medical service to all the people of the United States at costs which they can meet is a pressing one. At the present time, many persons do not receive service which is adequate either in quantity or quality, and the costs of service are inequably distributed. The result is a tremendous amount of preventable physical pain and mental anguish, needless deaths, economic inefficiency, and social waste. Furthermore, these conditions are...largely unnecessary. The United States has the economic resources, the organizing ability, and the technical experience to solve this problem. (Committee on the Costs of Medical Care, 1932/1970, p. 2)

The committee, chaired by Ray Lyman Wilbur, a past president of the American Medical Association, had been created in 1927 to look into the problems of the health care system. Strikingly, some would say tragically, the foregoing statement is entirely applicable today.

In the 1960s and 1970s, observers of the U.S. health care system, of different political persuasions, often spoke of the "crisis" in health care. Indeed, there have been numerous critical reports and studies going back many years. (For a bibliography of such reports, see the Appendix at the end of this chapter.)

In 1970, the editors of *Fortune* magazine, echoing the committee's final report, wrote:

> American medicine, the pride of the nation for many years, stands now on the brink of chaos. To be sure, our medical practitioners have their great moments of drama and triumph. But much of the U.S. medical care, particularly the everyday business of preventing and treating routine illnesses, is inferior in quality, waste-fully dispensed, and inequitably financed. Medical manpower and facilities are so maldistributed that large segments of the population, especially the urban poor and those in rural areas, get virtually no care at all even though their illnesses are most numerous and, in a medical sense, often easy to cure. (editors of *Fortune* magazine, 1970, p. 9)

Also echoing the CCMC's final report, and eerily presaging the problems of our own time, none other than President Richard M. Nixon (Nixon, 1994) in 1971 said:

> For a growing number of Americans, the cost of care is becoming prohibitive. Even those who can afford most care may find themselves impoverished by a catastrophic medical expenditure. The quality of medicine varies widely with geography and income. Because we pay so little attention to preventing disease and treating it early, too many people get sick and need intensive treatment. Costs have skyrocketed but values have not kept pace. We are investing more of our nation's resources in the health of our people, but we are not getting a full return on our investment. (p. 11)

In 1973, the Committee for Economic Development, with a board composed of representatives of many of the leading American corporations and banks, came to the following conclusions concerning the health care system:

> First, faulty allocation of resources is a major cause of inadequacies and inequalities in U.S. health services that result today

in poor or substandard care for large segments of the population. Second, the task of assuring all people the ability to cope financially with the costs of health care has been made realizable by the substantial base of coverage now provided by both private and public insurance plans. Third, unless step-by-step alterations are made in the means of delivering services and paying providers, closing the gaps in financing would overburden an inadequate system and offer little prospect of materially improving the quality and quantity of medical services of the health of the American people. (p. 17)

In 1990, perhaps the most prominent of a spate of reports and program proposals for health care reform issued that year had this to say (U.S. Bipartisan Commission on Comprehensive Health Care, 1990):

The American health care system is approaching a breaking point. Rapidly rising medical costs are increasing the numbers of people without health coverage and straining the system's capacity to provide care for those who cannot pay. The gap is widening between the majority of Americans, who can take advantage of the best medical services in the world, and the rest, who find it hard to get even basic needed care. As the gap increases, the weight of financing care for those without adequate coverage is undermining the stability of our health care facilities. Even for the majority, the explosive growth in health care costs is steadily eroding the private insurance system—the bulwark they count on as their defense against financial risk in case of illness. (p. 2)

Marking the advent of the 21st century, with many old themes still resonating, the Committee on the Quality of Health Care in America of the prestigious Institute of Medicine of the National Academy of Sciences (Institute of Medicine, 2001) came to the following conclusions:

The American health care delivery system is in need of fundamental change. Many patients, doctors, nurses, and health care leaders are concerned that the care delivered is not, essentially, the care we should receive. The frustration levels of both patients and clinicians have never been higher.... Health care today harms too frequently and routinely fails to deliver its potential benefits.

Americans should be able to count on receiving care that meets their needs and is based on the best scientific knowledge. Yet there is strong evidence that this is frequently not the case.... Between the health care we have and the health care we could have lies a chasm....

At no time in the history of medicine has the growth in knowledge and technologies been so profound....As medical science and technology have advanced at a rapid pace, however, the health care delivery system has floundered in its ability to provide consistently high-quality care to all Americans....The health care system as currently structured does not, as a whole, make the best use of its resources....What is perhaps most disturbing is the absence of real progress toward restructuring health care systems to address both quality and cost concerns, or toward applying advances in information technology to improve administrative and clinical processes....It is not surprising, then, that studies of patient experience document that the health system for some is a "nightmare" to navigate. (pp. 1–4)

The term *national health insurance* (NHI)[1] usually describes a single, country-wide health care financing system run by the government, at one or more jurisdictional levels. With varying prominence over time, proposals to create an NHI system have been on the United States' national political agenda since Teddy Roosevelt made it one of the planks of his Bull Moose Party platform in the presidential election of 1912.

It happened that the Reagan–Bush era (1981–1993) was one in which NHI faded almost completely from the health care political agenda. The prospect experienced a revival during the first 2 years of the Clinton administration (1993–1994) but with the defeat in the U.S. Congress of what came to be known as the Clinton health plan (CHP) (see later discussion), the issue receded again, through the second Clinton term and into the presidency of George W. Bush.

Nevertheless, the central problems of the U.S. health care delivery system that any comprehensive NHI program would address, from its high cost to the maldistribution of personnel and facilities to the lack of financial access for many people, to its lack of attention to health promotion and disease prevention, to its heavy emphasis on the use of expensive pharmaceuticals and medical/surgical procedures, remain. It also remains true that no fragmented, privately operated health care delivery system can by its nature address most of the major problems in the list. That is so because dealing successfully with most of them would require a comprehensive, coordinated, planned, national approach, something that is neither in the self-interest of nor within the competence of any of the private players presently on the field.

NATIONAL HEALTH INSURANCE AS SOLUTION

One of the major emphases of health care reformers throughout U.S. history has been to secure universal health coverage. In this section, we detail the history of this effort, beginning with a description of the world historical context in which the U.S. efforts have existed.

World Historical Background

The first NHI program appeared on the world stage in the 1880s. (Some readers may be distressed to learn that both the content and form of the arguments for and against NHI have remained largely fixed since that time [Boas, 1945/1958; Falk, 1973; McKittrick, 1940/1958; Schwartz, 1972]. This has been the case regardless of changed circumstances or new information.) It was introduced by Otto von Bismarck, the "Iron Chancellor" of Prussia and, after 1871, of the unified German state. Shortly after the bourgeois revolution of 1848 in Europe, he had said: "The social insecurity of the worker is the real cause of their being a peril to the state" (Roemer, 1960, p. 127). In 1881, the German Kaiser Wilhelm I, in a speech written by Bismarck, said "The healing of social evils cannot be sought in the repression of social democratic excesses exclusively but must equally be sought in the positive promotion of the workers' welfare" (Roemer, 1960, p. 129). In other words, "The workers are revolting; let's do something for them."

From the 1830s onward, various fragmented accident, workers' compensation, and sickness insurance schemes, both compulsory and voluntary, had come into existence in the several German states. Building on them, in 1883, Bismarck succeeded in ushering through the German Reichstag (Parliament) a Sickness Insurance Act (Roemer, 1960, pp. 121–131). Bismarck had wanted a uniform, national system, excluding those of the existing "sickness societies" that were for profit, retaining only the not-for-profit ones. Understandably, the former objected to the prospect of being put out of business. (In this regard, they had much in common with the present U.S. health insurance companies. Understandably as well, the insurers protest strongly against any proposed U.S. NHI plan that has no, or a limited, role for them.)

Bismarck settled for a plan that used the then-existing network of sickness societies, both for and not for profit. Nevertheless, it was a national program that certain categories of workers paid for medical care and provided cash support during periods of sickness and accidental injury. Two-thirds of the premiums were paid by the employees and one-third by the employers. Thus, it came to pass that the world's first NIH scheme was created, not by a progressive democratic or socialist government, but by a conservative constitutional monarchy.

By the 1920s, most of the European industrialized countries, as well as Japan, had some kind of NHI system. In each it usually began as a partial or voluntary system, generally progressing to a comprehensive and compulsory one (Douglas-Wilson & McLachlan, 1973, pp. 1–123, 211–230; Fry & Farndale, 1972; Glaser, 1978; Roemer, 1985). After World War II, the industrialized countries of the British Commonwealth gradually followed suit (Fry & Farndale, 1972; Lynch & Raphael, 1963; Roemer, 1985, 1991). As the new millennium began, the United States remained the only major industrialized country in the world not to have some sort of NHI system, but it was not for a lack of trying.

History of NHI in the United States

The Early Days[2]

The first campaign for a NHI program in the United States was undertaken by the American Association for Labor Legislation (AALL), a middle-class, liberal, reform-minded group founded in 1906 (Anderson, 1968, Part 2; Burrow, 1963, 1977, pp. 138–153; Goldfield, 2000, chapter 3). As noted, proposals for a broad social insurance plan were part of Teddy Roosevelt's Bull Moose (third) Party platform in 1912 (Burrow, 1963, p. 135). In 1916, proposing that the several states each adopt the program independently, the AALL put forward a standard bill for compulsory medical care and sickness benefits insurance. Their program would have covered persons earning below a certain income level and would have used existing insurance carriers. Employers, employees, and the states would have shared the costs (Anderson, 1968, pp. 62–65; Burrow, 1963, p. 136).

At first, support was widespread, extending to the American Medical Association (AMA) and even the National Association of Manufacturers (Burrow, 1963, pp. 138–145). Beginning in 1917, however, when the United States entry into World War I generally deflated the reform movement of the time, opposition began to surface from several quarters. Among the opponents were the American Federation of Labor and the commercial insurance industry (Anderson, 1968, p. 67; Burrow, 1977, pp. 148–153).

A battle ensued over the issue within the AMA (Anderson, 1968; Burrow, 1963, pp. 146–151). As part of an overall shift of power from the academic wing of the medical profession to the practitioner wing that was going on at the time, the latter, conservative, faction won out (Harris, 1966, p. 30).[3] In 1920, the AMA House of Delegates passed the following resolution (Burrow, 1963, p. 150):

> Resolved, that the American Medical Association declares its opposition to the institution of any plan embodying the system of compulsory contributory insurance against illness, or any other plan of compulsory insurance which provides for medical service to be rendered contributors or their dependents, provided, controlled, or regulated by any state or the Federal government.

In toto, that remained the AMA's position until the late 1960s (Harris, 1966). Even in the mid-1970s, by which time the AMA had adopted an NHI proposal of its own that ran counter to the bulk of the 1920 resolution, the noncompulsory principle was retained (Committee on Ways and Means, 1974). It was not until 1990 that the AMA had dropped the noncompulsory principle as well (American Medical Association [AMA], 1990).

During the New Deal and Its Aftermath

Serious consideration was next given to NIH during the development of the Social Security Act of 1935. This consideration was stimulated in part by the final report of the Committee on the Costs of Medical Care (1932; see also Anderson, 1968; Stevens, 1971, pp. 183–187). In 1934, President Franklin Roosevelt created the Committee on Economic Security to consider the whole question of social insurance. NHI was on the agenda (Goldfield, 2000, chapter 4). It did not stay there long (Goldfield, 2000, chapter 5).

The principal opposition again came from the AMA (Burrow, 1963, p. 193). Economic Security Committee Executive Director E. E. Witte wrote (Anderson, 1968, p. 108):

> When in 1934 the Committee on Economic Security announced that it was studying health insurance, it was at once subjected to misrepresentation and vilification. In the original social security bill there was one line to the effect that the Social Security Board should study the problem and make a report thereon to Congress. That little line was responsible for so many telegrams to the members of Congress that the entire social security program seemed endangered until the Ways and Means Committee unanimously struck it out of the bill.

The president wanted to make sure that the basic Social Security Act, conceived as one of the cornerstones of the New Deal, became law. It was eventually passed by Congress with no reference to NHI.

Senator Robert F. Wagner, Sr., of New York State initiated the next major legislative foray on behalf of NHI in the United States.[4] The landmark National Labor Relations Act of 1935 (referred to as the Wagner Act) had established the right to collective bargaining for all nonpublic employees in the United States. In 1939, Wagner introduced a bill (Roemer, 1960, pp. 189–190)

> to provide for the general welfare by enabling the several states to make more adequate provision for public health, prevention and control of disease, maternal and child health services, construction, and maintenance of needed hospitals and health centers, care of the sick, disability insurance, and training of personnel.

The bill, S. 1620, proposed to subsidize state public health programs (this later became federal policy through a series of separate acts), the construction of hospitals (enacted in 1946 as the Hill-Burton Act), and state programs for medical care for the poor (eventually enacted in part in 1960 as Kerr-Mills Medical Assistance for the Aged, then expanded as the federal/state Medicaid program, in 1965). The bill also proposed to provide cash sickness benefits (a standard feature of the European/ Japanese approach to NHI that has never made headway in the United States). Additionally, there was to be a program of federal subsidies to those states enacting comprehensive health insurance programs (Harris, 1966, pp. 31–32; Roemer, 1960, pp. 190–191). The bill died in committee, after being vigorously attacked by the AMA (Harris, 1966, pp. 38–40).

Senator Wagner tried again in 1943, this time in concert with Senator Murray and Representative John Dingell. Their bill, S. 1161, "advocated a national (i.e., Federal) compulsory system of health insurance, financed from payroll taxes and providing comprehensive health and medical benefits through entitlement to specified medical service benefits" (Stevens, 1971, p. 272). This was the first major legislative proposal for a federal rather than a state-based system. Once again, the AMA responded negatively, with vigor (Harris, 1966, pp. 40–42). The bill never got very far, although it was reintroduced in several successive Congresses (Anderson, 1968, pp. 112–113).

In 1947, Senator Robert Taft, Sr., introduced a proposal for federal subsidies to the states to pay for medical care for the poor similar to the one that was in Senator Wagner's 1939 package and would eventually see the light of day as the Medicaid program (Stevens, 1971, p. 273). Though sponsored by a conservative Republican, it also got nowhere.

In 1949 Harry Truman was reelected president with Democratic majorities in both houses of Congress (Goldfield, 2000, chapter 6). He decided to make enactment of NHI a major goal of his administration. He proposed a national, compulsory system, to be paid for by a combination of Social Security and general taxation, similar in many ways to the Wagner-Murray-Dingell bill of 1943. It was in 1945, just after he had succeeded to the presidency following Roosevelt's death in April of that year and the end of World War II shortly thereafter, that Truman had first enunciated the principles on which the proposed system would be based (Truman, 1945/1958):

> Everyone should have ready access to all necessary medical, hospital, and related services.... A system of required prepayment would not only spread the costs of medical care, it would also prevent much serious disease.... Such a system of prepayment should cover medical, hospital, nursing, and laboratory services. It should cover dental care [as far as] resources of the system permit...the nation-wide system must be highly decentralized in administration.... Subject to national standards,

methods and rates of paying doctors and hospitals should be adjusted locally....People should remain free to choose their own physicians and hospitals....Likewise physicians should remain free to accept or reject patients....Our voluntary hospitals and our city, county, and state general hospitals, in the same way, must be free to participate in the system to whatever extent they wish.... [W]hat I am recommending is not socialized medicine. Socialized medicine means that all doctors work as employees of government....No such system is proposed. (pp. 629–630)

The AMA mounted a furious attack on the plan, based primarily on the claim that it was indeed "socialized medicine" (Harris, 1966, pp. 40–62). The AMA used a major public relations firm and a war chest of over $2 million, a very substantial sum in those days. With allies from the drug and insurance industries (Stevens, 1971, pp. 273–274), it was once again successful in defeating an NHI plan in Congress. With the election of a Republican government in 1952, the AMA was able to breathe easily (Burrow, 1963, pp. 361, 385).

In the post–World War II climate of domestic and foreign anti-communism (Freeland, 1975), it was difficult for Truman to win support at home for a program consistently attacked as "communist" or "socialist," but in any case "Red" (Harris, 1966, p. 50). Thus, in 1951, on the recommendation of Oscar Ewing, the federal Social Security administrator, the Truman administration withdrew its support for NHI and began the campaign that eventually led to the passage in 1965 of Medicare (Goldfield, 2000, chapter 8; Harris, 1966, pp. 58–60; Stevens, 1971, p. 274).

Medicare and Medicaid

The campaign for Medicare was long and arduous (Harris, 1966; Stevens, 1971, pp. 432–443). Legislation creating it and its afterthought companion, Medicaid (Friedman, 1977), finally was passed by Congress in 1965 (Committee on Finance, 1970; Goldfield, 2000, chapter 8). Both had their historical antecedents, as previously noted. For example, the earliest AALL proposals contained the concept of beginning with partial coverage, aimed at the working poor. (In contrast, Medicaid covers primarily the nonworking poor.) Medicaid-like proposals had appeared in Senator Wagner's prewar bill and Senator Taft's postwar bills. Determination of an eligible population by age as in Medicare was, however, a relatively new twist, going back only to 1950.

However, failing to follow the example of the world's other industrialized countries, since 1965 the progression from some sort of partial coverage to comprehensive coverage, or close to it, just has never taken place in the United States. That has not been because of a lack of trying on behalf of the reform forces, but rather because of the strength of the political and health care system opponents of such change.

National Health Insurance in the 1960s and 1970s

Once Congress had passed Medicare and Medicaid, beginning in the late 1960s many new legislative proposals for NHI were made (Burns, 1971; Eilers, 1971; Falk, 1973, 1977; Goldfield, 2000, chapter 9; Hastings, 1972). In the 1970s, they were summarized by the Ways and Means Committee of the House of Representatives (Committee on Ways and Means, 1974) and the Senate Finance Committee (Committee on Finance, 1979; see also Karen Davis, 1975). In the wide-ranging debate on NHI, the basic arguments of the several sides had changed little over time.

As of 1975, a time when the passage of some sort of NHI seemed imminent to many observers, there were four major proposals before Congress. The constituencies represented were organized labor, the American Hospital Association, the Health Insurance Association of America, and, notably, the AMA itself. Because all of the major actors were on stage, it was believed that surely one of these proposals or some compromise among them would find its way through Congress.

One predicts the passage of NIH in the United States at one's peril, however. For example, in 1974, an observer wrote (Jonas, 1974):

> The United States of America is the only major country in the developed, capitalist world without some form of national health insurance programme. The struggle for national health insurance in the U.S., a long and bitter one, has been well described. It now appears as if there will be some form of national health insurance legislation in the U.S. before the Presidential elections of 1976. (p. 143)

There wasn't.

In the 1976 presidential campaign, candidate Jimmy Carter said, in his only speech on health policy:

> We must have a comprehensive program of national health insurance....The coverage must be universal and mandatory. We must lower the present barriers, in insurance coverage and otherwise, to preventive and primary care and thus reduce the need for hospitalization. We must have strong cost and quality controls, and...rates...should be set in advance....We must phase in the program as rapidly as revenues permit, helping first those who need help, and

achieving a comprehensive program well defined in the end. (quoted in Cavalier, 1979, p. 7)

Carter's administration never submitted such a proposal to Congress.

National Health Insurance Proposals in the 1980s

In 1979, the Congressional Research Service of the Library of Congress (Cavalier, 1979) stated that the major policy issues to be addressed in designing and NHI program were as follows:

- The rising costs of health care
- The gaps in present health insurance coverage, in terms of both services and populations
- Geographic maldistribution of personnel and facilities
- Access to health care service by ability to pay, social class, age group, and geography
- The impact, or lack thereof, of NHI on the population's health status

Once again, this list, published more than 30 years ago, has a familiar sound to it. It still describes the major problems facing the nation's health care delivery system.

In 1980, the same major NHI-proposal players were still on the field (Committee on Finance, 1979; Jonas, 1981, pp. 438–470; Kimble, 1979). However, with the election of Ronald Reagan in 1980, the whole movement just ran out of gas.

A measure of the enormous loss of energy suffered by the pro-NHI forces in the 1980s can be found in the contents of the "reform package" offered in 1985 by Senator Ted Kennedy (with Representative Fortney "Pete" Stark, House Ways and Means Committee, Health Subcommittee chair). They proposed ("Stark, Kennedy," 1985)

- to reduce the number of persons uninsured for health care costs by requiring employers to make health insurance available to former employees at group rates
- to reduce or eliminate "patient dumping" by hospitals
- to restrain increases in Medicare Part A premium costs
- to hold down Medicare payments to hospitals

This was a far cry from the sweeping changes proposed by Kennedy in several major bills he offered in the 1970s. (That weak cry of 1985 had an echo in 1996 with the eventual passage of a bill sponsored by Senators Kennedy and Nancy Landon Kassebaum providing that certain elements of portability from job to job become required for employer-provided health insurance [Goldfield, 2000, pp. 139–140; Hoppszallern & Arges, 2002; Kuttner, 1997].)

SOME CONTEMPORARY APPROACHES
TO HEALTH CARE REFORM

NHI by Contract, or the Personal Health Care System

The proponents of competitive reform did not go away, however. In the early 1980s, a proposal designed to deal with the problem list set out by the Congressional Research Service and many others was published (Jonas, 1980, 1984). First designated "NHI by contract," it was later called the personal health care system (PHCS). By 2002, it had yet to be put into legislative language per se, although some of its central concepts appeared as essential elements of the CHP (see later discussion).

The contract mechanism is the classic approach to the achievement of stated goals and objectives. The buyer and seller of a product agree on product or service specifications and costs, written down in a contract. The contract usually contains means of enforcement of its terms. A small-scale, partial prototype of such an approach to the financing, planning, and evaluation of health services (known colloquially as *ghetto medicine*) existed in New York City during the 1970s (Jonas, 1977).

Under NHI by contract, or PHCS, government would raise the funds necessary to pay for health services, from a variety of sources: general and special taxation, employer/employee contributions, and direct payments. It would also be responsible for negotiating a series of contracts with providers. The latter would agree to offer a set of services to the population for a given dollar amount. Most existing providers, whether institutional or individual, would be eligible to become either primary contractors or subcontractors. In this, the PHCS has much in common with the Health Care Corporation concept of the mid-1970s, an American Hospital Association plan dubbed "Ameriplan" (McMahon, 1975).

The composition of the service packages would be determined by health planning mechanisms. There would be free competition among the providers for the contracts, with bidders offering to provide the specified services at different prices. Primary contractors would be paid on a global budget basis. Much as MCOs do now, all contractors would then market their services to consumers.

All persons would be covered by a benefit package that would be determined nationally. Consumers would have free choice of contracting a provider, but once having made a choice, as in present multiple-choice situations, patients would have to stay with the selected provider for some specified period of time.

Advisory boards consisting of patients served by each contractor would be formed. The consumer role would focus on the evaluation of outcomes, that is, the extent to which contractors met their contract specifications. The boards would be party to contract negotiation and enforcement. There would be graded financial penalties for failure to meet contract specifications and rewards for excellent performance. Private ownership of the health services sector, including private medical practice, would be maintained. But the people, through both the government and the advisory boards, would have a strong voice in deciding how their money would be spent.

Government responsibilities would be distributed among the national, state, and local jurisdictions. Technology assessment, carried out at the federal level, would provide important data for health planning and priority setting. Insurance companies could be used as fiscal intermediaries.

The PHCS would provide the opportunity to deal directly with most of the principal problems presently facing the U.S. health care delivery system, including cost containment; quality improvement; implementing a comprehensive health promotion and disease prevention program; introducing rationality into the planning, development, distribution, and use of personnel and physical resources; and achieving equity of access. The PHCS would leave behind the present reliance on regulation and prayer to achieve program goals and objectives. It would enable the direct focusing of effort and payment, with a fair degree of fine tuning.

The rationale for the PHCS does not begin with benefit packages and decisions on copayment, as do so many other approaches to NHI. Rather, it starts with the establishment of planning principles. It assumes that benefit packages will be developed and decisions on copayment made after needs are assessed, goals and objectives are set, and the amount of available funds is determined. Then the contract specifications will be written, balancing needs, priorities, and available funds.

The PHCS would provide an integral link between the planning and financing of health services. As Rashi Fein, chair of the Institute of Medicine Committee on Health Planning Goals and Standards, noted some time ago, in his preface to the committee's report, this is essential to problem solving (Institute of Medicine, 1981, vol. 2, p. iii): "The committee believes that the forces at work in the American health care system, including the various reimbursement mechanisms, cannot be countered by a health planning effort that is divorced, among other limiting factors, from the flow of funds."

Using epidemiological methods in health services planning, the PHCS would carry out ongoing needs assessments, set priorities based on them, and, within the limits of available resources, make continual program adjustments to meet identified needs. The approach would allow for the direct application of planning information to health services system operation. Thus, the focus on meeting identified needs could always be maintained without direct government services operation.

An assumption underlying the PHCS approach is that the numerous individual and institutional health care providers are, by the very nature of their separateness and independence from one another, incapable of collectively engaging in rational, comprehensive planning on their own. The U.S. history of "voluntarism" in health planning and what happened in the completely unplanned, privately driven, pell-mell rush to for-profit managed care have shown that this is true. Thus, if comprehensive health planning is to be carried out, and if health care planning is to be linked with health care financing, government will have to take the lead.

The PHCS concept was developed before managed care became a major player in the system. Because it is at its core a sophisticated health care planning system, however, the PHCS could work equally well with the fee-for-service/indemnity insurance that predominated when it was originally conceived, or with managed care. The problems of implementation are political, economic, and financial, not conceptual.

Single-Payer System

Of all of the foregoing, it is the single-payer system that still deserves some attention because it is still very much on the national agenda of many people. A brief review of the single-payer system reveals the following features (Himmelstein & Wool-handler, 2001, chapter 12; see also Himmelstein & Woolhandler, 2002).

The program is modeled in part on the present Canadian system (Evans et al., 1989; Fuchs & Hahn, 1990; Himmelstein & Woolhandler, 2001, chapter 10; Igelhart, 1986, 1990; Katz et al., 2002; Tuohy, 2002). The program would be federally mandated and ultimately federally funded, but it would be administered primarily at the state and local levels. All U.S. residents would be covered for all medically necessary treatment and preventive medical, mental, and dental services, including acute, long-term, and rehabilitative care, in institutions, ambulatory care settings, and the home, with coverage for prescription drugs and medical supplies.

The program would have a single public system of administration, eliminating the present highly expensive multiple, fragmented, duplicative "system" operated by multiple government agencies and the private insurers now in place. Patient copayments would be limited. Hospitals would be paid on a global budgeting basis, much as public hospitals in both the civilian and military sectors are now and have been since their inception. Physicians and other independent practitioners would have their choice of payment options: fee for service, salary from institutions, or capitation. Capital spending would be planned under a national/regional system that would also supply the money.

The whole operation would be paid for by a combination of present Medicare and Medicaid expenditures, existing state and local expenditures for health services (including public health services), mandated employer contributions, and additional tax revenues equal to the amounts now spent by citizens out of pocket. These monies would be paid into the new national "single-payer" agency, which would then pay the monies out according to the provisions just outlined.

Although the single-payer system was still on the national health care reform agenda, it had not yet made it to the level of legislative consideration in Congress. In 1993, one such proposal did make it, what came to be known as the Clinton health plan, or CHP (Goldfield, 2000, chapter 10; White House Domestic Policy Council, 1993), which is the subject of the next section.

Clinton Health Plan

The Context: Change Was Already Coming

For a variety of reasons (primarily, continually escalating costs, a growing pool of uninsured persons, and declining health for certain portions of the population), in the early 1990s, NHI reappeared with prominence on the national political agenda. Once again, there were a whole series of proposals placed on the table, from such disparate groups as Senator Kennedy's Committee on Labor and Human Resources (1988), the National Association of Manufacturers (1989), the Heritage Foundation (1989), the National Leadership Commission on Health Care (cochaired by former Presidents Richard Nixon, Gerald Ford, and Jimmy Carter) (1989), the Oil, Chemical, and Atomic Workers (1989), the Committee for National Health Insurance (affiliated with the AFL-CIO) (1989), the American Medical Association (AMA, 1990), the American Public Health Association ("Insurance Plan," 1990), the U.S. Bipartisan Commission on Comprehensive Health Care of the U.S. Congress (also known as the Pepper Commission) (1990), and the Physicians for a National Health Program's "Single-Payor" system (Grumbach et al., 1991; Himmelstein & Woolhandler, 1989).

In 1994, the year that the CHP was debated and defeated in the U.S. Congress (Blumenthal, 1995; Goldfield, 2000, chapter 10; Skocpol, 1995), some form of managed care was already the reality for an increasing number of Americans; providers and patients alike (Freudenheim, 1994). Many of the changes that concerned providers the most, including being forced into some form of organized practice and seeing significant declines in their incomes, were happening whether or not the CHP or any of the other proposals then on the table were to be enacted. Many managed care-induced changes affecting patients, such as limiting their choices of plans and providers, were also already a reality. Many changes affecting both patients and providers, such as having insurance/managed care company representatives at the other end of an 800 line making treatment choices, were already a reality, too.

One real choice facing the country as a whole at the time of the debate of the CHP was whether this process would occur in a haphazard, unplanned way or be accomplished in a rational manner. In the latter case, the aim would be to achieve stated goals related to the health and health care of the people, not arising from the narrow interests of the insurance and managed care companies, many of them for-profit, and the provider networks. Another real choice was whether a system heavily dependent on public funds for its operations, such as the health care delivery system, should have a strong public voice in determining its policies and practices. The highly political nature of the debate on the CHP that ensued (Hacker, 1996) ensured that fundamental public policy questions such as these would never get a hearing.

The Clinton Health Plan: An Overview

In 1993, President Bill Clinton introduced his ill-fated Health Security Act. His words eerily sounded like those uttered by President Nixon when he presented his own NIH plan in 1971 (Nixon, 1994). Ironically, that plan was introduced in the Senate by none other than Senator Robert Dole, who in 1994 led the fight in Congress to kill the CHP.

President Clinton (White House Domestic Policy Council, 1993) had this to say when he offered his bill to the Congress:

> Americans are blessed with the world's finest doctors and nurses, the best hospitals, the most advanced medical technology, and the most promising research on the face of the earth. We cherish—and we will never surrender—our right to choose who treats us and how we get our care. But today our health care system is badly broken. Insurance has become a contest of finding only the healthiest people to cover. Millions of Americans are just a pink slip away from losing their health coverage, one serious illness away from losing their savings. Millions more are locked into jobs for fear of losing their benefits. And small business owners throughout our nation want to provide health care for their employees and families but can't get it or can't afford it. Next year we will spend more than one trillion dollars on health care—and still leave 37 million Americans without health insurance, and 25 million more with inadequate coverage.... In short, all the things that are wrong with our health care system threaten everything that's right. (p. iii)

Sounds familiar? Perhaps there has been only one speech writer for every speech of this type from the time of the final report of the Committee on the Costs of Medical Care to the present. If there is, surely he or she has a better health care plan than most Americans do.

Clinton's proposed Health Security Act had five primary features: guaranteed private insurance for everyone, choice of physician and health plan, elimination of unfair insurance practices, preservation of Medicare, and health benefits guaranteed through the work site (Goldfield, 2000, chapter 10; White House Domestic Policy Council, 1993). The act was based on six basic principles: security, savings, simplicity, choice, quality, and responsibility (White House Domestic Policy Council, 1993).

One of the CHP's principal public spokespersons, Irwin Redlener (1993), offered "11 Points" in describing/defending the plan:

1. It provided for a major overhaul based on the assumption of universal coverage
2. The plan created a federal framework with state adaptability
3. It offered a standardized national benefits package, to be prepared, reviewed, and modified from time to time by a National Health Board
4. It would be paid for by employer/employee contributions, special taxes (much as is done today), and internal savings in the system, primarily by a sharp reduction in the administrative costs of the current highly fragmented and markedly redundant revenue-raising/payment mechanisms
5. The plan would eliminate employer choice of an employee's health care provided for that employee
6. The plan would provide for health care coverage to be transportable, from job to job, from health to sickness, from illness to illness
7. The plan would create a new system of regional health plans (networks) for the provision of health services and not just a proliferation of HMOs
8. It would enable patients to make informed choices from among the plans, with the help of objective information provided by health care alliances (see later discussion)
9. It would improve medical care quality and reduce paperwork
10. It would make significant changes in the public health system
11. It would make significant changes in academic medicine

How the Clinton Health Plan Would Have Worked

A new series of agencies, called health care alliances, would be established by the states. Among other things, as noted by Redlener (1993), they would collect all of the money used to support health services from all sources. They would then contract with provider networks and groups in their region to provide a package of health care services for all persons enrolled (much like the approach of the PHCS).

The alliances would have oversight for all quality assurance activities. This system would presumably simplify both money flow and paperwork. It would guarantee a choice of plan and a system of quality assurance for the beneficiaries. For the providers, it would reunify authority and responsibility by putting medical decision making back in the hands of provider groups, along with fiscal responsibility for the viability of the plan.

A comprehensive benefit package was laid out, to be subject to fine-tuning and modification over time by the National Health Board (White House Domestic Policy Council, 1993). Its description took up 92 pages in the text of the CHP bill submitted to Congress. It included virtually all inpatient, outpatient, short- and long-term, institutional and home-based, preventive, diagnostic, treatment, rehabilitative, and follow-up services.

Each person would have been able to choose from among three types of coverage (White House Domestic Policy Council, 1993): an HMO with no deductible and a copayment of no more than $10 for each doctor visit; a PPO, with no deductible and a $10 copayment if the patient were to use network providers, deductibles and higher copayments for the use of physicians outside the PPO (which would be permitted); and a fee-for-service system (like the managed care point-of-service option), allowing completely free choice of doctor, with significant deductibles and copayments. (Under the last option, there would be a fee schedule for the physicians, and no balance billing would be allowed.)

For most businesses, large and small, participation would have been mandated (a major bone of contention). Because employers would have no say in plan choice by their employees, change from plan to plan would be only at the individual's option (unless a plan went out of business). Coverage would be portable from job to job and from job to no job.

Finally, the CHP would have linked payment and planning, under public rather than private control, the desideratum so eloquently set forth by Rashi Fein (IOM, 1981). That would have enabled (although not guaranteed) significant health care delivery system reform. This was, perhaps, what the opponents of the CHP were most afraid of.

The Opposition

The Republican ideologue William Kristol, former chief of staff to Vice President Dan Quayle and editor since its founding of *The Weekly Standard,* published by Rupert Murdoch, was an early leader of the opposition to the CHP. In the first of the then soon-to-be-famous "Kristol Memos" (1993), he said:

> The Clinton proposal is a serious political threat to the Republican Party. Republicans must therefore clearly understand the political strategy implicit in the Clinton plan—and then adopt an aggressive and uncompromising counterstrategy designed to delegitimize the proposal and defeat its partisan purpose.

On the provider/money transferor side, most of the medical, hospital, and insurance/managed care industry groups were arrayed against the CHP for a variety of reasons, ranging from an antagonism to "government regulation" to a concern with potential limitations on profit-making ability. On the public side, the "single-payer" forces were also arrayed against it; at least their leadership was (Navarro, 1994). They felt that it did not go far enough, that it left too many players in "Big Health Care" in place. They assumed that if the CHP went down to defeat, their approach would be next on the health care agenda. Unfortunately, on that point, history seems to have proved them wrong.

Finally, there was "big business." Represented by such groups as the U.S. Chamber of Commerce and the National Association of Manufacturers, it had originally been thought to be a major supporter of the CHP, at least by the Clinton administration. They were wrong. Industry groups, by and large, eventually came out in opposition (Hacker, 1996).

Also a factor in the defeat of the CHP was the fact that, although it appeared to be well thought out and adapted to the American political and health care delivery system realities, there was no comprehensive marketing plan prepared by the forces supporting it (Hacker, 1996). Thus, under a lengthy and expensive onslaught, the CHP went down to defeat in the summer of 1994 (Goldfield, 2000, chapter 10; Skocpol, 1995).

AFTER DEFEAT OF THE CLINTON HEALTH PLAN: 1994–2010

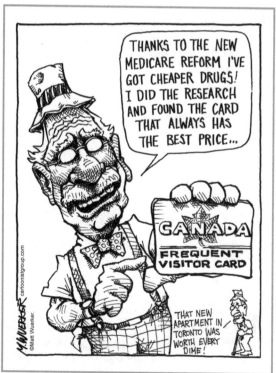

The period after the CHP was defeated, and before the Patient Protection and Affordable Care Act was enacted in 2010 under President Barack

Obama, was one of continued dissatisfaction and unrest among health care providers, patients and their advocates, and health policy makers. The problem list for the financing, distribution, and delivery of services had changed little since the time of the publication of the CCMC final report (except that the costs are incredibly higher). Indeed, certain problems considered important by the Committee on the Costs of Medical Care that were still pressing originated in our country and those of our European forebears well before the CCMC's time, in the 17th, 18th, and 19th centuries (Freymann, 1974, pp. 3–97). This was the case even though the advances in the science and technology of medicine had gone well beyond the wildest dreams of anyone giving thought to possibilities in 1932.

Interestingly enough, the one segment of the health care industry that seemed to be doing very well in this period was the for-profit hospitals/HMO sector. For example, a headline in the February 2002 issue of the American Hospital Association's journal *Hospitals and Health Networks* read, "Hospital Stocks Prove Health on Wall Street" (Carpenter, 2002). The popular companies were Tenet Healthcare Corp., Triad Hospitals Inc., and Humana. An article published on the aol.smartmoney.com website in April 2002 was headlined "What Health Care Crisis?" It reported that Lehman Brothers had noted that managed care stocks, which earlier were considered in "intensive care," had "popped 76% in the last year and 48% in 2002" (Bradford, 2002). In addition, the pharmaceutical companies have been highly profitable. As reported in the *British Medical Journal* in 2002: "Pharmaceuticals again ranked as the most profitable sector in the United States, topping the annual Fortune 500 ranking of America's top industries, released this month" (Gottlieb, 2002, p. 1054).

A story in the *New York Times* about pharmaceutical profits in 2006 stated: "Drug makers continued to post strong profit gains yesterday, led by Pfizer, the world's biggest pharmaceutical company, which reported that its third-quarter earnings had more than doubled from a year earlier" (Berenson, 2006). WellCare, a health care provider company, saw earnings double in the fourth quarter of 2006 and membership increase by 1.4 million, while Cynosure, the maker of cosmetic surgery systems, reported a 75% surge in earnings in the same quarter (Investor's Business Daily, 2007). Triad reported that, in the first 9 months of 2006, patient revenue per adjusted admission increased 7.7%, patient revenues increased 9.8%, and revenues increased 9.5%, compared to the same period in 2005 (Business Wire, 2006a). Humana reported that earnings for the third quarter of 2006 were up 64% over the same period in 2005. The company was projecting significant growth for 2007 (Business Wire, 2006b).

Nevertheless, looking at the larger picture, there was a fundamental conundrum facing health policy analysts, political leaders who would like to change things, and, above all, the American people. Unfortunately, this conundrum went unaddressed. To do so, one might have asked the following questions:

- Why is it that the plea of the Institute of Medicine (2001), made after it offered its litany of problems, for "all health care constituencies...[to] commit to a national statement of purpose for the health care system as a whole and to a shared agenda for improvement..." (p. 5) is likely to go entirely unheeded for the foreseeable future?
- Why is it that the findings and recommendations of a major report on health care issued in 1932 and echoed strongly in many, many similar efforts offered since have never been acted on?
- Why indeed, when it comes to issues such as coverage, distribution, the organization of health services, planning, quality assurance, and prevention, haven't things changed?

Or as Gordon Schiff and Quentin Young (2001) put it at the end of a friendly critique of the 2001 Institute of Medicine report quoted earlier:

> We indeed have a chasm to cross. With the current emphasis on incrementalism, many reformers believe they can succeed by first attending to quality and then reforming finance and delivery. Unfortunately, you cannot bridge a chasm in two jumps—health system reform must be pursued at the same time as quality reform. And you cannot bridge the gap between black and white or rich and poor health care by creating separate or stratified programs (which both Republicans and Democrats are proposing) based on ability to pay. Instead, we need a universal financing system that includes everyone, spreading the costs and the benefits in a fair and efficient way. (p. 401)

It is fascinating that, for the most part, these problems were not the result of a technical or scientific inability to deal with diseases or other health deficits. Nor were the problems caused by a lack of money, as is the case in so many other countries. In the United States, the principal problems, as determined by major system studies done since the 1930s, were as follows:

- As a nation we spent too much on health care, not too little (Berwick)
- The rate of increase in health care costs, which moderated somewhat in the late 1990s before gaining momentum again in the early 2000s, had been unaffected by any interventions tried to date
- The geographic and demographic distribution of health services was highly variable

- Much that could be done to prevent disease and promote health using available knowledge and techniques was not done
- Health care was widely misallocated and fragmented
- Many health care needs were undermet (e.g., not enough home health care for the infirm elderly), whereas others were overmet (e.g., too many hospital beds, too much surgery, too much diagnostic testing)
- Many people had no health care cost coverage of any kind
- There was an increasing focus on high-tech, increasingly expensive interventions that benefit a relatively small number of people
- Rationing of access, especially by race, was widespread
- There were serious problems with the quality of health care

In short, the problems were not the result of a lack of resources, but rather the misuse and misallocation of resources.

Public Health Concerns

In dealing with national health reform, rarely is much attention paid to public health and prevention. So let us stop for a moment and do so. According to the Centers for Disease Control and Prevention (CDC, 1999), the "Ten Great Public Health Achievements—United States, 1900–1999" were vaccination, motor vehicle safety, safer workplaces, control of infectious disease, decline in deaths from coronary heart disease and stroke, safer and healthier foods, healthier mothers and babies, family planning, fluoridation of drinking water, and recognition of tobacco use as a health hazard. One does not need to cite chapter and verse to recognize how important each of these interventions was to improving the health of the U.S. public in the century just past.

Jeffrey Koplan (a former director of the CDC) and David Fleming (2000) presented a list of public health challenges for the 21st century. First on the list is to "institute a rational health care system," the implication being that nothing effective can be done to deal with the outstanding public health problems unless that is done first. The implication is also that any such rational system will have to be organized in such a way that it can pay significant attention to the health of the public and to public health services.

Following on the list are "eliminate health disparities, focus on children's emotional and intellectual development, achieve a longer 'healthspan,' integrate physical activity and healthy eating into daily lives, clean up and protect the environment, prepare to respond to emerging infectious diseases, recognize and address the contributions of mental health to overall health and well-being, reduce the toll of violence in society, and use new scientific knowledge and technological advances wisely." Challenges indeed. The last alludes to the 800-pound gorilla in the room of any reform movement and effort—something that is little discussed but must be recognized: the high costs of increasingly high-tech medicine.

The Costs of Scientific and Technological Advance

As health services costs continued to escalate, much attention was paid to the overwhelming complexity of the extremely expensive payment/reimbursement system, the reorganization of which would save very significant sums of money (Woolhandler & Himmelstein, 1991, 1997). However, even if the payment/reimbursement system were to be reformed with the utmost efficiency in mind, there was an issue that was being blithely ignored: the totally unplanned, unregulated, poorly evaluated growth of technology and its use in medical care.

Some of the technology development was originally profit-driven, for example, the creation of high-tech hospital equipment that does not produce any better results than less expensive equipment. Some of the technology is driven by researchers who strive to find the "cure" for more and more difficult problems, such as the neonatologists who can now keep 2-pound newborns alive, but give no thought either to initial costs or to long-term consequences. Some high-tech systems are developed for the maintenance of life in a small number of persons with rare conditions, whereas large numbers of people with conditions like obesity and sedentary lifestyle are ignored, conditions that could be handled relatively cheaply with known health promotion and disease prevention methods.

Focusing solely on the issue of "medical progress," not the expensive mechanism we use to transfer the money to pay for health services, the economist Paul Krugman (2002), who writes a regular column for the *New York Times*, observed:

> Why do health care costs keep on rising? It's not because doctors and hospitals are greedy; it's because of medical progress. More and more conditions that once lay beyond doctors' reach can now be treated, adding years to the lives of patients and greatly increasing the quality of those years [only in certain instances, one must add]—but at ever greater expense. (p. A23)

Or listen to George Lundberg, former editor of the *Journal of the American Medical Association* (Rothman, 2001):

> Perhaps Lundberg's most consistent complaint about US medicine is that it does too much and therefore costs too much. He spreads the blame, indicting, among others, physicians, who have become too intent on making money [he disagrees with Krugman on that one], patients, who follow an "almost irrational chase for impossible cures," and legislators, who curry favor with constituents who are ill. The author is convinced that we must ration medical care to escape this dismal predicament. (p. 2604)

We have not even mentioned the costs of genome science and its potential clinical offspring of unproven benefit or perhaps even ultimately negative consequences.

The Case for Health Care Reform

David Blumenthal (1999) summarized the situation well. The primary factors that pushed for reform, he noted, were the declining access to care, the increasing costs of care, and the threats to the quality of care. Proposals for problem solutions abounded and had been available for decades, as previously noted numerous times. None of them were perfect in anyone's eyes. Nevertheless, some had more potential for solving the major problems than others. Those with the most potential had one key characteristic in common: proactive, not reactive, planning linked to financing.

A measure of how far the country was from any serious consideration of the overarching issues and problems that health care delivery faced in 2002 was the fact that the three principal issues that concerned Congress, and thus the political process in that year, were just how to go about implementing the complex requirements of the Health Insurance Portability and Accountability Act (HIPAA). Should patients be able to sue HMOs for alleged medical malpractice in the denial of services, and, if so, how should there be a prescription drug benefit of some sort under Medicare?

Potential Support for Reform From Providers

Health care providers (as opposed to the health care reimbursers or payers) were viewed as possible agents of change, out of necessity and self-protection. The for-profit insurance/managed care industry was becoming more powerful. Insurers had replaced the two traditionally most powerful groups, physicians and hospitals. In the past, major changes in the system had taken place only when physicians or hospitals wanted or needed those changes. Examples include the reinstitution of medical licensing laws and the reduction in the number of medical schools in the late 19th and early 20th centuries, and the development of hospital-sponsored voluntary hospital insurance during the Great Depression.

Health care reform might finally come when one or both of these groups wanted it or needed it. They then would have to be willing to make the compromises that would be necessary if they were to ally with consumers, as well as organized labor and academic, public health, public interest, and political forces that traditionally have been behind national health reform. Doing so would create a political coalition that might just be able to raise enough power to defeat the mighty for-profit insurance industry, which likes things pretty much just the way they are. An expensive fight indeed.

Private hospitals might want true national health care reform, as the AHA actually proposed in the mid-1970s (McMahon, 1975), as an increasing number of them faced bankruptcy in the face of uncontrolled cost increases and declining occupancy rates, as happened in Great Britain just before the enactment of the National Health Service in 1946. Physicians might want it when their numbers become so large that they are no longer able to sell all the products they collectively produce, or their incomes and control of the patient process are further hammered down by the MCOs.

However, many providers probably did not recognize that any NHI plan that did not tackle the causes of the health care delivery system problems head on, any plan that just paid in a different way for the system as it was, would, in the long run, make things worse, not better. We needed not just to pay differently for things; we needed to pay for different things.

"Patient Choice" and the "Free Market"

Henrik Blum asked in 1983: "Can there be meaningful health planning [in the United States] when so little else is planned?" Well, yes, there could be, and if we are to have meaningful, useful, cost-effective health care delivery system reform in the United States, a rational planning system will have to be a central element of it. However, one of the most powerful forces against rational planning was the ideology of the free market.

On the matter of the "free market" as the solution to stem the tide of rising medical and hospital costs, some influential policy groups such as the Heritage Foundation (1989), the Cato Institute (Blevins, 1997), and the AMA (Dickey & McMenamin, 1999) placed their major emphasis, not on any kind of national plan or system, but rather on the promotion of "competition" in the health care delivery system, to be stimulated by "consumer/patient choice."

Forget for a moment that the so-called market-driven managed care system had failed miserably in controlling costs. The theory treats the health care market as if it were a conventional one. Setting aside for a moment the understanding that competition is the antithesis of the planning mechanisms that the system is so much in need of, for competition to be effective even in such matters as lowering prices and improving quality, the consumer would have to have some reasonable knowledge of what he or she is buying. Furthermore, he or she would have to make the most of the purchasing decisions.

In health care, however, just the opposite is true. Most health services consumers know little or nothing about what they are buying and couldn't care less, just as long as they get better. Furthermore, it is in any case the health care providers (primarily the physicians), not the consumers, who make the majority of the decisions about what will be purchased on behalf of which consumers at what price.

There was another major element that these "market-based" proposals ignored as well. As Marcia Angell (1999), a former editor of the *New England Journal of Medicine*, pointed out:

> [When] health care is treated as a commodity provided by a huge number of competing organizations, the surest way for these organizations to thrive is to shift costs to one another by devising stratagems to avoid the most expensive patients— either those who are chronically ill, if payment is capitated, or those who are not insured for the services they need, if payment is on a fee-for-service basis. Other developed countries provide universal health care, considering it a social service, not a commodity. (p. 48)

THE PRESENT SITUATION: OBAMA HEALTH PLAN

Despite predictions of impending doom going back 40 years and more, no national catastrophe occurred (although millions of individuals have been affected) in the period between the defeat of the CHP and the enactment of the Patient Protection and Affordable Care Act in 2010 under President Obama. The system just kept barreling along, getting ever more expensive, and showing major defects in both the quality and the quantity of service provided (Institute of Medicine [IOM], 2000).

Yet the major problems in the U.S. health care delivery system, as outlined several times in this book, by many different voices, of a variety of political persuasions, speaking over many years, were national ones. They would require national solutions. That did not necessarily mean a federally run national health service. That approach would probably work poorly in this country for many reasons related to the ideology of the free market. But, as the single-payer proposal postulates, effective reform designed to deal with the consensus problem list does mean national principles and guidelines, and national programs for change.

When Barack Obama was elected president in 2008, he was determined to seek a national solution to the health care problems of the country, but without a national health service or NIH. He was open to a plan that was consistent with the private sector involvement in health care that had evolved during the 20th century, which, not surprisingly, was the kind of plan enacted. Nevertheless, the battle for passage of a bill was hard-fought for nearly two years. The bill that resulted, the Patient Protection and Affordable Care Act, was passed in March 2010 by the Democrats with no Republican votes. The final legislation was in every way a compromise that kept a place at the table for the complex mix of public and private stakeholders in the existing system. Many of its important and needed benefits were phased-in over many years, including prohibiting discrimination against persons with pre-existing health conditions and eliminating annual limits on insurance coverage, both of which do not go into effect until 2014. Other provisions will not be implemented until 2020 (healthcare.gov, 2012).

Yet the Patient Protection and Affordable Care Act (PPACA) is a national plan that will affect all Americans, and it addresses many of the shortcomings of the old health care delivery system. It represents a huge step toward solving some of the egregious problems of the old system. As Karen Davis (2010) wrote:

> A majority of Americans stand to gain under health reform. Primary beneficiaries include the uninsured and intermittently insured, the underinsured, those who cannot afford their out-of-pocket costs or health insurance premiums, small businesses and their employees, young adults who will be able to stay on their parents' policies until they find a job with health benefits, and those who are denied coverage because they have preexisting conditions or major health problems.... Most Americans fall into one of these categories and have personally experienced the shortcomings of our current system. (p. 7)

The Commonwealth Fund found that the new law delivers on President Obama's three goals for the legislation (Davis, 2010, p. 5):

- Expand access to affordable health insurance for those without coverage
- Improve the affordability of insurance for those who already have it
- Slow the rise in health care costs for individuals, families, and employers while not adding to the federal budget deficit

Major Features of the Obama Health Plan

The main features of the bill include (Davis, 2010, pp. 5–7):

New federal insurance market rules that prohibit restricting coverage or varying premiums based on health, set limits on the share of private premiums going for non-medical costs, and establish essential standard benefit packages that guarantee beneficiaries a comprehensive array of services with limits on levels of cost-sharing.

New health insurance exchanges that will more efficiently pool risk, lower administrative costs, and provide eligible individuals and small businesses a choice of affordable health plans.

Affordability provisions for low- and middle-income families, including an essential standard benefit package, premium assistance on a sliding scale up to four times poverty income (about $88,000 for a family of four), and expansion of Medicaid eligibility up to 133 percent of the federal poverty level (almost $30,000 for a family of four).

A commitment to shared responsibility that preserves employer-sponsored insurance, provides health insurance tax credits to small businesses, assesses a contribution from larger businesses whose employees receive government-financed premium subsidies, and requires that individuals have coverage.

Improvements to Medicare prescription drug benefits, including $250 rebates for seniors falling into the "doughnut hole" in 2010 and elimination of that coverage gap by 2020.

Creation of a new long-term care financing program to support community living for the disabled.

Investment in a stronger primary care foundation, one that includes increases in payment for primary care under Medicare and Medicaid, incentives for practices to organize as patient-centered medical homes providing more accessible and coordinated care, and investment in primary care training and expansion of community health centers and the National Health Service Corps.

Establishment of an innovation center within the Centers for Medicare and Medicaid Services to rapidly test and spread effective payment methods that reward quality of care, rather than volume of services. Additional payment and system reform provisions encourage accountability for patient outcomes and use of medical resources, and provide incentives for productivity improvement.

Creation of an Independent Payment Advisory Board with the authority to make recommendations for reducing cost growth and improving quality in both the Medicare program and the health system as a whole.

Investment in the infrastructure required for a high-performance health system, including publicly reported information on quality, cost, and performance of providers and insurers; use of modern information technology in medical care and health insurance; and national strategies and policies on disease prevention, public health, quality, safety, and the health care workforce.

Obama Health Plan From the Consumer Perspective

A brief description of the PPACA provisions from the consumer perspective follows, all taken from HealthCare.gov, a federal government website managed by the U.S. Department of Health & Human Services:

Rights and Protections

- Consumer Assistance Program
  State Consumer Assistance Programs will assist patients in filing complaints and appeals, enroll in health coverage, and learn about their rights and responsibilities as a health care consumer.

- Appealing Health Plan Decisions
  Patients have the right to ask their plan to reconsider a denial of payment for services.
- Preventive Care
  Patients may be eligible to receive recommended preventive health services at no cost.
- Patient's Bill of Rights
  The "Patient's Bill of Rights" outlines consumer protections and gives patients the knowledge needed to make informed choices about their health.
- Children's Preexisting Conditions
  Insurance companies can no longer limit or deny benefits to children under age 19 due to a preexisting health condition.
- Doctor Choice and Emergency Room Access
  Patients have the right to choose the doctor they want from their plan's network or seek emergency care at a hospital outside of their health plan's network.
- Grandfathered Health Plans
  Patients have the right to keep their "grandfathered" health plan if they were covered before the health care law was enacted. Grandfathered plans do not have to provide some of the rights and protections under the Affordable Care Act.
- Curbing Insurance Cancellations
  Insurance companies can no longer cancel coverage because the patient made a mistake on his or her application.

Insurance Provisions

- Preexisting Condition Insurance Plan (PCIP)
  Patients rejected for insurance due to a health condition or disability may be eligible for coverage through the Preexisting Condition Insurance Plan.
- Young Adult Coverage
  Persons under 26 may be eligible for health insurance coverage under their parent's plan.
- Affordable Insurance Exchanges
  Starting in 2014, persons will be able to shop for insurance and compare health plans in new state-based Affordable Insurance Exchanges.
- CO-OP Insurance Plans
  Starting in 2014, persons or small businesses may be able to buy insurance from a new type of nonprofit, consumer-run health insurer, called a Consumer Operated and Oriented Plan (CO-OP).

- Value for Premium Dollar
  The health care law limits how much of a premium dollar an insurer can spend on things other than providing and improving the quality of your health care.
- Lifetime and Annual Limits
  Lifetime limits on most benefits are banned for all new health insurance plans. Annual limits on health benefits are now restricted and will be phased out by 2014.
- Flexible Spending Account Changes
  Flexible spending account limits will be reduced.
- Rate Review
  Rate Review will be instituted. Insurance companies will have to justify any rate increase of 10% or more.
- Provisions for People 65 or Older
  The Affordable Care Act offers eligible seniors a range of preventive services with no cost-sharing, and provides discounts on drugs when in the coverage gap known as the "doughnut hole."
- Medicare Preventive Services
  Medicare beneficiaries are eligible for a number of cost-free preventive services.
- Medicare Drug Discounts
  Eligible seniors who are in the coverage gap known as the "doughnut hole" automatically receive a discount on prescription drugs in 2011 and beyond.

Employers

- Small Employer Tax Credits
  The law provides tax credits for small businesses and not-for-profits.
- Early Retiree Reinsurance Program (ERRP)
  A company that provides health insurance to retirees ages 55 to 64 may be eligible for financial help through the Early Retiree Reinsurance Program.

Future of the Obama Health Plan

At the time this book was written, the Obama Health Plan was being implemented according to the scheduled timetable, but Republicans were attempting to repeal the legislation. They explain themselves on the Republican website GOP.gov by saying that: "Because the new health care law kills jobs, raises taxes, and increases the cost of health care, we will immediately take action to repeal this law" (GOP.gov, 2012). Indeed, on January 19, 2011, the House of Representatives passed H.R. 2, which repealed the Patient Protection and Affordable Care Act, although repeal did not pass in the Senate. The vote in both the Senate and House was partisan. All Republicans in the House and Senate voted for repeal. In the House, all Democrats were opposed, except three from Arkansas, North Carolina, and Oklahoma. A bill is currently in progress in the House to replace the Patient Protection and Affordable Care Act:

> On January 20, 2011, the House passed H. Res. 9, a resolution instructing House committees to develop legislation replacing the job-killing health care law. Committees are currently doing their work to hold hearings and examine solutions to lower costs, increase access to quality care, and strengthen the doctor-patient relationship. (GOP.gov, 2012)

In addition, the constitutionality of PPACA has been brought to the Supreme Court, which agreed to hear appeals from only one decision, the United States Court of Appeals for the 11th Circuit in Atlanta, which struck down the individual mandate requiring individuals to purchase health insurance on the basis that "the mandate overstepped Congressional authority and could not be justified by the constitutional power 'to regulate commerce' or 'to lay and collect taxes'" (Liptak, 2011).

> Oral arguments are likely to be held in late February or March, with a ruling by June, assuring the blockbuster issue will become a hot-button political debate in a presidential election year.
> The high court agreed to hear two major questions: whether the law's key provision is unconstitutional, and if so, whether the entire law, with its 450 sections, must be scrapped. (Mears, 2011)

Stay tuned!

NOTES

1. As noted in Chapter 1, the term *health insurance* is a misnomer. Generically, *insurance* is a system that provides for the periodic collection of relatively small sums of money from large numbers of people to protect each of them against the financial consequences of a relatively rare negative event. However, over the course of a lifetime, for most people using health services is not a "relatively rare event." Thus, health insurance is not insurance in the conventional sense. Rather, it is a system for the collective, long-term prepayment for the costs of health services that each member of the group of people covered will, on average, use during the time period for which they are covered. Furthermore, the term is a misnomer in the sense that not much "health insurance" money actually pays for the maintenance and promotion of health. Rather, most of it goes to cover the costs of care during sickness. Nevertheless, the term as it is commonly used will be employed in this chapter.
2. Most of the references used in this section were published some time ago. They provide a great deal of detail about the events described here, some from quite a close-up perspective, and remain valid and useful. For a recently published overview of the history of

U.S. health care reform efforts, from the time of the Wilson presidency (1913–1921) to the present, see Goldfield (2000).
3. Both Burrow's book and the Harris articles contain detailed histories and analyses of the AMA's involvement in legislative battles over NHI. The Burrow (1963) book detailed those battles through the 1950s. The Harris (1966) articles covered the Medicare struggles. An excellent overall historical perspective was provided by Falk (1977), a man who had been at the center of the reform battles from the time he was staff director of the Committee on the Costs of Medical Care until the push for NHI was dropped at the end of the Truman administration.
4. The details of all major NHI proposals made between 1935 and 1957 are summarized in Brewster (1958).

REFERENCES

American Medical Association (AMA). (1990, March). *Health access America*. Chicago, IL: Author.

Anderson, O.W. (1968). *The uneasy equilibrium: Private and public financing of health services in the United States, 1875–1965*. New Haven, CT: College and University Press.

Angell, M. (1999). The American health care system revisited—A new series. *New England Journal of Medicine, 340*(1), 481.

Berenson, A. (2006, March 12). A cancer drug's big price rise is cause for concern. *The New York Times*. Retrieved from www.nytimes.com/2006/03/12/business/12price.html?pagewanted=all

Berenson, A. (2006, October 20). Pfizer and other drug makers report higher profits. *The New York Times*, Section C, Page 2, Column 1.

Blevins, S.A. (1997, December 12). Restoring health freedom: The case for a universal tax credit for health insurance. *Policy Analysis (The Cato Institute)*, No. 290.

Blumenthal, D. (1995). Health care reform—past and future. *New England Journal of Medicine, 332*, 465.

Blumenthal, D. (1999). Health care reform at the close of the 20th century. *New England Journal of Medicine, 340*(24), 1916–1920.

Boas, F. P. (1958). Why do we need national health insurance? In Committee on Medical Care Teaching of the Association of Teachers of Preventive Medicine. (1958). *Readings in medical care*. Chapel Hill: University of North Carolina Press. (Reprinted from Society for Ethical Culture, 1945.)

Bradford, S. L. (2002). *Stock watch: What health-care crisis?* Retrieved April 29, 2002, from www.aol.smartmoney.com

Brewster, A. W. (1958). *Health insurance and related proposals for financing personal health services*. Washington, DC: U.S. Government Printing Office.

Burns, E. M. (1971). Health insurance: Not if, or when, but what kind? *American Journal of Public Health, 61*(11), 2164–2175.

Burrow, J. G. (1963). *AMA: Voice of American medicine*. Baltimore, MD: Johns Hopkins University Press.

Burrow, J. G. (1977). *Organized medicine in the progressive era*. Baltimore, MD: Johns Hopkins University Press.

Business Wire. (2006a, October 30). Triad reports third quarter results. *Business Wire*.

Business Wire. (2006b, October 30). Humana Inc. reports third quarter 2006 financial results including earnings per share of $0.95. *Business Wire*.

Carpenter, D. (2002). For-profit health care. Hospital stocks prove health on Wall Street. *Hospitals and Health Networks, 76*(2), 22, 24.

Cavalier, K. (1979). *National health insurance*. Washington, DC: Congressional Research Service, Library of Congress.

Centers for Disease Control and Prevention (CDC). (1999). Ten great public health achievements—United States, 1990–1999. *Morbidity and Mortality Weekly Report, 48(12),* 241–243.

Committee for Economic Development. (1973, April). *Building a national health-care system: a statement on national policy by the research and policy committee of the committee for economic development.* New York, NY: Author.

Committee for National Health Insurance. (1989). *The health security partnership.* Washington, DC: Author.

Committee on Finance, U.S. Senate. (1970). *Medicare and Medicaid: Problems, issues and alternatives.* Washington, DC: U.S. Government Printing Office.

Committee on Finance, U.S. Senate. (1979). *Comparison of major features of health insurance proposals.* Washington, DC: U.S. Government Printing Office.

Committee on Labor and Human Resources, U.S. Senate. (1988, April 29). *Background information on S. 1265: The Minimum Health Benefits for All Workers Act of 1988.* Washington, DC: U.S. Government Printing Office.

Committee on the Costs of Medical Care. (1932). *Medical care for the American people.* Chicago, IL: University of Chicago Press. (Reprinted, Washington, DC: U.S. Department of Health, Education and Welfare, 1970.)

Committee on Ways and Means, U.S. House of Representatives. (1974). *National health insurance resource book.* Washington, DC: U.S. Government Printing Office.

Davis, K. (1975). *National health insurance: Benefits, costs, and consequences.* Washington, DC: Brookings Institution.

Davis, K. (2010). a *new era in American health care: Realizing the potential of reform.* New York, NY: The Commonwealth Fund.

Dickey, N. W., & McMenamin, P. (1999). Putting power into patient choice. *New England Journal of Medicine, 341(17),* 1305–1308.

Douglas-Wilson, I., & McLachlan, G. (1973). *Health service prospects: An international survey.* Boston, MA: Little, Brown.

Editors. (1970). Our ailing medical system: It's time to operate. *Fortune.* New York: Harper & Row.

Eilers, R. D. (1971). National health insurance: What kind and how much? (Parts 1 and 2). *New England Journal of Medicine, 284(15),* 881–886; *284(17),* 945–954.

Evans, R. G., Lomas, J., Barer, M. L., Labelle, R. J., Fooks, C., Stoddart, G. L., et al. (1989). Controlling health expenditures—the Canadian reality. *New England Journal of Medicine, 320(9),* 571–577.

Falk, I. S. (1973). Medical care in the USA, 1932–1972: Problems, proposals and programs from the Committee on the Costs of Medical Care to the Committee for National Health Insurance. *Milbank Memorial Fund Quarterly, Health and Society, 51(1),* 1–32.

Falk, I. S. (1977). Proposals for national health insurance in the USA: Origins and evolution, and some perceptions for the future. *Milbank Memorial Fund Quarterly, Health and Society, 55(2),* 161–191.

Freeland, R. M. (1975). *The Truman doctrine and the origins of McCarthyism.* New York, NY: Alfred Knopf.

Freudenheim, M. (1994, June 27). Health industry is changing itself ahead of reform. *New York Times,* p. 1.

Freymann, J. G. (1974). *The American health care system: Its genesis and trajectory.* New York, NY: Medcom.

Friedman, E. (1977, August–November). Medicaid Series, Parts 1–6. *Hospitals, 51(16, 17, 18, 19, 20, 21).*

Fry, J., & Farndale, W. A. J. (Eds.). (1972). *International medical care.* Oxford, UK: Medical & Technical Publishing Company.

Fuchs, V. R., & Hahn, J. S. (1990). How does Canada do it? A comparison of expenditures for physicians' services in the United States and Canada. *New England Journal of Medicine, 323(13),* 884–890.

Glaser, W. A. (1978). *Health insurance bargaining.* New York, NY: Gardner.

Goldfield, N. I. (2000). *National health reform American style: Lessons from the past.* Tampa, FL: American College of Physician Executives.

GOP.gov (the website of the Republican majority in Congress). (2012). *Repeal and replace the job destroying health care law.* Retrieved January 29, 2012, from www.gop.gov/indepth/pledge/healthcare

Gottlieb, S. (2002). Drug companies maintain "astounding" profits [News]. *British Medical Journal, 324*(7345), 1054.

Grumbach, K., Bodenheimer, T., Himmelstein, D. U., & Woolhandler, S. (1991). Liberal benefits, conservative spending: The physicians for a National Health Program proposal. *Journal of the American Medical Association, 265*(19), 2549–2554.

Hacker, J. S. (1996, Winter). National health care reform: An idea whose time came and went. *Journal of Health Politics, Policy and Law, 21*(4), 647–696.

Harris, R. (1966, July 2–23). Annals of legislation: Medicare. *The New Yorker.*

Hastings, J. E. (1972). Toward a national health program. Canadian experience. *Bulletin of the New York Academy of Medicine, 18*(1), 66–82.

HealthCare.gov (A federal government website managed by the U.S. Department of Health & Human Services). (2012). *Provisions of the Affordable Care Act, by Year.* Retrieved January 15, 2012, from www.healthcare.gov/law/timeline/full.html

Heritage Foundation. (1989). *Critical issues: A national health system for America.* Washington, DC: Author.

Himmelstein, D. U., & Woolhandler, S. (1989). A national health program for the United States. A physicians' proposal. *New England Journal of Medicine, 320*(2), 102–108.

Himmelstein, D. U., & Woolhandler, S. (with Hellander, I.). (2001). *Bleeding the patient: The consequences of corporate health care.* Monroe, ME: Common Coverale Press.

Himmelstein, D. U., & Woolhandler, S. (2002). Liberal benefits, conservative spending. *Archives of Internal Medicine, 162*(9), 973–975.

Hoppszallern, S., & Arges, G. (2002). Leveraging the high cost of HIPAA. *Hospitals and Health Networks, 76*(1), 56.

Igelhart, J. K. (1986). Canada's health care system. (Parts 1, 2, and 3). *New England Journal of Medicine, 315*(3, 12, 25), 202–208, 778–784, 1623–1628.

Igelhart, J. K. (1990). Canada's health care system faces its problems. *New England Journal of Medicine, 322*(8), 562–568.

Institute of Medicine (IOM), Committee on Health Planning Goals and Standards. (1981). *Health planning in the United States: Selected policy issues* (2 Vols.). Washington, DC: National Academies Press.

Institute of Medicine (IOM). (2000). *To err is human: Building a safer health system.* Washington, DC: National Academies Press.

Institute of Medicine (IOM). (2001). *Crossing the quality chasm: A new health system for the 21st century.* Washington, DC: National Academies Press.

Insurance plan stresses reform, prevention. (1990, March). *The Nation's Health,* p. 1.

Investor's Business Daily. (2007, February 14). Business briefs (Medical). *Investor's Business Daily,* p. A02.

Jonas, S. (1974). Issues in national health insurance in the United States of America. *Lancet, 2*(7873), 143–146.

Jonas, S. (1977). *Quality-control of ambulatory care.* New York, NY: Springer Publishing.

Jonas, S. (1980). Planning for national health insurance by objective: The contract mechanism. *Journal of Policy Studies, 9*(2), 250–260.

Jonas, S. (1981). National health insurance. In S. Jonas (Ed.), *Health care delivery in the United States* (2nd ed., pp. 438–470). New York, NY: Springer Publishing.

Jonas, S. (1984). The personal health care system. *New York State Journal of Medicine, 84*(4), 187–189.

Katz, S. J., Cardiff, K., Pascali, M., Barer, M. L., & Evans, R. G. (2002). Phantoms in the snow: Canadians' use of health care services in the United States. *Health Affairs, 21*(3), 19–31.

Kimble, C. (1979, November). Special report: Comparing the Carter and Kennedy national health insurance bills. *Washington Report on Medicine and Health.*

Koplan, J. P., & Fleming, D. W. (2000). Current and future public health challenges. *Journal of the American Medical Association, 284*(13), 1696–1698.

Kristol, W. (1993, December 2). *Defeating President Clinton's health care proposal* [Memo]. Washington, DC: Project for the Republican Future.

Krugman, P. (2002, March 19). Bad medicine. *The New York Times,* p. A23.

Kuttner, R. (1997). The Kassebaum-Kennedy Bill—The limits of incrementalism. *New England Journal of Medicine, 337*(1), 64–67.

Liptak, A. (2011, November 15). Justices to hear health care case as race heats up. *The New York Times,* p. A1.

Lynch, M. J., & Raphael, S. S. (1963). *Medicine and the state.* Springfield, IL: Charles C. Thomas.

McKittrick, L. S. (1958). Medical care for the American people: Is compulsory health insurance the solution? In Committee on Medical Care Teaching of the Association of Teachers of Preventive Medicine. (1958). *Readings in medical care.* Chapel Hill: University of North Carolina Press. (Reprinted from *New England Journal of Medicine,* 1940, 240, 998.)

McMahon, J. A. (1975, November 10). *Statement of the American Hospital Association on National Health Insurance before the Health Subcommittee of the House Committee on Ways and Means.* Washington, DC: American Hospital Association.

Mears, B. (2011, November 14). Supreme Court takes up challenge to health care reform law. *CNN Politics.* Retrieved January 15, 2012, fromhttp://articles.cnn.com/2011–11-14/politics/politics_health-care_1_oral-arguments-health-care-reform-law-affordable-care-act?_s=PM:POLITICS

National Association of Manufacturers. (1989). *Meeting the health care crisis.* Washington, DC: Author.

National Leadership Commission on Health Care. (1989). *For the health of a nation: A shared responsibility.* Ann Arbor, MI: Health Administration Press Perspectives.

Navarro, V. (1994). The need to mobilize support for the Wellstone-McDermott-Conyers Single-Payer Proposal. *American Journal of Public Health, 84*(2), 178–179.

Nixon, R. M. (1994, September 19–26). Health care now. Excerpts from speech given by Richard Nixon to Congress on 2/18/1971. *The New Republic,* p. 11.

Oil, Chemical, and Atomic Workers. (1989). *National health care: Pass it on!* Lakewood, CO: Author.

Redlener, I. (1993, November 10). *Presentation, Rockland County Democratic Forum,* New City, NY.

Roemer, M. I. (Ed.). (1960). *Henry E. Sigerist on the sociology of medicine.* New York, NY: MD Publications.

Roemer, M. I. (1985). I.S. Falk, the Committee on the Costs of Medical Care, and the drive for national health insurance. *American Journal of Public Health, 75*(8), 841–848.

Roemer, M. I. (1991). *National health systems of the world: The countries* (Vol. 1). New York, NY: Oxford University Press.

Rothman, D. (2001). [Book Review of *Severed trust: Why American medicine hasn't been fixed.*] *Journal of the American Medical Association, 286*(20), 2604–2605.

Schiff, G. D., & Young, Q. D. (2001). [Book Review of *You can't leap a chasm in two jumps*: The Institute of Medicine health care quality report.] *Public Health Reports, 116*(5), 396–403.

Schwartz, H. (1972). *The case for American medicine: A realistic look at our health care system.* New York, NY: David McKay.

Skocpol, T. (1995). The rise and resounding demise of the Clinton plan. *Health Affairs, 14*(1), 66–85.

Stark, Kennedy to propose health reforms. (1985, June 17). *Washington Report on Medicine and Health.*

Stevens, R. (1971). *American medicine and the public interest.* New Haven, CT: Yale University Press.

Truman, H. S. (1958). Message from the President of the United States. In Committee on Medical Care Teaching. (1958). *Readings in Medical Care.* Chapel Hill: University of North Carolina Press. (Reprinted from 79th Congress, 1st Session, 1945, Washington, DC: U.S. Government Printing Office.)

Tuohy, C. H. (2002, May–June). The costs of constraint and prospects for health care reform in Canada. *Health Affairs, 21*(3), 32–46.

U.S. Bipartisan Commission on Comprehensive Health Care. (1990, September). *A call for action.* Washington, DC: U.S. Government Printing Office.

White House Domestic Policy Council. (1993). *Health security: The President's report to the American people.* Washington, DC: The White House.

Woolhandler, S., & Himmelstein, D. U. (1991). The deteriorating administrative efficiency of the U.S. health care system. *New England Journal of Medicine, 324*(18), 1253–1258.

Woolhandler, S., & Himmelstein, D. U. (1997). Costs of care and administration at for-profit and other hospitals in the United States. *New England Journal of Medicine, 336*(11), 769–774.

APPENDIX

List of Critical Reports on the U.S. Health Care Delivery System, 1927–2006

Aday, L. A. (2001). *At risk in America: The health and health care needs of vulnerable populations in the United States.* San Francisco, CA: Jossey-Bass.

American health care: A system in crisis. (1983, October). *Healthline,* p. 7.

Citizen's Board of Inquiry into Health Services for Americans. (1971). *Heal yourself* [Report]. Washington, DC: Author.

The crisis in American medicine. (1960, October). *Harper's Magazine,* p. 123.

Ehrenreich, B., & Ehrenreich, J. (1971). *The American health empire: Power, profits, and politics.* New York, NY: Vintage Books.

Health Task Force of the Urban Coalition. (1969). *Rx for action* [Report]. Washington, DC: Author.

Himmelstein, D., & Woolhandler, S. (2001). *Bleeding the patient: The consequences of corporate health care.* Monroe, ME: Common Courage Press.

Institute of Medicine (IOM). (2000). *To err is human: Building a safer health system.* Washington, DC: National Academies Press.

Institute of Medicine (IOM). (2001). *Crossing the quality chasm: A new health system for the 21st century.* Washington, DC: National Academies Press.

Institute of Medicine (IOM). (2003). *Unequal treatment: Confronting racial and ethnic disparities in health care.* Washington, DC: National Academies Press.

Institute of Medicine (IOM). (2004). *Patient safety. Achieving a new standard for care.* Washington, DC: National Academies Press.

Jonas, S. (1978). *Medical mystery: The training of doctors in the United States.* New York, NY: W.W. Norton.

Kennedy, E. M. (1972). *In critical condition.* New York, NY: Simon & Schuster.

Kleinke, J. D. (2001). *Oxymorons: The myth of a U.S. health care system.* San Francisco, CA: Jossey-Bass.

Knowles, J. H. (Ed.). (1977). *Doing better and feeling worse.* New York, NY: W.W. Norton.

Moskin, J. R. (1964, November 3). The challenge to our doctors. *Look,* p. 26.

National Commission on Community Health Services. (1966). *Health is a community affair.* Cambridge, MA: Harvard University Press.

Ribicoff, A., with Danaceau, P. (1972). *The American medical machine.* New York, NY: Saturday Review Press.

Schorr, D. (1970). *Don't get sick in America.* Nashville, TN: Aurora Publishers.

Silver, G. A. (1976). *A spy in the house of medicine.* Germantown, MD: Aspen.

The $60-billion crisis over medical care. (1990, January 17). *Business Week,* [Special reprint].

Somers, A. R., & Somers, H. M. (1977). *Health and health care.* Germantown, MD: Aspen.

In a review of the Ehrenreich and Ehrenreich (1971) book, *The American Health Empire: Power, Profits, and Politics,* which appeared in the *International Journal of Health Services* (1972), Dr. Milton Roemer listed a series of other reports going back many more years. He said:

> Every few years, more recently in the last decade, there appears a book analyzing the serious defects of health care in America. In 1927, Harry H. Moore produced *American Medicine and the People's Health,* in the 1930s were the magnificent 27 volumes of the Committee on the Costs of Medical Care, in 1939 there was James Rorty's *American Medicine Mobilizes,* and in 1940 Hugh Cabot's *The Patient Dilemma.* After World War II, Carl Malmberg wrote *140 Million Patients* in 1947, Michael Davis wrote *Medical Care for Tomorrow* in 1955, and Richard Carter wrote *The Doctor Business* in 1958. In 1965, there was Selig Greenberg's excellent *The Troubled Calling: Crisis in the Medical Establishment.* The year after Medicare, 1966, saw two critical outputs: *The American Health Scandal* by Raul Tunley and *The Doctors* by Martin L. Gross. In 1967, there was Fred J. Cook's *Plot Against the Patient* and in 1970 Ed Cray's *In Failing Health.* (p. 119)

It is fascinating that, allowing for changes in magnitude, many of these analyses and the recommendations they make are similar in so many ways. It is also fascinating that three quarters of a century after Dr. Moore's book appeared, such books, referred to and cited in the text (e.g., the Institute of Medicine's *Crossing the Quality Chasm,* Himmelstein and Woolhandler's *Bleeding the Patient,* and Kleinke's *Oxymorons*) are still being written. This is the case because not only do many of the problems of cost, distribution, coverage, and quality that past works highlight remain with us, but because of the changes in their magnitude over time—they are only getting worse.

NINE

Epilogue: 2007

As discussed, as long ago as 1932, the findings of the first comprehensive study of health care in the United States deplored problems with health care quality, equity, and efficiency:

> The problem of providing satisfactory medical service to all the people of the United States at costs which they can meet is a pressing one. At the present time, many persons do not receive service which is adequate either in quantity or quality, and the costs of service are inequably distributed. The result is a tremendous amount of preventable physical pain and mental anguish, needless deaths, economic inefficiency, and social waste. Furthermore, these conditions are...largely unnecessary. The United States has the economic resources, the organizing ability, and the technical experience to solve this problem. (Committee on the Costs of Medical Care, 1970, p. 2)

These problems remain remarkably similar today despite recurring periods of intense dissatisfaction with the health care system, followed by calls for reform. No period of discontent with the U.S. health care system has resulted in major reform, whereby the problems of quality, equity, and efficiency are addressed systematically and in total. As discussed in Chapter 9, major change has always eluded reformers. Rather, the changes that have occurred may be characterized as "tinkering" with the system—varying from minor to major tinkering. "Major tinkering" occurred in the 1960s when the federal government created the Medicare and Medicaid programs. However, in most eras of dissatisfaction, "minor tinkering" with the system prevailed. A well-known example is the 1946 Hill-Burton Act to fund hospital construction in underserved areas, which was actually aimed at preventing government from taking a larger role in the provision of medical care for the general population:

> Supported by the medical establishment and guided through the Senate by Senator Robert Taft, [the Hill-Burton Act] deflected President Truman's proposal for a comprehensive health plan by limiting the government's role to the subsidy of voluntary nonprofit hospitals. The Hill-Burton Act eventually helped to finance 9,200 new hospitals and other facilities, assisting in financing almost one-third of all hospital projects in the nation. (Lipscomb, 2002, p. 109)

Another example of tinkering occurred in the 1990s. The Clinton health plan failed, as did all other proposals at the time, to overhaul the health care system. However, failure to bring major reform was followed later in the decade by passage of "minor tinkering" legislation. This included the Health Insurance Portability and Accountability Act, which patched the health insurance gap for people who were changing jobs, and the State Children's Health Insurance Program (SCHIP), which provided health insurance for low-income, uninsured children whose families were not poor enough to qualify for Medicaid.

A NEW ERA OF CHANGE?

As of the writing of this edition of *Jonas' Introduction to the U.S. Health Care System*, dissatisfaction with the health care system is rising again, and we may be entering another period of strong demand for change. Public confidence in the system appears to be waning. For example, the 2006 Health Confidence Survey (HCS) found that the public's increasing dissatisfaction with the U.S. health care system seems to be focused on rising costs and the negative effects on their financial well-being. People feel that steps should be taken to slow down increases in cost; 38% rate the health care system as fair, 31% as poor. The percentage of individuals rating the system poor has doubled since the inception of the HCS in 1998 (Helman & Fronstin, 2006).

The rising rate of those who are uninsured plays a large role in the public's dissatisfaction. The number of uninsured Americans is 47 million, which was almost one-sixth of the population in 2006. Much of this problem is related to the decrease in employer-based health insurance. The National Academies summarized recent findings of the Kaiser Family Foundation and the U.S. Census Bureau on this subject:

> Fewer employers are providing health insurance for their workers this year, according to the Kaiser Family Foundation and the Health Research and Educational Trust's 2005 Annual Survey of Employer Health Benefits. The main drop came from smaller companies that said they could not offer coverage because of high premiums.
>
> About 60 percent of businesses said they would offer health care plans in 2005, down from 69 percent in 2000. Since 2000, the number of uninsured adults [in 2006] has grown by more than 6 million, based on U.S. Census Bureau statistics for 2004. People who earn less are especially vulnerable because their health insurance is more prone to be cut and they are less likely to be able to afford their own coverage. (Pickoff-White, 2006)

Further, poor access to health care has been related to the declaration of personal bankruptcies (Himmelstein, Warren, Thorne, & Woolhandler, 2005) because individuals are

> emotionally and financially exhausted, hoping to stop the collection calls, save their homes, and stabilize their economic circumstances. Many of the debtors detailed ongoing problems with access to care. Some expressed fear that their medical care providers would not continue their care...several had used credit cards to charge medical bills they had no hope of paying...the co-occurrence of medical and job problems was a common theme...a second common theme was sounded by parents of premature infants or chronically ill children...many of the insured debtors blamed high co-payments and deductibles for their financial ruin. (pp. W5–W64)

In addition to the rising rate of those who are uninsured, national health care spending is again growing at a rapid rate (National Coalition on Health Care, 2004), a concern for patients, providers, payers, and policymakers:

> By several measures, health care spending continues to rise at the fastest rate in our history. In 2004 (the latest year data

are available [for this report]), total national health expenditures rose 7.9 percent—over three times the rate of inflation. Total spending was $1.9 TRILLION in 2004, or $6,280
per person. Total health care spending represented 16 percent of the gross domestic product (GDP)....U.S. health care
spending is expected to increase at similar levels for the
next decade reaching $4 TRILLION in 2015, or 20 percent
of GDP.

The costs of health care are particularly hard on state budgets. States
apportion a tremendous proportion of their budgets to Medicaid. In
2005, the average was 22.9% of a state's total expenditures. The range
was 7.7% in Wyoming to 34.3% in Missouri, with most states (31 of
the 50 states) over 20% (National Association of State Budget Officers
[NASBO], 2006). Although Medicaid spending growth slowed in 2006
and state revenues continued to recover after the economic downturn
of the early 2000s (Smith et al., 2006), the amount devoted to Medicaid
spending by the states is major:

> Despite dramatic slowing of Medicaid spending and enroll-
> ment growth, pressure to control Medicaid spending growth
> remains strong. Requirements to balance state budgets each
> year, rising health care costs, increasing numbers of Americans
> without health insurance and the aging population (contrib-
> uting to more elderly and more persons with disabilities) all
> continue to impose demands on Medicaid. States may be fac-
> ing additional strains around Medicaid financing as formula
> driven changes continue to push down federal match rates
> and as the Centers for Medicare and Medicaid Services (CMS)
> continues to scrutinize state financing practices regarding what
> expenditures qualify for federal matching dollars. (Smith et al.,
> 2006, p. 9)

The SCHIP program is a looming problem for states. Authorization
for SCHIP ended in 2007, and the program may not be renewed because
of the fiscal priorities of the current administration:

> In fiscal year 2007, the final year of SCHIP's original ten-year
> authorization, many states are expected to have inadequate
> SCHIP funds to cover the same number of beneficiaries as in
> 2006. We estimate, based on states' most recent SCHIP spend-
> ing projections for fiscal year 2007 and taking into account
> stop-gap SCHIP legislation enacted in December 2006, that
> 14 states will face a combined shortfall this year of nearly

$745 million—equivalent to the average annual cost of covering 510,000 children through SCHIP in 2007. (Broaddus & Park, 2007)

Finally, physicians are increasingly discontent with their profession due to decreasing autonomy and income growth and increasing intrusion of management into the doctor–patient relationship. Many feel that they cannot practice the kind of medicine they believe is appropriate and necessary. As Zuger writes:

> The profession of medicine has taken its members on a wild ride during the past century: a slow, glorious climb in well-being followed by a steep, stomach-churning fall. In the decades after World War II, sociologists portrayed American doctors as the lucky heirs to a golden age of medicine. They were surrounded by admiring assistants, loyal patients, and respectful colleagues and had full autonomy in their work, job security, and a luxurious income. This era was short-lived. By the 1980s, newspaper headlines proclaimed that many of the nation's "dispirited doctors" were considering bailing out of medicine, and subsequent observers have continued to describe a profession in retreat, plagued by bureaucracy, loss of autonomy, diminished prestige, and deep personal dissatisfaction. (2004, p. 69)

In summary, dissatisfaction with the health care system is growing among many stakeholders, including the general public, physicians, and payers, and it seems likely to result in change over the next decade.

WHAT KIND OF CHANGE?

What will be the nature of the response to current problems is a fundamental question for policymakers and stakeholders. For although we may agree on goals, we will often disagree on how to reach them. At present, for example, there is a fair amount of agreement among health policymakers that we need to reengineer our health care system based on population needs to improve health care quality through utilization management, care management, and evidence-based medicine; to eliminate inequities in the quality of and access to health care; and to increase efficiency so that our health care expenditures are reasonable for the outcomes they produce (e.g., Kindig, 1997; Shortell et al., 2000). How this might be accomplished and by whom are other matters entirely. Given the historical importance of the relationship between the public and private sectors in the United States, the answers to these questions are likely to involve this linkage.

One of the major differences between policy approaches in the United States is the preferred role of the public and private sectors, particularly the for-profit private sector. For this reason, one of the themes in this book is the increasing involvement of for-profit corporations in the delivery of health care. The tension between public and private sectors is a remarkably salient issue in the United States. The U.S. health care system is a "mixed enterprise," one in which there is a strong private sector wielding enormous power as well as a large and influential public sector (Rosenberg, 2006). The "mixed enterprise" has historical roots that transcend health care:

> There is nothing more fundamental in the history of American health care than the mixture of public and private. In this regard, American distinctiveness lies not in some unique devotion to the market and individualism, but in a widespread inattention to a more complex reality. From the canal and railroad land grants in antebellum America to support for the aircraft industry in the twentieth century, from tariff policy to the creation of the corporation in the nineteenth century to today's outsourcing of military functions, the interactive and mutually constitutive mixture of public and private has been so ubiquitous in American history as to be almost invisible; it is as true for medicine as it is and has been for transportation or the military-industrial complex. All have been clothed with a sense of collective responsibility that implies—if not demands—the active role of government. Since the Second World War, the public sector (and especially the federal government) has supported medicine in all of its aspects—basic research and the training of biomedical scientists and clinicians, the provision of care, and the management of medically defined dependency. It is a tradition with roots older than the nation itself. (Rosenberg, 2006, pp. 14–15)

Although a mixed public and private health care system has existed throughout U.S. history, prior to the mid-1960s, government was involved mainly in four areas of health care: providing money to train physicians and other health care workers; funding medical research, primarily through the National Institutes of Health (NIH); funding public health activities such as epidemic control at the federal, state, and local levels; and providing medical services to special populations, principally the military, both active and retired, and the mentally ill. Public involvement did not interfere with the basic nature of medical care delivery for the general population. Prior to the mid-1960s, medical care delivery was primarily a "cottage industry" made up of individual or small groups of providers paid for their services directly by patients, or their employer-based insurance, on a fee-for-service basis.

In the mid-1960s, the Medicare and Medicaid legislation brought about a momentous shift in public sector involvement in the health care system, moving it beyond its traditional purview of medical research, workforce training, public health, and provision of medical care for certain special populations. By funding medical care for the elderly (Medicare) and the poor (Medicaid), these programs brought the public sector into the business of providing medical care for large sections of the general population. Moreover, both programs have grown steadily in size of expenditures, number of people served, and influence on hospitals, physicians, and other providers since their inception.

During this period from the mid-1960s to today, however, the private sector, particularly the profit-making sector, was not stagnant. There has been tremendous growth since the mid-1960s among for-profit health care companies in traditional service areas such as supply of therapeutics including pharmaceuticals, medical supplies, and medical devices; and new service areas such as supply of information technology. In addition, for-profit insurance companies such as Prudential and Aetna entered the health insurance market, changing it from a mainly private, nonprofit arena based on community rating to a profit-making one, based on experience rating.[1] Finally, companies such as United Health Care, Tenet, Triad, and Humana were developed to provide direct medical care through integrated systems of care from ambulatory, hospital, rehabilitation, home health, to nursing home. These profit-making corporations stand in sharp contrast to the "cottage industry" providers of the past. Much as local banks have been replaced by large, national and international banking corporations, United Health Care, Tenet, and others with Wall Street money exemplify the same trend in the direct provision of medical care.

Returning then to the question of what kind of change might result from the present period of discontent, we need to assess the power of each sector—public and private—and their interest in promoting certain directions in reform, and the likelihood that one will be more successful than the other. In a sense, both public and private sectors are now more competitive, rather than complementary, than they were prior to the advent of Medicare and Medicaid. Will the mixed system prevail, or will one sector become dominant?

A PRIVATE SYSTEM?

The strong, historical incentives to maintain a mixed health care system have prevented the United States from following our peer countries. All of them have primarily public systems, whereby the government ensures health care for all residents through direct provision of services (e.g., United Kingdom), universal health insurance (e.g., Canada), or a mix of these.

However, there are signs that the United States may be on the threshold of developing a nonmixed health care delivery enterprise. Playing to a strong current of anti-government sentiment in the United States, conservative stakeholders since the 1980s have pressed toward privatization of public functions. Although anti-government sentiment among Americans is not uncritical or necessarily a primary motivation (Goldsteen, Goldsteen, Kronenfeld, & Hann, 1997), it has been a useful political device for ideologues to promote a private sector–only agenda. The "framing" of issues in anti-government terms has succeeded in limiting public sector involvement in health care as well as other areas. This "crafted approach" is working to move health care and other public activities away from the mixed enterprise system.

We are in an era in which privatization of public sector functions is widespread. There is "privatization creep" in health care as well as other sectors. For example, private companies have been given long-term leases for public roads in Northern Virginia on the Dulles Greenway, in Indiana on the East-West Toll Road, and on a 157-mile highway running east from Chicago to the Ohio border. The idea has been considered in New Jersey, Illinois, Ohio, Texas, and other locales.

Commodification of water is occurring throughout the world, including the United States. Many municipalities are looking to private corporations for long-term leasing of water supplies. The transnational private water corporations including Suez, Vivendi, and Nestle/Perrier have annual revenues of over a trillion dollars and have privatized many formerly public water sources. As water shortages and conflicts increase, water is more and more being transformed from a public good to a privately owned commodity that is sold and traded for profit. It is an increasingly alluring idea to municipalities faced with expensive infrastructure costs.

Major functions of the military have been privatized in recent years. There are advocates for privatizing military maintenance and other functions traditionally performed by the military itself. Blackwater USA, by its own statement "the most comprehensive professional military, law enforcement, security, peacekeeping, and stability operations company in the world" (Blackwater USA, 2007), has been used heavily in the Iraq War. A review of privatizing military training by Deborah Avant summarizes the current situation:

- Private military companies (PMCs), performing an array of security tasks for a variety of clients, have proliferated.
- In pursuing its war on terrorism, the Pentagon is increasingly relying on the services of PMCs, as overseas training programs expand.

- Although private military companies have long performed covert and unsavory tasks, today's PMCs are seeking to polish their image as legitimate firms. (Avant, 2002, p. 1)

In the realm of health care delivery, a number of pieces of recent legislation have given elements of the Medicare program to the private sector. The development of a means test for Medicare Part B destroys Medicare's universal aspect. The Medicare Modernization Act of 2003 is another example. Part D, the drug program, requires that all Medicare recipients get prescription drug coverage from a private insurance company, which then receives a government subsidy to provide coverage. Dual eligibles, those Medicare recipients who also qualify for Medicaid, have been forced into the Part D program as well. Further, the legislation does not permit the Medicare program to bargain with drug companies for lower prices. Prescription drug coverage for Medicare recipients is now a private enterprise, eroding public-sector involvement in health care delivery in favor of the private sector.

The Medicare Modernization Act of 2003 also authorized the Medicare program to subsidize private HMOs for Medicare recipients, so that these plans would become attractive to more and more people who would then select them over the less costly traditional Medicare. Called the Medicare Advantage plans, the motivation for this legislation was clearly not fiscal restraint, but the desire to move health care delivery to the private, for-profit sector, as evidenced by its excess cost:

> According to the Medicare Payment Advisory Commission, an independent federal body that advises Congress on Medicare issues, Medicare Advantage now costs 11% more per beneficiary than traditional Medicare. According to the Commonwealth Fund, which has a similar estimate of the excess cost, the subsidy to private HMOs cost Medicare $5.4 billion in 2005. (Krugman, 2007)

It seems likely that the private sector will continue in traditional service areas, such as supply of therapeutics, and provide new services such as information technology. There is also little doubt that the public sector will continue supporting medical research, healthy workforce training, and public health functions such as epidemic control because of their high cost and lack of profitability. At issue is whether the mixed system will prevail in the direct provision of health care—ambulatory, hospital, long-term care, and so forth. The balance between private and public for the delivery of direct services to the general population may be shifting in favor of the private, profit-making sector.

Although we could address the problems of quality, equity, and efficiency by expanding the highly successful Medicare program to all

Americans, we may be moving instead toward a totally integrated delivery system owned by a few large companies such as Humana, Triad, and United Healthcare, and a small public sector to serve those deemed "unaffordable" by the private sector companies. Employer-based health insurance, the private health insurance market, and public programs for special groups, such as the poor, elderly, and veterans, would be eliminated. Thus, health care delivery might be integrated and "single payer," but the provider would be a profit-making corporation rather than a public or nonprofit entity.

A PUBLIC SYSTEM IS PREFERABLE

There is sufficient reason to doubt that a primarily private, profit-making health care system would achieve the goals of most Americans—health care quality, equity, and efficiency—because of fundamental incompatibilities with the nature of health care (e.g., Kaveny, 1999; Pellegrino, 1999). As we have argued throughout this book (see Chapters 8 and 9), the large profit-making health care companies have put profits before quality and equity, as might be expected because they must answer to their stockholders first. Therefore, it is of grave concern that the United States may have even more privatization of health care than it does now, even moving to dominance of profit-making enterprises in the direct delivery of health care. As Pellegrino (1999) argues, health care is fundamentally about healing, which is necessarily a public good, not a commodity. Treating health care as a commodity is injurious to the ethics of patient care and we, as a society, have an obligation to protect health care from the "market ethos":

> Understanding health care to be a commodity takes one down one arm of a bifurcating pathway to the ethic of the marketplace and instrumental resolution of injustices. Taking health care as a human good takes us down a divergent pathway to the resolution of injustice through a moral ordering of societal and individual priorities.
>
> One thing is certain: if health care is a commodity, it is for sale, and the physician is, indeed, a money-maker; if it is a human good, it cannot be for sale and the physician is a healer. [There is] only one ethically defensible answer. (p. 262)

If we move to market-driven health care delivery, we would be undoing 4,000 years of history in which profit was not the first priority of the system. This possibility is of the greatest concern, particularly for health care equity. As Martin Luther King, Jr., said, "Of all the forms of inequality, injustice in health care is the most shocking and inhumane."

EPILOGUE UPDATE: FEBRUARY 2012

Nearly 5 years have passed since the preceding epilogue was written for the 6th edition, and the public and private sector roles in the U.S. health care delivery system are still unsettled; an unsettling fact in itself. On one hand, we have seen under President Obama the first major health care system reform since the Medicare and Medicaid legislation in the 1960s. The new bill—the Patient Protection and Affordable Care Act of 2010—maintains all previous private sector participants in health care delivery, but also increases government involvement in health care through mandates on individuals, employers, health insurance companies, health care providers including physicians, hospitals, and long-term care facilities, and pharmaceutical companies. An example of the reach of the bill's mandates is the overall approach to expanding access to health care coverage:

> Require most U.S. citizens and legal residents to have health insurance. Create state-based American Health Benefit Exchanges through which individuals can purchase coverage, with premium and cost sharing credits available to individuals/ families with income between 133–400% of the federal poverty level (the poverty level is $18,310 for a family of three in 2009) and create separate Exchanges through which small businesses can purchase coverage. Require employers to pay penalties for employees who receive tax credits for health insurance through an Exchange, with exceptions for small employers. Impose new

regulations on health plans in the Exchanges and in the individual and small group markets. Expand Medicaid to 133% of the federal poverty level. (Kaiser Family Foundation, 2011)

In addition, there will be an expansion of the public programs Medicaid and SCHIP under the new legislation, as well as creation of state-based health insurance exchanges—American Health Benefit Exchanges and Small Business Health Options Program (SHOP) Exchanges—that will be "administered by a government agency or nonprofit organization through which individuals and small businesses with up to 100 employees can purchase qualified coverage" (Kaiser Family Foundation, 2011). Therefore, in February 2012 we can say that public sector involvement in the health care delivery system is substantial.

However, during this same 5-year period, the rhetoric of Americans who wish to limit government has been perhaps more explicit and strident than at any time in memory, and anti-government sentiment appears more widespread and powerful. The rise of the Tea Party as the most influential representative of conservative America has been a hallmark of this period. The mission and core principles of the Tea Party movement, in its own words, are:

> The Tea Party Patriots' mission is to restore America's founding principles of Fiscal Responsibility, Constitutionally Limited Government and Free Markets. (Tea Party Patriots, 2012)

OUR CORE PRINCIPLES

Fiscal responsibility means not overspending, and not burdening our children and grandchildren with our bills. In the words of Thomas Jefferson: "the principle of spending money to be paid by posterity (is) swindling futurity on a large scale." A more fiscally responsible government will take fewer taxes from our paychecks.

Constitutionally limited government means power resides with the people and not with the government. Governing should be done at the most local level possible where it can be held accountable. America's founders believed that government power should be limited, enumerated, and constrained by our Constitution. Tea Party Patriots agree. The American people make this country great, not our government.

Free-market economics made America an economic superpower that for at least two centuries provided subsequent generations of Americans more opportunities and higher standards of living. An erosion of our free markets through government intervention is at the heart of America's current economic decline, stagnating jobs, and spiraling debt and deficits. Failures in government programs and government-controlled financial markets helped spark the worst financial crisis since the Great Depression. Further government interventions and takeovers have made this Great Recession longer and deeper. A renewed focus on free markets will lead to a more vibrant economy, creating jobs and higher standards of living for future generations.

As an example of the rhetoric and goals of present-day conservatives and the effectiveness of the Tea Party, read the words of three of the candidates who ran for the Republican presidential nomination in February 2012—Mitt Romney, Newt Gingrich, and Ron Paul. Mitt Romney is quoted on his own website—America Needs Mitt: Romney for President 2012—as denouncing government participation in the economy, in general (America Needs Mitt: Romney for President 2012, 2012):

> The country needs to believe in free enterprise, capitalism, limited government, federalism.
> The idea of government running anything and thinking it will do a better job than the private sector is a very bad idea indeed, and suggests a lack of understanding of how our economy works.

Newt Gingrich (Newt, 2012) expressed a similar view toward government:

> *Remove obstacles to job creation imposed by destructive and ineffective regulations, programs, and bureaucracies.* Steps include: *Repealing the Sarbanes-Oxley Act*, which did nothing to prevent the financial crisis and is holding companies back from making new investments in the U.S; *Repealing the Community Reinvestment Act*, the abuse of which helped cause the financial crisis; *Repealing the Dodd-Frank Law* which is killing small independent banks, crippling loans to small businesses and crippling home sales; *Breaking up Fannie Mae and Freddie Mac*, moving their smaller successors off government guarantees and into the free market; *Replacing the Environmental Protection Agency* with an Environmental Solutions Agency that works collaboratively with local government and industry to achieve better results; and *Modernizing the Food and Drug Administration* to get lifesaving medicines and technologies to patients faster.

Ron Paul is another Republican candidate whose orientation is anti-government. His website (Ron Paul 2012: Restore America Now, 2012) leaves little doubt about his beliefs. It states that:

> High taxes stifle innovation, prevent saving, destroy production, crush the middle class and the poor, and discourage

investment. Every American is entitled to the fruits of his labor, especially during these tough economic times.

Lowering taxes will leave you more money to take care of yourself and your family, and it will allow businesses greater opportunities to hire new workers, increase current salaries, and expand their companies.

As President, Ron Paul will support a Liberty Amendment to the Constitution to abolish the income and death taxes. And he will be proud to be the one who finally turns off the lights at the IRS for good.

Capital gains taxes, which punish you for success (and interfere with your efforts to hedge against inflation by purchasing gold and silver coins), should also be immediately repealed.

Struggling college students and those working to support their families would be greatly benefited and receive an immediate pay raise by eliminating taxes on tips.

As a congressman, Ron Paul has consistently endorsed legislation to let Americans claim more tax credits and deductions, including on educational costs, alternative energy vehicles, and health care. He also believes it is immoral to tax senior citizens twice by requiring them to include Social Security benefits in their gross income at tax time. A first step to eliminating that requirement would be to repeal the 1993 increase in taxes on Social Security benefits. Then we must abolish that tax entirely.

While a Flat Tax or a Fair Tax would each be a better alternative to the income tax system, Congressman Paul believes we would have to guarantee the 16th Amendment is repealed to avoid having both the income tax and one of these systems as an additional tax.

But there is a better way. Restraining federal spending by enforcing the Constitution's strict limits on the federal government's power would help result in a 0% income tax rate for Americans.

The answer to spending and debt is to return to a constitutionally limited government that protects liberty—not one that keeps robbing Peter to pay Paul.

All three candidates are opposed to the Patient Protection and Affordable Care Act, citing government involvement, and each has promised to repeal it if elected president. Ron Paul's website (Ron Paul 2012: Restore America Now, 2012) states that he would:

Repeal ObamaCare and end its unconstitutional mandate that all Americans must carry only government-approved health insurance or answer to the IRS.

Mr. Gingrich's website (Newt 2012, 2012) states:

> The big government Obamacare approach does not address
> the root causes of America's health care crisis. Instead, it cre-
> ates layers of new taxes, regulations, and bureaucracies that
> will ultimately make our problems worse, not better. Newt
> proposes a "Patient Power" plan that will save lives and save
> money.

As a result of the extreme schism between anti-government Americans and those who desire a role for the public sector in health care and
other endeavors, we are unable to say how the questions we posed in 2007
about health system reform will be answered in the coming years. At this
time, a case could be made that the Patient Protection and Affordable Care
Act will be repealed, or at least seriously weakened, and replaced by the
previous health care delivery system or one with a smaller, even nonexistent, government role. Much depends upon the 2012 elections that will
determine the next president of the United States and the majority party
in Congress. Should a Republican president be elected, the new legislation
is surely endangered. If President Obama is re-elected, and faced with a
Republican Congress, the law will certainly be challenged and perhaps
overturned. The road to health care reform remains full of potholes, and
its destination is still uncertain.

POSTSCRIPT

As *Jonas' Introduction to the U.S. Health Care System* was about to go to
press, a historic Supreme Court decision was handed down that had enormous impact on the Affordable Care Act (ACA) and the efforts to provide
all Americans with health insurance. As we noted earlier in the Epilogue,
the attorneys general of 26 states and the National Federation of Independent Businesses had asked the Supreme Court to hear a case against the
ACA, particularly the individual mandate and Medicaid expansion.

The individual mandate was crucial to the law's success. For its supporters, the main purpose of the ACA was to provide all Americans with
health insurance. However, the expense of providing health insurance for
all would increase an already expensive system unless the legislation had
cost-containment provisions. If costs could not be controlled, any health
care legislation would be unsustainable. Because other options for insuring
every American were not supported by conservative legislators, the ACA
addressed this problem in three ways: (1) to spread the costs of health care
over all people by requiring all persons to have health insurance through
the individual mandate and Medicaid expansion, (2) to seek efficiencies in
the system of delivering care; and (3) to promote prevention and thereby
reduce the demand for this costly service.

The case brought before the Supreme Court sought to cripple the ACA's ability to contain costs by striking down the individual mandate and Medicaid expansion. As Karlan (2012) wrote:

> The federal government's ability to regulate economic and social life stems largely from four powers in the Constitution. Under the commerce clause, Congress can "regulate" national economic activity. Under the taxing power, it can "lay and collect Taxes." Under the spending power, it can "provide for the common Defence and general Welfare of the United States." And under the enforcement powers, it can enact "appropriate legislation" to enforce the 14th Amendment's equal protection and due process clauses and the 15th Amendment's guarantee of the right to vote regardless of race.

The Obama administration defended the individual mandate as permissible under the Commerce Clause. During the period of March 26–28, 2012, the Supreme Court considered this case *National Federation of Independent Businesses et al. v. Sebelius, Secretary of Health and Human Services, et al.* In a 5 to 4 decision, the Court upheld the constitutionality of the ACA in a decision that was awaited anxiously by both sides. However, in a surprise to most observers, the Court did not justify its ruling with the Commerce Clause. Rather, the authority of the federal government to impose taxes was the basis of the Court's ruling, and the Chief Justice, a highly conservative justice known for favoring limited government, wrote the decision. Roberts wrote in a split-the-difference decision, "The federal government does not have the power to order people to buy health insurance. The federal government does have the power to impose a tax on those without health insurance." Chief Justice John Roberts Jr. sided with Justices Ruth Bader Ginzberg, Stephen Breyer, Sonja Sotomayor, and Eleanor Kagan to form the majority opinion. As a result of the Supreme Court decision, the ACA will continue to be implemented.

The decision was another episode in the curious, complicated, and long tale of America's attempt to achieve universal access to health care, as all developed nations of the world have done. However, the Supreme Court victory for the ACA is not the end of the story. The elections in November 2012 may deliver a Republican president and legislative majority that will repeal the ACA. Republican presidential candidate, Mitt Romney, has pledged to overturn it if elected, as have most current leaders of the Republican party, even though the ACA is virtually the same as the legislation that Mr. Romney enacted as governor of Massachusetts and the Heritage Foundation recommended as a means of keeping government out of health care. Indeed, the Supreme Court decision has galvanized conservative political action to prevent re-election of President Obama, maintain a Republic majority in the House of Representatives, and create a Republican majority in the Senate.

Further, the Supreme Court decision, although it allows the present survival of the ACA on the basis of the federal government's taxing authority, may have established legal precedent for future threats to federal programs that have been justified by the Commerce Clause. As Karlan (2012) noted:

> What, then, to make of the court's landmark decision to uphold the individual mandate? Chief Justice Roberts construed the mandate not as a requirement that individuals purchase health insurance but as a choice: buy insurance or pay a tax. But the conservatives surely know that a Congress that can tax but not do much else—spend money, regulate the economy or enforce civil rights—will be hamstrung. Taxes are unpopular and nearly every Republican member of Congress has promised to oppose any additional taxes on individuals or businesses.
>
> A Congress that can advance national priorities only through its taxing power is a Congress with little power at all. That is the real legacy of the last term. The Supreme Court has given Americans who care about economic and social justice a reason to worry this Fourth of July. The court's guns have been loaded; it only remains to be seen whether it fires them.

Our original ending to the new Epilogue still holds. Health policy in the United States is still pulled taut between those who want government to take an active role in assuring equal rights and opportunities for Americans and those who believe that equalities will occur naturally, with little government action, as an offshoot of private enterprise. The most recent Supreme Court decision does nothing to resolve this basic tension in American society.

NOTE

1. Community rating means that the cost of a health insurance premium is the same for everyone regardless of differences in their health status, prior utilization of health care, or other factors that increase the risk of requiring health care in the future. With experience rating, people pay different amounts based on these factors, with people at low risk paying less than people at high risk.

REFERENCES

America Needs Mitt: Romney for President 2012. (2012). *Mitt Romney notable quotes.* Retrieved February 6, 2012, from http://americaneedsmitt.com

Avant, D. (2002). Privatizing military training. *Foreign Policy in Focus, 7*(6), 1–4.

Blackwater USA. (2007). *Blackwater.* Retrieved on March 20, 2007, from www.blackwaterusa.com

Broaddus, M., & Park, E. (2007). Freezing SCHIP funding in coming years would reverse recent gains in children's health coverage. *Center on Budget and Policy Priorities*. Retrieved March 11, 2007, from www.cbpp.org/6-5-06health.htm

Committee on the Costs of Medical Care. (1932/1970). *Medical care for the American people*. Chicago, IL: University of Chicago Press. (Reprinted, Washington, DC: USDHEW, 1970.)

Goldsteen, R. L., Goldsteen, K., Kronenfeld, J. J., & Hann, N. (1997). Anti-government sentiment and support for public health goals: Are they compatible? *American Journal of Public Health, 87*(1), 25–28.

Helman, R., & Fronstin, P. (2006). 2006 Health Confidence Survey: Dissatisfaction with health care system doubles since 1998. *EBRI Notes, 27*(11), 2–10.

Himmelstein, D. U., Warren, E., Thorne, D., & Woolhandler, S. (2005). Illness and injury as contributors to bankruptcy. *Health Affairs* [Web Exclusive, pp. W5–63–W5–73]. Retrieved March 18, 2007, from www.healthaffairs.org/WebExclusives.php

Kaiser Family Foundation. (2011, February 15). *Focus on health reform: Summary of new health reform law*. Retrieved February 6, 2012, from www.kff.org/healthreform/upload/8061.pdf

Karlan, P. S. (June 30, 2012). No Respite for Liberals. The New York Times: Sunday Review. Retrieved July 5, 2012 from http://www.nytimes.com/2012/07/01/opinion/sunday/no-respite-for-liberals.html?pagewanted=all

Kaveny, M. C. (1999). Commodifying the polyvalent good of health care. *Journal of Medicine and Philosophy, 24*(3), 207–223.

Kindig, D. A. (1997). *Purchasing population health: Paying for results*. Ann Arbor, MI: The University of Michigan Press.

Krugman, P. (2007, January 5). First, do less harm. *The New York Times*, Op-Ed Column.

Lipscomb, C. E. (2002). Lister Hill and his influence. *Journal of the Medical Library Association, 90*(1), 109–110.

National Association of State Budget Officers (NASBO). (2006). *State Expenditure Report: Fiscal Year 2005*. Washington, DC: NASBO.

National Coalition on Health Care. (2004). *Health insurance cost*. Retrieved March 11, 2007, from www.nchc.org

Newt 2012. (2012). *Solutions: 21st century contract with America*. Retrieved February 6, 2012, from www.newt.org/solutions

Pellegrino, E. D. (1999). The commodification of medical and health care: The moral consequences of a paradigm shift from a professional to a market ethic. *Journal of Medicine and Philosophy, 24*(3), 243–266.

Pickoff-White, L. (2006, September 20). Number of uninsured in U.S. increases. *The National Academies [Science in the Headlines]*. Retrieved March 11, 2007, from www.nationalacademies.org/headlines/20050920.html

Ron Paul 2012: Restore America Now. (2012). *Issues*. Retrieved February 6, 2012, from www.ronpaul2012.com

Rosenberg, C. E. (2006). Anticipated consequences: Historians, history, and health policy. In R. A. Stevens, C. E. Rosenberg, & L. R. Burns (Eds.), *History and health policy in the United States: Putting the past back in* (pp. 13–31). New Brunswick, NJ: Rutgers University Press.

Shortell, S. M., Gillies, R. R., Anderson, D. A., Erickson, K. M., & Mitchell, J. B. (2000). *Remaking health care in America: The evolution of organized delivery systems* (2nd ed.). San Francisco, CA: Jossey-Bass.

Smith, V., Gifford, K., Ellis, E., Wiles, A., Rudowitz, R., O'Malley, M., & Marks, C. (2006). *Low Medicaid spending growth amid rebounding state revenues: Results from a 50-state Medicaid budget survey. State fiscal years 2006 and 2007*. Washington, DC: Kaiser Family Foundation.

Tea Party Patriots. (2012). *About Tea Party Patriots*. Retrieved February 7, 2012, from www.teapartypatriots.org/about

Zuger, A. (2004). Dissatisfaction with medical practice. *New England Journal of Medicine, 350*(1), 69–75.

Index

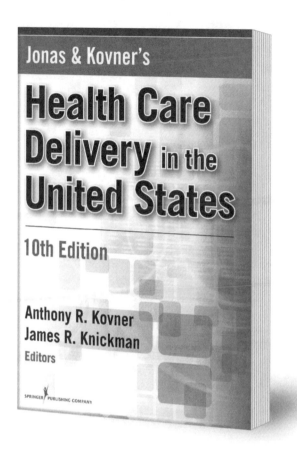